D1616313

CONSTRUCTIVE DIVORCE

Procedural Justice and Sociolegal Reform

PENELOPE EILEEN BRYAN

American Psychological Association
Washington, DC

The LAW AND PUBLIC POLICY: PSYCHOLOGY AND THE
SOCIAL SCIENCES series includes books in three domains:

Legal Studies—writings by legal scholars about issues of relevance to
psychology and the other social sciences, or that employ social
science information to advance the legal analysis;

Social Science Studies—writings by scientists from psychology and
the other social sciences about issues of relevance to law and public
policy; and

Forensic Studies—writings by psychologists and other mental health
scientists and professionals about issues relevant to forensic mental
health science and practice.

The series is guided by its editor, Bruce D. Sales, PhD, JD, ScD(*hc*),
University of Arizona; and coeditors, Bruce J. Winick, JD, University of
Miami; Norman J. Finkel, PhD, Georgetown University; and
Valerie P. Hans, PhD, University of Delaware.

* * *

Published by
American Psychological Association
750 First Street, NE
Washington, DC 20002
www.apa.org

To order
APA Order Department
P.O. Box 92984
Washington, DC 20090-2984
Tel: (800) 374-2721
Direct: (202) 336-5510
Fax: (202) 336-5502
TDD/TTY: (202) 336-6123
Online: www.apa.org/books/
E-mail: order@apa.org

In the U.K., Europe, Africa, and the Middle
East, copies may be ordered from
American Psychological Association
3 Henrietta Street
Covent Garden, London
WC2E 8LU England

Typeset in Goudy by World Composition Services, Inc., Sterling, VA

Printer: Edwards Brothers, Inc., Ann Arbor, MI
Cover Designer: Naylor Design, Washington, DC
Project Manager: Debbie Hardin, Carlsbad, CA

The opinions and statements published are the responsibility of the authors, and such opinions and statements do not necessarily represent the policies of the American Psychological Association.

Library of Congress Cataloging-in-Publication Data

Bryan, Penelope Eileen
    Constructive divorce : procedural justice and sociolegal reform / Penelope Eileen Bryan.
        p. cm. — (Law and public policy)
    Includes bibliographical references and index.
    ISBN 1-59147-279-2
    1. Divorce—Law and legislation—United States. 2. Justice, Administration of—United
States. 3. Divorce—Psychological aspects. I. Title. II. Series.

    KF535.B79 2005
    346.7301′66—dc22   2004031071

British Library Cataloguing-in-Publication Data
A CIP record is available from the British Library.

Printed in the United States of America
First Edition

To Eileen and John Bryan, my parents,
whose lives informed my sense of justice and
my commitment to family law,
and my children, Benjamin, Candice, Hillary, and Matthew,
who tolerate that commitment with affection.

CONTENTS

ACKNOWLEDGMENTS

I thank my editors Bruce Winick and Bruce Sales, who believed in this project and patiently waited for its completion even when I struggled. Throughout the process, the staff and editors at the American Psychological Association provided excellent guidance. My successive deans at the University of Denver—Dennis Lynch and Mary Ricketson—afforded years of unwavering support. My students offered enthusiasm and inspiration. And my children, Candice, Hillary, Benjamin, and Matthew, provided the necessary balance in my life. I am grateful to everyone who helped bring this book to fruition.

CONSTRUCTIVE
DIVORCE

INTRODUCTION

Divorce outcomes threaten the well-being of millions of adults and children each year. Divorced women and their dependent children live financially compromised lives that restrict their individual potential and their collective contributions. Financial stress, role strain, and bitterness affect the psychological health of many divorced custodial mothers and, in turn, their children.

Children suffer in high conflict divorced families. Previously involved fathers ultimately fade from the lives of their children, and those fathers and their children grieve their losses. Courts threaten the physical and mental health of children when they order children to live, or visit, with physically or sexually abusive parents. Battered women frequently lose custody of their children to the very persons who abused them, and many times their children. Some commentators have described divorce as a public health crisis.[1]

The procedures used to resolve divorce disputes contribute to these poor outcomes.[2] Inept judges spawn unjust results, and appellate courts defer. Inefficiencies contribute to lengthy divorces that drain the emotional and financial resources of the parties. Divorced adults and children complain about the treatment they receive from judges, lawyers, mediators, guardians ad litem, and custody evaluators.[3] Lawyers negotiate, and judges decide, divorce cases based on inaccurate or inadequate information. Scholars, professionals, and participants acknowledge that a broken system needs fixing.[4]

Yet meaningful reform eludes us. Some reformers offer procedural alternatives to our current system. Unified family courts allegedly promote efficiency and provide extended services to troubled families.[5] Mediation, or perhaps collaborative divorce,[6] promises a civil alternative to hostile, destructive, and expensive litigation. These procedural alternatives, however, generally ignore the individual and social importance of quality outcomes in divorce and offer no theoretical, empirical, or practical link to improved results. Behind a mask of attractive rhetoric, these alternatives simply perpetuate or exacerbate many of the deficiencies of the current system.[7]

Other reformers seek to improve divorce outcomes through changes in substantive divorce law. Many suggest changes to spousal maintenance law, property law, or both in order to alleviate the economic plight of divorced women and dependent children.[8] Others advocate custody laws that honor the caretaking that parents actually perform during the marriage.[9] Although substantive reform certainly has merit, it alone cannot improve divorce outcomes. Many diverse factors systematically interact to produce dysfunctional results, not just substantive law.[10] Moreover, without substantial reform of the procedures that systematically fail to protect legal rights, changes to those rights will not substantially improve results.

This book uses procedural justice criteria, as defined by social scientists, to critique and propose procedural reforms for divorce. Part I justifies this approach. First, citizens perceive a justice system as legitimate if it offers procedural justice and dispenses substantive justice. Identification and correction of the system's procedural deficiencies offer to enhance the legitimacy of our justice system generally. Second, for decades researchers have established a link between the public's perception of procedural justice and the willingness of citizens to comply with the law. Enhanced procedural justice might decrease noncompliance with divorce decrees and settlements. Third, and most importantly, our current family law system produces results that threaten the collective good as well as the individual well-being of millions of adults and children. The procedures used to resolve legal disputes inevitably influence the quality of outcomes and, in turn, the effect of those outcomes on the financial and psychological well-being of participants.

Part II of this book evaluates the current family law system through the prism of procedural justice. It includes an assessment of whether the system

1. provides decision makers with respected authority;
2. allows participants adequate voice or participation;
3. fosters efficiency;
4. preserves the disputants' relationship or reduces hostilities between them;
5. offers an opportunity for the correction of error;
6. suppresses bias;

7. operates consistently;
8. provides decision makers who treat disputants with respect and show concern for their rights; and
9. ensures that accurate information informs decisions.

Throughout, the link between procedural deficiencies and poor results emerges.

In Part III, this book offers procedural reforms based on the critique performed in Part II. These reforms enhance procedural justice, improve outcomes, and promote the psychological and emotional well-being of participants. The Conclusion justifies the reliance on procedure and ends with a brief exploration of changes in substantive law that would complement the proposed procedural reforms.

A nod seems appropriate to a related body of thought. Therapeutic jurisprudence recognizes that the manner in which a legal system processes disputes determines whether the law has a positive or negative impact on the psychological and emotional well-being of participants.[11] Substantive laws, legal procedures, and legal and quasi-legal actors all play important roles in the therapeutic or anti-therapeutic effects of the law.[12] Therapeutic jurisprudence promotes many of the procedural justice criteria mentioned earlier, particularly respectful treatment and party participation,[13] because these criteria promise better results and enhance the psychological well-being of participants. Therapeutic jurisprudence thus also would support many of the reforms proposed here because of their potential therapeutic effect on participants.

The author hopes that this book will help the many diverse professionals who work in the divorce arena to understand the importance of procedural justice, to detect and to reduce system weaknesses, to improve the assistance they provide to divorcing families, and, ultimately, to generate better results.

NOTES

1. See Andrew Schepard, *Parental Conflict Prevention Programs and the Unified Family Court: A Public Health Perspective*, 32 FAM. L.Q. 95, 96–106 (1998).

2. See Donald J. MacDougall, *Negotiated Settlement of Family Disputes, in* THE RESOLUTION OF FAMILY CONFLICT: COMPARATIVE LEGAL PERSPECTIVES 26, 32 (John M. Eekelaar & Sanford N. Katz eds. 1984) (recognizing that none of the available methods for resolving divorce disputes adequately protects the social interests at stake).

3. See Marsha Kline Pruett & Tamara D. Jackson, *The Lawyer's Role During the Divorce Process: Perceptions of Parents, Their Young Children, and Their Attorneys*, 33 FAM. L.Q. 283, 289, 295 (1999); Larry R. Spain, *Collaborative Law: A Critical*

Reflection on Whether a Collaborative Orientation Can Be Ethically Incorporated Into the Practice of Law, 56 Baylor L. Rev. 141, 145 & n.25 (2004).

4. *See, e.g.*, Oregon Task Force on Family Law, Final Report to Governor John A. Kitzhaber & The Oregon Legislative Assembly 2 (1997); *Developments: Unified Family Courts and the Child Protection Dilemma*, 116 Harv. L. Rev. 2099, 2099–2100 (2003); William Howe, III & Maureen McNight, *Oregon Task Force on Family Law: A New System to Resolve Family Law Conflicts*, 33 Fam. & Concil. Cts. Rev. 173 (1995); Gary B. Melton, *Children, Families, and the Courts in the Twenty-First Century*, 66 S. Cal. L. Rev. 1993, 2012 (1993); Schepard, *supra* note 1, at 95–96; Spain, *supra* note 3, at 143–45.

5. *See, e.g.*, Catherine J. Ross, *The Failure of Fragmentation: The Promise of a System of Unified Family Courts*, 33 Rev. Jur. U.I.P.R. 311 (1999).

6. *E.g.*, Pauline H. Tesler, Collaborative Law: Achieving Effective Resolution in Divorce Without Litigation (2001); James K.L. Lawrence, *Collaborative Lawyering: A New Development in Conflict Resolution*, 17 Ohio St. J. Disp. Resol. 431 (2002); Pauline H. Tesler, *Collaborative Law: Achieving Effective Resolution in Divorce Without Litigation*, 40 Fam. Ct. Rev. 403 (2002); Pauline H. Tesler, *Collaborative Law: What It Is and Why Family Law Attorneys Need to Know About It*, 13 Am J. Fam. L. 215 (1999); Pauline H. Tesler, *Collaborative Law: A New Paradigm for Divorce Lawyers*, 5 Psychol. Pub. Pol'y & L. 967 (1999).

7. *See* Penelope Eileen Bryan, *Women's Freedom to Contract at Divorce: A Mask for Contextual Coercion*, 47 Buff. L. Rev. 1153 (1999); Penelope Eileen Bryan, *Collaborative Divorce: Meaningful Reform or Another Quick Fix?*, 5 Psychol. Pub. Pol'y & L. 1001 (1999); Penelope E. Bryan, *Killing Us Softly: Divorce Mediation and the Politics of Power*, 40 Buff. L. Rev. 441 (1992). *See also* MacDougall, *supra* note 2.

8. *See, e.g.*, Katharine T. Bartlett, *Feminism and Family Law*, 33 Fam. L.Q. 475, 479–80 (1999); Martha M. Ertman, *Commercializing Marriage: A Proposal for Valuing Women's Work Through Premarital Security Agreements*, 77 Tex. L. Rev. 17 (1998); Jana B. Singer, *Alimony and Efficiency: The Gendered Costs and Benefits of the Economic Justification for Alimony*, 82 Geo. L.J. 2423 (1994); Cynthia Starnes, *Divorce and the Displaced Homemaker: A Discourse on Playing with Dolls: Partnership Buyouts and Dissociation Under No-Fault*, 60 U. Chi. L. Rev. 67 (1993); Amy L. Wax, *Bargaining in the Shadow of the Market: Is There a Future for Egalitarian Marriage?*, 84 Va. L. Rev. 509, 656–64 (1998); Joan Williams, *Is Coverture Dead? Beyond a New Theory of Alimony*, 82 Geo. L.J. 2227 (1994).

9. *See, e.g.*, American Law Institute, Principles of the Law of Family Dissolution §2.08 (2002).

10. As Garrison notes

These various examples make it clear that the achievement of equitable outcomes when families break up cannot be achieved either through broad grants of discretion, or even through the substitution of rules for discretionary standards. Changes in the law of family dissolution will not produce equity improvements unless two preliminary criteria are met: legal change must reflect public values and familial expectations, and it must also reflect a detailed understanding of current outcomes and the process by which they are produced.

Marsha Garrison, *The Economic Consequences of Divorce: Would Adoption of the ALI Principles Improve Current Outcomes?*, 8 Duke J. Gender L. & Pol'y 119, 123 (2001). *See also* Gary Skoloff & Robert J. Levy, *Custody Doctrines and Custody Practice: A Divorce Practitioner's View*, 36 Fam. L.Q. 79, 79–85 (2002) (acknowledging numerous factors that influence custody outcomes and openly doubting whether custody doctrine can alter those factors). *See generally* Mary Becker, *Patriarchy and Inequality: Towards a Substantive Feminism*, 1999 U. Chi. Legal F. 21, 23–24.

11. *See* Bruce J. Winick, *The Jurisprudence of Therapeutic Jurisprudence*, 3 Psychol. Pub. Pol'y & L. 184, 188, 190, 191 (1997).

12. *See* Barbara A. Babb, *An Interdisciplinary Approach to Family Law Jurisprudence: Application of an Ecological and Therapeutic Perspective*, 72 Ind. L.J. 775, 798 (1997); Winick, *supra* note 11 at 201–02.

13. *See* Tom R. Tyler, *The Psychological Consequences of Judicial Procedures: Implications for Civil Commitment Hearings*, 46 SMU L. Rev. 433 (1992).

I

JUSTIFICATIONS FOR
A PROCEDURAL
JUSTICE ASSESSMENT

1

LEGITIMACY AND COMPLIANCE

Legal theory and doctrine long have recognized the importance of procedural fairness to the legitimacy of our legal system.[1] Several decades ago, researchers confirmed that procedures as well as substantive outcomes influenced the public's perception of justice.[2] Early researchers reasoned that people want a procedural opportunity to exert influence over third-party decision makers, because they expect this opportunity to produce more favorable outcomes.[3] More recent work by Tyler and others indicates that disputants consider procedural fairness important, independent of the substantive outcome.[4]

Some researchers and philosophers occasionally imply that procedural trumps substantive justice.[5] Decisions made according to the procedural criteria discussed in this book will create systemwide legitimacy, no matter the result.[6] Therefore, we need pay little attention to substantive justice. Disconnecting procedures from the results they produce might provide comfort in a heterogeneous society that offers little consensus on substantive norms.[7] We at least can agree on procedures, even if we cannot agree on what outcomes the legal system should favor. No matter how comforting, however, this reasoning ignores research that indicates that the public considers substantive justice an important component of a legitimate legal system.[8] People find procedural justice important precisely because they expect "fair" procedures to produce just results.[9] If the results from a procedural system consistently seem unfair, eventually the public will consider the procedures themselves to be illegitimate. Most importantly, as the subsequent discussion clarifies, procedures substantially affect outcomes. And, in the divorce arena, those outcomes have great significance to the individuals involved and to society at large. In the end, a justice system that promotes voluntary compliance and commands public respect must dispense substantive as well as procedural justice.[10]

LEGITIMACY

Public respect for the family law system seems particularly important to the legitimacy of the legal system generally. Millions of adults and children of all classes and races divorce in our courts each year.[11] Their experiences during divorce undoubtedly affect their beliefs about the legitimacy of the legal system generally.[12] This concern seems particularly salient when we note the public's current low level of confidence in our legal system and low regard for lawyers and judges.[13] As we explore procedural justice in Part II, we learn that current divorce procedures fail to provide it. Procedural inadequacies also contribute substantially to poor outcomes, which raise significant concerns about substantive justice. Understandably, the millions who divorce each year complain bitterly about their experiences and often express shock at the system's deficiencies.[14] The procedural reforms proposed in Part III enhance the legitimacy of the entire legal system, because they promote substantive as well as procedural justice in divorce.

COMPLIANCE

Compliance provides a second reason to use procedural justice to assess the divorce system. Divorced parties frequently fail to comply with judicial orders or agreements regarding child support, spousal maintenance, and child custody and visitation.[15] Noncompliance with child support awards has become a national scandal.[16] For instance, parents in the United States owe over $84 billion in child support arrearages.[17] Swank further reports that

> As of 1998, there were approximately 14 million parents in the United States who had custody of 22.9 million children who were eligible to receive child support. Only fifty-six percent of these custodial parents, however, had some type of child support order or agreement. Of these, fifty-nine percent received either none or only part of the ordered or agreed upon amount of child support. All told, $29.1 billion in child support was owed in 1997, but only $17.1 billion—fifty-nine percent—was paid. Thirty-two percent of custodial parents received no

child support at all in 1997. By fiscal year 2000, the amount of child support paid dropped to fifty-six percent of what was owed.[18]

In frustration, and in response to federal mandates,[19] today states attempt to enforce child support awards through a variety of mechanisms.[20] For example, statutes authorize Florida courts to subject child support orders to garnishment[21] and income deduction orders.[22] Absent parental agreement and judicial approval, noncustodial parents must pay child support through state-monitored depositories.[23] Many states subject those in arrears to possible contempt,[24] suspension or denial of professional licenses and certificates,[25] and suspension of driver licenses and motor vehicle registrations.[26] Despite increasingly coercive efforts,[27] however, enforcement procedures remain only marginally effective,[28] and, as indicated earlier,[29] many custodial parents with child support orders receive no child support or only partial payment.[30] Spousal maintenance awards meet a similar fate. Only a few women awarded spousal maintenance actually receive the amount awarded,[31] and coercive enforcement statutes have little effect. In addition to the financial and social problems created by noncompliance, government efforts to coerce payment require the state to expend extensive resources and threaten the legitimacy of a democracy that relies upon the consent of the governed.[32]

Divorce participants also resist compliance with child custodial decrees and agreements. Parental kidnappings in defiance of custody decrees and intractable child visitation disputes reveal disdain for judicial mandates regarding children.[33] Researchers estimate that 203,900 children fell victim to family abduction in 1999.[34] Biological fathers and mothers accounted for 159,200 of theses abductions.[35] Forty-four percent of family-abducted children had not yet reached six years of age.[36] Shara Pang, assistant to former Senator Alan Dixon (D-Ill.), estimates that foreign countries hold 10,000 American children as hostages, and custody disputes provoke most of these abductions.[37] International child abductions have spawned desperate self-help measures by wronged parents. Despite the illegality of such measures, Corporate Training Unlimited, composed of ex-Delta Force commandos, locates missing children, helps them to escape, and returns them to wronged parents. These commandos frequently risk imprisonment or execution by authorities in the countries that retain the children. Their fees can reach as much as $100,000 for foreign services.[38]

Clearly our family law system has a major compliance problem. Moreover, noncompliance has a significant effect on the psychological and emotional well-being of all concerned. Research, fortunately, establishes a positive correlation between procedural justice and people's willingness to comply with the law.[39] I suggest here that a more procedurally just system might enhance compliance. I do not, however, want to claim too much.

For instance, people undoubtedly resist child support orders for reasons other than procedural deficiencies in the system that generates them. Lingering hostilities, as well as a belief that the ordered support benefits the custodial parent more than the children, may impair the noncustodial parent's motivation to comply.[40] The obligation to support one's children no longer has the same moral currency in society.[41] We now accept divorce and its frequency; which in turn has changed our expectations about lifelong obligations generally. Short-term have replaced long-term commitments, and these commitments intuitively seem less important. Our individualistic ideology reinforces our intuition by casting doubt on the worthiness of any obligation that interferes with our individual interests. Certainly child support and spousal maintenance obligations can interfere significantly with individual financial, and sometimes relationship, goals.[42]

In the past, children contributed valuable labor to their families, particularly in rural areas. Parents also expected children to support and care for them as they aged. Today children rarely live on family farms, and today's younger generation likely will earn less than its parents. A gloomier financial future, coupled with geographic dispersion and a waning sense of moral responsibility for aged parents, diminishes parental expectations of future support from children. Today's parents, then, cannot expect the same economic return on investments they make in their children that past generations of parents could. When parents divorce, a noncustodial parent likely expects no return on his economic investment in his child. Hence a reluctance to pay child support.

The diminished economic value of children suggests that today's parents value children primarily because of their affective bonds with them, the societal approval of the parental role, and the creative accomplishment of raising successful children. Divorce threatens the value of the noncustodial parent's relationship to the child on all three fronts. "Visitation" rather than "life" with one's child compromises affective bonds.[43] Some noncustodial parents find the "visiting" relationship so painful that they avoid contact, breaking all bonds with the child.[44] Noncustodial parents who remain close to their children can continue to receive social validation for participating in the parental role, but their noncustodial status makes them second-class parents.[45] And, finally, although noncustodial parents can take personal satisfaction in their children's accomplishments, custodial parents receive most of the credit. As Fineman notes, a father's relationship to the mother mediates his membership in the "family" and, consequently, his relationship to his children.[46] When the father–mother dyad splinters in divorce, we conceptually expel the noncustodial parent from the family, and that parent becomes physically and emotionally distant from the children. Under such circumstances, the obligation of the expelled parent to support the children loses the moral and social force exerted by the norms that govern the "normal" family.[47] Any one or all of these factors may contribute to any particular noncustodial parent's unwillingness to comply with child support orders.[48]

Just as complex motives influence noncompliance with child support orders,[49] so too do numerous factors influence noncompliance with custody and spousal support orders. Consequently, a more procedurally just system likely will produce only an incremental increase in, rather than widespread compliance with, support and custody orders. Given the current state of affairs, however, any increase seems a desirable goal to pursue, particularly if procedural reforms also produce better outcomes.

NOTES

1. *See* Judith Resnik, *Tiers*, 57 S. Cal. L. Rev. 837, 845–58 (1984); Tom R. Tyler, *Multiculturalism and the Willingness of Citizens to Defer to the Legal and Legal Authorities*, 25 L. & Soc. Inquiry 983, 988–89 (2000). *See also* Lawrence M. Friedman, Total Justice 43 (1985) (noting that people expect procedural and substantive fairness).

2. John Thibaut & Laurens Walker, Procedural Justice: A Psychological Analysis (1975).

3. Tom R. Tyler, Why People Obey the Law 6–7, 115–16 (1990).

4. See *id.* at 115–24. Subgroup identification, however, tempers this claim. When people identify exclusively with their particular subgroup, they focus more on whether the results favor their subgroup than the fairness of the procedures used to reach the result. Tyler, *supra* note 1, at 1009–13.

5. Ronald Dworkin notes that,

   Some philosophers deny the possibility of any fundamental conflict between justice and fairness because they believe that one of these virtues in the end derives from the other. Some say that justice has no meaning apart from fairness, that in politics, as in roulette, whatever happens through fair procedures is just. That is the extreme of the idea called justice as fairness.

   Ronald Dworkin, Law's Empire 177 (1986).

6. See Tyler, *supra* note 1, at 997–98 (noting the possibility for abuse of procedural justice to promote satisfaction with undesirable results).

7. *See* Tyler, *supra* note 3, at 109; Resnik, *supra* note 1, at 841–42; Thomas D. Rowe, Jr., *American Law Institute Study on Paths to a 'Better Way': Litigation, Alternatives, and Accommodation: Background Paper*, 1989 Duke L.J. 824, 827. Moreover, in a democratic society, the legitimacy of law depends on the consent of the governed. A focus and consensus on procedure can, to some extent, enhance law's legitimacy, even when consensus on substance seems unlikely. This observation does not, however, justify our continued reluctance to face our substantive problems, especially when those problems tear at the fabric of our society.

8. *See* TYLER, *supra* note 3, at 214–15; Jonathan D. Casper et al., *Procedural Justice in Felony Cases*, 22 L. & Soc'y Rev. 483, 486, 503 (1988); Deborah R. Hensler, *Suppose It's Not True: Challenging Mediation Ideology*, 2002 J. Disp. Resol. 81, 94 & n.45 (2002) (noting research that indicates when parties have information that helps them assess fairness of outcomes before they resolve their dispute, they use that information, rather than process information, to determine fairness of outcomes) (citing K. Van de Bos et al., *Procedural and Distributive Justice: What is Fair Depends More on What Comes First than on What Comes Next*, 72 J. PERSONALITY & Soc. PSYCHOL. 95 (1997)); Tom R. Tyler, *Citizen Discontent with Legal Procedures: A Social Science Perspective on Civil Procedure Reform*, 45 Am. J. COMP. L. 871, 882–83 (1997) (hereinafter *Citizen Discontent*); Tom R. Tyler, *What is Procedural Justice?: Criteria Used by Citizens to Assess the Fairness of Legal Procedures*, 22 L. & Soc'y Rev. 103, 117 (1988).

9. *See* TYLER, *supra* note 3, at 165.

10. *See* Deborah R. Rhode, *The Rhetoric of Professional Reform*, 45 MD. L. REV. 274, 286–87 (1986) ("Informed decisions about the appropriate structure[s] of dispute resolution must depend on greater attention to the social, political, and legal culture in which they function. Analysis should center not only on the comparative efficiencies of available processes, but also on the collective values to be served."). *See also* TYLER, *supra* note 3; Lon L. Fuller, *Positivism and Fidelity to Law—A Reply to Professor Hart*, 71 HARV. L. REV. 630, 670 (1958); Richard D. Schwartz, *Law, Society, and Moral Order: Introduction to the Symposium*, 1980 B.Y.U. L. REV. 721, 726.

11. In 1995, 20% of first marriages ended within five years, whereas 33% ended within 10 years. *See* Matthew D. Bramlett et al., *First Marriage Dissolution, Divorce, and Remarriage: United States*, Advance Data No. 323, Department of Health & Human Servs., Centers for Disease Control & Prevention, National Center for Health Statistics, May 31, 2001. In 1994, 1,191,000 marriages ended in divorce, a rate of 20.5 divorces per 1,000 married women. *See* Laura Gatland, *Putting the Blame on No-Fault*, 83 A.B.A. J. 50, 52 (1997) (citing the National Center for Health Statistics). In 1988, the rate was higher—37 divorces per every 1,000 married women. Nevertheless, every year since the late 1970s, more than 1 million marriages have ended in divorce. *See* Patricia H. Shiono & Linda Sandham Quinn, *Epidemiology of Divorce*, 4 THE FUTURE OF CHILDREN: CHILDREN AND DIVORCE 14, 18 (Richard E. Behrman, ed., 1994). Some predict that more than half of all marriages in the United States will end in divorce. *See, e.g.*, Arland Thornton, *Comparative and Historical Perspectives on Marriage, Divorce and Family Life*, 1994 UTAH L. REV. 587, 595. Others predict an even higher percentage. *See* Gary B. Melton, *Children, Families, and the Courts in the Twenty-First Century*, 66 S. CAL. L. REV. 1993, 2011 n.87 (1993) (stating that two out of every three first marriages will end in divorce or separation) (citing Teresa Castro Martin & Larry L. Bumpass, *Recent Trends in Marital Disruption*, 26 DEMOGRAPHY 37, 40–41 (1989)). Approximately 60% of these divorcing couples will have minor children. *See* Mary Ann Glendon, *Family Law Reform in the 1980's*, 44 LA. L. REV. 1553, 1555 & n.9 (1984) (citing U.S. BUREAU

OF THE CENSUS, U.S. DEP'T OF COMMERCE, SPECIAL STUDIES SERIES P-23, No. 84, DIVORCE, CHILD CUSTODY, AND CHILD SUPPORT (1979)). Second and third marriages have even higher divorce rates, and remarried couples with children have higher rates still. *See* E. MAVIS HETHERINGTON & JOHN KELLY, FOR BETTER OR FOR WORSE: DIVORCE RECONSIDERED 178 (2002) (noting that remarriages with stepchildren have a 50% higher divorce rate than remarriages without children); Melton, *supra*, at 2011 n.87 (citing Lynn K. White & Alan Booth, *The Quality and Stability of Remarriage: The Role of Stepchildren*, 50 AM. SOC. REV. 689 (1985)). *See* SUSAN MOLLER OKIN, JUSTICE, GENDER, AND THE FAMILY 4 (1989) (citing U.S. BUREAU OF THE CENSUS, U.S. DEP'T OF COMMERCE, CURRENT POPULATION REPORTS, HOUSEHOLD AND FAMILY CHARACTERISTICS, at 79 (1987)). *See also* MAUREEN BAKER, CANADIAN FAMILY POLICIES: CROSS-NATIONAL COMPARISONS 305 (1995) (acknowledging that divorce and separation now account for most single-parent families).

12. *See* Rudolph J. Gerber, *Recommendation on Domestic Relations Reform*, 32 ARIZ. L. REV. 9, 13 (1990); Catherine J. Ross, *The Failure of Fragmentation: The Promise of a System of Unified Family Courts*, 33 REV. JUR. U. I. P. R. 311, 312 (1999) (noting that family law cases provide the point of contact for many citizens with the justice system and that such contact undoubtedly influences citizens' respect for or alienation from legal system generally).

13. *See, e.g.*, LYNN MATHER ET AL., DIVORCE LAWYERS AT WORK: VARIETIES OF PROFESSIONALISM IN PRACTICE 21 (2001); *Citizen Discontent, supra* note 8, at 871–72.

14. *See, e.g.*, KAREN WINNER, DIVORCED FROM JUSTICE: THE ABUSE OF WOMEN AND CHILDREN BY DIVORCE LAWYERS AND JUDGES (1996); Gerber, *supra* note 12, at 13 (noting one woman's statement: "[I] hate the legal system more than I hate [my husband]. It's disgusting to me how these attorneys and judges sit around and don't do what they're supposed to do for you.").

15. *See* HETHERINGTON & KELLY, *supra* note 11, at 55–56 (noting a California study by Eleanor Maccoby and Robert Mnookin of Stanford University that found that only approximately one-third of divorced couples adhered to their settlement agreements about support, custody, and visitation). Beck and Sales note that, during the 1980s, more than 40% of postdivorce parties in the United States failed to comply with support and custody orders. Connie J.A. Beck & Bruce Sales, *A Critical Reappraisal of Divorce Mediation Research and Policy*, 6 PSYCHOL. PUB. POL'Y & L. 989, 990 (2000).

16. *See* Drew A. Swank, *The National Child Non-Support Epidemic*, 2003 MICH. ST. DCL L. REV. 357 (2003). *See also* ACHIEVING EQUAL JUSTICE FOR WOMEN AND MEN IN THE CALIFORNIA COURTS: FINAL REPORT 133, 136 (Gay Danforth & Bobbie L. Welling eds., 1996); CONNECTICUT TASK FORCE ON GENDER JUSTICE AND THE COURTS 143 (1991) (hereinafter CONNECTICUT TASK FORCE); HETHERINGTON & KELLY, *supra* note 11, at 48; FINAL REPORT OF THE MICHIGAN SUPREME COURT TASK FORCE ON GENDER ISSUES IN THE COURTS 50, 60 (1989) (hereinafter MICHIGAN TASK FORCE); REPORT OF THE OREGON SUPREME COURT/ OREGON STATE BAR TASK FORCE ON GENDER FAIRNESS 47, 51–52 (1998);

David L. Chambers, *Fathers, the Welfare System, and the Virtues and Perils of Child-Support Enforcement*, 81 VA. L. REV. 2575, 2588–89 (1995); Ronald K. Henry, *Child Support at a Crossroads: When the Real World Intrudes Upon Academics and Advocates*, 33 FAM. L.Q. 235, 238 (1999).

17. *See* Swank, *supra* note 16, at 358. Swank notes that this amount exceeds the annual gross national product of Ireland. *Id.*

18. Swank, *supra* note 16, at 358–59. Nonpayment does not present a new problem. For instance, in 1989, 26% of custodial mothers who had child support orders received no support at all, and another 26% obtained only partial payment. *See* Paula G. Roberts, *Child Support Orders: Problems with Enforcement*, 4 THE FUTURE OF CHILDREN: CHILDREN AND DIVORCE 101, 110 (1994). Moreover, fathers' refusals to support their children has caused states problems for nearly 100 years. In the early 20th century, for instance, states passed legislation that criminalized desertion and nonsupport. *See* ANN MASON, FROM FATHER'S PROPERTY TO CHILDREN'S RIGHTS: THE HISTORY OF CHILD CUSTODY IN THE UNITED STATES 94–95 (1994). Then, as now, however, these laws largely proved ineffective at providing children with needed funds, and courts sent few deserting fathers to jail. *Id.* at 95–96. Mason argues that poor mothers likely would have fared better without these tougher laws. Widows became almost the exclusive recipients of mother's pensions, because the toughened laws encouraged the belief that deserting fathers, not the state, should provide for their families. *Id.* at 96. Rather than provide aid to deserted mothers and their children, state agencies unsuccessfully pursued the deserting father. *Id.* By the mid 1930s, courts no longer proved reluctant to jail deserting, nonsupporting fathers. *Id.* at 115. Judges, however, responded ambivalently to a divorced father's obligation to support his children over whom he no longer had custody. Some courts reasoned that the father's obligation to support his children arose from the father's right to complete custody and control of the children. If the father no longer had this right to custody, perhaps he also should no longer have the obligation of support. *Id.* at 115. Most courts, however, created new rationales to justify a father's continuing obligation to support children over whom he had lost custody at divorce. *Id.* at 116. Some courts found that "divine law" supported the father's obligation; others reasoned that fathers could fulfill the duty of support better than mothers. *Id.* at 116.

19. *See* Melton, *supra* note 11, at 2038 (citing *U.S. Commission on Interstate Child Support, Summary of Recommendations to Congress*, 18 FAM. L. REP. 2105 (1992)); Roberts, *supra* note 18, at 108–110 (citing 42 U.S.C. §666(a)(2); 45 C.F.R. §303.101(b)(2); 42 U.S.C. §§666(b)(3)(A); 666 (a)(8); 664; 666(a)(3)).

20. Many argue that preservation of state and federal welfare funds motivates governmental efforts to collect child support rather than the desire to improve the financial circumstances of children. *See, e.g.*, BAKER, *supra* note 11, at 327–28.

21. FLA. STAT. §61.12(1) (2002).

22. *Id.* §61.1301(1)(a) (2002).

23. *Id.* §161.301(1)(b)(4) (2002). Many states now route payments through a state agency that forwards money to the custodial parent. MAUREEN BAKER,

CANADIAN FAMILY POLICIES: CROSS-NATIONAL COMPARISONS 305, 326 (1995).

24. FLA. STAT. §61.1301 (2002).

25. *Id.* §61.13015 (2002).

26. *Id.* §61.13016 (2002).

27. Enforcement services also include the location of absent parents and the establishment of paternity. *See* BAKER, *supra* note 23, at 327.

28. Swank reviews the research on the suspension of drivers license, the booting of cars, and the incarceration of the defiant parent and concludes that these three enforcement mechanisms have successfully increased child support payments. Swank, *supra* note 16, at 366–78. *See also* Marsha Garrison, *Child Support and Children's Poverty,* 28 FAM. L.Q. 475 (1994) (reviewing ANDREA H. BELLER & JOHN W. GRAHAM, SMALL CHANGE: THE ECONOMICS OF CHILD SUPPORT (1993) & DONALD J. HERNANDEZ, AMERICA'S CHILDREN: RESOURCES FROM FAMILY, GOVERNMENT AND THE ECONOMY (1993)); Henry, *supra* note 16, at 239, 246–47; Roberts, *supra* note 18, at 114–15.

29. *See* Swank, *supra* note 16, at 358–59.

30. *See also* Roberts, *supra* note 18, at 103.

31. *See, e.g.,* CONNECTICUT TASK FORCE, *supra* note 16, at 144–45; REPORT OF THE GENDER BIAS STUDY OF THE SUPREME JUDICIAL COURT, COMMONWEALTH OF MASSACHUSETTS 31 (1989) (noting 1981 nationwide statistics that indicate that only 43% of women awarded maintenance received full payment and that 33% of women awarded maintenance received no payment at all) (citing U.S. BUREAU OF THE CENSUS, U.S. DEP'T OF COMMERCE); MICHIGAN TASK FORCE, *supra* note 16, at 55; LESLIE A. MORGAN, AFTER MARRIAGE ENDS: ECONOMIC CONSEQUENCES FOR MIDLIFE WOMEN 30 (1991) (noting that only 14% to 15% of women receive maintenance awards and that in 1985 only 73.3% of women awarded maintenance received at least part of the amount awarded).

32. *See, e.g.,* TYLER, *supra* note 3, at 22–23, 26 & n.11 (1990); Tyler, *supra* note 1, at 984–86. *See also, e.g.,* Marc Galanter & Mia Cahill, *"Most Cases Settle": Judicial Promotion and Regulation of Settlements,* 46 STAN. L. REV. 1339, 1381 (1994); Gerald Turkel, *Legitimation, Authority, and Consensus Formation,* 8 INT'L L.J. SOC. L. 19, 22–23 (1980).

33. Some child abductions relate directly to judicial incompetence. For instance, some parents choose to hide their children rather than allow court-ordered visitation with a sexually abusive parent. *See* Meredith Sherman Fahn, *Allegations of Child Sexual Abuse in Custody Disputes, Getting to the Truth of the Matter,* 25 FAM. L.Q. 193, 196–97 (1991).

34. *See* Heather Hammer, et al., *Children Abducted by Family Members: National Estimates and Characteristics,* in U.S. DEP'T OF JUSTICE, NATIONAL INCIDENCE STUDIES OF MISSING, ABDUCTED, RUNAWAY, AND THROWNAWAY CHILDREN 2 (Oct. 2002), available at http://www.ojjdp.ncjrs.org. Biological fathers abducted 53% of these children, whereas biological mothers abducted 25%. *Id.* at 4. Grandparents accounted for 14%. *Id.* Forty-six percent of family-abducted children returned within one week, and 26% within one day. *Id.* at 6. Twenty-

one percent remained missing for one month or longer, 6% remained missing for six months or more, and 6% remained missing at the time of the survey interview. *Id.*

35. *Id.* at 4, 6 & tab. 5. Family members account for 49% of juvenile kidnappings. David Finkelhor & Richard Ormrod, *Kidnapping of Juveniles: Patterns from NIBRS*, 3 Juvenile Justice Bull. 3 (U.S. Dep't of Justice, June 2000). Earlier researchers estimate that the number of kidnappings by noncustodial parents range from 25,000 to 100,000 per year. Daniel Oberdorfer, Comment, *Larson v. Dunn: Toward a Reasoned Response to Parental Kidnapping*, 74 Minn. L. Rev. 1701, 1703 n.17 (1991) (noting that people most frequently estimate that 100,000 parental kidnappings per year occur); Christopher L. Blakesley, *Child Custody—Jurisdiction and Procedure*, 35 Emory L.J. 291, 296 & n.25 (1986) (estimate made before the effective date of the Parental Kidnapping Prevention Act, 28 U.S.C. §1738(A) (1982)). Some parents lack the sometimes substantial financial resources necessary to recover their children. *See* Linda K. Girdner & Patricia M. Hoff, Obstacles to the Recovery and Return of Parentally Abducted Children 17 (1994).

36. *See* Hammer et al., *supra* note 34, at 4, 5 & tab. 3. According to Grief and Hegar's studies, three-quarters of all abducted children were six years of age or younger when abducted, having an average age of two years. *See* Neil C. Livingston, Rescue My Child 96 (1992) (citing work by Geoffrey L. Grief and Rebecca Hegar that found three-quarters of abducted children had not yet reached the age of 6).

37. *See* Livingston, *supra* note 36, at 95–96.

38. *See* Cara L. Finan, Comment, *Convention of the Rights of the Child: A Potentially Effective Remedy in Cases of International Child Abduction*, 34 Santa Clara L. Rev. 1007, 1030 & n.175 (1994) (citing generally Neil C. Livingston, Rescue My Child (1992)).

39. *See, e.g.*, Raymond Paternoster et al., *Do Fair Procedures Matter? The Effect of Procedural Justice on Spouse Assault*, 31 L. & Soc'y Rev. 163, 167–68 (1997); Tyler, *supra* note 1; Tom R. Tyler & Kenneth Rasinski, *Procedural Justice, Institutional Legitimacy, and the Acceptance of Unpopular U.S. Supreme Court Decisions: A Reply to Gibson*, 25 L. & Soc'y Rev. 621 (1991); Tyler, *supra* note 3.

40. *See generally* Jay D. Teachman, *Who Pays? Receipt of Child Support in the United States*, 53 J. Marriage & Fam. 759, 760 (1991).

41. As one commentator stated

> Americans no longer hold strong and universal convictions about the solemn duties of men to their children—or to the children's mother. The cultural pressures that once pushed men into accepting lifelong family obligations have grown weak. Far too many men have abandoned the responsibilities their own fathers and grandfathers took for granted.

Stephen Chapman, *Deluding Ourselves about the Doctrine of the Family*, Chi. Trib., Feb. 19, 1995, §4, at 3. *See also* Thornton, *supra* note 11, at 603–04.

42. *See* HETHERINGTON & KELLY, *supra* note 11, at 48–49. Judges have shown reluctance to overburden men with support obligations partially because financial obligations to first families can interfere with men's ability to establish and support new families. Child support guidelines that allow a divorced parent to reduce his or her obligation to a previous family based on support obligations to a new family also reflect this attitude. Deborah L. Rhode & Martha Minow, *Reforming the Questions, Questioning the Reforms: Feminist Perspectives on Divorce Law, in* DIVORCE REFORM AT THE CROSSROADS 191, 205 (Stephen D. Sugarman & Herma Hill Kay eds. 1990).

43. In their study, Maccoby and Mnookin found a positive correlation between the amount of contact a father had with his child and the father's compliance with a child support order. ELEANOR E. MACCOBY & ROBERT H. MNOOKIN, DIVIDING THE CHILD: SOCIAL AND LEGAL DILEMMAS OF CUSTODY 251–57 (1992).

44. *See* DAVID BLANKENHORN, FATHERLESS AMERICA 151 (1995).

45. As one commentator notes: "If you win the child you are good so you confirm yourself as an individual. If you lose the child you lose your self esteem." *Contested Custody and the Courts, in* ABA SECTION ON FAMILY LAW, CHILD CUSTODY DISPUTES: SEARCHING FOR SOLOMON, 18, Wingspread Conference (Oct. 1988–Aug. 1989).

46. *See* MARTHA ALBERTSON FINEMAN, THE NEUTERED MOTHER, THE SEXUAL FAMILY AND OTHER TWENTIETH CENTURY TRAGEDIES (1995).

47. Dworkin notes that

> Most people think that they have associative obligations just by belonging to groups defined by social practice, which is not necessarily a matter of choice or consent, but that they can lose these obligations if other members of the group do not extend them the benefits of belonging to the group.

DWORKIN, *supra* note 5, at 196. Associative obligation, argues Dworkin, relies primarily on reciprocity. *Id.* at 198–200.

48. *See* Harry D. Krause, *Child Support Reassessed: Limits of Private Responsibility and the Public Interest, in* DIVORCE REFORM AT THE CROSSROADS 166, 178–183 (Stephen D. Sugarman & Herma Hill Kay eds. 1990).

49. One might argue that the social problems created by noncompliance with child support orders provide a welcome and necessary precursor of much needed social change. If enough noncustodial parents refuse to pay child support and alarm about the postdivorce economic deprivation of children continues to grow, people might require the government to take some responsibility for children. Some already suggest that the federal government should establish a child support assurance system, which would provide a national guideline for determining child support, automatic payroll deduction of the ordered support, and a federal guarantee of support in the event the noncustodial parent defaults. *See* Irwin Garfinkel et al., *Child Support Orders: A Perspective on Reform*, 4 THE FUTURE OF CHILDREN: CHILDREN AND DIVORCE 84, 91–96 (1994). This proposal emphasizes our collective responsibility for the well-being of divorced children

rather than the responsibility of the individual noncustodial parent. Conceivably this approach would provide more support for children than pursuit of deadbeat dads. Some also suggest the superior morality of this approach, because of the diminished value of the parent–child relationship to the noncustodial parent and the importance of healthy children to society generally. *See* Krause, *supra* note 48, at 189. The current political commitment to reduce public expenditures to needy families and the approval of that commitment by most of our citizenry suggest that years will pass before this country will recognize our collective responsibility for the well-being of children in single-parent households. In the interim, I hope that the reforms suggested here will provide more politically palatable solutions to the noncompliance problem.

2

DYSFUNCTIONAL RESULTS

Justice is the first virtue of social institutions, as truth is of systems of thought. A theory however elegant and economical must be rejected or revised if it is untrue; likewise laws and institutions no matter how efficient and well-arranged must be reformed or abolished if they are unjust.

—John A. Rawls, A *Theory of Justice*

A legitimate legal system must produce just results. Consensus on what results a legal system should promote, however, proves difficult. Legal scholars debate the moral and logical premises for holding some values superior to others in law.[1] Moral relativism, skepticism, and individualism pervade society and suggest that individual, not collective, conscience determines morality.[2] The mantle of privacy that envelops "the family" heightens the importance of individualism in the context of family dissolution.[3] Concepts of "right" and "just" lose force, because justice has no collective meaning.[4] Our fractured sense of justice provides little guidance in the choice of the values that a legal system should support.

Justice proves particularly difficult to define in divorce law. Many influential justice theorists ignore how gender roles within the family promote inequality between spouses inside and outside the family.[5] Others simply assume, without explanation, the naturalness of injustice within families, or conversely the justness of that institution.[6] This theoretical deficit persists among elite men despite significant insights about injustice in the family offered by feminist scholars.[7] Feminists themselves also differ on what divorce outcomes the law should promote.[8]

Add to theoretical inadequacies the tense social reality to which the legal system must respond. Strained gender relations permeate our families and our society generally;[9] interest groups intensify these differences.[10] Fathers' rights groups seek increased access for fathers to their children upon divorce.[11] Their strident advocacy distorts discussions on what type of custody and visitation arrangements best serve children's interests.[12] Similarly, feminists fear that candid discussion of the problems that confront single-parent families will fuel the political and rhetorical attacks on single mothers, because most divorced children live with their mothers and mother-blaming commonly occurs.[13] These groups might have legitimate concerns, but their cynicism and entrenchment inhibit clear thought and consensus about what results the family law system can and should produce.[14]

Racial diversity and tension complicate further any search for consensus.[15] Families of different racial groups have unique histories and live in divergent social conditions.[16] Their family resources and relationship patterns differ, creating different levels and types of interests. Presumably one group's perceptions of appropriate results may differ from that of another. Racial tension between groups and diversity among groups also inhibit consensus. The White majority may have difficulty taking seriously the plight of poor, divorced African American or Hispanic families,[17] because they do not care or they believe themselves immune to poverty. Nonetheless, many middle-class White children suffer poverty or economic deprivation after divorce,[18] and the poverty of any child affects us all.[19]

Gendered attitudes of the divorce disputants themselves raise more difficulties. A wife who devotes her life to home and hearth likely will expect her husband to continue to provide for her after divorce. In contrast, the husband who has labored for years outside the home may see his hard-earned income as primarily his. This wife likely will perceive a short-term rehabilitative maintenance award as inadequate, whereas the husband likely will perceive such an award as unjustified. Neither spouse experiences the result as fair. We can say the same for many contested divorce issues.[20]

General consensus in the abstract, of course, might come easier than consensus between former spouses regarding a specific outcome. For instance, let us assume that few husbands would support the general proposition that wives should live in poverty after divorce. Yet, when asked to part with some of his income to prevent his former wife's poverty, any particular husband might balk. Consensus on general fairness norms, however, remains important. Presumably, a lawyer might persuade a reluctant husband to provide spousal maintenance to his former wife by reference to the general norm, articulated in the law, that wives should not live in poverty after divorce, particularly if the husband previously agreed with that abstract proposition.[21]

Although identification of the values our divorce system should support proves daunting,[22] we no long can afford to ignore or politicize this issue: the individual and collective costs are too great. At a minimum, our legal system should strive to avoid outcomes that promote the dysfunctionality of postdivorce families, because those results threaten individual and the collective well-being.[23]

Far too many divorce outcomes threaten our social foundations and our future well-being. Families, we maintain, provide the bedrock for society.[24] Whether wise or not,[25] we rely on the family to provide material and emotional support for its members[26] and to nurture, educate, and properly socialize the young. The results produced in divorce cases, however, frequently impair the ability of postdivorce families[27] to perform their traditional functions. Consider the current state of divorce affairs.

THE CHILDREN

As noted earlier, the divorce rate in the United States remains high,[28] supporting the prediction that before they reach age 16 approximately 40% to 50% of America's children will experience the divorce of their parents.[29] At divorce these children frequently experience a precipitous drop in their standard of living.[30] Many sink into poverty.[31] Bianchi and McArthur found that children are nearly twice as likely to live in poverty after a divorce than before; specifically, the percentage of impoverished children increased from 19% to 36% within 4 months of divorce.[32]

Financial deprivation inhibits the academic, social, and psychological development of divorced children.[33] Many become depressed[34] and perform poorly at school,[35] compromising their success.[36] Inadequate food,[37] housing,[38] and medical care[39] threaten children's physical health.[40] Many divorced children grow angry and bitter at the financial discrepancy between their homes and the homes of their fathers.[41] Multiple moves, undertaken for economic reasons, deprive children of familiar peers, neighborhoods, and schools.[42]

Divorced children's diminished financial circumstances often depress their social status and their self-esteem. One mother reports

> I had $950 a month, and the house payment was $760, so there was hardly anything left over. So there we were: my son qualified for free lunches at school. We'd been living on over $4,000 a month, and there we were. That's so humiliating. What that does to the self-esteem of even a child is absolutely unbelievable. And it isn't hidden; everybody knows the situation. They knew at his school that he was the kid with the free lunch coupons. . . . My son is real tall and growing. I really didn't have any money to buy him clothes, and attorneys don't think school clothes are essential. So he was wearing these sweatshirts that were too small for him. Then one day he didn't want to go to school because the kids had been calling him Frankenstein because his arms

and legs were hanging out of his clothes—they were too short. That does terrible things to a kid, it really does. We just weren't equipped to cope with it.[43]

Loss of social status may cause divorced children to join more marginal groups of children,[44] and criminal behavior increases.[45]

Divorced children from middle-class families frequently receive no financial assistance for college and consequently do not go.[46] Most of the youngsters in Wallerstein and Blakeslee's study, for instance, came from middle-class families where one or both parents had college degrees, and most of the children attended high schools where 85% of all students attended college. Yet, at 10-year follow-up interviews, only half of the divorced children were attending or had completed a two-year or four-year college. One-third of them, including many highly intelligent children, had dropped out of high school or college. Of the children who attended college, only 1 in 10 received full financial support from one or both parents. Others received no help at all, or only limited financial help—even from wealthy fathers who could afford to help much more. Among the fathers in the study who could afford to help with college expenses, only one third assisted their children. Two thirds provided nothing.[47]

Divorced children whose economic situations do improve over time typically face years of interim hardship.[48] They cannot reclaim the potential lost during those years.[49] A highly intelligent child, for instance, might perform poorly in school for three of his four high-school years because of stress and depression caused by his family's financial hardship. Even if his custodial mother improves the family's financial position by remarriage at the end of his junior year, he cannot change his earlier grades. His choice of college becomes restricted, and he may not achieve what he could have achieved had his family remained economically sound.

Although a child's positive relationship with the custodial parent, as well as that parent's well-being, positively affect a child's divorce adjustment,[50] many divorced children live with financially and logistically stressed single parents who become less available to the children than before the divorce.[51] Not only must these children adjust to less contact with noncustodial parents,[52] they also must cope with the diminished caretaking capacity[53] and availability of the custodial parent.[54] The logistical strains on their households force many divorced children to assume adult responsibilities,[55] sometimes compromising their academic achievement and their social development. Moreover, many children are caught in the hostile crossfire between parents,[56] stressing further their emotional reserves.[57]

Courts order children into confusing visitation patterns that compromise them even more.[58] Despite numerous studies indicating that when parents remain conflicted children fare poorly when they retain frequent contact with both parents,[59] courts continue to place children in joint physical custody arrangements with hostile parents.[60] Far too frequently courts order children to visit parents who have sexually or physically abused them,[61] despite experts who note that an important healer of sexually abused children is their use of the judicial system to halt the abuse.[62] Worse yet, with shocking frequency courts award custody of children to the abusive parent[63] or to a father who has abused the child's mother.[64] Some children never recover[65]—they are lost to themselves and to us.

Court cases provide numerous examples of destructive custody decisions. In a Massachusetts case, the court granted visitation rights to a father who fired a gun into the home of his ex-girlfriend, killed her friend, and was charged with attempted murder of his child. In another Massachusetts's case, the court asked a man who pled guilty to rape whether he wanted visitation rights to the child conceived as the result of the rape.[66] Many more similar cases exist.

The suffering and lost potential of divorced children should prompt humanist concern.[67] Surely the idea that children should have the right to a standard of living adequate to ensure their proper growth and development, the right to an education, the right to adequate health care, and the right to protection from torture, mistreatment, and sexual exploitation is not novel or controversial.[68] A more selfish concern, however, also is warranted. We all suffer when the results reached in divorce cases compromise the physical and mental health and the academic achievement of these children. They may not grow into productive and responsible citizens. Even if they do, their full potential may remain undeveloped.[69] Sometimes they become embittered, dysfunctional adults, unable to help themselves or contribute to our collective well being.[70] Likewise, we all suffer when many divorced children engage in criminal behavior. The costs to police and punish juvenile offenders keeps rising. And some of us, undoubtedly, will become their victims.

THE ADULTS

We not only lose the potential of our children, we also needlessly harm many divorced adults.[71] Women, trapped in the poverty or economic deprivation that frequently follows divorce,[72] have difficulty obtaining the job experience and education that would help them contribute what they otherwise could to themselves,[73] their children, and society.[74]

Many divorced mothers struggle to find work and make ends meet.[75] Not all succeed.[76] Financial desperation keeps many women trapped in low-paying jobs.[77] Rising numbers of divorced mothers must hold two jobs to survive.[78] Their financial worries compromise their physical[79] and emotional health,[80] as well as their parenting skills.[81] Divorced mothers agonize as they watch their children suffer.[82] Their anger at ex-husbands mounts as they and their children go without resources and opportunities that they once had—and that the ex-husband often retains.[83] Men, frequently severed from meaningful day-to-day relationships with their children,[84] grieve their loss and sometimes emotionally and financially abandon their children.[85] As Blankenship observes

> The Visiting Father is hard to see. He is a shadow dad, a displaced man trying not to become an ex-father. He is a father who has left the premise. He still stops by, but he does not stay. He is on the outside looking in. No longer the man of the house, he has been largely de-fathered. He is a father once removed. He has become a visitor.
>
> As a visitor, he is part father, part stranger. Physical distance, combined with estrangement from his children's mother, has radically diminished his paternity. Now a weekend and holiday dad, a treat father, a telephone father, he is frequently filled with resentment and remorse. He mourns the loss of his fatherhood much as one would mourn the loss of health.
>
> He loves his children, but he did not stay with them. He wants to be a good father, but in the ways that matter most, he cannot be. He cannot raise his children. He can only visit them.[86]

Perhaps we do not take the plight of divorced women and men seriously because we expect them to recover.[87] Some women, of course, do manage to improve their financial situation by obtaining education, training, or higher paying jobs, or by increasing their work hours.[88] Yet the financial desperation of many others induces them to take whatever low-paying jobs they can find.[89] Many women under age 30, and some women under 40, remarry[90] and improve their financial positions.[91] Yet they, like their children, face interim years of hardship that compromise their lives.[92] Moreover, many divorced women never remarry,[93] particularly older women and women with custody of children.[94] Others remarry out of economic desperation[95] and enter into poor relationships with men who abuse them, their children, or both.[96] Many remarriages create adaptation problems for children[97] and adults.[98] Remarriages frequently end in divorce,[99] perpetuating the cycle and again disrupting the children's lives.[100] Many women and their children simply do not recover from the financial hardships of divorce.[101] Our failure to take seriously the economic deprivation of divorced women and their dependent children seems at best shortsighted, and at worst inhumane.[102]

Divorced men, too, are expected to remarry and establish new families. Yet the loss of meaningful contact with their children from their first families haunts many divorced fathers.[103] Their children also suffer from substantially diminished exposure to, or abandonment by, these fathers.[104] Moreover, we stigmatize adults who do not maintain meaningful relationships with their children by harboring unspoken suspicions about their morality.[105] Our vision of the happily remarried divorced father, then, is superficial and encourages us to trivialize his loss and that of his children.

All of this suggests that the current family law system far too frequently produces results that threaten our foundations by crippling postdivorce families. Moreover, the postdivorce dysfunctionality of families primarily seems related to two results: economic deprivation[106] and insensitive custody and visitation arrangements.[107] Because divorce restructures so many people's lives in this country, the state simply must promote the functionality of these "families." The procedural justice critique that follows exposes many of the factors that contribute to poor outcomes and suggests what procedural reforms might generate better ones. A procedurally just system can also encourage compliance with results that do not necessarily benefit individual interests[108] and can enhance the legitimacy of the legal system.

NOTES

1. *See* Richard H. Fallon, Jr., *Of Speakable Ethics and Constitutional Law: A Review Essay*, 56 U. Chi. L. Rev. 1523 (1989) (reviewing Michael J. Perry, Morality, Politics, and Law: A Bicentennial Essay (1988)).

2. *Id.* at 1527, 1536.

3. *See generally* Daniel A. Krauss & Bruce D. Sales, *Legal Standards, Expertise, and Experts in the Resolution of Contested Custody Cases*, 6 Psychol. Pub. Pol'y & L. 843, 845–46 (2000).

4. *See* Carl Schneider, *Moral Discourse and the Transformation of American Family Law*, 83 Mich. L. Rev. 1803 (1985) (noting the decline in moral discourse in family law); Lee E. Teitelbaum, *Moral Discourse and Family Law*, 84 Mich. L. Rev. 430, 431 (1985) ("Where courts and agencies once felt confident in relying on their judgments regarding what 'good' and 'moral' parents should do for their children, those 'value judgments' now seem insensitive to non-middle-class families.").

5. *See* Susan Moller Okin, Justice, Gender, and the Family 9 (1989) (including in this category Bruce A. Ackerman, Social Justice in the Liberal State (1980); Ronald Dworkin, Taking Rights Seriously (1977); William Galston, Justice and the Human Good (1980); Alasdair MacIntyre, After Virtue (1984); Alasdair MacIntyre, Whose Justice? Whose Rationality? (1988); Robert Nozick, Anarchy, State, and Utopia (1974); Roberto Unger, Knowledge and Politics (1975); and Roberto Unger, The Critical Legal Studies Movement (1983)). *See id* at 7–109 for fuller development of this argument. *See generally* Carole Pateman, The Sexual Contract (1988).

6. *See* Okin, *supra* note 5, at 9 (arguing that John Rawls assumes that the family is just).

7. *Id.* at 7; PATEMAN, *supra* note 5, at 19. Feminists, for instance, have challenged the patriarchal presumption that the domination of women by men is natural or inevitable. *See* OKIN, *supra* note 5, at 7. Feminists also challenge the presumption that the husband's postdivorce income belongs exclusively to him. They argue for wives' entitlement to a portion of that income, because the wife has helped him earn it. Many seek to commodify wives' service contributions to the family rather than assume that the wife "donates" such services out of love and altruism. Commodification of household services supports their financial relevance at divorce.

8. *See* Penelope E. Bryan, *Reasking the Woman Question at Divorce*, 75 CHI.-KENT L. REV. 713, 733–53 (2000). *See generally* Mary Becker, *Patriarchy and Inequality: Towards a Substantive Feminism*, 1999 U. CHI. LEGAL F. 21.

9. *See* Ellen Goodman, *Media Blamed for a Resegregation of the Sexes*, CHI. TRIB., Mar. 14, 1995, §1, at 15 (media focus on and exploitation of differences between men and women help to create and sustain tension between men and women).

10. The National Organization for Women (NOW), for instance, offers an educational program for judges on child sexual abuse allegations in custody disputes. Rather than recognize the needed service NOW provides, father's rights groups remain suspicious. *See* David E. Rovella, *Sex-Abuse Charge in Custody Fights Perplexes Courts: New NOW Curriculum Gives Judges Guidance, But Fathers' Groups are Wary*, NAT'L L.J., Nov. 11, 1996, at A1, A20. Moreover, fathers' rights groups ignore evidence to the contrary and continue to maintain that mothers fabricate most allegations of child sexual abuse. *Id.* Many commentators acknowledge child custody issues as fertile ground for gender wars. *See* MARY ANN MASON, THE CUSTODY WARS: WHY CHILDREN ARE LOSING THE LEGAL BATTLE AND WHAT WE CAN DO ABOUT IT 2 (1999); Herma Hill Kay, *No-Fault Divorce and Child Custody: Chilling out the Gender Wars*, 36 FAM. L.Q. 27 (2002).

11. *See* MAUREEN BAKER, CANADIAN FAMILY POLICIES: CROSS-NATIONAL COMPARISONS 329 (1995); Kay, *supra* note 10, at 35–37. Blankenhorn provides an apt description of the fervor and the political organization of fathers' rights groups in the United States. *See* DAVID BLANKENHORN, FATHERLESS AMERICA: CONFRONTING OUR MOST URGENT SOCIAL PROBLEM 161–63 (1995). These groups advocate for the importance of fathers to children generally and decry what they perceive as the marginalization of fathers. *E.g.*, *id.* *See also* Jed H. Abraham, *Why Men Fight for Their Kids: How Bias in the System Puts Dads at a Disadvantage*, 17 FAM. ADVOC. 48 (1994); Ronald K. Henry, *"Primary Caretaker": Is It a Ruse?*, 17 FAM. ADVOC. 53 (1994).

12. Schepard et al. provide one illustration. They argue that mediators should promote joint custody before the authors establish that joint custody facilitates children's best interests. They cite research that indicates children, in general, benefit from contact with both parents after divorce to justify their position. Andrew Schepard et al., *Ground Rules for Custody Mediation and Modification*, 48 ALBANY L. REV. 616, 625 (1984). Nothing, however, justifies their leap from the cited research to their conclusion that joint physical custody necessarily benefits divorced children. Moreover, Wallerstein and Kelly conducted one

of the studies they cite. The researchers themselves specified that their study concerned only 60 California families and that only a few other studies of divorced children existed. They then cautioned

> One of the unhappy consequences is that the findings of this study in California, drawn primarily, but not entirely, from a white and middle-class population, must await comparison with those families from other significant segments of the population whose experience may resemble or may diverge from these in important regards. For the present, we cannot know.

JUDITH S. WALLERSTEIN & JOAN BERLIN KELLY, SURVIVING THE BREAKUP: HOW CHILDREN AND PARENTS COPE WITH DIVORCE 5 (1980). The researchers then painstakingly explain that their sample of divorced children does not represent the larger population and that their results suffer from the lack of a control group, standard methodological problems. *Id.* at 7–10. In their advocacy for joint custody, these limitations and cautions have escaped Schepard et al.'s attention.

13. *E.g.,* NANCY CHODOROW, THE REPRODUCTION OF MOTHERING: PSYCHOANALYSIS AND THE SOCIOLOGY OF GENDER (1978); NANCY E. DOWD, IN DEFENSE OF SINGLE-PARENT FAMILIES xii–xviii, 3–15 (1997); P. Caplan & I. Hall-McCorquodale, *Mother Blaming in Major Clinical Journals,* 55 AM. J. ORTHO-PSYCHIATRY 345 (1985); Bernardine Dohrn, *Bad Mothers, Good Mothers, and the State: Children on the Margins,* 2 U. CHI. L. SCH. ROUNDTABLE 1 (1995); M. Laurie Leitch, *The Politics of Compromise: A Feminist Perspective on Mediation,* 14/15 MEDIATION Q. 163, 167 (1986–87). Martha Fineman argues that society especially stigmatizes and scorns single mothers as deviant. Martha L.A. Fineman, *Masking Dependency: The Political Role of Family Rhetoric,* 81 VA. L. REV. 2181, 2182, 2190–93, 2206–08 (1995). Some poverty theorists blame mothers for the poverty of mother-led families. *See* BAKER, *supra* note 11, at 348.

14. *See* Bryan, *supra* note 8, at 733–53. The report of the Missouri Task Force on Gender and Justice illustrates this problem. Victims of domestic violence and their attorneys report that the legal system responds poorly to their needs. Alleged perpetrators and their attorneys claim that women frequently make allegations of domestic violence to gain an advantage in divorce negotiations and that the legal system discriminates against men on issues of domestic violence. *Report of the Missouri Task Force on Gender and Justice,* 58 MO. L. REV. 485, 500–527 (1993) (hereinafter *Missouri Task Force*).

15. *See* JUNE CARBONE, FROM PARTNERS TO PARENTS 68–84 (2000). *See generally* BAKER, *supra* note 11, at 342.

16. *See* CARBONE, *supra* note 15, at 68–84; Rukalie Jayakody et al., *Family Support to Single and Married African American Mothers: The Provision of Financial, Emotional, and Child Care Assistance,* 55 J. MARRIAGE & FAM. 261 (1993); Cynthia R. Mabry, *African Americans "Are not Carbon Copies" of White Americans: The Role of African American Culture in Mediation of Family Disputes,* 13 OHIO ST. J. DISP. RESOL. 405 (1998).

17. *See* CARBONE, *supra* note 15, at 80, 81.

18. *See* E. MAVIS HETHERINGTON & JOHN KELLY, FOR BETTER OR FOR WORSE: DIVORCE RECONSIDERED 9–10 (2002) (noting that many women, even middle-class women, become impoverished as a result of divorce); LENORE J. WEITZMAN, THE DIVORCE REVOLUTION: THE UNEXPECTED SOCIAL AND ECONOMIC CONSEQUENCES FOR WOMEN AND CHILDREN IN AMERICA 352 (1985).

19. Tyler makes the interesting observation, based on research, that an individual who identifies himself or herself as an American citizen rather than exclusively as a member of a subgroup likely will accept outcomes generated by authorities in a system the individual perceives as procedurally just. Tom R. Tyler, *Multiculturalism and the Willingness of Citizens to Defer to Law and to Legal Authorities*, 25 L. & SOC. INQUIRY 983, 1004–13 (2000). Our acknowledgment, then, of our interdependence and our membership in society at large enhances the ability of a procedurally just system to promote acceptance and compliance with outcomes that do not necessarily satisfy our individual interests.

20. *See* Lynn Hecht Schafran, *Gender Bias in Family Courts*, 17 FAM. ADVOCATE 22, 22 (1994) (fathers and mothers perceive state courts as biased against them in custody cases). *See also* Jerry W. McCant, *The Cultural Contradiction of Fathers as Nonparents*, 21 FAM. L.Q. 127 (1987); Nancy D. Polikoff, *Why Are Mothers Losing: A Brief Analysis of Criteria Used in Child Custody Determinations*, 7 WOMEN'S RTS. L. REP. 235 (1982). The family law system, much as the entire justice system, has grown increasingly reliant on settlement rather than adjudication as a means to resolve disputes. *See* Marc Galanter & Mia Cahill, *"Most Cases Settle": Judicial Promotion and Regulation of Settlements*, 46 STAN. L. REV. 1339 (1994). Some argue that settlements, particularly those reached in mediation, generate results superior to those reached in adjudication. *Id.* at 1371–78. One need not agree with Galanter and Cahill that settlement deserves a more critical appraisal to recognize that this reliance on settlement to generate superior justice alleviates the pressure on the family law system to examine the values that its procedures and laws should promote.

21. As Galanter and Cahill note

> [L]aw may change behavior by influencing estimations of the correctness or feasibility of various sorts of behaviors. We learn what society condones from courts and from law-related activities. Communication by a court about the existence of a law or its application may change other actors' moral evaluation of an item of conduct.

Galanter & Cahill, *supra* note 20, at 1382.

22. *See* BAKER, *supra* note 11, at 343 (acknowledging the difficulty of building consensus on family issues in a country that offers cultural diversity, a tradition of individual rights, and an ideology of family privacy).

23. Therapeutic jurisprudence also supports the concerns raised in this section. Therapeutic jurisprudence demands empirical evaluation of the law's effect on those it purportedly serves. When the law's intervention fails to promote or undermines therapeutic goals, reforms must occur. Moreover, when the law does intervene in families, it must do so competently and with public accountability. *See Developments: Unified Family Courts and the Child Protection Dilemma*,

116 Harv. L. Rev. 2099, 2104 (2003). The reforms in this book, however, do not seek to provide therapeutic services to families of divorce. Rather than offer therapeutic services, the author asserts that the procedural reforms in this book will improve the psychological, emotional, and economic condition of many divorced families.

24. As Thornton explains

> [T]he age of European exploration revealed some central facts about the nature of human lifestyles around the world. One of the most important conclusions emanating from these explorations was the discovery of the universal importance of family institutions. Family and kinship relations historically have been central principles of social organization throughout the world. Kinship structures have been central features of virtually every society studied by several generations of explorers and scholars.

Arland Thornton, *Comparative and Historical Perspectives on Marriage, Divorce, and Family Life*, 1994 Utah L. Rev. 587, 599. Thornton also explains, however, that in modern society, many nonfamily institutions also hold sway over individuals, organizing their time, determining their well-being, and exercising authority over them. *Id.* Despite inroads by other institutions, Thornton argues that scholarly literature continues to reflect the importance of families in organizing the activities and in promoting the well-being of individuals. *Id.* at 600, 602.

25. Placement of the burden of childrearing exclusively within the nuclear family discourages the larger society from assuming, or even considering the assumption of, any responsibility for the children of others. Fineman argues that placement of the burden for dependent care within the private family allows the state to ignore the existence of dependency and to employ a rhetoric that idealizes capitalistic individualism, independence, self-sufficiency, and autonomy. Fineman, *supra* note 13, at 2205–06. *See also* Baker, *supra* note 11, at 350 (acknowledging that family values rhetoric that places sole responsibility for family members within the family itself provides a mechanism for governments to save their resources); Kathryn Abrams, *Choice, Dependence, and the Reinvigoration of the Traditional Family*, 73 Ind. L.J. 517, 519, 530 (1998). At a time when many, if not most, nuclear families find fulfillment of all of their traditional roles difficult to impossible, see Gary B. Melton, *Children, Families, and the Courts in the Twenty-First Century*, 66 S. Cal. L. Rev. 1993, 2011 (1993), our collective refusal to acknowledge any responsibility for the children of others seems shortsighted and counterproductive to our societal well-being.

26. Martha L.A. Fineman, *Masking Dependency: The Political Role of Family Rhetoric*, 81 Va. L. Rev. 2181, 2182–83 (1995); Thornton, *supra* note 24, at 599–600.

27. Throughout this book I refer to the relationships between divorced children and their custodial and noncustodial parents as "families." Traditional state notions of family frequently exclude single-parent families. This exclusion allows the state to pay inadequate attention to the needs of millions of divorced children and adults—a highly undesirable situation. Moreover, exclusion of the noncustodial parent from the concept of family discourages the noncustodial

parent's involvement with the children and implicitly absolves that parent from responsibility for the children—both insensitive and undesirable results. Because divorce restructures so many people's lives in the United States, the state simply must acknowledge the importance of these "families."

28. Numerous factors contribute to the rise in divorce rates in modern societies. Industrialization caused young persons to leave home to find work or obtain education. Moving loosened family and community restrictions and increased people's expectations regarding their personal development and fulfillment. Individualism undermined the traditional views of marriage as a lifelong obligation. People began to expect personal happiness, fair treatment, and love in marriage. Married women's participation in the labor force exposed them to numerous people and increased their ability to support themselves without a husband. Birth control allowed people to separate sex and marriage, fostering discreet nonmarital relations for both men and women and straining traditional marriages. State legislatures moved to no-fault divorce, allowing people easy exits from marriage. *See* BAKER, *supra* note 11, at 57–58. Other influences include marriages between persons of dissimilar backgrounds and the decline in the influence of formal religion. *Id.* at 60. *See also* CARBONE, *supra* note 15, at 18 (noting that financial independence, particularly of younger women, contributes to their willingness to divorce).

29. *See* WEITZMAN, *supra* note 18, at 352; Frank F. Furstenberg, Jr., *History and Current Status of Divorce in the United States*, in THE FUTURE OF CHILDREN: CHILDREN AND DIVORCE 29, 35 (1994); Alfred J. Kahn & Sheila B. Kamerman, *Child Support in the United States: The Problem*, in CHILD SUPPORT: FROM DEBT COLLECTION TO SOCIAL POLICY 10, 10 (Alfred J. Kahn & Sheila B. Kamerman eds. 1988); Krauss & Sales, *supra* note 3 (citing S. Bahr et al., *Trends in Child Custody Awards: Has the Removal of the Maternal Preference Made a Difference?*, 28 FAM. L.Q. 247 (1994)); Sara S. McLanahan, *Parent Absence or Poverty: Which Matters More?*, in CONSEQUENCES OF GROWING UP POOR 35 (Greg J. Duncan & Jeanne Brooks-Gunn eds. 1997).

30. *See, e.g.*, TERRY ARENDELL, MOTHERS AND DIVORCE: LEGAL ECONOMIC AND SOCIAL DILEMMAS 154–56 (1986); BAKER, *supra* note 11, at 295–96; OKIN, *supra* note 5, at 4; WEITZMAN, *supra* note 18, at 323–56; Ruth A. Brandwein et al., *Women and Children Last: The Social Situation of Divorced Mothers and Their Families*, 36 J. MARRIAGE & FAM. 498, 500 (1974) (explaining that financial difficulties plague most single mothers); Margaret F. Brinig, *"These Boots Are Made for Walking": Why Most Divorce Filers Are Women*, 2 AM. L. & ECON. REV. 126, 127–28 (2000); Mary Corcoran et al., *The Economic Fortunes of Women and Children: Lessons from the Panel Study of Income Dynamics*, 10 SIGNS 232, 240–41, 244, 247 (1984); Marsha Garrison, *The Economic Consequences of Divorce: Would Adoption of the ALI Principles Improve Current Outcomes?*, 8 DUKE J. GENDER L. & POL'Y 119, 121 n.5 (2001) (citing DIANE DODSON & JOAN ENTMACHER, WOMEN'S LEGAL DEFENSE FUND, REPORT CARD ON STATE CHILD SUPPORT GUIDELINES 94, 97–98 (1994) (finding that application of 1989–1990 U.S. child support guidelines, on average, caused children's

living standards to decline by 26%, whereas those of noncustodial parents improved by 34%) (hereinafter *Economic Consequences*); Marsha Garrison, *Equitable Distribution in New York: Results and Reform: Good Intentions Gone Awry: The Impact of New York's Equitable Distribution Law on Divorce Outcomes*, 57 BROOK. L. REV. 621, 720–23 tab. 55 (1991) (noting that average postdivorce per capita income of wives and children approximates 68% of their pre-divorce per capita income, whereas per capita income of husbands increases by 182% after divorce); JAMES B. McLINDON, *Separate But Unequal: The Economic Disaster of Divorce for Women and Children*, 21 FAM. L.Q. 351 (1987); Melton, *supra* note 25, at 2011 (disruption of the traditional family unit threatens economic well-being of women and children); Robert S. Weiss, *The Impact of Marital Dissolution on Income and Consumption in Single-Parent Households*, 46 J. MARRIAGE & FAM. 115, 116–17 (1984); Jason DeParle, *Child Poverty Twice as Likely After Family Split, Study Says*, N.Y. TIMES, Mar. 2, 1991, §1, at 8 (noting a study by Suzanne Bianchi and Edith McArthur that found that within 16 months of divorce, after adjusting for the decrease in family size, the income of the family in which the child lived dropped by 29%). *See generally* LESLIE A. MORGAN, AFTER MARRIAGE ENDS: ECONOMIC CONSEQUENCES FOR MIDLIFE WOMEN (1991). The postdivorce decline in standard of living affects women at all socioeconomic levels and has the most severe impact on women of upper socioeconomic status. Paul R. Amato, *The Impact of Divorce on Men and Women in India and The United States*, 25 J. COMP. FAM. STUD. 207, 211 (1994).

31. *E.g.*, ARENDELL, *supra* note 30, at 153–57; CHILDREN'S DEFENSE FUND, THE STATE OF AMERICA'S CHILDREN 23, 25 (1991) (showing that approximately 1 in 5 children in the United States lives in poverty, 1 in 2 children who live in a female-headed, one-parent home lives in poverty, and that approximately 1 in 10 children who live with both parents lives in poverty); Jay D. Teachman & Kathleen M. Paasch, *Financial Impact of Divorce on Children and Their Families*, 4 THE FUTURE OF CHILDREN: CHILDREN OF DIVORCE 63 (Richard E. Behrman ed. 1994). Approximately 65% of single-parent families result from marital separation or divorce. *See* OKIN, *supra* note 5, at 4 (1989) (citing U.S. BUREAU OF THE CENSUS, U.S. DEP'T OF COMMERCE, CURRENT POPULATION REPORTS, HOUSEHOLD AND FAMILY CHARACTERISTICS, at 79 (1987)). *See also* BAKER, *supra* note 11, at 340–41 (noting that Canada has higher child poverty rates than most industrialized countries, except for the United States). *See also* Greer Litton Fox, *Children's Well-Being: Clues and Caveats from Social Research*, 39 SANTA CLARA L. REV. 1075, 1079 (1999) (noting the multiple negative effects poverty has on children's well-being).

32. *See* DeParle, *supra* note 30.

33. For example, in a 2-year study of a random nationwide sample of 699 elementary school children, Guidubaldi and Perry found that divorced children performed more poorly on 9 of 30 mental health measures than children from intact families. Divorced children showed higher frequencies of dependency, irrelevant talk, withdrawal, blaming, inattention, decreased work effort,

inappropriate behavior, unhappiness, and maladaptive symptoms. When the researchers controlled for income level of custodial households, the group of divorced children scored differently on only two mental health measures. Boys from divorced homes, however, performed lower on four mental health measures than boys from intact families. The only difference remaining between girls from divorced homes and girls from intact families concerned internal locus of control, a self-esteem measure. Girls from divorced households actually exhibited higher internal locus of control than did girls from intact families. See John Guidubaldi & Joseph D. Perry, *Divorce and Mental Health Sequelae for Children: A Two-Year Follow-Up of a Nationwide Sample*, 24 J. AM. ACAD. CHILD PSYCHIATRY 531, 533–34 (1985). See also WEITZMAN, *supra* note 18, at 354; Alan C. Acock & K. Jill Kiecolt, *Is it Family Structure or Socioeconomic Status? Family Structure During Adolescence and Adult Adjustment*, 68 SOC. FORCES 553, 556–57 (1989); David H. Demo, *Parent–Child Relations: Assessing Recent Changes*, 54 J. MARRIAGE & FAM. 104, 110 (1992); E. Mavis Hetherington et al., *Marital Transitions: A Child's Perspective*, 44 AM. PSYCHOL. 303, 304 (1989) (citations omitted) (reporting that the most common problems of divorced children are aggression, noncompliance, acting-out behaviors, decreases in prosocial behavior, poorer academic achievement and school adjustment, and disruptions in peer and heterosexual relations); William F. Hodges et al., *The Cumulative Effect of Stress on Preschool Children of Divorced and Intact Families*, 46 J. MARRIAGE & FAM. 611, 614 (1984) (explaining that children of divorced families with inadequate income had substantially higher levels of anxiety and depression); Lawrence A. Kurdek, *An Integrative Perspective on Children's Divorce Adjustment*, 36 AM. PSYCHOL. 856, 858, 860 (1981); Judith A. Seltzer, *Consequences of Marital Dissolution for Children*, 20 ANN. REV. SOC. 235, 244 (1994). Baker notes that several Canadian parliamentary committees have acknowledged that children who live in poverty are likely to develop social and psychological problems that will prove costly to resolve in the future. BAKER, *supra* note 11, at 340–41. Despite the overwhelming number of studies that identify how divorce harms many children, a cautionary note seems appropriate. Some of the negative research findings on divorced children come from populations of children in therapy. Moreover, many early studies do not compare the findings on divorced children to findings on children from intact families. Others fail to control for socioeconomic variables or assess the effects on children of their downward financial mobility. See ARENDELL, *supra* note 30, at 88. Some studies suggest that many of the negative symptoms of divorced children existed before the divorce. See, e.g., Jeanne H. Block et al., *The Personality of Children Prior to Divorce: A Prospective Study*, 57 CHILD DEV. 827 (1986); Hetherington et al., *supra*, at 304–05; J. M. Jenkins & M. A. Smith, *A Prospective Study of Behavioural Disturbance in Children Who Subsequently Experience Parental Divorce: A Research Note*, 19 DIVORCE & REMARRIAGE 143 (1993). Others suggest that not all children respond poorly to divorce. See ARENDELL, *supra* note 30, at 81 (finding that children from abusive households especially may prosper in their less stressful postdivorce homes); HETHER-

INGTON & KELLY, *supra* note 18, at 5, 7–8 (claiming that literature has overestimated the negative effect of divorce on children, particularly when divorce rescues adults and children from domestic violence); Demo, *supra*, at 110; Guidubaldi & Perry, *supra*, at 531 (stating that some children respond well to divorce); Hetherington et al., *supra*, at 304 (citations omitted) (explaining that researchers consistently find that children adapt better in a well-functioning single-parent family than in a conflict-ridden two-parent family); Seltzer, *supra*, at 239. Nevertheless, result replication and recent methodological refinements have confirmed that many divorced children suffer as noted in this text. *See* Judith Wallerstein et al., The Unexpected Legacy of Divorce: A 25 Year Landmark Study (2000); Daniel A. Krauss & Bruce D. Sales, *Legal Standards, Expertise, and Experts in the Resolution of Contested Custody Cases,* 6 Psychol. Pub. Pol'y & L. 843, 850–54 (2000) (chronicling the methodological limitations of research on children of divorce, but concluding that research does provide important insights relevant to child custody decisions). Even divorced mothers who express outrage at the negative stereotypes of divorced children also recognize the hardships their children experience as a result of financial impoverishment. *See* Arendell, *supra*, at 49, 100–101; Dowd, *supra* note 13, at 25–27.

34. Researchers have found, for instance, that preschool children of divorced families with inadequate income exhibit higher levels of anxiety and depression than do other preschoolers. When family income is adequate, these differences disappear. *See* Weitzman, *supra* note 18, at 354. *See also* Arendell, *supra* note 30, at 124–25; Hodges et al., *supra* note 33, at 614 (explaining that children of divorced families with inadequate income had substantially higher levels of anxiety and depression).

35. *See* Arendell, *supra* note 30, at 124–26; Seltzer, *supra* note 33, at 238. One researcher, for instance, found that children in single-mother and in single-father households performed equally well in school, but that both groups performed more poorly than did children from intact families. Economic deprivation explained the poor performance of children in single-mother households, whereas interpersonal deprivation explained the poor performance of children in single-father households. *See* Douglas B. Downey, *The School Performance of Children From Single-Mother and Single-Father Families,* 15 J. Fam Issues 129, 144–45 (1994). *See also* Sara McLanahan, *Family Structure and the Reproduction of Poverty,* 90 Am. J. Soc. 873, 888–89, 897 (1985) (finding that the economic deprivation of white children living in single-mother households substantially decreased the children's success in school).

36. Divorced children attain lower levels of educational and economic achievement than children raised in intact families. *See* Dowd, *supra* note 13, at 25–26 (1997); Judith S. Wallerstein & Sandra Blakeslee, Second Chances: Men, Women, & Children a Decade After Divorce 160 (1989) (noting that divorce chills the hopes, aspirations, and achievements of children). *See also* Paul R. Amato & Bruce Keith, *Separation From a Parent During Childhood and Adult Socioeconomic Attainment,* 70 Soc. Forces 187, 193–98, 200, 202–03

(1991); Verna M. Keith & Barbara Finlay, *The Impact of Parental Divorce on Children's Educational Attainment, Marital Timing, and Likelihood of Divorce*, 50 J. MARRIAGE & FAM. 797, 798–99 (1988); Sheila Fitzgerald Krein & Andrea H. Beller, *Educational Attainment of Children From Single-Parent Families: Differences by Exposure, Gender, and Race*, 25 DEMOGRAPHY 221, 222–24 (1988).

37. Consider, for example, the voices of mothers in Weitzman's study:

> We ate macaroni and cheese five nights a week. There was a Safeway special for 39 cents a box. We could eat seven dinners for $3.00 a week. . . . I think that's all we ate for months. I applied for welfare. . . . It was the worst experience of my life. . . . I never dreamed that I, a middle class housewife, would ever be in a position like that. It was humiliating . . . they make you feel it. . . . But we were desperate, and I had to feed my kids. You name it, I tried it—food stamps, soup kitchens, shelters. It just about killed me to have the kids live like that. . . . I finally called my parents and said we were coming . . . we couldn't have survived without them.

WEITZMAN, *supra* note 18, at 339.
Weitzman observes

> In addition to scaled-down budgets for food ("We learned to love chicken backs") and clothing ("At Christmas I splurged at the Salvation Army—the only "new" clothes they got all year"), many spoke of cutting down on their children's school lunches ("I used to plan a nourishing lunch with fruit and juice; now she's lucky if we have a slice of ham for a sandwich") and school supplies and after-school activities ("he had to quit the Little League and get a job as a delivery boy").

Id. at 340.

38. As Joan Williams explains

> A family's housing is intimately tied to its creation of an environment suitable for raising children. In the classic scenario, the children of divorced parents move to an apartment with their mother. This relocation takes the children away from their friends and support network during a time of acute stress. Moreover, since the quality of schools is often tied to the price of housing, cutting the children off from their father's wealth may affect their long-term future. (citations omitted)

Joan Williams, *Is Coverture Dead? Beyond a New Theory of Alimony*, 82 GEO. L.J. 2227, 2233–34 (1994).

39. *See* ARENDELL, *supra* note 30, at 17, 40; PETER J. CUNNINGHAM & BETH A. HAHN, 4 THE FUTURE OF CHILDREN: CRITICAL HEALTH ISSUES FOR CHILDREN AND YOUTH 24 (1994).

40. *See* Joan S. Tucker et al., *Parental Divorce: Effects on Individual Behavior and Longevity*, 73 J. PERSONALITY & SOC. PSYCHOL. 381, 381–83 (1997) (noting the link between parental divorce and poorer health for children and adolescents).

41. *See* WALLERSTEIN & KELLY, *supra* note 12, at 231; WEITZMAN, *supra* note 18, at 353; Seltzer, *supra* note 33, at 244.

42. *See* Dowd, *supra* note 13, at 26. *See also* Hetherington & Kelly, *supra* note 18, at 88; Wallerstein & Kelly, *supra* note 12, at 183; Fox, *supra* note 31, at 1082; Seltzer, *supra* note 33, at 245. High degrees of environmental change also correlate with children's depression, social withdrawal, aggression, and delinquency. *See* Kurdek, *supra* note 33, at 858.

43. Arendell, *supra* note 30, at 17, 49.

44. Melton notes, "poverty accounts for the greatest portion of variance in community rates of delinquency and child maltreatment, neighborhood quality accounts for much of the remainder." Melton, *supra* note 25, at 2003 (citations omitted).

45. *See* Dowd, *supra* note 13, at 25–26 (noting that poverty in single-parent families correlates with children's criminal activity); Demo, *supra* note 33, at 110; Seltzer, *supra* note 33, at 238. In the United States, more than 70% of all juveniles in state reform institutions come from fatherless homes. After controlling for income, boys from single-mother homes are significantly more likely than others to commit crimes that place them in the criminal justice system. The relationship between crime and one-parent families is so strong that when researchers control for family configuration, the relationships between race and crime and between low income and crime disappear. *See* Lynn D. Wardle, *The Use and Abuse of Rights Rhetoric: The Constitutional Rights of Children*, 27 Loy. U. Chi. L.J. 321, 329 (1996) (citing Barbara D. Whitehead, *Dan Quayle Was Right*, Atlantic Monthly, Apr. 1993, at 47, 77). Professor Melton notes, "Poverty accounts for the greatest portion of variance in community rates of delinquency and child maltreatment, neighborhood quality accounts for much of the remainder." Melton, *supra* note 25, at 2003.

46. *See* Arendell, *supra* note 30, at 25, 44; Wallerstein et al., *supra* note 33, at 249.

47. *See* Wallerstein & Blakeslee, *supra* note 36, at 156. *See also* Arendell, *supra* note 30, at 25, 44; Weitzman, *supra* note 18, at 353; Barbara Grissett & L. Allen Furr, *Effects of Parental Divorce on Children's Financial Support for College*, 22 J. Divorce & Remarriage 155, 159–61 (1994) (finding that divorced children attending college received significantly less parental financial support than children from intact families and that the custodial parent likely provided whatever support they did receive); Barbara Bennett Woodhouse, *Towards a Revitalization of Family Law*, 69 Tex. L. Rev. 245, 269 (1990). The economic disadvantage of all children, whether or not they experience divorce, strongly influences their educational attainment. Robert Crosnoe et al., *Economic Disadvantage, Family Dynamics, and Adolescent Enrollment in Higher Education*, 64 J. Marriage & Fam. 690, 690, 692 (2002). The economic disadvantage of single-parent families compared to intact families, however, accounts for a significant amount of the difference in academic achievement of divorced children compared to those from intact families. Kathryn S. Schiller et al., *Economic Development and the Effects of Family Characteristics on Mathematics Achievement*, 64 J. Marriage & Fam. 730, 731 (2002).

48. When their mothers remarry, the financial situation of divorced children generally improves. *See* Hetherington et al., *supra* note 33, at 307. More than half

of the children whose parents divorce, however, spend at least six years with only one parent. *See* Demo, *supra* note 33, at 109. Moreover, a high percentage of remarriages end in divorce, especially those with stepchildren, HETHER-INGTON & KELLY, *supra* note 18, at 171–72, 179–97, again exposing children to financial worries.

49. *See* WEITZMAN, *supra* note 18, at 352–54. *See generally* BAKER, *supra* note 11, at 59 (noting that divorced children may live in single-parent households for only a few years, but those years might represent an influential portion of their lives).

50. *See* HETHERINGTON & KELLY, *supra* note 18, at 9; Toni L. Thiriot & Eugene T. Buckner, *Multiple Predictors of Satisfactory Post-Divorce Adjustment of Single Custodial Parents*, 17 J. DIVORCE & REMARRIAGE 27, 28 (1991).

51. *See, e.g.*, ARENDELL, *supra* note 30, at 61–68, 90, 151–52 (1986); DOWD, *supra* note 13, at 26; HETHERINGTON & KELLY, *supra* note 18, at 46; WALLERSTEIN ET AL., *supra* note 33, at 6–9; Paul R. Amato & Sonia Partridge, *Widows and Divorcees with Dependent Children: Material, Personal, Family, and Social Well-Being*, 36 FAM. RELATIONS 316, 316 (1987); Nancy Donohue Colletta, *Stressful Lives: The Situation of Divorced Mothers and Their Children*, 6 J. DIVORCE 19, 23–27 (1983); Demo, *supra* note 33, at 110–11; Hetherington et al., *supra* note 33, at 308; Leslie N. Richards & Cynthia J. Schmiege, *Problems and Strengths of Single-Parent Families: Implications for Practice and Policy*, 42 FAM. REL. 277, 280 fig. 6. (1993).

52. Some noncustodial fathers find intermittent parenting painful and withdraw from their children, and most noncustodial fathers rapidly become less available to their children. *See* Hetherington et al., *supra* note 33, at 309; Seltzer, *supra* note 33, at 254–55, 258; Judith S. Wallerstein & Shauna B. Corbin, *Father–Child Relationships After Divorce: Child Support and Educational Opportunity*, 20 FAM. L.Q. 109, 114 (1986). *See also* ARENDELL, *supra* note 30, at 109–24 (describing the psychological difficulties divorced children have when their fathers seem disinterested in or abandon them). Noncustodial fathers become even less available after they remarry. Hetherington et al., *supra*, at 309.

53. *See* DOWD, *supra* note 13, at 26–27; WALLERSTEIN ET AL., *supra* note 33, at 6–13, 24, 26; Seltzer, *supra* note 33, at 254; Judith S. Wallerstein, *The Over-burdened Child: Some Long-Term Consequences of Divorce*, 30 SOC. WORK 116, 117 (1985).

54. *See* ARENDELL, *supra* note 30, at 80–81, 61–64, 152; WALLERSTEIN ET AL., *supra* note 33, at 24–25; WALLERSTEIN & KELLY, *supra* note 12, at 25; WEITZMAN, *supra* note 18, at 319; Hetherington et al., *supra* note 33, at 304. In many instances, however, successful adjustment does occur. *See* ARENDELL, *supra* note 30, at 82–88; HETHERINGTON & KELLY, *supra* note 18, at 229–30; Kurdek, *supra* note 33, at 859–60.

55. *See* ARENDELL, *supra* note 30, at 91–92; WALLERSTEIN ET AL., *supra* note 33, at 6–13, 26–27; Hetherington et al., *supra* note 33, at 305, 308. Although the early assumption of responsibilities can lead to maturity, approximately one third of older children and adolescents disengage from their families. *See* Hetherington et al., *supra*, at 305. If these disengaged children become involved in

pro-social peer groups, academic achievement, or constructive relationships, their disengagement can be a positive coping mechanism. On the other hand, if these disengaged children become involved with anti-social groups and activities without adult monitoring, destructive results can occur. *See id.*

56. *See* ARENDELL, *supra* note 30, at 106, 123–27 (explaining that children frequently suffer when divorced parents remain hostile); HETHERINGTON & KELLY, *supra* note 18, at 138 (finding that six years after divorce, 20% to 25% of divorced parents still participated in high conflict behaviors); WALLERSTEIN ET AL., *supra* note 33, at 5 (noting that one third of the couples in their study still fought intensely 10 years after divorce); Janet R. Johnston, *Building Multidisciplinary Professional Partnerships With the Court on Behalf of High-Conflict Divorcing Families and Their Children: Who Needs What Kind of Help?*, 22 U. ARK. LITTLE ROCK L. REV. 453, 454–55 (2000) (noting that many divorced children experience unremitting hostility and chaos throughout their childhoods). Many studies establish that intense conflict between divorced parents strongly correlates with children's poor adjustment to divorce. *See, e.g.,* Christy M. Buchanan et al., *Adolescents and Their Families After Divorce: Three Residential Arrangements Compared,* 2 J. RES. ADOLESCENCE 261, 287–88 (1992); Andre P. Derdeyn & Elizabeth Scott, *Joint Custody: A Critical Analysis and Appraisal,* 54 AM. J. ORTHOPSYCHIATRY 199, 204 (1984); Denise Donnelly & David Finkelhor, *Does Equality in Custody Arrangements Improve the Parent–Child Relationship?,* 54 J. MARRIAGE & FAM. 837, 843–44 (1992); Fox, *supra* note 31, at 1082–83; Hetherington et al., *supra* note 33, at 307; Marsha Kline et al., *The Long Shadow of Marital Conflict: A Model of Children's Postdivorce Adjustment,* 53 J. MARRIAGE & FAM. 297 (1991); Seltzer, *supra* note 33, at 253–54.

57. Children inevitably suffer in high conflict postdivorce families. *See* E. MARK CUMMINGS & PATRICK DAVIES, CHILDREN AND MARITAL CONFLICT: THE IMPACT OF FAMILY DISPUTE AND RESOLUTION (1994); *High-Conflict Custody Cases: Reforming the System for Children—Conference Report and Action Plan,* 34 FAM. L.Q. 589, 589–90 (2001).

58. *See* WALLERSTEIN ET AL., *supra* note 33, at 174–85.

59. *See* Krauss & Sales, *supra* note 33, at 856–57; Janet R. Johnston et al., *Ongoing Postdivorce Conflict: Effects on Children of Joint Custody and Frequent Access,* 59 AM. J. ORTHOPSYCHIATRY 576 (1989).

60. Robert H. Mnookin et al., *Private Ordering Revisited: What Custodial Arrangements are Parents Negotiating?, in* DIVORCE REFORM AT THE CROSSROADS 37, 54–55 (Stephen D. Sugarman & Herma Hill Kay eds. 1985); Laurie C. Kadoch, *Five Degrees of Separation: A Response to Judge Sheldon's The Sleepwalker's Tour of Divorce Law,* 49 ME. L. REV. 321, 352 n.165 (1997) (discussing Rodrigue v. Brewer, 667 A.2d 605 (Me. 1995)). As Hetherington and Kelly note: "Moreover, visits from an alcoholic, abusive, depressed, or conflict-prone parent do nothing for a troubled child, except possibly make the child more troubled." HETHERINGTON & KELLY, *supra* note 18, at 134.

61. *See* REPORT OF THE GENDER BIAS STUDY OF THE SUPREME JUDICIAL COURT, COMMONWEALTH OF MASSACHUSETTS 69–70 (1989) (hereinafter MASSACHUSETTS GENDER BIAS REPORT); Meredith Sherman Fahn, *Allegations of Child*

Sexual Abuse in Custody Disputes, Getting to the Truth of the Matter, 25 Fam. L.Q. 193, 195 (1991); *Report of the Florida Supreme Court Gender Bias Study Commission*, 42 Fla. L. Rev. 803, 867 (1990) (hereinafter *Florida Gender Bias Report*); *Missouri Task Force, supra* note 15, at 513, 567. For numerous reasons, negotiated settlements reflect this pattern. An abused mother, for instance, may agree to a custody or visitation arrangement that fails to protect her and her child because she fears losing custody altogether. Moreover, guardians ad litem and custody evaluators frequently disbelieve or minimize a mother's allegations of abuse. They consequently may recommend that the alleged perpetrator receive custody. With no support from these professionals, the mother may agree to generous visitation in order to avoid losing custody altogether.

62. *See* David Finkelhor & Angela Browne, *The Traumatic Impact of Child Sexual Abuse: A Conceptualization*, 55 Am. J. Orthopsychiatry 530, 532 (1985).

63. One Missouri attorney observed: "Judges and attorneys have difficulty believing sex abuse allegations by women and children and sometimes place children back with abusers. In a recent case, the male guardian ad litem didn't want to believe allegations of sex abuse against the father because he seemed like a nice guy." *Missouri Task Force, supra* note 14, at 568. Court cases provide additional examples. In one case, the Massachusetts Department of Social Services substantiated the mother's allegations of child sexual abuse of the daughter by the father. *See In re* A.F. v. N.F., 549 N.Y.S.2d 511, 513 (N.Y. App. Div. 1989). The trial court ignored this and other evidence of sexual abuse and awarded custody to the father. *See id.* at 513, 514. In a rare moment, the appellate court substituted its judgment for that of the trial court and ordered that custody be returned to the mother and that the father have only supervised visitation with the child. *See id.* at 513, 515. *See also* Fahn, *supra* note 61, at 194–95.

64. *E.g.*, Phyllis Chesler, Mothers on Trial: The Battles For Children and Custody 79 (1987) (finding that in her study 59% of the fathers who won custody in litigation had abused their wives and that 50% of the fathers who obtained custody through private negotiations had abused their wives). *See also* Philip C. Crosby, Comment, *Custody of Vaughn: Emphasizing the Importance of Domestic Violence in Child Custody Cases*, 77 B.U. L. Rev. 483 (1997) (discussing a case in which the trial court awarded the abusive husband custody of the child).

65. *See* Wallerstein et al., *supra* note 33 (concluding that children continue to experience the negative effects of their parents' divorces well into adulthood).

66. *See* Massachusetts Gender Bias Report, *supra* note 61, at 69.

67. In a sense I present here what Resnik and Ruddick call "maternal thinking:"

> Ruddick is not wedded to mothers as a condition dependent upon gender. For her, "'maternal' is a social category" and there can be "mothers of both sexes," but the essential experience of mothering must not be lost in the translation. Moreover, the lesson of maternal thinking is not simply how to care for children on an individual basis; rather the primary goal is to "bring a transformed maternal thought into the public realm, to make the preservation and growth of all children a

work of public conscience . . . [and to] join in articulating a theory of justice shaped by and incorporating maternal thinking."

Judith Resnik, *On the Bias: Feminist Reconsiderations of the Aspirations for Our Judges*, 61 S. Cal. L. Rev. 1877, 1917–18 (1988) (citing Sara Ruddick, *Maternal Thinking*, 6 Feminist Studies 342 (1980)).

68. Each of these rights is enumerated in the United Nations' Convention on the Rights of the Child. *See* Cara L. Finan, Comment, *Convention on the Rights of the Child: A Potentially Effective Remedy in Cases of International Child Abduction*, 34 Santa Clara L. Rev. 1007, 1023–24 (1992). Every nation in the world community, with the exception of the United States, has adopted this convention. Barbara Bennett Woodhouse, *Talking About Children's Rights in Judicial Custody and Visitation Decision-Making*, 36 Fam. L.Q. 105, 108 (2002).

69. *See* Henrik H.H. Andrup, *Divorce Proceedings: Ends and Means, in* The Resolution of Family Conflict: Comparative Legal Perspectives 163, 166 (John M. Eekelaar & Sanford N. Katz eds. 1984). *See also* Dowd, *supra* note 13, at 17 (acknowledging that our punitive approach to children who live in single-parent families is socially destabilizing).

70. *See* Hetherington & Kelly, *supra* note 18, at 228–29, 269 (finding that 20% of the children in their study who experienced one divorce of their parents remained substantially impaired and that 38% of children who experienced multiple divorces of their custodial parents never recovered). *See also* Donald S. Moir, *No Fault Divorce and the Best Interests of Children*, 69 Denv. U. L. Rev. 663, 672 (1992) (noting that if Wallerstein and Kelly are correct, that more than one third of divorced children are chronically impaired, and if 50% of our children experience the divorce of their parents, then one sixth of our population will face a disabled adulthood because of divorce); Tucker et al., *supra* note 40 (finding parental divorce predictive of premature mortality for men and women).

71. Weitzman explains

Data from national samples consistently document the disruptive effects of divorce on the mental and physical health of both sexes. . . . divorce and marital separation consistently rank second and third in a list of 42 stressful life events: the death of a spouse is the only event considered to require greater readjustment. The psychological distress engendered by divorce is revealed by the fact that divorced men and women exhibit more symptoms (such as "nervous breakdown" and "inertia"), and in more serious degree, than do persons of other marital statuses. Divorced and separated people have the highest admission rates to psychiatric facilities (compared to married, widowed, and never married people), and this holds true across different age groups, for both sexes, and for blacks and whites alike. Divorce also takes a toll on the physical well-being of both sexes. Divorced people have more illness, higher mortality rates (in premature deaths), higher suicide rates, and more accidents than those who are married. In fact, the marital status of a person is one of the best predictors of his or her health, disease, and death profile. While both sexes "share" some of the psychic and physical distress of divorce, women seem to experience the greater stress and their stress seems to take a higher toll. Beyond question, much of the women's stress is attributable to their economic condition. This is to be expected in light of the well-known relationship between low socioeconomic status and both mental and physical illness. Three decades of research have shown a strong correlation between low income and both stress and psychiatric disability. Having a low socioeconomic status and being a single mother is "additively and cumulatively associated with physical morbidity among mothers." (citations omitted)

WEITZMAN, *supra* note 18, at 349–50. *See also* HETHERINGTON & KELLY, *supra* note 18, at 59–60.

72. *See* MORGAN, *supra* note 30, at 3–4, 25–28; MASSACHUSETTS GENDER BIAS REPORT, *supra* note 61, at 19; WEITZMAN, *supra* note 18; Brandwein et al., *supra* note 30, at 500; Corcoran et al., *supra* note 30, at 240–41, 244, 247; Peggy S. Draughn, *Divorcees' Economic Well-Being and Financial Adequacy as Related to Interfamily Grants*, 22 J. DIVORCE & REMARRIAGE 23, 24–25 (1994) (citing numerous studies establishing that women's economic well-being suffers more than men's at divorce). As Brinig notes, even the most conservative accounts of the postdivorce financial circumstances of women reveal that the average divorced woman's standard of living declines, whereas divorced men's standard of living often increases. Brinig, *supra* note 30, at 127–28. *See also* BAKER, *supra* note 11, at 304–305 (noting Canadian research that indicates that, in the first year after divorce, women's family income declined by 50%, whereas men's declined by 25%, but when these figures were adjusted for family size, men's economic well-being increased, whereas women's economic well-being dropped by 50%) (citations omitted); HETHERINGTON & KELLY, *supra* note 18, at 9, 48 (noting that women's economic resources decline three times more than men's after divorce).

73. *See* ARENDELL, *supra* note 30, at 50–51; DOWD, *supra* note 13, at 22.

74. In her study of 60 divorced mothers, Terry Arendell found that 10 mothers did not experience serious depression or despair after divorce. She comments

But the reasons they gave simply reemphasize the central importance of economic loss in the lives of divorced women. Four of these ten had various sources of income that protected them from poverty and enabled them to work actively toward improving their situation. Two of them were using income from the divorce property settlement to attend graduate school, and they hoped to regain their former standard of living by pursuing professional careers. Two were receiving financial support from their parents while they sought employment and planned for the possible sale of their homes as part of the property settlement. The remaining six said they were generally optimistic in spite of their poor economic positions. Like the others, they found the financial hardships imposed by divorce surprising and difficult to handle; they simply found these hardships easier to cope with than the despair they had known in their marriages.

ARENDELL, *supra* note 30, at 51. *See also* MORGAN, *supra* note 30, at 35.

75. *See* ARENDELL, *supra* note 30, at 53–79. Seventy-eight percent of the single-parent mothers studied by Richards and Schmiege identified financial difficulties as a major problem. All of these single-parent mothers came from middle class backgrounds. One mother who remarried quickly noted "financially it got pretty bad towards the end. It was like I was selling a lot of our stuff like the freezer, and whatever else we had, just to keep going. It was a trying time." Richards & Schmiege, *supra* note 51, at 280. In contrast, only two of the 11 single-parent fathers in their study mentioned financial problems. One of these fathers complained that he had to reinvest too quickly in order to avoid capital gains tax. *See id.*

76. One study found that before divorce, 33% of wives worked full time. At four months and at one year after divorce, the percentage of divorced women working full time reached 41%. The study also indicated that, within four months of divorce, wives who had not worked during the marriage had found part-time employment, decreasing wives' overall unemployment rate from 43% to 31%. This change did not last, however. Within a year of divorce, ex-wives' unemployment rate had returned to 43%. *See* DeParle, *supra* note 30. *See also* MORGAN, *supra* note 30, at 34–35.

77. *See* ARENDELL, *supra* note 30, at 55–61; DOWD, *supra* note 13, at 19–22; MASSACHUSETTS GENDER BIAS REPORT, *supra* note 61, at 33. Arendell notes that of the 60 mothers she interviewed

> Being underemployed was common: nearly a third of the women doing clerical work had college degrees, as did the one blue-collar worker. One woman earned over $2,000 a month and another less than $600, but these extremes were the exception. The majority had net incomes of between $800 and $1,200 a month, or $9,600 to $14,400 a year.

ARENDELL, *supra* note 30, at 56. The mothers' dependency on their meager earnings made them reluctant to ask for higher wages. *See id.* at 59. *See also* BAKER, *supra* note 11, at 303 (noting that single-parent mothers do not work full time as frequently as single-parent fathers, nor do they earn wages comparable to their male counterparts).

78. *See* Peter T. Kilborn, *For Many Women, One Job Just Isn't Enough*, N.Y. TIMES, Feb. 15, 1990, at A1. *See also* ARENDELL, *supra* note 30, at 63–64.

79. Generally, divorced adults experience more alcoholism, drug abuse, depression, psychosomatic problems, and accidents than nondivorced adults. Moreover, marital disruption depresses the immunologic system, making divorced persons more vulnerable to disease, infection, chronic and acute medical problems, and death. Hetherington et al., *supra* note 33, at 307–08.

80. *See* WEITZMAN, *supra* note 18, at 349–50. *See also* ARENDELL, *supra* note 30, at 46–52, 61–63; Hetherington et al., *supra* note 33, at 307–08; Gay C. Kitson

& Leslie A. Morgan, *The Multiple Consequences of Divorce: A Decade Review*, 52 J. MARRIAGE & FAM. 913, 913–14 (1990). *But see* WEITZMAN, *supra* note 18, at 345–49 (stating that within one year of their divorce, women and men report higher self-esteem and competence); Alan Booth & Paul Amato, *Divorce and Psychological Stress*, 32 J. HEALTH & SOC. BEHAVIOR 396, 400–405 (1991) (illustrating that two years after divorce, psychosomatic symptoms, depression, and unhappiness of divorced persons become comparable to those of married persons).

81. *See generally* ARENDELL, *supra* note 30, at 49, 90, 93–101; HETHERINGTON & KELLY, *supra* note 18, at 60; Hetherington et al., *supra* note 33, at 308. As Baker notes

> Receiving custody of children may soften the initial blow of marital separation because the children are a source of affection and companionship. Nevertheless, divorced women with custody often report a difficult readjustment to single life because children require continual supervision and financial support. They also require considerable emotional support, especially at the time of parental separation, if they witness parental disputes or violence, were unprepared for the breakup, or blame themselves for the divorce. In addition, the presence of children constantly reminds separated women of their family status and former married life and therefore lengthens the transition period from married to single life. Attempting to provide children with a stable environment on a low income may occupy much of the time and energy of separated and divorced parents, especially mothers.

BAKER, *supra* note 11, at 302. Baker further explains

> Although living with children can be fulfilling and rewarding, having no other adults to talk to, especially about child-rearing issues, can be isolating. Loneliness can be aggravated if you cannot afford to hire a sitter in order to search for a job or go out with friends. Work overload and role strain are problems for lone parents of either gender, who may be attempting to fulfill the role of both mother and father, to earn a living, and to perform household and child care tasks that are often done by two people. The demands of paid work, parenting, and care of a home can be exhausting. In addition, many lone parents are involved in custody or child support disputes, even years after the separation or divorce occurred.

Id. at 303. *See generally* Karen Czapanskiy, *Interdependencies, Families, and Children*, 39 SANTA CLARA L. REV. 957, 962 (1999) (noting the interdependency between the caregiver's well-being and that of the child). *But see* Richards & Schmiege, *supra* note 51, at 281 (finding that many single parents take pride in their parenting skills and in their ability to communicate well with their children).

82. *See* HETHERINGTON & KELLY, *supra* note 18, at 87; Brinig, *supra* note 30, at 129 n.5.

83. *See* ARENDELL, *supra* note 30, at 40–41, 44, 46–52 (1986); WALLERSTEIN & KELLY, *supra* note 12, at 231; WEITZMAN, *supra* note 18, at 347, 353; *Economic Consequences*, *supra* note 30, at 121 (noting that "parents and children typically measure the fairness of a support award in relation to their current circumstances; if a support award leaves the smaller segment of the divided family with the lion's share of the income, the other segment is likely to feel aggrieved."). *See also* MASSACHUSETTS GENDER BIAS REPORT, *supra* note 61, at 33 (noting the lifestyle differences between middle-aged (40- to 50-year-old) women and their ex-husbands).

84. Thompson explains

> The absence of the visiting parent from the ordinary variety of daily activities that children experience—from helping with homework to sharing domestic tasks— undoubtedly contributes to the artificiality of their relationship and the feeling that the visiting parent has ceased to function as a genuine parent in the child's life.

Ross A. Thompson, *The Role of the Father After Divorce, in* 4 THE FUTURE OF CHILDREN: CHILDREN AND DIVORCE 210, 222 (1994).

85. Two researchers explain

> At its core, the visiting relationship is ambiguous and therefore stressful. A visiting father is a parent without portfolio. He lacks a clear definition of his responsibility or authority. He often feels unneeded, cut off from the day-to-day issues in the child's life that provide the continuing agenda of the parent-child relationship. The narrow constraints of the visit are often reflected in the need to schedule a special time and place to be with one's child, the repeated leave-taking, and the need to adapt flexibly to the complex changing needs of the child. The forced interface with new adult figures within what sometimes is the father's former home, and the continued crossing and recrossing of new family boundaries in the child's life, are murky and burdensome aspects of the visiting parent's role because they are largely undefined and therefore unsupported by social convention. They generate a changing mix of frustration, anxiety and gratification. The conflicting psychological strains on the visiting father usually pull him between the need to remain close to his children out of his love, dependence, sense of commitment, and legal obligation, and the countervailing desire to take flight in order to escape the painful feelings associated with the failed marriage. For a significant number of fathers, the urge to take flight can be irresistible.

Wallerstein & Corbin, *supra* note 52, at 114. *See also* ARENDELL, *supra* note 30, at 109–24; Hetherington et al., *supra* note 33, at 309. Noncustodial fathers become even less available after they remarry. *Id.* One divorced father compellingly reports: "I lost my center when I lost my family. I don't know who I am or where I'm going. I don't recognize myself." HETHERINGTON & KELLY, *supra* note 18, at 60.

86. BLANKENHORN, *supra* note 11, at 148.

87. *See* WEITZMAN, *supra* note 18, at 150 (explaining how a Los Angeles judge stated that he "would think she is entitled to some severance pay . . . that's probably not the right terminology but something to give her an opportunity to have a year or two where she's not hurting and maybe she'll find some other doctor to marry her and/or get a chance to try to get herself reoriented to her new status."); MORTON DEUTSCH, DISTRIBUTIVE JUSTICE: A SOCIAL–PSYCHOLOGICAL PERSPECTIVE 59 (1985) (explaining that the belief that a victim's situation will improve can inhibit action to assist the victim).

88. *See generally* ARENDELL, *supra* note 30, at 44–45, 51 (1986); HETHERINGTON & KELLY, *supra* note 18, at 62–64.

89. *See* ARENDELL, *supra* note 30, at 55–59.

90. *See id.* at 142–45 (explaining that many divorced women, however, express extreme ambivalence about remarriage); Paul C. Glick & Sung-Ling Lin, *Recent Changes in Divorce and Remarriage*, 48 J. MARRIAGE & FAM. 737, 739–44 (1986); Richards & Schmiege, *supra* note 51, at 278 (finding in their study of 60 single parents from middle-class backgrounds that 57% of the women and 55% of the men had remarried).

91. *See* Hetherington et al., *supra* note 33, at 307 (finding that remarriage tends to improve the financial status of single-parent mothers and their children, although the new family faces other difficult issues). *But see* Margorie Engel, *Pockets of Poverty: The Second Wives Club—Examining the Financial Insecurity of Women in Remarriages*, 5 WM. & MARY L. REV. 309 (1999) (noting that remarriage can increase the financial marginalization of women). Some might argue that divorce outcomes that force women to remarry in order to survive financially provide a conservative solution to the feminization of poverty. *See* BAKER, *supra* note 11, at 347.

92. *See* ARENDELL, *supra* note 30, at 46–52; MORGAN, *supra* note 30, at 128–29. Morgan also notes that remarriage does not guarantee that a woman will improve her financial well-being. *Id.* at 135, 140.

93. *See* ARENDELL, *supra* note 30, at 144; MORGAN, *supra* note 30, at 28–29.

94. *See* Brinig, *supra* note 30, at 128; HETHERINGTON & KELLY, *supra* note 18, at 52. *But see* MORGAN, *supra* note 30, at 37 (noting that recent research indicates that the presence of children may lengthen the time before remarriage, but no longer serves as a serious deterrent to remarriage).

95. *See* ARENDELL, *supra* note 30, at 143; HETHERINGTON & KELLY, *supra* note 18, at 164–65 (finding that one-third of the remarried women in their study remarried, at least partially, for financial reasons); MORGAN, *supra* note 30, at 35–38 (citing numerous studies that find or imply that divorced women frequently remarry in order to improve their financial circumstances); Glick & Lin, *supra* note 90, at 743 (speculating that the greater financial needs of divorced women with children likely encouraged them to remarry more quickly than their childless counterparts).

96. *See generally* Teresa Puente, *Boy Set Afire Over Missing Food Stamps*, CHI. TRIB., Mar. 26, 1995, §2, at 1 (10-year-old boy set on fire by his mother's fiancé for refusing to confess to stealing $20 worth of food stamps). The current conserva-

tive solution to the feminization of poverty, i.e., marriage for women, seems short-sighted and potentially destructive.

97. *See, e.g.*, HETHERINGTON & KELLY, *supra* note 18, at 179–97 (explaining why children require a longer period to adjust to step families than to the initial divorce and why children require even longer periods to adjust to complex step families); WALLERSTEIN ET AL., *supra* note 33, at 236–48; Neil Kalter et al., *School-Based Developmental Facilitation Groups for Children of Divorce: A Preventive Intervention*, 54 AM. J. ORTHOPSYCHIATRY 613, 619–20 (1984).

98. *See* HETHERINGTON & KELLY, *supra* note 18, at 168.

99. *See* WALLERSTEIN ET AL., *supra* note 33, at 28–29 (noting that only 7 of the original 131 children studied experienced stable second marriages with a good stepparent relationship). Divorce rates for second marriages exceed those of first marriages. *See* HETHERINGTON & KELLY, *supra* note 18, at 171–72 (noting that the divorce rate for remarriages in their study approached the 60% national average); MORGAN, *supra* note 30, at 38, 139–40; Engel, *supra* note 91, at 313.

100. *See* MORGAN, *supra* note 30, at 139–40; Melton, *supra* note 25, at 2011 n.87 (stating that remarried couples divorce more frequently than first-married couples and that remarried couples with children show a higher rate of divorce than remarried couples without children) (citing Lynn K. White & Alan Booth, *The Quality and Stability of Remarriage: The Role of Stepchildren*, 50 AM. SOC. REV. 689 (1985)). Because divorce occurs more rapidly in remarriages, sometimes a child confronts a second divorce before adapting to the remarriage.

101. *See* ARENDELL, *supra* note 30, at 44–45, 50–52; MORGAN, *supra* note 30, at 27, 143–44 (1991).

102. Arguably law could ameliorate the problems associated with divorce by promoting the stability of intact families. Law could deter divorce by increasing its negative effects. However, the financial devastation that currently awaits women and children as well as the uncertainty of mother custody have not deterred women from seeking divorce. Our system must respond to the actual, rather than the hypothetical, behavior of those it governs.

103. Men who remain single six years after divorce seem particularly vulnerable to anxiety, anger, depression, accidents, drug abuse, alcoholism, and health problems. *See* HETHERINGTON & KELLY, *supra* note 18, at 97.

104. *See* BLANKENHORN, *supra* note 11 at 9–10, 19–20. *See also* Kalter et al., *supra* note 97, at 618.

105. *See generally* BLANKENHORN, *supra* note 11, at 160 (citing James H. Bray & Charlene E. Depner, *Perspectives on Nonresidential Parenting, in* NONRESIDENTIAL PARENTING: NEW VISTAS IN FAMILY LIVING 184–85 (James H. Bray & Charlene E. Depner eds. 1994).

106. *See* WEITZMAN, *supra* note 18, at 354 (noting the strong relationship between the economic deprivation that follows divorce and the psychological well-being of divorced children). Research consistently finds a positive correlation between financial-well being and women's postdivorce adjustment. *E.g.*,

Jeanne M. Tschann et al., *Resources, Stressors, and Attachment as Predictors of Adult Adjustment after Divorce: A Longitudinal Study*, 51 J. MARRIAGE & FAM. 1033, 1034, 1041, 1044 (1989).

107. *See generally* Joan B. Kelly, *Psychological and Legal Interventions for Parents and Children in Custody and Access Disputes: Current Research and Practice*, 10 V. J. Soc. Pol'y & L. 129, 130–31 (2002) (citing diminished parent support and contact, continued high interparental hostility, violence, loss of economic and psychological resources, disruptive life changes, and remarriages and re-divorces as risk factors for children of divorce).

108. *See* Tyler, *supra* note 19.

II

INTRODUCTION TO PROCEDURAL JUSTICE

This part defines procedural justice and exposes the current family law system's procedural inadequacies. The link between these deficiencies and the poor outcomes that compromise the financial and psychological functionality of postdivorce families also emerges, and many insights suggest meaningful reform.

Researchers have spent decades teasing out what criteria represent procedural fairness to the public.[1] Their work confirms that the public perceives legal procedures as just if they

1. provide decision makers with respected authority;[2]
2. allow participants adequate voice or participation;[3]
3. foster efficiency;[4]
4. preserve the disputants' relationship or reduce hostilities between them;[5]
5. offer an opportunity for the correction of error or unfair results;[6]
6. suppress bias;[7]
7. operate consistently;[8]
8. provide decision makers who treat disputants with respect;[9]

9. provide decision makers who show concern for disputants' rights;[10] and

10. ensure quality decisions based on accurate information.[11]

Chapter 3 explores the procedural justice criteria related to decision maker characteristics—respected authority, impartiality, and respectful treatment of disputants and their legal rights. Chapter 4 turns to the procedural characteristics of the system itself—adequate voice, efficiency, correction of error, reduction of hostilities, procedural consistency, and decisions based on accurate information.

NOTES

1. *See* Tom R. Tyler, Why People Obey the Law 71–84 (1990).

2. Dworkin also recognizes that, in H.L.A. Hart's jurisprudence, a rule can never be binding unless the person or body issuing the rule has the authority to do so. Ronald Dworkin, Taking Rights Seriously 20 (1977).

3. *See, e.g.,* Deborah R. Hensler, *Suppose It's Not True: Challenging Mediation Ideology*, 2002 J. Disp. Resol. 81, 95 (2002); E. Allan Lind et al., *In the Eye of the Beholder: Tort Litigants' Evaluation of Their Experiences in the Civil Justice System*, 24 L. & Soc'y Rev. 953, 972–73 (1990); Raymond Paternoster et al., *Do Fair Procedures Matter? The Effect of Procedural Justice on Spouse Assault*, 31 L. & Soc'y Rev. 163, 167 (1997); Tom R. Tyler, *What is Procedural Justice?: Criteria Used by Citizens to Assess the Fairness of Legal Procedures*, 22 L. & Soc'y Rev. 103, 111, 122, 128 (1988). *See also* Lawrence M. Friedman, Total Justice 81 (1985).

4. *See* Lind et al., *supra* note 3, at 955 (noting that policy makers frequently assume that litigation costs and delay contribute to public dissatisfaction with the civil justice system). Results obtained by Lind et al., however, indicate that costs and delay have less effect on litigants' perceptions of procedural justice than other process variables. *Id.* at 969–72, 975.

5. *See* Kwok Leung, *Some Determinants of Reactions to Procedural Models for Conflict Resolution: A Cross National Study*, 53 J. Personality & Soc. Psychol. 898 (1987).

6. *See* Paternoster et al., *supra* note 3, at 167–68; Tyler, *supra* note 3, at 113, 122, 127–28. *See also* Friedman, *supra* note 3, at 81.

7. *See* E. Barrett-Howard & Tom R. Tyler, *Procedural Justice as a Criterion in Allocation Decisions*, 50 J. Personality & Soc. Psychol. 296 (1986); Hensler, *supra* note 3, at 95; Gerald S. Leventhal, *What Should Be Done with Equity Theory?, in* Social Exchange: Advances in Theory and Research (K. J. Gergen, M. S. Greenberg, & R. H. Weiss eds. 1980); Paternoster et al., *supra* note 3, at 167–68; Tyler, *supra* note 3, at 112, 122, 127–28.

8. *See* Paternoster et al., *supra* note 3, at 167–68; Tyler, *supra* note 3, at 105–107 (referring to G. S. Leventhal, *What Should Be Done with Equity Theory?, in*

Social Exchange: Advances in Theory and Research (K. J. Gergen, M. S. Greenberg, & R. H. Weiss eds. 1980) as well as other studies). *See generally* Friedman, *supra* note 3, at 43. *But see* Tyler, *supra* note 3, at 122–23, 130 (noting that consistency of treatment did not predict perceptions of procedural justice).

9. *See* Paternoster et al., *supra* note 3, at 167–68; Lind et al., *supra* note 3, at 972–73, 978–81; Tom R. Tyler, *Multiculturalism and the Willingness of Citizens to Defer to the Legal and Legal Authorities*, 25 L. & Soc. Inquiry 983 (2000); Tyler, *supra* note 3, at 129.

10. *See* Paternoster et al., *supra* note 3, at 167–68; Tyler, *supra* note 3, at 113, 129–30.

11. *See* Paternoster et al., *supra* note 3, at 167–68; Tyler, *supra* note 1; Tyler, *supra* note 3, at 106, 112–13, 126–27. A note of caution: empirical research has not addressed what, specifically, the public wants in divorce procedures, and Tyler's research indicates that the meaning of procedural justice does vary from context to context. *See* Tyler, *supra* note 3, at 107–08. Enough similarity exists, however, in what procedures the public wants in different contexts to support this analysis. *See* Tyler, *supra* note 9, at 997–99. Moreover, Tyler's research receives substantial support from scholars who have written about the legitimating potential of procedure. *See, e.g.,* Judith Resnik, *Tiers*, 57 S. Calif. L. Rev. 837 (1984); Lon L. Fuller, *The Forms and Limits of Adjudication*, 92 Harv. L. Rev. 353 (1978).

3

DECISION-MAKER CHARACTERISTICS

Citizens want unbiased decision makers with respected authority to decide legal cases. They also expect decision makers to treat them with respect and to honor their legal rights. An assessment of these characteristics in the divorce context requires consideration of many different decision makers. Certainly judges decide some divorce cases,[1] but lawyers settle many more through negotiation.[2] Because of judicial reliance on guardians ad litem and custody evaluators in custody cases, these individuals, in effect, decide many custody and visitation disputes. Consequently, a thorough consideration of decision maker characteristics and their link to divorce outcomes must address all of these possibilities.[3]

This procedural justice analysis deliberately omits people who settle their divorces without the involvement of legal or quasi-legal actors. Increasing numbers of parties resolve their divorce disputes by themselves[4] or in mediation, but they effectively remove themselves from the formal legal system, and their divorce experiences have limited impact on their procedural justice perceptions. Certainly these settlements influence overall outcomes and deserve attention.[5] Critics claim that divorce mediation, for instance, disadvantages the less powerful[6]—particularly abused wives[7]—and leads to unfair results. We know little about the outcomes reached by pro se litigants. One can surmise, however, that the same power dynamics that influence mediated settlements also affect pro se agreements and that unfair results emerge.[8] Although this part excludes these alternative informal procedures, the reforms ultimately proposed do anticipate and mitigate the substantive problems noted for pro se parties. When these informal processes fail to achieve settlement and the pro se parties turn to the formal system, the disputants will have the same problems with the authority of legal actors that represented parties experience.

RESPECTED AUTHORITY OF JUDGES, GUARDIANS AD LITEM, AND CUSTODY EVALUATORS

We now assess the respected authority of judges, guardians ad litem, and custody evaluators. Although judges decide only 5% to 10% of divorce cases,[9] they remain important decision makers. Preliminary judicial rulings frequently affect cases ultimately settled by lawyers.[10] A judge's refusal early in a divorce to grant the wife temporary maintenance or attorney fees may strain the wife's financial resources and force her lawyer to settle. Although the lawyer becomes the ultimate decision maker, the judge's preliminary ruling significantly affects the lawyer's decision about settlement. Likewise, a judge's preliminary custody and visitation decision may influence any custody–visitation agreement reached by the parties. A judge's decision to appoint a guardian ad litem for the children and the guardian's subsequent recommendation can shape a lawyer's settlement decision even though the judge does not decide the custody issue. Just the reputation of a particular judge may inform a lawyer's decisions about settlement.[11] Consequently, even though judges infrequently decide final divorce outcomes, they do exert significant influence over the choices of the final decision makers. Whether the public respects the authority of judges on divorce issues remains important to a procedural justice critique.

Because of their legal expertise and their formal affiliation with the justice system, judges have institutional authority to resolve legal disputes.[12] In divorce cases, however, the norm of family privacy as well as the incompetence and behavior of judges invite divorce disputants to disrespect this authority.

The pervasive belief that family matters should remain private[13] suggests that the authority of husbands and wives, rather than judges, deserves respect in the resolution of family issues.[14] Numerous U.S. Supreme Court decisions reinforce the norm of family privacy by recognizing that privacy restricts state authority in the family realm.[15]

Privacy concerns seem particularly salient in child-related decisions. Although the state claims a parens patriae power over children, parents may resist that authority more strongly than state power over financial issues. With rare exception, our society demands that parents take full responsibility for the care and proper socialization of their children. Total responsibility suggests a corresponding parental, not state, right to control.[16] The emotional bond between parents and their children, and the parental experience of their children as extensions of themselves, also suggest that parents may disrespect state authority to reorder parent–child relationships.[17] One commentator notes

> Parents have, and should have, the primary responsibility for raising their children. Judges as a group possess no qualities that make them inherently more capable than parents of making intelligent decisions as to a child's best interests after the termination of a marriage. On the contrary, because they brought the child into the world, have far more knowledge of the child's needs and desires, and carry the financial and emotional burden of raising the child, the parents ought to enjoy a presumption in favor of their judgment.[18]

The personal and often embarrassing nature of the information revealed during divorce trials intensifies privacy concerns. Trial frequently exposes parties to public ridicule that threatens their self-esteem, their social identity, or both.[19] Sexual preferences and indiscretions, questionable parental behaviors, embarrassing statements or acts, mental instability, and sexual and physical abuse of spouses and children provide relevant evidence in contested divorce cases. Litigants may well resent rather than respect judges who preside over these invasive proceedings.

When an individual possesses expertise on a subject, people generally respect that person's authority on that topic.[20] Judges could bolster their suspect authority with expertise on the critical issues they must decide.[21] States, however, frequently assign judges to family rotations without relevant training or education. Judges usually serve in the family division for only limited time periods, restricting their ability to acquire expertise through experience. Many judges have little interest in acquisition of the expertise necessary to legitimate their authority, because they dislike and disrespect divorce cases.[22]

Initially, parties have reason to anticipate judicial expertise on and to accept judicial authority over financial issues, thus mitigating privacy concerns. Judges have access to financial knowledge in law school and in practice, and judges routinely preside over cases that present sophisticated financial issues. Moreover, income tax and Social Security programs condition people to accept some state control over family finances.[23] Yet sophisticated financial issues unique to divorce precipitate blatant judicial errors by untrained judges. Judges also routinely fail to recognize the economic vulnerability of women, particularly those with custody of children.[24] Whatever expectation of financial expertise disputants might anticipate evaporates in the face of their exposure to judicial incompetence.

Even if a judge does possess financial expertise relevant to divorce, his or her authority probably receives less respect from the spouse (usually the husband) who has exercised financial control within the marriage. Because of his historical control, reinforced by family privacy, the husband may only grudgingly accept judicial authority. Men's resistance to judicial authority may provide a partial explanation for their noncompliance with support orders.

Most judges also lack the expertise on child issues necessary to enhance their authority. Few judges receive education in the psychology or developmental needs of children,[25] and many openly acknowledge their incompetence.[26] Only a few judges know anything about domestic violence, an issue that significantly affects the well-being of children. Judges seem particularly incompetent in cases where allegations of child sexual abuse occur.[27] The media have done much to expose judicial deficiencies in contested custody issues.[28] One mediator expresses his contempt:

> A judge, after all, has to know what a child's best interests are before he can make a decision based upon those interests. But what qualifies a judge to know this? Surely there is nothing either in his training or in his experience that would give him those qualifications. Nor will the legal rules that he will turn to provide him with that guidance; for they are, at best, a very poor instrument by which to determine those best interests. That is why a judge's declaration that his decision represents what is in a child's best interest is not judicial wisdom, but judicial arrogance. A judge makes this decision, not because he is qualified to, but because he has to—because Barbara and Bill, in being unable to decide it themselves, have left him with no choice.[29]

Judicial behavior reinforces perceptions of incompetence. Judges often pressure divorce disputants to settle their cases[30] or resolve them in mediation, implying that individual authority trumps judicial authority in divorce. Judges often display discomfort with divorce issues,[31] which encourages disputants to wonder about judicial competence. Some judges insist that parents, rather than judges, should resolve child issues. In the words of one judge,

> The two of you are before me as parents. We are getting to what frequently happens in this case, that you are acting as if the other was some stranger . . . . Has any effort been made to resolve this? I never understand why parents want to spend all their money on lawyers' fees for something between themselves. I could care less about the parties. I look at the children. This is a custody issue. If anyone is using the children as a pawn to get at the other, I have little sympathy. I can't

resolve marital problems. You two are probably going to fight on and on. We're here and you brought it . . . I'm going to have to have two parents be told by me what to do about their children. Here I am a total stranger and I'm going to have to tell you when the children can see the other parent. It's utterly ridiculous.[32]

Another judge stated, "I would rather send someone to life in the penitentiary for a criminal act than make a custody decision about a child."[33] When state agents openly question their own authority to act in family matters, they invite the public to disrespect that authority.

Disrespect for judicial competence provides a link between procedural justice and outcomes. We can predict that judges who lack knowledge about the very issues they must decide will make bad decisions. As shown in chapter 2, academic literature and reported cases amply support this expectation.

Their unease, and perhaps their intuitive recognition of their suspect authority, prompts many judges to turn for guidance to professed experts on child issues.[34] Judges routinely seek assistance from guardians ad litem[35] and mental health custody evaluators.[36] Judicial reliance on these individuals, however, has not solved the problem of respected authority[37] or poor outcomes. Many of these experts make inaccurate judgments,[38] and judges rarely challenge their findings.[39] Many guardians ad litem have no expertise on children's issues: lay persons with minimal training, or lawyers, frequently fill these positions.[40] Mental health professionals who serve in this capacity carry an aura of expertise that might create respect for their authority, yet literature suggests that many mental health professionals lack expertise relevant to custody decisions.[41] Many know little about domestic violence or child abuse.[42] Evaluators administer and rely on psychological instruments unsuitable for custody issues[43] or use unreliable tests that claim relevance.[44] Some professionals ascribe to psychological theories that lack scientific verification.[45] Many do not adequately investigate their cases and make recommendations based on faulty or inadequate information. Parents may initially respect the authority of the mental health professional, but their experiences eventually spawn disillusionment.

Guardians ad litem and custody evaluators, just as judges, do not provide decision makers with enough respected authority to override privacy concerns. These unaware or misinformed decision makers also generate poor results.[46] Note the following example.

Marilyn and Steve divorced after nine years of a troubled marriage that included several incidents of domestic violence by Steve against Marilyn. The couple had one 5-year-old child, Amanda. Although Steve pushed Marilyn down the stairs during her pregnancy, he stopped his physical aggression against Marilyn after Amanda's birth. At age 5 Amanda's personality and mind sparkled, and she looked like a modern-day version of Shirley Temple. Under Marilyn's guidance, Amanda had learned to read at age 3 and to subtract and add at age 5. Both of her parents worked outside their attractive middle-class home. Marilyn and Steve agreed that Marilyn should have custody of Amanda and that Steve should have liberal visitation. The court incorporated their settlement agreement into the final judgment of dissolution.

After the divorce, Steve regularly exercised his liberal visitation rights. Several months later, however, Amanda complained to her baby-sitter and to her teacher that her father hurt her. The teacher and baby-sitter informed Marilyn of Amanda's complaints. Amanda began to have nightmares, screaming out, "No, Daddy, no!" The nightmares became severe, and Marilyn had difficulty comforting Amanda. Marilyn consulted her sister Linda, a pediatric nurse. Linda cautioned Marilyn to keep a close watch on Amanda's behavior, suggesting that Amanda's nightmares represented more than a child's normal reaction to divorce. Amanda's teacher and baby-sitter reported that Amanda engaged in inappropriate sexual behavior at school with herself and with other children. Marilyn began to record Amanda's nighttime screams. Two months later, Amanda developed a vaginal discharge. Marilyn took her to a doctor at a children's hospital. The doctor asked many questions, obviously suspicious that some form of sexual abuse had occurred. The physician's questions further alarmed Marilyn.

Marilyn, with Linda's guidance, finally questioned Amanda who gave alarming answers. Marilyn refused to allow Steve to see Amanda. Steve filed an emergency petition asking for enforcement of his visitation rights or for a change of custody. He alleged that Marilyn had interfered with his access to Amanda and had alienated his daughter from him. At the hearing on Steve's emergency petition, the court appointed a guardian ad litem and rescheduled the hearing in two weeks.

During the two-week period, the guardian ad litem interviewed Steve. She refused Marilyn's requests that she talk with Amanda's baby-sitter, teacher, and Aunt Linda. She never interviewed Marilyn or Amanda. Alarmed at the guardian's refusal to investigate, Marilyn took Amanda to a child sexual abuse unit at the children's hospital. On the basis of physical and psychological evaluations, the physicians concluded that Amanda had suffered sexual abuse.

At the hearing two weeks later, the attorney guardian ad litem presented Steve as a charming, intelligent man who had a good relationship with his daughter. On the basis of her interview of Steve, she told of trips to the zoo, soccer games in the park, bedtime stories, and a flower garden Steve and Amanda had planted. Despite her lack of expertise, the attorney guardian stated that Steve showed none of the characteristics common among those people who sexually abuse children. Instead, she testified that

Marilyn had fabricated the sexual abuse allegations and actively had undermined Amanda's relationship with Steve. She concluded that Marilyn suffered from parental alienation syndrome, a syndrome that has no acceptance within the scientific community,[47] and was an unfit parent.

On the basis of this testimony the judge refused to allow Marilyn's medical experts, Amanda's teacher, Amanda's baby-sitter, and Linda to testify. The court also refused to allow Marilyn to introduce the tapes of Amanda's nighttime screams. The court awarded Steve custody of Amanda and allowed Marilyn one hour per week of supervised visitation.

A year later, Amanda still slept in Steve's bedroom. She became a poor student. She gained weight, and her eyes dulled. She lost most of her hair. During her one hour per week with her mother, Amanda refused to talk above a whisper, as though she feared that her mother would evaporate entirely if she again dared to speak out loud. Needless to say, this mother had nothing but contempt for the authority of the guardian ad litem and the judge. All those prepared to testify on Amanda's behalf felt similar outrage. And, very importantly, the judge's reliance on this incompetent guardian ad litem produced a horrific result. Reliance on others provides no substitute for judicial education, responsibility, and accountability.

This discussion suggests that judicial education and accountability, rather than judicial reliance on others, would enhance the respect for external authority in divorce cases and undoubtedly would produce better results. Moreover, to the extent that judges continue to rely on other experts for assistance in child custody disputes, the education and accountability of these experts would enhance their authority and generate better results. Meaningful parental involvement in the decision-making process and fewer adversarial trials also would soften state intrusion on family privacy and enhance respected authority. We turn now to the respected authority of lawyers as decision makers.

RESPECTED AUTHORITY OF LAWYERS

Lawyers have institutional authority based on their role as officers of the courts.[48] As with judges, the norm of family privacy, however, invites disrespect for their authority to decide divorce cases.[49] One contemptuous mediator states

> If lawyers, who, after all, are simply people who went to law school, did not have some special provence that qualified them to make the decisions in our lives when we married, they do not now mysteriously acquire that expertise because we have decided to divorce. Similarly, if we would never have considered it appropriate to regulate our personal affairs by the application of abstract legal rules before, these legal principles do not now

suddenly become relevant or appropriate simply because we have decided to change the direction of our lives. On the contrary, we have every reason to continue to regulate our lives based upon the same personal considerations that we have always looked to in the past. Again, our common sense is enough to tell us this.[50]

Attentive lawyers can minimize the negative effect of family privacy by sharing decision-making authority with their clients. Although some lawyers insist on client participation throughout the case,[51] many others do not.[52] Professional ethics do require lawyers to obtain client approval of any settlement. Ethical rules, however, do not prevent lawyers from exercising a great deal of control over their clients and over what goals their clients ultimately pursue.[53] Unsurprisingly, clients complain that lawyers actively coerce them into settlements that the lawyers think appropriate.[54] The settlement may represent the best result a lawyer can obtain for the client, but many clients make little to no real contribution to the settlement decision. If lawyers encouraged more client participation, they could enhance the respected authority of divorce decision makers generally.

Lawyers also can enhance their authority by acquiring expertise through education and experience during and after law school.[55] A well-educated and seasoned divorce lawyer might actually command more client respect for his or her authority than that commanded by the judge.[56] Many lawyers who represent divorce clients, however, lack the expertise necessary to bolster respect for their authority.[57]

Some lawyers lack competence[58] or incompetently represent some clients. Others take divorce cases only when more desirable cases do not materialize.[59] Solo practitioners sometimes "specialize" in mass-production, by-the-numbers divorces,[60] because a steady stream of divorce clients pays the bills. Only within the past three decades have high quality law firms that specialize in divorce become a common feature of the legal landscape.[61] For the most part, these firms represent a few wealthy clients,[62] many of them husbands, and leave most parties with lawyers of lesser expertise.

Just as with judges, parties likely will respect the authority of lawyers over financial more than custody issues. Clients routinely turn to lawyers for advice in budget development, preparation of financial affidavits, transfer and valuation of property, declarations of bankruptcy, formation of settlement agreements to maximize tax advantages, and evaluation of settlement proposals under the current law. Because of the lawyer's expertise and the parties' dependence, disputants likely will recognize and respect the lawyer's expert authority on financial issues. The authority of lawyers on monetary issues, however, probably will receive less respect from financially sophisticated spouses (usually husbands) who have exercised financial control within the marriage. Even unsophisticated dependent spouses may grow to disrespect the authority of incompetent lawyers who advocate for or coerce them into poor financial settlements.[63]

Lawyers confront the same impediments to respected authority on child issues as judges. Moreover, most lawyers lack the expertise on child issues that could enhance parental respect for their authority. Few lawyers receive education in the psychology of children,[64] domestic violence, and physical and sexual abuse of children.[65] Lawyer ignorance can precipitate poor custody decisions, inviting the scorn, rather than the respect, of those who employed them.

In the end, numerous divorce clients complain vociferously about their divorce lawyers,[66] strongly suggesting little respect for lawyer authority. The link between this procedural deficiency and poor divorce outcomes seems obvious. We can expect incompetent lawyers who do not meaningfully include their divorce clients in important decisions to produce poor results. To circumvent this procedural and substantive deficiency, a procedural system, at a minimum, should intercept lawyer ineptitude and encourage client participation in important decisions. We turn now to an assessment of decision maker impartiality.

IMPARTIALITY

A decision maker's bias inhibits his or her ability to listen with an open mind and to make decisions based on the information the disputants present.[67] Bias ultimately can lead to incorrect or unjust results.[68] Not surprisingly, people want their justice system to suppress decision maker bias.[69] Authorities exhibit bias when they base their decisions on the personal characteristics—such as gender, race, or age—of one or both parties or when they favor one party over another.[70]

Divorce disputants raise many claims of bias by judges, guardians ad litem, mental health custody evaluators, and lawyers. Women claim that these decision makers discriminate against them in financial and custody awards,[71] whereas men claim bias against them in custody issues.[72] Gay and lesbian biological parents married to heterosexual spouses claim discrimination against them on custody and visitation issues. No one seems to perceive decision makers as impartial.[73]

Claims of bias present complex issues. Just as gendered expectations influence perceptions of appropriate outcomes in divorce, they also undoubtedly affect perceptions of bias. A father might attribute a judge's refusal to award him custody to gender bias,[74] even though most would find the mother a more appropriate custodial parent.[75] Likewise, a wife may attribute a judge's refusal to award permanent maintenance to gender bias against women, whereas most would find permanent maintenance inappropriate under the circumstances. No legal system, no matter how procedurally sound, can eradicate these gender-driven perceptions of bias. It can, however, temper them.

Divorce disputants also may mistake an incompetent decision maker as biased. For instance, a judge might award primary custodial responsibility to an abusive parent, because he or she does not know that abuse of a spouse harms the children. The mother, however, may attribute the decision to the judge's bias against women, particularly abused women, rather than judicial incompetence. Undoubtedly, judicial ignorance invites "perceptions" of bias. Simply put, an ignorant decision maker, as opposed to an expert, invites an already suspicious public to believe that decisions rest on bias rather than knowledge.

Ignorance also facilitates and perpetuates actual bias. Unconstrained and unchallenged by expert knowledge, an ignorant decision maker remains free to believe in the accuracy of his or her stereotypical beliefs.

These observations reinforce the importance of judicial education in a legitimate procedural system. Education cannot curb all bias, and no judge can[76] or should achieve actual neutrality.[77] The goal is to moderate the worst forms of bias that severely strain procedural legitimacy and generate some of the dysfunctional results discussed here.

JUDICIAL BIAS IN FINANCIAL ISSUES

The divorce outcomes noted earlier suggest judicial bias against women on financial issues. A closer look supports this claim more directly.[78] For many reasons, wives become financially dependent on their husbands.[79] In order to survive during the pendency of divorce, wives need temporary support.[80] Despite statutory authorization, many judges refuse to make such awards.[81]

Many wives also need spousal maintenance after the dissolution of their marriages. Wives tend to subordinate their careers to those of their husbands and to assume the bulk of homemaking and childcare responsibilities.[82] Wives lose income for each year they do not participate in the work force,[83] and a wife's market work during marriage has little to no effect on her financial well-being after divorce.[84] Unless the wife remarries, she will suffer long-term economic costs attributable to divorce.[85] Many women thus need spousal maintenance to keep their financial heads above water, to obtain education or job training, to avoid hasty and ill-conceived remarriages, to compensate for their marginalized work force participation, to provide their children with adequate supervision and quality parenting, and to mitigate the psychological and emotional traumas associated with financial problems.[86]

At the final divorce hearing, maintenance statutes authorize judges to award various forms of maintenance, and these statutes typically show sensitivity to the financial dependency that results from the caregiving that wives and mothers provide before and after dissolution.[87] Although maintenance statutes invite judges to respond to the economic and social realities of divorced women,[88] judges typically refuse that invitation.[89] Approximately 60% of divorcing couples have children, and mothers receive custody approximately 90% of the time;[90] yet only 10% to 17% of divorced women receive an alimony award.[91] Less than half of the wives married for more than 15 years receive maintenance,[92] and custodial mothers with dependent children receive maintenance only 25% of the time.[93] Even when wives do obtain a maintenance award, the award is small[94] and for a short duration.[95]

Judges find that wives who earn $12,000 to $20,000 per year have no need of maintenance, regardless of their husbands' ability to pay.[96] Others find maintenance inappropriate based on their belief that the wife will remarry.[97] Rather than honor the wife's caretaking contributions that marginalize her work force participation, judges typically underestimate a wife's financial vulnerability at divorce[98] and continue to view the husband's income as rightfully his.[99]

Many studies indicate that the husband's inability to pay[100] rarely accounts for the inadequacy of maintenance awards.[101] For instance, in a 1984 study of three New York counties, Garrison found that, in contested divorce cases, the wives married for 20 or more years who received permanent maintenance had an average income of $5,757 after divorce, whereas their husbands had an average postdivorce income of $52,679. Wives in this same group who received durationally limited maintenance had an average income of $7,458 after divorce, whereas their husbands had an average postdivorce income of $77,358.[102]

Certainly simple ignorance can contribute to a judge's misapprehension of the wife's economic vulnerability at divorce.[103] The lack of judicial education and training invites this ignorance. Cases and studies suggest, however, that bias as well as ignorance support the tendency of judges to award inadequate maintenance awards.[104] In the candid words of one judge,

> Alimony was never intended to assure a perpetual state of secured indolence. It should not be suffered to convert a host of physically and mentally competent young women into an army of alimony drones, who neither toil nor spin, and become a drain on society and a menace to themselves.[105]

As one lawyer observed to his male divorce client,

We ought not to be offering too much. Precedent seems to be more generous than judges are in paying spousal support. As much as you are concerned right now about what she might be getting, the judges are really not generous at all. This is a somewhat conservative county and there's a backlash for a woman to go out and do whatever a man can. So why not? Why can't she go and take care of herself? You take care of yourself.[106]

As a final example, consider the following. A Massachusetts attorney represented a wife with two children under age six. One of the children had a chronic illness. The wife worked part time and earned less than $100 per week; her husband made $55,000 per year. The attorney told the Massachusetts Gender Bias Task Force that the judge stated, "it was unconscionable for her to be taking a job like this. It was about time women learned that they had to work. His daughters were going to work." The judge awarded the wife $200 a week for six months. He reduced the award to $100 per week after six months so that "she could learn a lesson."[107]

Judicial bias also taints the distribution of marital property.[108] Most states subject marital property[109] to equitable distribution.[110] The unspoken "he who earns it owns it" rule seems to dictate what judges find equitable,[111] resulting in wives' frequent receipt of fewer marital assets than husbands.[112] Even in equitable distribution states that employ a presumption in favor of an equal division of marital property, wives still receive less than half of the marital assets.[113] Moreover, if judges did equally divide marital assets, as they do in some community property states,[114] equality might mask inequity.[115] Most divorcing couples have little marital property to distribute.[116] Aside from wealthy couples, the marital property of a couple married for many years generally consists of equity in a marital home.[117] With spousal maintenance disfavored and infrequent, the dependent spouse with financial prospects inferior to those of her husband may need more than half of the marital property.[118]

Judicial bias on financial issues links directly to the poor economic results noted earlier. A system that promotes judicial impartiality also undoubtedly would produce better results. Lawyers, too, exhibit bias.

LAWYER BIAS IN FINANCIAL ISSUES

Lawyers face numerous obstacles when they attempt to obtain maintenance for their clients. Judicial attitudes toward maintenance hamper a lawyer's ability at trial to obtain an award. Lawyers also face practical impediments to maintenance in settlement negotiations. Husbands typically resist spousal maintenance,[119] and a lawyer cannot credibly threaten trial on the issue when everyone knows the judge likely will not award maintenance[120] or will not award enough to make the struggle worthwhile.[121] Consequently, lawyers find settlements that include maintenance difficult to obtain.

These practical impediments, however, do not completely explain why lawyers fail to obtain maintenance for their clients. Lawyers can and do obtain maintenance when they pursue it. In her 1984 study of divorce cases in three New York counties, Garrison found that not one unrepresented wife received spousal maintenance, whereas 30% of represented wives obtained an award.[122] Just as with judges, ignorance and bias shape lawyer attitudes and behaviors related to maintenance. Rather than pursue maintenance, attorneys for wives most commonly counsel their clients to forgo maintenance and get on with their new lives.[123] The Massachusetts Gender Bias Task Force discovered that reluctant attorneys sought alimony in only 29% of their divorce cases.[124]

Gender bias of lawyers also affects property settlements.[125] Settlements, just as judicial decisions, reveal that wives receive fewer marital assets than do husbands.[126] Certainly women complain bitterly about the representation they receive from their lawyers,[127] supporting a conclusion of lawyer bias and incompetence. Although many lawyers claim to seek "fair settlements,"[128] numerous cases in which wives seek to set aside settlement agreements graphically reveal the gender bias, incompetence, or both in their lawyers.[129] These cases also illustrate the link between biased decision makers and poor financial outcomes for women and dependent children—outcomes that trigger the social problems noted earlier.

BIAS ON CUSTODY ISSUES

Custody issues also raise concerns about bias. Fathers' rights groups vociferously argue that judges discriminate against them on custody issues,[130] yet, on the surface, studies seem to belie their claims. Whereas mothers still receive custody far more frequently than fathers,[131] many custody arrangements simply reflect the father's wishes or requests.[132] Moreover, a Massachusetts gender bias study found that fathers who actually seek custody obtain either primary or joint physical custody in more than 70% of cases.[133] Judges in Wisconsin report that they "about equally" award custody to men and women in contested custody cases.[134] Many other studies confirm that fathers who pursue custody—particularly those who batter their wives[135]—have greater success than their wives.[136] Despite these studies, some observers harbor no doubt that some judges cling to the belief that mothers make better parents, regardless of what role the father actually played in the family.[137]

Mothers also claim judicial bias against them in custody cases, and research confirms such claims.[138] Judges typically devalue the nurturing that mothers provide[139] and favor the superior economic resources of fathers.[140] On the other hand, if the mother and father work, courts believe her employment conflicts with the children's best interests.[141] Judges find mothers with ambitious careers even more suspect.[142] In contrast, judges believe the father's employment benefits the children.[143]

Courts hold mothers to higher standards of parenting than fathers.[144] If a mother temporarily relinquishes custody to the father for any reason, courts find her an improper custodian.[145] In one extreme example, the wife, advised by counsel to be "friendly" to the children's father, allowed her husband frequent contact with the children. At the final divorce hearing, the court granted the husband primary residential custody of the children, reasoning that the mother did not really want the children because she allowed the father to see them so often.[146] In stark contrast, courts encourage uninvolved or long-absent fathers to reestablish their relationships with their children.[147] Additionally, the illicit sexual relations of mothers compromise their custody claims far more severely than do those of fathers.[148]

Judicial bias also compounds judicial ignorance[149] about spousal violence in the custody context. The law of many states now provides that evidence of spousal violence has relevance in a custody determination.[150] Many judges, however, routinely ignore these provisions.[151] Frequently, judges do not believe the wife's allegations of domestic violence.[152] Judges who do believe that violence occurred generally minimize its importance[153] and its relevance to child custody.[154] This belief that the father's violence against the mother has no relevance persists in the face of compelling evidence that children who witness the abuse[155] exhibit numerous and sometimes severe behavioral and psychological problems[156] and that spouse abusers frequently physically and sexually abuse their children.[157] A New York court stated, for example: "Although defendant abused plaintiff wife in the presence of the child, the only incident directly affecting the child was when defendant threw a television set on the floor when his daughter disobeyed him."[158]

More perversely, judges who do believe that spouse abuse harms children sometimes blame the mother for her failure to remove and protect the children,[159] or they perceive her failure to leave and avoid the violence as a pathology[160] that makes her an unsuitable child custodian.[161] Conversely, if she does attempt to protect herself and the children and flees with them to a shelter, the judge may find her living arrangements inferior to those of her husband and award the husband custody.[162] Her flight to a shelter also interferes with the batterer's access to the children, making her, in biased judicial eyes, an unfriendly parent. On the other hand, if she flees and leaves the children behind, she risks claims of abandonment,[163] instability,[164] and insensitivity to her children's needs.

Biased judges misinterpret battered women's reactions to abuse and question their ability to parent. Some abused women exhibit symptoms of posttraumatic stress disorder (PTSD),[165] including (a) hyperarousal, a consistent alert for danger that may cause excessive irritability and explosive aggression; (b) intrusion, a reexperience of the original violence through flashback and nightmare; and (c) constriction, a dissociation, trance, or numbness that protects against experiencing a terrifying memory.[166] A battered wife who suffers from PTSD, or from various aspects of PTSD, may repress memories of violent events, relate her story in convoluted fragments, exhibit inappropriate affect while testifying about abusive incidents,[167] minimize the magnitude and impact of the abuse,[168] overreact to a batterer's seemingly insignificant behavior or remark, and testify inconsistently with other evidence such as medical records.[169] Bias invites judges to view these symptoms as indications of parental unfitness rather than the products of the husband's abuse. The Commission on Gender Bias for the State of Georgia reported the following:

> A frequent complaint to the Commission was the batterer's tactic in divorce proceedings of "going on the offensive" and attempting to demonstrate that the victim is unstable, is not self-sufficient, or is unable to care for their children. Judges who do not understand the syndrome often fulfill the batterer's threat and the victim's worst nightmare by awarding custody to the father, interpreting the victim's erratic behavior as neurotic.[170]

When a mother alleges that a father has physically or sexually abused a child, judicial bias frequently produces tragic results for children. Judges typically discount a mother's allegation of child abuse,[171] commonly believing that the mother has fabricated the abuse to gain an advantage in divorce negotiations.[172] Dismissive of mothers' complaints about fathers' abuse of children,[173] judges also routinely order children to visit with those who have abused them.[174] Judges label women who try to protect their children the "unfriendly" parent[175] and frequently award custody to the abuser.[176] In a Maryland case, for example, the judge denied the mother custody of two preteen daughters because he felt that the father's sexual abuse of the girls had not damaged them as much as the mother's decision to report it. According to the judge, the mother's report to authorities "showed [that] her hatred for the father took precedence over the children's need to hold a high image of their father.'"[177] In another case, the mother accused the father of sexual abuse of their daughter. The trial court found that the mother overreacted, that the father posed no danger to the child, and that overnight visitation was appropriate provided one of four persons close to the father supervised. When it entered this order, the trial court ignored evidence that the father admitted to his sexual abuse of the wife's older daughter by a previous marriage, that he inflicted excessive punishment on the older daughter, that he denied that he needed treatment for this conduct, and that he had physically and sexually abused the mother.[178] In another case, the Massachusetts Department of Social Services substantiated the mother's allegations of child sexual abuse of the daughter by the father.[179] The trial court ignored this and other evidence of sexual abuse and awarded custody to the father.[180] In a rare moment, the appellate court substituted its judgment for that of the trial court and ordered the trial court to return custody to the mother and to allow the father only supervised visitation.[181] A Florida case provides a final example. A father, uncle, and grandfather sexually assaulted a five-year-old girl in front of her eight-year-old brother. The past president of the board of Women in Distress stated

> It took us 18 months—this happened in the last two years—18 months to be able to stop the man from visitation rights[,] during which time he continued to abuse the child. . . . But the judge said to me: "Do you as a counselor, do you as a professional, believe that this child [has been abused]"—"Yes, absolutely." She said, "Okay, thank you," and went ahead and let him visit her alone.[182]

Judicial reliance on mental health professionals[183] does little to hinder bias. Mental health professionals have a long history of discrimination against women generally, and against mothers in particular.[184] Mental health professionals strongly believe in shared parenting[185] and the participation of both parents in the postdivorce lives of their children,[186] despite little evidence that supports the benefits of shared parenting.[187] Their bias encourages them to presume that men and women make equal parental contributions, exaggerates the importance of fathers, and undervalues the mother's primary caretaking role.[188]

Mental health professionals, just as judges, exhibit a particular bias against women who have suffered abuse.[189] Abused wives commonly perform poorly on psychological tests, encouraging biased mental health professionals to evaluate them negatively.[190] In contrast, batterers tend to perform better than their victims on psychological tests,[191] and their skill at manipulation may result in a favorable psychological evaluation.[192]

Many mental health professionals treat women's claims of physical or sexual abuse of children with a skepticism similar to that of judges.[193] Bias leads other mental health professionals to unquestioned application of false syndromes to mothers, such as "parental alienation syndrome,"[194] and to tragic custody recommendations. Just as with judges, their bias compounds their ignorance.[195] Courts also employ guardians ad litem to assist in custody decision making.[196] No reason exists to assume that court-appointed guardians ad litem exhibit less bias against women and mothers than other types of professionals.[197]

Decision maker bias independently generates poor and even tragic custody results, but so too does the mere anticipation of this bias. A dedicated mother's realistic fear of losing custody altogether, because of decision maker bias, may induce her to agree to a custody or visitation arrangement that compromises both her and the children's interests.[198] This same fear may hinder her ability to demand fairness in financial negotiations,[199] particularly if she lacks the economic resources to hire an attorney or to build a good custody case.[200] Perversely, the worse the father's parenting during the marriage, the more the mother may desire custody in order to protect the children, and the more vulnerable she may become to financial manipulation.

Lawyers, too, exhibit bias on custody issues. Because lawyers operate in the privacy of their offices rather than in open court and do not write opinions, their custody biases prove more difficult to detect than those of judges. Moreover, when a lawyer advises a father to forgo a request for custody, the lawyer may base this advice on a realistic anticipation of the father's failure in court before a biased judge rather than the lawyer's private belief that mothers make better custodians of children. Similarly, a lawyer may advise a mother not to make allegations of domestic violence, fearing that, as a consequence, the court will find the mother an "unfriendly parent" and award custody to the father.

Nonetheless, parties do perceive lawyers as biased on custody issues. Mothers claim that the gender bias causes their lawyers to misapprehend the danger to children in domestic violence situations.[201] A gender bias study in Oregon suggests that male lawyers have significantly less empathy for the plight of battered women than their female counterparts.[202] Undoubtedly some lawyers do advise deserving fathers to forgo custody, particularly of infants. And, finally, no reason exists to suspect that a lawyer differs from any other legal decision maker whose personal biases and preferences influence behavior.[203] Sometimes that bias will favor the lawyer's client, other times not.

RESPECTFUL TREATMENT

Disputants also want legal decision makers to treat them with respect and to show concern for their rights.[204] Respectful treatment of disputants and their rights implicates their social status and self-worth and influences their feelings of self-respect.[205] We now consider whether legal actors fulfill these procedural concerns.

Judges do not like divorce cases[206] and often treat parties with disrespect. Certainly parties, primarily women, complain about judicial treatment.[207] For example, a Colorado judge routinely called battered women liars and screamed at them. A few times he actually threw things onto the floor and stomped out of the courtroom. Despite attempts to prepare the women for this judicial abuse, they left his courtroom shell-shocked, regardless of favorable outcomes. Although this behavior might seem extreme, the discomfort many judges feel with divorce cases and the unsavory issues these cases frequently present encourage judges to act disrespectfully toward the parties.

As illustrated earlier, judges also frequently fail to respect the legal rights of parties. The indeterminate nature of divorce law, however, complicates this claim of disrespect. For instance, the "best interests of the child" standard governs custody decisions,[208] and a typical statute lists 10 to 12 relevant factors.[209] Similarly, spousal support[210] and property distribution[211] statutes mandate that courts consider several criteria when they make awards. Statutory indeterminacy gives judges a great deal of discretion to define the legal rights available under these statutes. Parties seem to have no definitive legal rights until a judge actually makes an award; therefore we cannot argue that any judicial award disrespects those rights. This argument, however, is unsatisfactory. Surely state legislatures intended their divorce statutes to do more than grant judges the right to award whatever suits them. The very existence of these statutes suggests legal rights worthy of judicial respect.

Whether attributable to ignorance or bias, we have seen that judges neglect the legal rights of divorce disputants. Statutes mandate custody and visitation arrangements that serve the best interests of children, yet judges and those on whom judges rely produce results that do not honor that mandate. Statutes require consideration of domestic violence in custody cases, yet judges and their appointed experts routinely discount or ignore allegations of domestic violence. Statutes provide for temporary maintenance, attorneys' fees, and spousal maintenance for financially dependent spouses, yet judges fail to make these awards. Many states presume that an equal distribution of marital property is equitable, yet judges make lopsided distributions that favor men. In essence, the law may suggest a legal right, but that right frequently evaporates in its judicial application. Judicial enthusiasm for settlement also may convey the impression of judicial disinterest in the vindication of legal rights.[212]

Judges not only disrespect substantive legal rights, they also fail to honor legal procedures. For instance, the rules of civil procedure provide numerous discovery mechanisms that allow parties to gather the information they need from adverse parties. If a party fails to respond to a discovery request, the requesting party can motion the court to compel the reluctant party to respond. In most civil cases, judges typically grant motions to compel. In divorce cases, however, judges do not take formal discovery seriously and are reluctant to grant motions to compel.[213] Colorado law allows parties to obtain an initial and a supplemental custody evaluation in contested custody cases.[214] Yet I stood in the home of a Denver judge and heard him proudly relate to the gathering that he had refused to allow the parties in a case to obtain a custody evaluation. He hoped his refusal would force the parents to settle.

Judicial failure to respect the substantive and procedural rights of parties provides a direct link to poor outcomes. Judicial failure to give effect to the financial legal rights of women produces results that contribute to the social and psychological problems noted earlier. Judges who ignore statutory mandates concerning custody, particularly those that pertain to domestic violence, produce deplorable results. Without formal discovery, a party may enter into an unfair settlement based on ignorance. Without a formal custody evaluation, an abused child may remain unprotected. Once again, a procedural justice criteria implicates substantive justice as well.

Lawyers also often insufficiently respect clients and their legal rights. Certainly parties, particularly women, do not believe that their divorce lawyers respect them or their rights.[215] The nature of the lawyer–client relationship offers some explanation for client discontent.[216] Many times divorce lawyers refuse to empathize too strongly with clients, because they know that clients commonly distort reality and too much client reinforcement can encourage litigation rather than an advantageous settlement.[217] A lawyer's necessary reconstruction of a client's reality to fit within relevant legal criteria might offend a client's sense of personal dignity.[218] Clients bring unrealistic expectations to the divorce arena that lawyers must adjust before trial or before settlement can occur.[219] Clients may perceive such adjustments as disrespectful of them or their legal rights. A lawyer may ignore multiple daily calls from a client in order to actually work on that or another client's case, but that client may perceive this as neglect. Although legitimate representation techniques may explain some client dissatisfaction, undoubtedly many divorce lawyers simply do not, in their client's eyes, treat their clients respectfully.[220] For example, to persuade their clients to accept their advice, some divorce lawyers yell at them, call them names, and ridicule them[221]—the antithesis of respectful treatment.

Lawyers also often do not show respect for the legal rights of their clients.[222] As Sarat and Felstiner note, divorce clients

> [c]ome to the divorce lawyer's office believing in the efficacy of rights in the legal system only to encounter a process that not only is 'inconsistent,' but cannot be counted on to protect fundamental rights or deal in a principled way with the important matters that come before it.[223]

These authors then relate an illustrative exchange between a female divorce client, Jane, and her attorney, Peter:

> Jane: I just really cannot quite believe this. Part of me is still incredulous. It's nothing else than property rights. I don't even have the rights of a landlord, to go to a home that I own 50 percent of, to make sure it's not being destroyed. I don't understand that. I always thought that, in some way or another, if one's human rights were not protected, one's property rights were.
>
> Peter: No.[224]

Attorneys, for practical, emotional, and financial reasons,[225] often would rather settle than try divorce cases.[226] Settlement becomes the primary focus rather than protection of a client's legal rights.[227] Nevertheless, many argue that attorneys negotiate divorce agreements in the "shadow of the law,"[228] implying that lawyers protect legal rights in settlement negotiations.[229] Yet studies suggest that divorce lawyers frequently encourage their clients to settle with little or no reference to legal principles.[230] Moreover, as already noted, lawyers routinely coerce women into poor agreements unreflective of legal rights.[231] Lawyers sometimes misrepresent a client's interests in child custody, regardless of what arrangement might best serve a child's interests.[232] Indeterminate law helps lawyers to persuade their clients to accept their advice.[233] Lawyers simply seem more interested in securing a settlement than in protection of a client's legal rights.

Clients also complain that settlements fail to reflect their legal rights because lawyers neglect their cases.[234] Many lawyers only passively prepare and process the agreements the clients independently have reached with their spouses rather than pursue the client's legal rights.[235] Sarat and Felstiner tell the story of Kathy, whom they label "The Unsupported Wife." Wendy, a self-styled feminist lawyer, represented Kathy. Wendy insisted that Kathy required spousal maintenance to survive financially. Wendy also realized that Kathy never stood up to her husband Nick. Indeed, whenever Kathy thought about confronting Nick, she cringed. Nevertheless, Wendy sent Kathy to negotiate with Nick alone, and Kathy predictably failed to secure Nick's agreement to pay spousal maintenance.[236]

Many times lawyers cannot protect their clients' right to maintenance and equitable distribution without first conducting financial discovery.[237] Yet many lawyers settle cases without discovery.[238] Settlement terms often simply reflect the parties' stamina and vulnerability to the pressures of prolonged negotiations[239] rather than their legal rights.

When a lawyer does respect and pursue his or her client's legal rights, however, the settlement may not reflect them. Financial pressures sometimes persuade clients to accept settlement proposals that their lawyers consider unfair.[240] Judicial reluctance to honor legal rights also can make trial futile and hamper a lawyer's ability to obtain a settlement that respects those rights. For instance, a lawyer will have difficulty obtaining half of the marital assets for the wife in negotiations if the other lawyer knows that the judge likely will not equally distribute the marital property.

Some lawyers may have good reason to counsel their clients to forgo legal rights. Even lawyers who abhor domestic violence and understand its effect on children, for instance, may discourage a client from raising the issue because of fear of judicial backlash. Consequently, lawyer-brokered settlements sometimes may reflect judicial rather than lawyer disrespect for legal rights. Nevertheless, lawyers frequently broker agreements that are less protective of legal rights than judicial decrees. Judges, for instance, seem more inclined to divide marital property equally and to provide spousal maintenance than litigants who settle their cases.[241] Many cases that uphold settlement agreements also illustrate that judges frequently do not consider the negotiated settlement as fair or reflective of the law.[242]

For many reasons, disrespect for divorce disputants and their rights permeates the divorce system. This disrespect contributes to poor results that do not reflect what the law intends. Again we have the link between procedural and substantive justice.

NOTES

1. Studies indicate that courts decide only 6% to 20% of custody cases. *See* Daniel A. Krauss & Bruce D. Sales, *Legal Standards, Expertise, and Experts in the Resolution of Child Custody Cases*, 6 Psychol. Pub. Pol'y & L. 843, 843 (2000).

2. As Galanter and Cahill note, most cases settle, Marc Galanter & Mia Cahill, *"Most Cases Settle": Judicial Promotion and Regulation of Settlements*, 46 Stan. L. Rev. 1339, 1339 (1994), and Ross argues that "the principle institution of the law in action is not trial: it is settlement out of court." H. L. Ross, Settled Out of Court 3 (2d ed. 1980). *See also* Marc Galanter, *Worlds of Deals: Using Negotiation to Teach About Legal Process*, 34 J. Legal Educ. 263, 269 (1984). One study found that 217 of 349 Wisconsin divorce cases settled without judicial involvement. Marygold S. Melli et al., *The Process of Negotiation: An Exploratory Investigation in the Context of No-Fault Divorce*, 40 Rutgers L. Rev. 1133, 1142 (1988). And, scholars observe that the overwhelming majority of divorce cases settle in negotiation. *See* Lynn Mather et al., Divorce Lawyers at Work: Varieties of Professionalism in Practice 75, 114, 121–22 (2001); Robert H. Mnookin, *Divorce Bargaining: The Limits on Private Ordering*, in The Resolution of Family Conflict: Comparative Legal Perspectives 364, 364 (John M. Eekelaar & Sanford N. Katz eds. 1984). Lind et al. note the importance of the lawyer as a source of litigant impressions of procedural justice. E. Allan Lind et al., *In the Eye of the Beholder: Tort Litigants' Evaluation of Their Experiences in the Civil Justice System*, 24 L. & Soc'y Rev. 953, 972–73 (1990), at 959, 972.

3. *See* Melli et al., *supra* note 2, at 1162.

4. *See* Connie J.A. Beck & Bruce D. Sales, *A Critical Reappraisal of Divorce Mediation Research and Policy*, 6 PSYCHOL. PUB. POL'Y & L. 989, 993 (2000); Nancy Thoennes et al., *The Impact of Child Support Guidelines on Award Adequacy, Award Variability, and Case Processing Efficiency*, 25 FAM. L.Q. 325, 342 tab. 11 (1991) (noting that in 1986–1987, 23% of mothers and 48% of fathers proceeded pro se in a Colorado sample; 27% of mothers and 51% of father proceeded pro se in a Hawaii sample; and 8% of mothers and 30% of fathers had no legal representation in an Illinois sample); Marsha Garrison, *Equitable Distribution in New York: Results and Reform: Good Intentions Gone Awry: The Impact of New York's Equitable Distribution Law on Divorce Outcomes*, 57 BROOK. L. REV. 621, 646 tab. 2 (1991) (finding that, in one New York county, 25% of wives and 31% of husbands proceeded pro se and that in another New York county 14% of wives and 33% of husbands had no legal representation).

5. As Nolan-Haley notes

> Under prevailing criteria, mediation is evaluated generally in terms of self-determination, participant satisfaction, and efficiency. As applied to court mediation, these criteria may be useful indicators for evaluating process, but are less helpful when evaluating outcome. These criteria tell us only that litigants were doing something, that they felt good about it, and that dockets were cleared as a result. They tell us little about whether litigants actually knew what they were doing or why they were doing it. Thus, these criteria tell us little about justice in court mediation.

   Jacqueline M. Nolan-Haley, *Court Mediation and the Search for Justice Through Law*, 74 WASH. U. L.Q. 47, 85–86 (1996).

6. *E.g.*, Penelope Eileen Bryan, *Reclaiming Professionalism: The Lawyer's Role in Divorce Mediation*, 28 FAM. L.Q. 177 (1994) (hereinafter *Reclaiming Professionalism*); Penelope E. Bryan, *Killing Us Softly: Divorce Mediation and the Politics of Power*, 40 BUFF. L. REV. 441 (1992) (hereinafter *Killing Us Softly*); Trina Grillo, *The Mediation Alternative: Process Dangers for Women*, 100 YALE L.J. 1545, 1601 (1991); Christopher Honeyman, *Patterns of Bias in Mediation*, 1985 J. DISPUTE RESOL. 141; M. Laurie Leitch, *The Politics of Compromise: A Feminist Perspective on Mediation*, 14/15 MEDIATION Q. 163, 167 (1986–1987).

7. *See* Desmond Ellis, *Marital Conflict Mediation and Post-Separation Wife Abuse*, 8 L. & INEQ. J. 317, 327–39 (1990); Karla Fischer et al., *The Culture of Battering and the Role of Mediation in Domestic Violence Cases*, 46 S.M.U. L. REV. 2117, 2118, 2165–71 (1993); Barbara Hart, *Gentle Jeopardy: The Further Endangerment of Battered Women and Children in Custody Mediation*, 7 MEDIATION Q. 317 (1990); Lisa G. Lerman, *Mediation of Wife Abuse Cases: The Adverse Impact of Informal Dispute Resolution on Women*, 7 HARV. WOMEN'S L.J. 57 (1984); Dianne Post, *Mediation Can Make Bad Worse*, NAT'L L.J., June 8, 1992, at 15. *See also* Beck & Sales, *supra* note 4, at 996–98.

8. *See generally* Penelope Eileen Bryan, *Women's Freedom to Contract at Divorce: A Mask for Contextual Coercion*, 47 Buff. L. Rev. 1153 (1999); *Killing Us Softly*, *supra* note 6.

9. *See, e.g.*, Robert J. Levy, *Comment on the Pearson-Thoennes Study and on Mediation*, 17 Fam. L.Q. 525, 530 (1983) (noting that 85% to 90% of divorce cases settle); Melli et al., *supra* note 2, at 1142 (finding that 217 of 349 Wisconsin divorce cases settled); Mnookin, *supra* note 2, at 364, 364 (observing that the vast majority of divorce cases are resolved by negotiation). The rate of settlement for divorce cases mimics the rate for civil cases generally. *See* Marc Galanter, *Reading the Landscape of Disputes: What We Know and Don't Know (and Think We Know) About Our Allegedly Contentious and Litigious Society*, 31 UCLA L. Rev. 4, 27 (1983).

10. Galanter & Cahill caution that resolution without trial does not always mean resolution without judicial involvement:

> Oft-cited figures estimating settlement rates of between 85 and 95 percent are misleading; those figures represent all civil cases that do not go to trial. But that is not quite the same as limiting the definition of cases that "settle" to those resolved solely by agreement between the parties without authoritative decisions in ways other than by trial. Herbert Kritzer, analyzing 1649 cases in five federal judicial districts and seven state courts, found that although only 7 percent of cases went to trial and reached a jury verdict or court decision, another 15 percent terminated through some other form of adjudication, such as arbitration or dismissal. Another 9 percent settled following a ruling on a significant motion.

Galanter & Cahill, *supra* note 2, at 1339–40 (citing Herbert M. Kritzer, *Adjudication to Settlement: Shading in the Gray*, 70 Judicature 161, 162–64 (1986)).

11. *See* Mather et al., *supra* note 2, at 99–100.

12. *See, e.g.*, Joseph Raz, The Authority of Law 216–17 (1979); Charles W. Collier, *The Use and Abuse of Humanistic Theory in Law: Reexamining the Assumptions of Interdisciplinary Legal Scholarship*, 41 Duke L.J. 191, 215–23 (1991).

13. *See* Robert J. Levy, *The Rights of Parents*, 1976 BYU L. Rev. 693; Carl E. Schneider, *Moral Discourse and the Transformation of American Family Law*, 83 Mich. L. Rev. 1803, 1833–46 (1985); Janet Maleson Spencer & Joseph P. Zammit, *Mediation–Arbitration: A Proposal for Private Resolution of Disputes Between Divorced or Separated Parents*, 1976 Duke L.J. 911, 919; Arland Thornton, *Comparative and Historical Perspectives on Marriage, Divorce, and Family Life*, 1994 Utah L. Rev. 587, 596. *See also* Beck & Sales, *supra* note 4, at 1032 (noting research that indicates parties have a strong dislike for the exposure of private matters in divorce hearings).

14. Many commentators note that family law doctrine currently extends less protection to family privacy than in the past. *See, e.g.*, Martha Albertson Fineman, The Illusion of Equality: The Rhetoric and Reality of Divorce Reform

6 (1991). And certainly Americans have come to accept the necessity of state intrusion into the family in order, for example, to protect children from various forms of abuse and neglect. But state intrusion into family privacy during divorce, when no obvious physical threat to individual members exists, remains highly suspect. *See* Krauss & Sales, *supra* note 1, at 845–46. The divorce mediation movement has gained acceptance partially because it offers divorce disputants the ability to avoid the intrusive formal legal system. *Id.* at 849. And, some commentators question whether the state recently has reached too deeply into family privacy when it prosecutes parents for the crimes of their children, *see, e.g.*, Jill Smolowe, *Parenting on Trial: A Michigan Couple is Fined for a Son's Crimes*, TIME, May 20, 1996, at p. 50, and prescribing what kind and how much physical discipline parents may inflict on their children.

15. *E.g.*, Troxel v. Granville, 530 U.S. 57 (2000); Roe v. Wade, 410 U.S. 113 (1973); Griswold v. Connecticut, 381 U.S. 479, 483 (1965).

16. This suggestion has a deep historical link to children's incapacity. In the 17th century, Locke argued that a child's irrationality required parental control until the child attained reason. JOHN LOCKE, SECOND TREATISE OF CIVIL GOVERNMENT 45, 49 (Henry Regnery Co. 1955 (original volume published 1658)). *See generally* Katherine Hunt Federle, *Looking for Rights in All the Wrong Places: Resolving Custody Disputes in Divorce Proceedings*, 15 CARDOZO L. REV. 1523, 1528–32 & nn.18–22 (1994). The idea that children become the property of those who make them—primarily their mothers—receives theoretical support from Nozick's entitlement theory. *See* SUSAN MOLLER OKIN, JUSTICE, GENDER, AND THE FAMILY 79–86 (1989) (discussing ROBERT NOZICK, ANARCHY, STATE, AND UTOPIA (1974)). United States Supreme Court decisions that recognize parents' constitutional right to a relationship with their biological children also intimate that parental responsibility justifies control. *See, e.g.*, Lehman v. Lycoming County Children's Servs. Agency, 458 U.S. 502, 511 (1982); Santosky v. Kramer, 455 U.S. 745, 753 (1982); Lassiter v. Department of Social Servs., 452 U.S. 18, 27 (1981). The Court's privacy jurisprudence also recognizes the primacy of parental, rather than state, rights to control and socialize children in certain contexts. *See* Karen Brandon, *Parents Ask: Who Controls Our Kids?: Colorado Proposal Fuels Rights Debate*, CHI. TRIB., Oct. 6, 1996, §1, at 1, 20.

17. The parent with closer bonds to the child may be especially resistant to lawyers and judges who suggest custody and visitation arrangements with which he or she disagrees.

18. Spencer & Zammit, *supra* note 13, at 918.

19. Generally, taking one's personal problems to court lessens one's respectability. Sally Engle Merry & Susan Silbey, *What Do Plaintiffs Want? Reexamining the Concept of Dispute*, 9 JUST. SYS. J. 151, 160 (1984).

20. *See Killing Us Softly, supra* note 6, at 490 n.213.

21. *See, e.g.*, LENORE J. WEITZMAN, THE DIVORCE REVOLUTION: THE UNEXPECTED SOCIAL AND ECONOMIC CONSEQUENCES FOR WOMEN AND CHILDREN IN AMERICA 395–98 (1985).

22. *See id.* at 398; *Report of the Missouri Task Force on Gender and Justice*, 58 MO. L. REV. 485, 537–39 (1993) (noting judicial dislike of family law cases)

(hereinafter *Missouri Task Force*); Catherine J. Ross, *The Failure of Fragmentation: The Promise of a System of Unified Family Courts,* 33 Rev. Jur. U.I.P.R. 311, 312–13 (1999). Jacob studied the Circuit Court of Cook County, Illinois, the largest unified court in the nation with 400 judges serving a population of 5.1 million. Herbert Jacob, *The Governance of Trial Judges,* 31 L. & Soc'y Rev. 3, 8 (1997). He found that judicial assignments varied in prestige and desirability according to the nature of the cases, the quality of the attorneys appearing in the courtroom, and the volume of the caseload. *Id.* at 10. Large financial claims, the appearance of attorneys from elite law firms, and low-volume courts spelled prestige. *Id.* at 10–11. Prestigious assignments began in the chancery and law divisions, descended to the criminal division, to the jury courtrooms in the municipal districts, and descended still further to domestic relations and juvenile court, and landed at the bottom in traffic court. *Id.* at 11. The low prestige of domestic relations courts helps to explain why judges do not like divorce cases and why many young judges hope that their good performance will result in assignment to a "better" courtroom. *Id.* at 12.

23. Although many citizens complain about the amount of taxes they must pay, few seriously contest the authority of state and federal governments to tax. Mandatory social programs such as Social Security also condition the public to accept governmental authority over their financial resources.

24. Baker notes

> Because Canadian family law is written to be gender neutral, many judges have implied equal access to earned income in their divorce decisions. Yet the vast majority of North American husbands have higher earning power than their wives. Taking time off work to bear and raise children appears to place women at a permanent economic disadvantage. Evidence of this appears in numerous studies both in Canada and the United States which indicate that women and children tend to live on reduced incomes after marriage breakdown, while men tend to acquire a higher personal standard of living. For these reasons, the division of matrimonial property and payment of spousal support remain contentious areas of policy reform in both countries.

Maureen Baker, Canadian Family Policies: Cross-National Comparisons 295–96 (1995) (citations omitted).

25. *See* Wallace J. Mlyniec, *A Judge's Ethical Dilemma: Assessing a Child's Capacity to Choose,* 64 Fordham L. Rev. 1873 (1996).

26. Lawyers and judges themselves acknowledge their lack of competence in custody issues. *See generally* Kenneth Kressel, The Process of Divorce: How Professionals and Couples Negotiate Settlements 49 (1985); William Rich, *The Role of Lawyers: Beyond Advocacy,* 1980 B.Y.U. L. Rev. 767, 770.

27. *See* Karen Czapanskiy, *Domestic Violence, the Family, and the Lawyering Process: Lessons from Studies on Gender Bias in the Courts,* 27 Fam. L.Q. 247, 256, 268–69 (1993). *See also* Anna Quindlen, *Legal System Turning a Blind Eye to Sexual Abuse of Our Children,* Chi. Trib., Dec. 12, 1994, §1, at 15 (discussing similar cases throughout the United States); David E. Rovella, *Sex-Abuse Charge in*

Custody Fights Perplexes Courts: New NOW Curriculum Gives Judges Guidance, But Fathers' Groups are Wary, NAT'L L.J., Nov. 11, 1996, at 1.

28. E.g., Bob Green, *The Law Is Not Indecent*, CHI. TRIB., Mar. 8, 1995, §5, at 1 (criticizing the Illinois Supreme Court's decision in the highly publicized Baby Richard case); Jan Crawford Greenburg et al., *Love and War: "Richard" Case Reads Like a Novel, But For Those Involved—Especially One Small Boy—It's Very Real*, CHI. TRIB., Jan. 29, 1995, §1, at 1.

29. LENARD MARLOW, DIVORCE AND THE MYTH OF LAWYERS 29–30 (1992).

30. *See* Melli et al., *supra* note 2, at 1153–54 (noting the judicial pressure to settle divorce disputes).

31. *See generally* Janet R. Johnston, *Building Multidisciplinary Professional Partnerships with the Court on Behalf of High-Conflict Divorcing Families and Their Children: Who Needs What Kind of Help?*, 22 U. ARK. LITTLE ROCK L. REV. 453, 458 (2000).

32. Linda K. Girdner, *Adjudication and Mediation: A Comparison of Custody Decision-Making Processes Involving Third Parties*, 8 (3/4) J. DIVORCE 33 (1985).

33. Risa J. Garon et al., *From Infants to Adolescents: A Developmental Approach to Parenting*, 38 FAM. & CONCILIATION CTS. REV. 168, 183 (2000) (citation omitted).

34. Strauss and Sales note that many scholars and critics argue that courts need guidance from mental health professionals in custody decision making, because judges have difficulty adjudicating child custody cases. Ultimately they hope that mental health professionals will provide what judges lack. Krauss & Sales, *supra* note 1, at 862.

35. *See* Roy T. Stuckey, *Guardians Ad Litem as Surrogate Parents: Implications for Role Definition and Confidentiality*, 64 FORDHAM L. REV. 1785, 1785–93 (1996).

36. *See* PETER G. JAFFE ET AL., CHILDREN OF BATTERED WOMEN: 108 (1990); MYRA SUN & ELIZABETH THOMAS, CUSTODY LITIGATION ON BEHALF OF BATTERED WOMEN (1987) (finding that in custody disputes judges followed the recommendations of mental health professionals 90% of the time); Martha Fineman, *Dominant Discourse, Professional Language, and Legal Change in Child Custody Decisionmaking*, 101 HARV. L. REV. 727, 740–44, 764–65 (1988); Daniel W. Shuman, *The Role of Mental Health Experts in Custody Decisions: Science, Psychological Tests, and Clinical Judgment*, 36 FAM. L.Q. 135, 136–37, 158–59 (2002).

37. *See* Johnston, *supra* note 31, at 454 (noting the widespread distress, frustration, anger, alienation, and cynicism that divorcing parents and children experience with family courts and the professionals that allegedly serve them).

38. Shuman explains the dangers in unstructured expert clinical decision making:

> [O]ne of the most consistent findings of decision making research is that the actuarial method of judgment and decision making outperforms the clinical method of judgment. The research on human judgment and decision making reveals that judgments of experienced clinicians are as susceptible to error as lay judgments and that experts, like untrained, lay decision makers, use decision making strategies or mental shortcuts known as heuristics, in arriving at decisions that contribute

to the error rate. Decision makers often ignore the importance of sample size and base rates and assume that isolated incidents are representative and capable of being generalized to a broader range of activities. Decision makers also tend to err by giving inappropriate weight to information based on its availability, such as relying on more dramatic recent stories or anecdotes to the exclusion of known statistical information. Decision makers often overestimate their knowledge about a decision. Decision makers evaluate information and attribute causality in very different ways based upon the framing of the information and tend to anchor their decisions stereotypically and select information to support them based on conclusions reached before receiving data about those decisions. There is no correlation between confidence and accuracy of clinical decision making by either lay or expert decision makers. Strategies for reducing these errors, such as warning decision makers about them, have not proven effective to correct these error inducing strategies in lay or expert decision-makers. Thus, the certainty that well-qualified experts bring to their clinical judgments reveals nothing about the likelihood that they are correct and forensic decision-making is just as flawed as typical clinical judgment.

Daniel W. Shuman, *What Should We Permit Mental Health Professionals to Say About "The Best Interests of the Child"?: An Essay on Common Sense, Daubert, and the Rules of Evidence*, 31 FAM. L.Q. 551, 553–54 (1997) (footnotes omitted).

39. *See* Shuman, *supra* note 36, at 138–39. *See also* Krauss & Sales, *supra* note 1, at 866. Courts typically defer to court-ordered custody evaluations despite their inadequacies. *Id.* at 863 (noting that recent studies indicate that judges rely heavily on psychological evaluations in custody decision making). Shuman notes that, throughout the judicial system, judges have begun to hold expert witnesses more accountable—except in the areas of child custody and visitation. *See* Shuman, *supra* note 36, at 138–39; Shuman, *supra* note 38. For instance, courts accept syndrome testimony despite the lack of scientific support for the existence of the syndrome. *See id.* at 564–65. Moreover, Marc and Melissa Ackerman's survey of psychologists who perform custody evaluations revealed that one third of these experts used two tests, the MCMI–II and the MCMI–III, on divorcing parents and ignored that the tests were designed for a clinical rather than a normal population. *See* Marc J. Ackerman & Melissa C. Ackerman, *Child Custody Evaluation Practices: A 1996 Survey of Psychologists*, 30 FAM. L.Q. 565, 573 (1996). Interestingly, one survey indicated that family law attorneys thought mental health experts provided little help in child custody decisions. These lawyers presented expert testimony largely to discredit their opponent's expert. *See* Robert D. Felner et al., *Child Custody Resolution: A Study of Social Science Involvement and Impact*, 18 PROF. PSYCHOL. RES. & PRAC. 468 (1987).

40. For a scathing indictment of guardians ad litem, see Richard Ducote, *Guardians Ad Litem in Private Custody Litigation: The Case for Abolition*, 3 LOY. J. PUB. INT. L. 106 (2002).

41. Krauss and Sales note the intense debate within the psychological field itself regarding "expertise" related to custody decision making.

Some commentators have argued that psychologists and other MHPs (mental health professionals) have no expertise in assessing a child's best interest and, consequently, that it is unethical for psychologists to offer "expert" opinions that have no real scientific basis. However, others have contended that psychologists should participate in child custody proceedings and should present expert testimony concerning an appropriate child custody placement, because this psychological information can incrementally increase the validity of judicial opinions. Melton et al. (1987) has suggested that "there is probably no forensic question on which overreaching by mental health professionals has been so common and egregious" as MHP's participation in child custody disputes.

Krauss & Sales, *supra* note 1, at 863. The conclusions of mental health experts seem particularly suspect when based exclusively on their clinical experience rather than scientific research. *See* Daniel W. Shuman & Bruce D. Sales, *The Admissibility of Expert Testimony Based Upon Clinical Judgment and Scientific Research*, 4 Psychol. Pub. Pol'y & L. 1226, 1228–32 (1998).

42. *See* Jaffe et al., *supra* note 36, at 108. To support their contention that evaluating mental health professionals may know little about domestic violence, Jaffe et al. call attention to a 1986 book about custody assessments that contained nothing about domestic violence except the warning to exercise caution about women's exaggerated reports of violence. *See id.* at 108 (citing R. Parry et al., *Custody Disputes: Evaluation and Intervention* (1986)); Kathleen Coulborn Faller, *Child Maltreatment and Endangerment in the Context of Divorce*, 22 U. Ark. Little Rock L.J. 429, 431–35 (2000); Daniel G. Saunders, *Child Custody Decisions in Families Experiencing Woman Abuse*, 39 Soc. Work 51, 54 (1994) (noting that therapists fall prey to the same misunderstandings of battered women's behavior as do judges).

43. *See* Shuman, *supra* note 36, at 142–50 (questioning the use of the Minnesota Multiphasic Personality Inventory (MMPI–2), the Million Clinical Multiaxial Inventory (MCMI), the Rorschach Inkblot Technique, and the Thematic Apperception Test (TAT) in custody evaluations). *See also* Ann M. Haralambie, Child Sexual Abuse in Civil Cases: A Guide to Custody and Tort Actions 41 (1999).

44. *See* Shuman, *supra* note 36, at 150–54 (discussing the serious shortcomings of the Bricklin Scales (BPS) and the Ackerman-Schoendorf Scales for Parent Evaluation of Custody (ASPECT)). Ironically, these tests claim reliability based on the similarity of their results to judicial custody decisions. *Id.* at 151–52. Shuman concludes that, at most, psychological tests should play a limited rather than central role in child custody evaluations and that many tests should play no role at all. *Id.* at 153. Krauss and Sales agree. Krauss & Sales, *supra* note 1, at 869. *See also id.* at 867–70 (discussing the severe limitations of the BSP and the ASPECT in child custody evaluations and the failure of these instruments to meet the evidentiary standards for expert testimony set forth by the U.S. Supreme Court in Daubert v. Merrell Dow Pharmaceuticals, 509 U.S. 579 (1993)).

45. *See* HARALAMBIE, *supra* note 43, at 33–34; Faller, *supra* note 42, at 431; Sharon R. Lowenstein, *Child Sexual Abuse in Custody and Visitation Litigation: Representation for the Benefit of Victims*, 60 UMKC L. REV. 227, 245–57 (1991).

46. *See* Robert F. Kelly & Sarah H. Ramsey, *Monitoring Attorney Performance and Evaluating Program Outcomes: A Case Study of Attorneys for Abused and Neglected Children*, 40 RUTGERS L. REV. 1217, 1238–40 (1988) (finding that attorneys routinely represent children incompetently); Robert E. Shepherd Jr. & Sharon S. England, *"I Know the Child Is My Client, But Who Am I?"*, 64 FORDHAM L. REV. 1917, 1924–32, 1933–43 (1996) (explaining that many children do not receive competent legal advocacy and that confusion over the proper role of those appointed to represent children compounds incompetence). *See also* Emily Buss, *"You're My What?" The Problem of Children's Misperceptions of Their Lawyers' Roles*, 64 FORDHAM L. REV. 1699, 1699–1706 (1996); Katherine Hunt Federle, *The Ethics of Empowerment: Rethinking the Role of Lawyers in Interviewing and Counseling the Child Client*, 64 FORDHAM L. REV. 1655 (1996) (discussing empowerment as the key element in defining a lawyer's relationships to a child client); Martin Guggenheim, *A Paradigm for Determining the Role of Counsel for Children*, 64 FORDHAM L. REV. 1399, 1399 (1996); Peter Margulies, *The Lawyer as Caregiver: Child Client's Competence in Context*, 64 FORDHAM L. REV. 1473 (1996); Jean Koh Peters, *The Roles and Content of Best Interests in Client-Directed Lawyering for Children in Child Protective Proceedings*, 64 FORDHAM L. REV. 1505 (1996); Stuckey, *supra* note 35, at 1785–93.

47. *See, e.g.,* Carol S. Bruch, *Parental Alienation Syndrome and Parental Alienation: Getting It Wrong in Child Custody Cases*, 35 FAM. L.Q. 527 (2001); Ducote, *supra* note 40, at 140–42.

48. Some suggest that the meaning of law is found in lawyer–client interaction, as opposed to judicial decisions and legislation. *See* Austin Sarat & William L.F. Felstiner, *Law and Social Relations: Vocabularies of Motive in Lawyer/Client Interaction*, 22 L. & SOC'Y REV. 737, 739 (1988) (discussing the implication of Martin Shapiro's assertion that law is what lawyers tell their clients); Martin Shapiro, *On the Regrettable Decline of Law French, or Shapiro Jettet le Brickbat*, 90 YALE L.J. 1198, 1201 (1981).

49. One mediator expresses his contempt for lawyer authority as follows:

> Did Bill's attorney raise any of the questions, or invoke any of the considerations, that he and Barbara had previously discussed, when they were confronted with this same issue [whether to send their son John to summer camp] the year before? The answer, of course, is no. After all, what could he possibly have added that would have been of any significance? He was not a financial planner. Nor was he a child psychologist, let alone an authority on what was in John's best interests. In fact, he had no special provence that would have qualified him to participate in those discussions during their marriage. If that was the case, what would suddenly make him an expert in these matters now, simply because they had decided to get a divorce?

MARLOW, *supra* note 29, at 13.

50. *See id.* at 1–2.

51. *See* MATHER ET AL., *supra* note 2, at 56 (finding that lawyers who specialize in divorce, primarily women, seem more likely to encourage client participation).

52. *See id.* at 50.

53. *See id.* at 87–96. A study of divorce lawyers in Maine and New Hampshire, for instance, reveals that lawyers use a variety of techniques to set what lawyers deem "reasonable" expectations and demands throughout representation. *Id.* at 96–107 (2001) (noting that lawyers use verbal persuasion, references to what judges will do, delay, fees and expenses, threats to part ways with clients, and actual dismissal of clients to influence client expectations and demands).

54. Winner notes that divorce lawyers frequently urge their women clients to accept the agreements women do not want, explaining that the agreements are "for [the client's] own good." KAREN WINNER, DIVORCE FROM JUSTICE: THE ABUSE OF WOMEN AND CHILDREN BY DIVORCE LAWYERS AND JUDGES 69, 91 (1996). *See also* Bryan, *supra* note 8, at 1259–62; *Reclaiming Professionalism*, *supra* note 6, at 177–88 (providing an example of a lawyer coercing her resistant female client into a very poor financial settlement); Melli et al., *supra* note 2, at 1158–59. Sarat and Felstiner studied interactions between divorce lawyers and their clients. Their work provides numerous examples of lawyers using evasive predictions of what a court would do in order to manipulate clients into acceptance of particular settlements. AUSTIN SARAT & WILLIAM L.F. FELSTINER, DIVORCE LAWYERS AND THEIR CLIENTS: POWER AND MEANING IN THE LEGAL PROCESS 124–26 (1995).

55. *See* MATHER ET AL., *supra* note 2, at 79–81, 85.

56. *See* Beck & Sales, *supra* note 4, at 1032 (noting a suggestive study in which 70% of divorce litigants expressed satisfaction with their lawyers, but had strong negative opinions of their court experiences).

57. *See* MATHER ET AL., *supra* note 2, at 47–48 (noting that large numbers of lawyers in New Hampshire and Maine take only an occasional divorce case). Moreover, with the exception of a limited number of specialists, divorce lawyers do not appreciate or pursue knowledge of complex divorce laws. *Id.* at 80–81.

58. *See* WINNER, *supra* note 54, at 18.

59. Sarat and Felstiner explain that client emotionalism and dissatisfaction, low professional prestige, lack of financial rewards, and unpleasantness of tasks discourage lawyers from enthusiastic representation of divorce clients. *See* SARAT & FELSTINER, *supra* note 54, at 3–4. *See also Reclaiming Professionalism*, *supra* note 6, at 177–88 (relating the story of a divorce lawyer's incompetent representation of the wife).

60. *See* MATHER ET AL., *supra* note 2, at 25–30 (describing the practice of such a lawyer); PATRICIA PHILLIPS, DIVORCE: A WOMAN'S GUIDE TO GETTING A FAIR SHARE 58 (1995).

61. *See* MATHER ET AL., *supra* note 2, at 25, 52. Retention of a high status divorce firm, however, does not guarantee adequate representation. I have seen many clients poorly represented by such firms.

62. *See id.* at 52, 60.

63. For instance, after an 11-year marriage, Ms. Phillips and Dr. Curtis filed for divorce and entered into a property settlement agreement. *In re* Marriage of Curtis, 23 P.3d 13, 15 (Wash. 2001). Both parties had legal counsel during settlement negotiations. *Id.* At the final hearing, Ms. Phillips' new lawyer argued that the trial court should vacate the settlement agreement, because Ms. Phillips' first lawyer did not value Dr. Curtis' medical practice properly and the agreement was unfair. *Id.* at 16. The trial court refused to vacate the settlement agreement and incorporated the agreement into the final judgment of dissolution. Ms. Phillips' appealed. *Id.* at 15. The appellate court found that the first lawyer's failure to properly evaluate Dr. Curtis' medical practice and an unfair settlement were insufficient grounds to vacate a settlement agreement incorporated into a final judgment of dissolution. *Id.* at 16–17. *See* MATHER ET AL., *supra* note 2, at 46 (noting that dissatisfaction with divorce settlements sometimes prompts clients to file grievances against their former attorneys).

64. *See* Mlyniec, *supra* note 25.

65. *But see* MATHER ET AL., *supra* note 2, at 38, 79, 80, 178 (noting that Maine and New Hampshire attorneys who specialize in divorce often have a broad range of knowledge).

66. *See* MATHER ET AL., *supra* note 2, at 46 (noting that clients in Maine and New Hampshire file grievances against divorce attorneys more frequently than in other types of cases). *See also* Marsha Kline Pruett & Tamara D. Jackson, *The Lawyer's Role During the Divorce Process: Perceptions of Parents, Their Young Children, and Their Attorneys*, 33 FAM. L.Q. 283, 289, 295 (1999); Larry R. Spain, *Collaborative Law: A Critical Reflection on Whether a Collaborative Orientation Can Be Ethically Incorporated Into the Practice of Law*, 56 BAYLOR L. REV. 141, 145 & n.25 (2004). *See generally* WINNER, *supra* note 54.

67. *See* Judith Resnik, *Tiers*, 57 S. CALIF. L. REV. 837 (1984).

68. Tom Tyler assessed the importance of impartiality or neutrality in his research by asking (a) whether race, sex, age, nationality, or some other personal characteristic of the respondents influenced the treatment or the outcomes the respondents experienced; (b) whether the authorities behaved improperly or dishonestly; (c) whether the authorities had lied to respondents; and (d) how hard the authorities had attempted to show fairness. Tom R. Tyler, *What is Procedural Justice?: Criteria Used by Citizens to Assess the Fairness of Legal Procedures*, 22 L. & SOC'Y REV. 103, 111, 122, 128 (1988), at 112. *See also* MICHAEL D. BAYLES, PROCEDURAL JUSTICE: ALLOCATING TO INDIVIDUALS 135 (1990); Resnik, *supra* note 67, at 852; Judith Resnik, *On the Bias: Feminist Reconsiderations of the Aspirations for Our Judges*, 61 S. CAL. L. REV. 1877, 1885 (1988).

69. *See* Donald N. Bersoff, *Judicial Deference to Nonlegal Decisionmakers: Imposing Simplistic Solutions on Problems of Cognitive Complexity in Mental Disability Law*, 46 SMU L. REV. 329, 366–67 (1992); Raymond Paternoster et al., *Do Fair Procedures Matter? The Effect of Procedural Justice on Spouse Assault*, 31 L. & SOC'Y REV. 163, 167 (1997) at 167–68; Tyler, *supra* note 68, at 112. *See also* Ralph Cavanagh & Austin Sarat, *Thinking About Courts: Toward and Beyond a Jurisprudence of Judicial Competence*, 14 L. & SOC'Y REV. 371, 378 (1980) (noting that judicial competence requires judicial impartiality).

70. *See* Paternoster et al., *supra* note 69, at 168. *See generally* Resnik, *supra* note 67, at 1885.

71. *See generally* WINNER, *supra* note 54; Bryan, *supra* note 8.

72. *See* DAVID BLANKENHORN, FATHERLESS AMERICA: CONFRONTING OUR MOST URGENT SOCIAL PROBLEM (1995); Jed H. Abraham, *Why Men Fight for Their Kids: How Bias in the System Puts Dads at a Disadvantage*, 17 FAM. ADVOC. 48 (1994); Ronald K. Henry, *Primary Caretaker': Is It a Ruse?*, 17 FAM. ADVOC. 53 (1994).

73. *But see* MATHER ET AL., *supra* note 2, at 73 (noting that many Maine and New Hampshire divorce lawyers did not perceive judges as biased).

74. *See* Young v. Hector, 740 So. 2d 1153 (Fla. Dist. Ct. App. 1998).

75. *Id.* The father's attribution of bias also protects him from the ego-damaging realization that the mother offered superior parenting. See Amy D. Ronner, *Women Who Dance on the Professional Track: Custody and the Red Shoes*, 23 HARV. WOMEN'S L.J. 173 (2000) for comment on *Young*.

76. *See* Resnik, *supra* note 68, at 1905.

77. *Id.* (exploring the more nuanced concept of impartiality offered by feminists, as opposed to the cold and unrealistic detachment advocated by traditionalists).

78. Resnik notes the pervasiveness of gender bias in the legal system generally:

> Over the past few years, states have commissioned studies of how women fare in courts. The findings—across jurisdictional boundaries—have been notably uniform: Women are stereotyped and disadvantaged when they appear as litigants, witnesses, or lawyers. The Report of the New York Task Force on Women in the Courts is illustrative. The task force concluded that "gender bias against women . . . is a pervasive problem with grave consequences. . . . Cultural stereotypes of women's role in marriage and in society daily distort courts application of substantive law. Women uniquely, disproportionately and with unacceptable frequency must endure a climate of condescension, indifference and hostility." The documentation provided by New York, New Jersey, and the other states now considering the issue paints a picture of partiality, of prejudgment, of judges ready to translate racial and sexist views into law.

> *Id.* at 1904.

79. *See* Bryan, *supra* note 8, at 1172–73, 1211–12.

80. *See id.* at 1173.

81. *See* REPORT OF THE GENDER BIAS STUDY OF THE SUPREME JUDICIAL COURT, COMMONWEALTH OF MASSACHUSETTS 21 (1989) (hereinafter MASSACHUSETTS GENDER BIAS REPORT); Czapanskiy, *supra* note 27, at 250 n.11; *Report of the Florida Supreme Court Gender Bias Study Commission*, 42 FLA. L. REV. 803, 887–88 (1990) (hereinafter *Florida Gender Bias Report*); Missouri Task Force, *supra* note 22, at 550–51.

82. *See* Joan Williams, *Is Coverture Dead? Beyond a New Theory of Alimony*, 82 GEO. L.J. 2227, 2245–47 & n.91 (1994). Williams describes how wives tend

to sacrifice their own market participation in order to facilitate the ideal worker status of their husbands. *Id.* at 2236–67. Williams also explains that even in two-career families, couples commonly engage in a game of "chicken" over who will provide housekeeping and child care services. Because of socialization that accords high priority to homemaking and child care, the wife typically loses this game and performs most of these functions. *See id.* at 2240–41. Statistics from 1995 indicate that women spend more than three times as many hours caring for children and substantially more time at household tasks than do men. *See* Laura Shapiro, *The Myth of Quality Time,* Newsweek, May 12, 1997, at 62, 68. As noted by Fuchs,

> In the early years of the sex-role revolution there was a hope that differences in homemaking and childcare responsibilities would disappear, but this is not occurring on a large scale. There are some households in which the father does as much as or more than the mother, but they are the exception, not the rule. Moreover, almost one child in four is raised in a household without a father or stepfather. Children are still predominately women's concern.

Victor R. Fuchs, Women's Quest for Economic Equality 72 (1988). Fuchs concludes that women's disproportionate responsibility for child care provides the most powerful explanation of the difference in men and women's earnings. *See id.* at 60–62. Although the gap between men and women's wages closed by an unprecedented 7% between 1980 and 1986, Fuchs explains that the improvement was caused largely by the increased percentage of women workers who were born after 1946 and had fewer children. *See id.* at 65–66. *See also* Martha Albertson Fineman, The Neutered Mother, The Sexual Family and Other Twentieth Century Tragedies 161–65 (1995); Massachusetts Gender Bias Report, *supra* note 81, at 61; Winner, *supra* note 54, at 47; *Florida Gender Bias Report, supra* note 81, at 821.

83. Williams notes that wives who interrupt their careers lose an average of 1.5% of income for each year they do not participate in market labor, with college-educated wives losing as much as 4.3%. Williams, *supra* note 82, at 2257 n.148 (1994) (citing Jacob Mincer & Solomon Polachek, *Family Investments in Human Capital: Earnings of Women, in* Economics of the Family 397 (Theodore W. Schultz eds. 1974)). *See also* Elizabeth Smith Beninger & Jeanne Wielage Smith, *Career Opportunity Cost: A Factor in Spousal Support Determination,* 16 Fam. L.Q. 201, 206 (1982); Jacob Mincer & Solomon Polachek, *Family Investment in Human Capital: Earnings of Women,* 82 J. Pol. Econ. 576, 583 (1974). Estin reports a study that found a typical wage gap of 33% the first year women returned to work, with a portion of the gap made up over time. *See* Ann Laquer Estin, *Maintenance, Alimony, and the Rehabilitation of Family Care,* 71 N.C. L. Rev. 721, 746 n.87 (1993) (discussing a study by Laurence Levin and Joyce Jacobsen) (citing Laura Myers, *Women Who Interrupt Career Fall Into Pay Gap,* Boulder Daily Camera, Jan. 11, 1992, at 1A, 11A).

84. *See* Pamela J. Smock, *The Economic Costs of Marital Disruption for Young Women Over the Past Two Decades,* 30 Demography 353, 367 (1993).

85. *See id.* at 366–67. *See also* Williams, *supra* note 82, at 2256–57 (noting that a mother's decreased earning capacity because of child care responsibilities extends beyond the children's majority).

86. *See* Massachusetts Gender Bias Report, *supra* note 81, at 31 (noting that education and training for future employment may necessitate maintenance). Some feminists resist the idea of spousal maintenance, arguing that these awards perpetuate women's dependence on men and help sustain patriarchy. *See generally* Fineman, *supra* note 14, at 21–22 (noting that in the face of growing opposition, many feminist legal scholars continue to argue that true equality for women requires legal rules that ignore gender as a distinguishing characteristic); David L. Kirp et al., Gender Justice 178–82 (1986); Weitzman, *supra* note 21, at 359. *But see* Betty Friedan, It Changed My Life 325–26 (1976) (defending women's need of and right to spousal maintenance). Feminists who oppose maintenance overlook the reality of most women. Some dependence on an ex-spouse seems better than poverty or severe economic deprivation. Support may be essential to the woman's physical and psychological health. *See* Celvia Stovall Dixon & Kathryn D. Rettig, *An Examination of Income Adequacy for Single Women Two Years After Divorce,* 22 J. Divorce & Remarriage 55, 60 (1994) (citations omitted). *See also* Terry Arendell, Mothers and Divorce: Legal Economic and Social Dilemmas 68–70 (1986) (noting that work generally provides divorced mothers with income, increased self-esteem, contact with other adults, and personal growth). In one study, educational attainment and income accounted for 66% of the well-being of single-parent mothers. *See* Mary E. Duffy, *Mental Well-Being and Primary Prevention Practices in Women Heads of One-Parent Families,* 13 J. Divorce 45 (1989). Moreover, women can use spousal maintenance to achieve greater financial independence by seeking education, job training, or business opportunities. Divorced women instead often remain trapped in menial jobs, poverty, or both. *See* Arendell, *supra,* at 42–50; Weitzman, *supra* note 21, at 208–09. Finally, the desperate financial positions of divorced women frequently lead them to remarry, sometimes very unwisely. *See* Arendell, *supra,* at 132; E. Mavis Hetherington & John Kelly, For Better or for Worse: Divorce Reconsidered 164–65 (2002) (finding that one third of the remarried women in their study remarried, at least partially, for financial reasons); Leslie A. Morgan, After Marriage Ends: Economic Consequences for Midlife Women 35–38 (1991) (citing numerous studies that find or imply that divorced women frequently remarry in order to improve their financial circumstances); Paul C. Glick & Sung-Ling Lin, *Recent Changes in Divorce and Remarriage,* 48 J. Marriage & Fam. 737, 743 (1986) (speculating that the greater financial needs of divorced women with children likely encouraged them to remarry more quickly than their childless counterparts). Because of inadequate postdivorce support, these women become "more" rather than "less" dependent on men. Although spousal maintenance perpetuates some dependence, it can also facilitate women's financial independence and alleviate postdivorce poverty.

87. *See* Weitzman, *supra* note 21, at 149; Estin, *supra* note 83, at 727–29 (noting that maintenance statutes in more than 20 states acknowledge that a parent's custodial obligations may influence his or her need for maintenance).

88. *See* Estin, *supra* note 83, at 748 & n.93, 749–54; Cynthia Starnes, *Divorce and the Displaced Homemaker: A Discourse on Playing With Dolls, Partnership Buyouts and Dissociation Under No-Fault*, 60 U. Chi. L. Rev. 67, 95–96 (1993); Williams, *supra* note 82, at 2234, 2252.

89. *See* Wisconsin Equal Justice Task Force: Final Report 229–39 (1991) (hereinafter Wisconsin Task Force Report); Estin, *supra* note 83, at 728–30 & n.20; Laurie C. Kadoch, *Five Degrees of Separation: A Response to Judge Sheldon's The Sleepwalker's Tour of Divorce Law*, 49 Me. L. Rev. 321, 345–51 (1997) (noting ineffective judicial application of Maine alimony law, rather than the law itself, results in inadequate awards). *See also* Baker, *supra* note 24, at 295 (noting a similar reluctance by Canadian judges).

90. In a study of 908 divorcing families in California, only 20% of the divorce petitions indicated a conflict between the mother's and the father's custody request. *See* Robert H. Mnookin et al., *Private Ordering Revisited: What Custodial Arrangements are Parents Negotiating?*, in Divorce Reform at the Crossroads 37, 51 (Stephen D. Sugarman & Herma Hill Kay eds. 1985). In the 693 uncontested cases, the mother received sole custody 90% of the time. *See id.* at 52. In the contested cases, mothers' requests were granted twice as often as those of fathers. More specifically, in the 190 contested cases, mothers received what they asked for in 115 cases, fathers received what they requested in 50 cases, and a compromise was reached in 25 cases. *See id.* at 53. Many other sources confirm that mothers receive custody more often than fathers. *See, e.g.*, Massachusetts Gender Bias Report, *supra* note 81, at 61 (noting that Massachusetts mothers have primary physical custody in the great majority of cases). However, when mothers and fathers dispute custody, findings from other studies differ significantly from Mnookin's. For instance, in Massachusetts, when fathers and mothers dispute custody, the father receives either primary or joint physical custody more than 70% of the time. *See id.* at 59.

91. *See, e.g.*, Massachusetts Gender Bias Report, *supra* note 81, at 30 (noting that, nationwide, only 12.4% of people divorced between 1980 and 1985 obtained an alimony award) (citing U.S. Bureau of The Census, U.S. Dep't of Commerce (1989)); Weitzman, *supra* note 21, at 167, 362 (noting that, in 1977, only 17% of wives in two California counties received maintenance); Terry J. Arendell, *Women and the Economics of Divorce in the Contemporary United States*, 13 Signs 121, 133 (1987); Garrison, *supra* note 4, at 697 (finding that wives in three different New York counties received maintenance in only 4%, 15%, and 18% of divorce cases, respectively); *id.* at 634 n.44 (citing studies in which 30%, 18%, 10.9%, and 7% of wives were awarded alimony at divorce); Deborah L. Rhode & Martha Minow, *Reforming the Questions, Questioning the Reforms: Feminist Perspectives on Divorce Law*, in Divorce Reform at the Crossroads 191, 202 (Stephen D. Sugarman & Herma Hill Kay eds. 1990) (noting that approximately one sixth of divorced women receive alimony and

that two thirds of the awards are for a short duration); U.S. Census Bureau, U.S. Dep't of Commerce, Series P-23, No. 167, Child Support and Alimony: 1987 (1990) (hereinafter *1990 Census Report*) (showing that, in a 1988 U.S. Census survey, 17% of the divorced women reported that their divorce decree entitled them to spousal maintenance). Moreover, Weitzman found that more than half of the older housewives in her study received no maintenance. *See* WEITZMAN, *supra* note 21, at 183.

92. *See* WEITZMAN, *supra* note 21, at 187; Garrison, *supra* note 4, at 669–700 (explaining that only 34% of wives married for 20 or more years received spousal maintenance, and more than half of them were awarded maintenance for a limited time); Garrison, *supra* note 4, at 669–703 (finding that, in 1984, unemployed wives married for 20 or more years received permanent maintenance in only 32% of contested divorce cases). Weitzman also found that older long-term homemakers are expected to live on much smaller incomes than their ex-husbands. In 1977, in California, wives married 18 years or more with predivorce family incomes of $20,000 to $30,000 per year had, on the average, a median income of $6,300 per year after the divorce, versus a median income of $20,000 for their husbands. *See* WEITZMAN, *supra*, at 8. Moreover, these women are more likely to have dependent children with whom they must share their income. *See id.* at 191. An estimate from the Displaced Homemakers Network suggests that 57% of displaced homemakers earn income at or near the poverty line. *See* Starnes, *supra* note 88, at 79 & n.50 (citing NATIONAL DISPLACED HOMEMAKERS NETWORK, THE MORE THINGS CHANGE . . . A STATUS REPORT ON DISPLACED HOMEMAKERS AND SINGLE PARENTS IN THE 1980s 20–21 (1990)).

93. *See, e.g.,* ELEANOR E. MACCOBY & ROBERT MNOOKIN, DIVIDING THE CHILD 123–24 (1992) (finding that wives received alimony in 30% of cases in which the divorced couple had at least one child under the age of 16); MASSACHUSETTS GENDER BIAS REPORT, *supra* note 81, at 30 (finding that, in Massachusetts families with minor children, wives receive alimony in only 10% to 20% of the cases); WEITZMAN, *supra* note 21, at 185 (demonstrating that, in two California counties in 1977, only 22% of mothers with custody of minor children received maintenance, and only 13% of mothers with preschool children received maintenance); Garrison, *supra* note 4, at 704–06 (stating that, in New York in 1984, only 25% of divorced mothers with custody received spousal maintenance). The Massachusetts Gender Bias Task Force discovered that implementation of child support guidelines negatively affected the frequency of maintenance awards. Evidently, judicial officers conflate child and family support and believe that maintenance is unnecessary. *See* MASSACHUSETTS GENDER BIAS REPORT, *supra*, at 19.

94. *See* WEITZMAN, *supra* note 21, at 171 (revealing that in 1977 the median maintenance award was $210 per month); Garrison, *supra* note 4, at 711–12 & n.270 (noting that census data and other time-series studies uniformly report declining alimony awards); *1990 Census Report, supra* note 91 (finding that the mean alimony award received by women was $3,730 per year).

95. *See* Lynn Hecht Schafran, *Gender and Justice: Florida and the Nation*, 42 Fla. L. Rev. 181, 188 (1990). Weitzman's study revealed that in 1977 one third of the alimony awards were open-ended or permanent, whereas two thirds were for a limited duration. The median duration of a transitional award was 25 months. *See* Weitzman, *supra* note 21, at 164–65. *See also* Garrison, *supra* note 4, at 634 n.45, 697–98 (citing numerous studies, including her own, that indicate a dramatic decline in permanent alimony awards). Weitzman comments that these meager awards thrust wives into the job market without affording them the time and financial resources to gain the education, career counseling, and training that they need to improve their job prospects. Weitzman, *supra*, at 7. Not only do just a few wives receive meager and short-term maintenance awards, but husbands refuse to pay approximately half of those awards. *See* Rhode & Minow, *supra* note 91. These statistics stand in stark contrast to survey results indicating that 81% of women assume they will be able to obtain spousal maintenance if they need it. *See* Lynn A. Baker & Robert E. Emery, *When Every Relationship Is Above Average: Perceptions and Expectations of Divorce at the Time of Marriage*, 17 L. & Hum. Behav. 439, 443 (1993).

96. *See* Massachusetts Gender Bias Report, *supra* note 81, at 30–32; Williams, *supra* note 82, at 2252 n.120 (1994) (citing Luedke v. Luedke, 487 N.E.2d 133 (Ind. 1985); Rohling v. Rohling, 379 N.W.2d 519 (Minn. 1986)).

97. One attorney in Missouri reported that two different judges refused to order spousal maintenance for his client because she was young and attractive and the judges believed she would remarry. *See* Missouri Task Force, *supra* note 22, at 542.

98. *See* Massachusetts Gender Bias Report, *supra* note 81, at 63; *Florida Gender Bias Report*, *supra* note 81, at 814–16.

99. *See* Weitzman, *supra* note 21, at 163, 183. *See also* Jana B. Singer, *Husbands, Wives, and Human Capital: Why the Shoe Won't Fit*, 31 Fam. L.Q. 119, 124 (1997); Williams, *supra* note 82, at 2250–52. Devaluation of women's work within the family undoubtedly shapes attitudes toward maintenance. The desirability of optimal child caretaking services partially justifies spousal maintenance. Mothers who receive maintenance could remain at home or work part time, retaining sufficient time and energy for quality child caretaking. If we generally devalue caretaking, however, maintenance seems less justified. Many commentators argue that "work associated with child rearing within the private sphere of the family has been systematically devalued." *See* Kathleen Gerson, Hard Choices: How Women Decide About Work, Career, and Motherhood 211–12 (1985). *See also* Fineman, *supra* note 82; Ann Laquer Estin, *Love and Obligation: Family Law and the Romance of Economics*, 1995 Wm. & Mary L. Rev. 989, 993–95; Alicia Brokars Kelly, *The Marital Partnership Pretense and Career Assets: The Ascendancy of Self Over the Marital Community*, 81 B.U. L. Rev. 59, 108–11 (2001).

100. The Massachusetts Gender Bias Task Force found that judges assume, without factual verification, that husbands who pay child support cannot afford maintenance. Massachusetts attorneys maintain, however, that courts cannot assess

accurately what a husband can afford without proper discovery and adequate factual findings. *See* MASSACHUSETTS GENDER BIAS REPORT, *supra* note 81, at 30.

101. *See* Garrison, *supra* note 4, at 707–09 (finding that the husband's income did not correlate with maintenance awards to low-earning wives or wives married for 20 years or more). The discrepancy between men and women's standard of living after divorce strongly suggests that men could pay more spousal maintenance. *See* MASSACHUSETTS GENDER BIAS REPORT, *supra* note 81, at 28; Garrison, *supra* note 4, at 633 n.42 (citing numerous studies indicating that women's standard of living dropped precipitously at divorce, whereas men's standard of living increased); *id.* at 720–21 tab. 55 (noting that the average postdivorce per capita income of wives and children was approximately 68% of their predivorce per capita income, whereas the per capita income of husbands increased by 182% after divorce); James B. McLindon, *Separate But Unequal: The Economic Disaster of Divorce for Women and Children*, 21 FAM. L.Q. 351, 386–88 tab. 26 (1987) (noting that, in New Haven, Connecticut, the per capita income of divorced women in the early 1980s was 69% of predivorce per capita median income, whereas the average per capita income of divorced men was 190% of predivorce per capita median income); Williams, *supra* note 82, at 2227 n.1; Ruth Wishik, *Economics of Divorce: An Exploratory Study*, 20 FAM L.Q. 79, 97–98 tab. 5 (1986) (finding that the per capita income of women in Vermont dropped 33% after divorce, whereas the per capita income of Vermont men increased 120% after divorce). *See also* WEITZMAN, *supra* note 21, at 338–39 fig. 3. Weitzman elaborates,

> Where the discrepancy [in the standard of living] is smallest—namely, in lower-income families—the husband and every member of his post-divorce family each have about twice as much money as his former wife and every member of her postdivorce family (i.e., typically, his children). Where the discrepancy is the greatest—in higher-income families—it is enormous: among families with predivorce incomes of $40,000 or more a year, the wife is expected to live at 42 percent of her former per capita standard of living, while her husband is allowed 142 percent of his former per capita level. . . . In addition, each person in the husband's new household—a new wife, or cohabitor, or possibly a child—has three times as much disposable income as those living with his former wife. Inasmuch as the other members of his former wife's household are almost always his own children, the discrepancy between the two standards of living is especially striking.

Id. at 191. Some argue that Weitzman's research suffers from "skewed statistical analyses" and researcher bias. Jed H. Abraham, *"The Divorce Revolution" Revisited: A Counter-Revolutionary Critique*, 9 N. ILL. U. L. REV. 251, 296 (1989). *See generally* Williams, *supra*, at 2227 n.1 (1994) (citing commentators who criticize and defend Weitzman's findings). However, even those who criticize Weitzman's work generally agree that women's economic position after divorce is substantially worse than that of men. *See, e.g.*, Stephen D.

Sugarman, *Dividing Financial Interests on Divorce, in* DIVORCE REFORM AT THE CROSSROADS 130, 149–52 (Stephen D. Sugarman & Herma Hill Kay eds., 1990).

102. *See* Garrison, *supra* note 4, at 708 n.261.

103. Many attorneys believe that many judges have an unrealistic view of the dependent spouse's ability to become self-sufficient. *See Missouri Task Force, supra* note 22, at 546–50.

104. In her study of discretionary decision making by divorce judges, Garrison found a judge's political affiliation a strong predictor of the duration of spousal maintenance awards, whereas none of the statutory factors governing spousal maintenance predicted durational outcomes. Marsha Garrison, *How Do Judges Decide Divorce Cases? An Empirical Analysis of Discretionary Decision Making,* 74 N.C. L. REV. 401, 488 tab. 29, 489–90 (1996).

105. *See* Samuel H. Hofstadter & Shirley R. Levittan, *Alimony—A Reformulation,* 7 J. FAM. L. 51, 55 (1967). For an illustrative example of judicial ignorance and bias regarding spousal maintenance, see Olsen v. Olsen, 557 P.2d 604, 606–16 (Idaho 1976) (Justice Shepard's dissent).

106. SARAT & FELSTINER, *supra* note 54, at 125. *See also* Melli et al., *supra* note 2, at 1143–44.

107. *See* MASSACHUSETTS GENDER BIAS REPORT, *supra* note 81, at 33.

108. *See id.* at 33–36; Williams, *supra* note 82, at 2273–75.

109. Nearly every state defines as marital all property acquired by either spouse during the marriage, with the exceptions of property obtained by gift or through inheritance. During the past several decades most jurisdictions have expanded their definition of marital property to encompass property titled solely in one spouse's name, pension and retirement plans, business and celebrity goodwill, and in a few jurisdictions, increased value of separate assets. Under extreme circumstances, a few states allow judges to award the separate property of one spouse to the other spouse upon divorce.

110. *See, e.g., In re* Marriage of Harding, 545 N.E.2d 459, 465 (Ill. App. Ct. 1989). Community property states now commonly permit deviation from an equal division of property, making them similar to equitable distribution states. *See* Linda D. Elrod & Robert G. Spector, *A Review of the Year in Family Law: Of Welfare Reform, Child Support, and Relocation,* 30 FAM. L.Q. 765, 808, tab. 5 (1990).

111. *See* Williams, *supra* note 82, at 2251.

112. *See* MASSACHUSETTS GENDER BIAS REPORT, *supra* note 81, at 33–36; *Florida Gender Bias Report, supra* note 81, at 816–18; Isabel Marcus, *Locked In and Locked Out: Reflections on the History of Divorce Law Reform in New York State,* 37 BUFF. L. REV. 375, 462–67 & n.342 (1988–1989) (finding that appellate cases reveal that wives receive fewer marital assets than do husbands and that settlements reflect this pattern); Schafran, *supra* note 95, at 188.

113. *See* IRA MARK ELLMAN ET AL., FAMILY LAW: CASES, TEXT, PROBLEMS 234 (2d ed. 1991). *See also* WINNER, *supra* note 54, at 41–42. Some researchers, however, have detected a trend toward equal distribution of marital assets in

equitable distribution states. *See* Garrison, *supra* note 4, at 673. *But see* WEITZ-
MAN, *supra* note 21, at 106–07 (citing studies by researchers who have not
detected this trend). Courts constantly remind that equitable distribution does
not require an equal distribution. *See, e.g., In re* Harding, 545 N.E.2d 459,
465 (Ill. App. Ct. 1989).

114. *See* Garrison, *supra* note 4, at 636 & n.55 (noting that California, Louisiana,
and New Mexico mandate equal property division).

115. *See* Suzanne Reynolds, *The Relationship of Property Division and Alimony: The
Division of Property to Address Need*, 56 FORDHAM L. REV. 827, 854–57, 861–64
(1988) (observing that courts rarely distribute property to address financial
need, despite statutory authorization to do so).

116. *See* Garrison, *supra* note 4, at 662, 667 (finding a median net worth of $23,591
in marital property in a 1984 sample of contested divorce cases and that much
of that property consisted of nonliquid assets like furniture and cars); Rhode
& Minow, *supra* note 91, at 191, 202 (noting that more than 50% of divorcing
couples have no significant marital assets); *Florida Gender Bias Report, supra*
note 81, at 818; Starnes, *supra* note 88, at 84–87 (noting that marital assets
rarely are sufficient to ease the financial problems of divorced women). As
Singer explains,

> Feminist analysis and human capital theory have also combined to
> demonstrate that traditional definitions of marital property fail to ac-
> count for a substantial portion of the assets accumulated during mar-
> riages. Thus, relying on equitable distribution principles is unlikely to
> achieve an equitable sharing of costs and benefits in a substantial number
> of divorces.

Singer, *supra* note 99, at 122.

117. *See* WEITZMAN, *supra* note 21, at 66, 78–79. Weitzman explains that the most
valuable, or only, marital property of middle-income couples (who make up
approximately half of the divorcing population) is usually the marital home.
Lower-income couples in short marriages typically do not own homes, whereas
wealthy couples have other assets in addition to the marital home. *See id.* at
66. Specifically, Weitzman found that the family home was the major asset
for 46% of divorcing couples and that the median equity in the family home
was approximately $33,000 in 1978 dollars, or $53,100 in 1984 dollars. *See
id.* at 61–62. Moreover, less than one quarter of the divorcing couples had a
pension, and only one in nine had a business or other real estate. *See id.* at
80. *See also* MASSACHUSETTS GENDER BIAS REPORT, *supra* note 81, at 33–34
(finding that the marital estate often consists of a marital home and few other
assets); WINNER, *supra* note 54, at 38–39; Garrison, *supra* note 4, at 665
(finding in her 1984 study of New York divorce cases that the marital home
was by far the most valuable asset in most contested cases).

118. *See* Schafran, *supra* note 95, at 189–90.

119. *See* WEITZMAN, *supra* note 21, at 160–61.

120. Massachusetts attorneys complain that inconsistency in judicial maintenance
awards hampers considerably their ability to predict a judge's response to a

maintenance request. *See* MASSACHUSETTS GENDER BIAS REPORT, *supra* note 81, at 33.

121. An expectation of what a court will award provides a bargaining chip in negotiation. *See* Galanter, *supra* note 2, at 268–69.

122. Garrison, *supra* note 4, at 710.

123. *See* WEITZMAN, *supra* note 21, at 162.

124. *See* MASSACHUSETTS GENDER BIAS REPORT, *supra* note 81, at 30.

125. For a graphic example of gender bias on the part of the wife's female lawyer, see *Reclaiming Professionalism*, *supra* note 6, at 177–88.

126. *See* Marcus, *supra* note 112, at 462–67 & n.342.

127. In Terry Arendell's study of 60 divorced mothers, only 7 of the mothers failed to complain vehemently about their lawyers. *See* ARENDELL, *supra* note 86, at 13. Of those seven, three of the mothers had proceeded pro se, three had reached an agreement with their husbands before they hired lawyers, and one had entered law school and obtained her divorce with the help of one of her professors. *See id.* For a scathing indictment of lawyers' representation of wives during divorce, see WINNER, *supra* note 54.

128. *See* MATHER ET AL., *supra* note 2, at 114 (noting that 35% of the Maine and New Hampshire divorce lawyers studied defined their primary goal as fair settlement).

129. *See* Bryan, *supra* note 8, at 1253–70. *See also, e.g., In re* Marriage of Curtis, 23 P.3d 13, 16–17 (Wash. 2001) (inadequate legal representation and overall unfairness provided insufficient reasons to vacate a property settlement agreement incorporated into final judgment of dissolution); *In re* Marriage of Foster, 451 N.E.2d 915, 919 (Ill. App. Ct. 1983) (Kasserman, J., dissenting) (noting that the husband received at least $100,000 more than the wife); *In re* Marriage of Beck, 404 N.E.2d 972, 975 (Ill. App. Ct. 1980) (noting that the trial court characterized the settlement as a "bad deal," yet denied the wife's petition to vacate). *See generally* WINNER, *supra* note 54.

130. *See* BLANKENHORN, *supra* note 72; Abraham, *supra* note 72; Henry, *supra* note 72.

131. In one California study, 693 of 908 divorcing families did not contest custody, and in those 693 uncontested cases the mother received sole custody 90% of the time. *See* Mnookin et al., *supra* note 90, at 37, 52. In the contested cases, courts granted mothers' requests twice as often as those of fathers. More specifically, in the 190 contested cases, mothers received what they asked for in 115 cases, fathers received what they requested in 50 cases, and a compromise was reached in 25 cases. *Id.* at 37, 53. Many other sources confirm that mothers receive custody more often than fathers. *See, e.g.,* MASSACHUSETTS GENDER BIAS REPORT, *supra* note 81, at 61 (noting that Massachusetts mothers have primary physical custody in the great majority of cases).

132. Mothers continue to provide far more child caretaking than fathers and remain more invested in the parental role than fathers. In her study of the California divorce courts, Weitzman found that 96% of the divorced women, compared to 57% of divorced men, reported that they wanted custody of their children.

Only 38% of the divorced men, however, spoke of custody with their lawyers, and only 13% requested custody in their divorce petition. Weitzman concludes that most divorcing fathers are not seriously interested in having custody of their children, whereas most divorcing mothers are. WEITZMAN, *supra* note 21, at 243–44. In a study of 908 divorcing families in California, only 20% of the divorce petitions indicated a conflict between the mother's and the father's custody request. *See* Mnookin et al., *supra* note 90, at 37, 51. The researchers sought to explain the discrepancy between what type of custody fathers said they wanted and what custody they actually requested. They speculated that fathers may not have wanted custody as passionately as mothers, that fathers may have conformed to the social expectation that women "should" have custody, that fathers may have perceived their wishes as unrealistic because they were less experienced parents than their wives, or that fathers ultimately may have perceived their desire for custody as inconsistent with the demands of their work. *See id.* at 37, 72.

133. MASSACHUSETTS GENDER BIAS REPORT, *supra* note 81, at 59, 62–63.

134. *See* WISCONSIN TASK FORCE REPORT, *supra* note 89, at 197.

135. *See, e.g.,* PHYLLIS CHESLER, MOTHER ON TRIAL: THE BATTLE FOR CHILDREN AND CUSTODY 81 (1987) (finding that 59% of the fathers who won custody in litigation and 50% of the fathers who obtained custody through private negotiations had abused their wives).

136. *See* Nancy D. Polikoff, *Why Are Mothers Losing: A Brief Analysis of Criteria Used in Child Custody Determinations,* 7 WOMEN'S RTS. L. REP. 235, 236–37 (1982); *Florida Gender Bias Report, supra* note 81, at 821–22 & n.101. *See also* CHESLER, *supra* note 135, at 78–80 tab. 4 (1987) (finding that in 70% of disputed custody cases fathers won custody); *id.* at 65–66 (noting that many studies, including her own, indicate that fathers who contest custody are more likely than their wives to win); WEITZMAN, *supra* note 21, at 233–34 tab. 22; Martha L. Fineman & Anne Opie, *The Uses of Social Science Data in Legal Policymaking: Custody Determinations at Divorce,* 1987 WIS. L. REV. 107, 120 & n.37; Lenore J. Weitzman & Ruth B. Dixon, *Child Custody Awards: Legal Standards and Empirical Patterns for Child Custody, Support and Visitation After Divorce,* 12 U.C. DAVIS L. REV. 471, 502–04 (1979) (finding that in 63% of disputed custody cases in Los Angeles in 1977, fathers won custody). *But see* Mnookin et al., *supra* note 90, at 37, 53 (finding that when mothers' and fathers' requests for custody conflicted, courts granted mothers' requests approximately twice as often as those of fathers). Yet, when both parents requested sole custody, mothers received what they requested in only 46.2% of the cases. *See* Mnookin et al., *supra,* at 26, 54 tab. 2.6.

137. *See, e.g.,* ACHIEVING EQUAL JUSTICE FOR WOMEN AND MEN IN THE CALIFORNIA COURTS: FINAL REPORT 144–45 (1996) (hereinafter CALIFORNIA EQUAL JUSTICE REPORT); THE GENDER BIAS TASK FORCE OF TEXAS FINAL REPORT 51–55 (1994) (hereinafter TEXAS GENDER BIAS REPORT); REPORT OF THE OREGON SUPREME COURT/OREGON STATE BAR TASK FORCE ON GENDER FAIRNESS 49–50 (1998) (hereinafter OREGON GENDER FAIRNESS REPORT). Mary Ann Mason, for instance, describes a case in which the court awarded custody

to the mother, despite the primary caretaker status of the father. MARY ANN
MASON, THE CUSTODY WARS 30–32 (1999).

138. *See* MASSACHUSETTS GENDER BIAS REPORT, *supra* note 81, at 62–66, 69–73;
CHESLER, *supra* note 135, at 210–23; GENDER BIAS TASK FORCE REPORT OF
SOUTH DAKOTA 4 (1994) (finding that those surveyed perceived gender bias
against women as most prevalent in four areas: rape, custody, sentencing, and
child support); WINNER, *supra* note 54, at 46–49; Christopher P. Gilkerson,
*Theoretics of Practice: The Integration of Progressive Thought and Action: Poverty
Law Narratives: The Critical Practice and Theory of Receiving and Translating
Client Stories*, 43 HASTINGS L.J. 861, 880–81 (1992); Linda R. Keenan, Note,
Domestic Violence and Custody Litigation: The Need for Statutory Reform, 13
HOFSTRA L. REV. 407, 412 (1985); *Florida Gender Bias Report*, *supra* note 81,
at 819–23.

139. *See* TEXAS GENDER BIAS REPORT, *supra* note 137, at 56; Polikoff, *supra* note
136, at 237–38.

140. *See* CHESLER, *supra* note 135, at 83–84; WINNER, *supra* note 54, at 47–48;
Mary Becker, *Patriarchy and Inequality: Towards a Substantive Feminism*, 1999
U. CHI. LEGAL F. 21, 51; Gilkerson, *supra* note 138, at 880–81; Susan Beth
Jacobs, *The Hidden Gender Bias Behind "The Best Interest of the Child" Standard
in Custody Decisions*, 13 GA. ST. U. L. REV. 845, 858–63, 880–83 (1997);
Polikoff, *supra* note 136, at 237–39.

141. *See* CALIFORNIA EQUAL JUSTICE REPORT, *supra* note 137, at 148; NANCY E.
DOWD, IN DEFENSE OF SINGLE-PARENT FAMILIES 6–8 (1997); MASSACHUSETTS
GENDER BIAS REPORT, *supra* note 81, at 63; WINNER, *supra* note 54, at 46–47;
Becker, *supra* note 140, at 51; Jacobs, *supra* note 140, at 863–68; Polikoff,
supra note 136, at 237–39. Our society expects mothers to devote themselves
to rearing children. Because an employed mother does not devote her entire
self to rearing the children, her motherhood becomes suspect. On the other
hand, our society does not expect fathers to devote themselves to rearing
children. His employment, then, does not make his fatherhood suspect. *See*
Gilkerson, *supra* note 138, at 880–81. *See generally* CHESLER, *supra* note 135,
at 49–63. Prejudice against working mothers persists despite studies that indicate that children benefit from their mothers' work and greater economic
independence. *See* DOWD, *supra*, at 33.

142. *See* Jacobs, *supra* note 140, at 868–71; Ronner, *supra* note 75.

143. *See* Polikoff, *supra* note 136, at 237–39.

144. *See* MASSACHUSETTS GENDER BIAS REPORT, *supra* note 81, at 63–64; Jacobs,
supra note 140, at 857; *Florida Gender Bias Report*, *supra* note 81, at 822;
Schafran, *supra* note 95, at 192.

145. *See* MASSACHUSETTS GENDER BIAS REPORT, *supra* note 81, at 64.

146. *See Florida Gender Bias Report*, *supra* note 81, at 819–23. *See also* Joanne
Schulman & Valerie Pitt, *Second Thoughts on Joint Custody: Analysis of Legislation and Its Implications for Women and Children*, 12 GOLDEN GATE U. L. REV.
538, 554–56, 572–77 (1982) (discussing friendly parent provisions).

147. *See* MASSACHUSETTS GENDER BIAS REPORT, *supra* note 81, at 64–65.

148. *See id.* at 65; Jacobs, *supra* note 140, at 872–74, 892–93; Schafran, *supra* note 95, at 192.

149. *See The Family Violence Project of the National Council of Juvenile and Family Court Judges: Family Violence in Child Custody Statutes: An Analysis of State Codes and Legal Practice*, 29 FAM. L.Q. 197, 212–14, 216–18 (1995) (hereinafter *Family Violence in Child Custody Statutes*); Catherine F. Klein & Leslye E. Orloff, *Providing Legal Protection for Battered Women: An Analysis of State Statutes and Case Law*, 21 HOFSTRA L. REV. 801, 811–14 (1993).

150. *See* Naomi R. Cahn, *Civil Images of Battered Women: The Impact of Domestic Violence on Child Custody Decisions*, 44 VAND. L. REV. 1041, 1058–59 (1991); *Family Violence in Child Custody Statutes*, *supra* note 149, at 199–201, 208–10; Leslie D. Johnson, *Caught in the Crossfire: Examining Legislative and Judicial Response to the Forgotten Victims of Domestic Violence*, 22 L. & PSYCHOL. REV. 271, 276–77 (1998); Lynne R. Kurtz, Comment, *Protecting New York's Children: An Argument for the Creation of a Rebuttable Presumption Against Awarding a Spouse Abuser Custody of a Child*, 60 ALB. L. REV. 1345, 1348 (1997) (noting that the custody statutes of 44 states and the District of Columbia have provisions that relate to domestic violence); Joan S. Meier, *Notes From the Underground: Integrating Psychological and Legal Perspectives on Domestic Violence in Theory and Practice*, 21 HOFSTRA L. REV. 1295, 1304, 1309 (1993); Mildred Daley Pagelow, *Justice for Victims of Spouse Abuse in Divorce and Child Custody Cases*, 8 VIOLENCE & VICTIMS 69, 76 (1993). Eleven states have presumptions against an award of custody to a batterer. *See* Kurtz, *supra*, at 1350. Many of these presumptions, however, provide trial courts with wide discretion, which diminishes their effectiveness. *See id.* at 1367 & nn.151–55, 1368–72.

151. *See* Czapanskiy, *supra* note 27, at 249, 255–58; Klein & Orloff, *supra* note 149, at 958 (concluding that gender bias studies suggest that half of the sitting judiciary resists considering domestic violence in custody litigation). *See also* CHESLER, *supra* note 135, at 81 (finding that 59% of the fathers who won custody in litigation and 50% of the fathers who obtained custody through private negotiations had abused their wives).

152. *See* Mary E. Becker, *Double Binds Facing Mothers in Abusive Families: Social Support Systems, Custody Outcomes, and Liability for Acts of Others*, 2 U. CHI. L. SCH. ROUNDTABLE 13, 17 (1995); Czapanskiy, *supra* note 27, at 249, 252, 254–56 & n.19; Martha R. Mahoney, *Legal Images of Battered Women: Redefining the Issue of Separation*, 90 MICH. L. REV. 1, 11–12 (1991) (noting that denial of wife abuse permeates the legal system); Meier, *supra* note 150, at 1308, 1310; Pagelow, *supra* note 150, at 73.

153. *See* Becker, *supra* note 152, at 17; Czapanskiy, *supra* note 27, at 249, 252, 254–56 & n.19; Mahoney, *supra* note 152, at 11–12; Meier, *supra* note 150, at 1308, 1310; Pagelow, *supra* note 150, at 73; Lynn Hecht Schafran, *There's No Accounting for Judges*, 58 ALB. L. REV. 1063, 1063–67 (1995). The report of the Florida Gender Bias Commission provides extreme examples of judicial attitudes toward battered women:

Upon learning that a husband had poured lighter fluid on his wife and set her afire, one Palm Beach County judge, in open court, sang, "You light up my wife" to the tune of the song, "You Light Up my Life." When the judge in a recent first-degree murder case learned that the defendant had tried to kill his wife, the judge asked, in open court, "Is that a crime here in Dade County?"

Florida Gender Bias Report, supra note 81, at 863 (footnotes omitted).

154. *See* Becker, *supra* note 152, at 17, 23; Cahn, *supra* note 150, at 1073; Czapanskiy, *supra* note 27, at 257 & n.30; Meier, *supra* note 150, at 1308; Schafran, *supra* note 95, at 192; Elizabeth M. Schneider, *Particularity and Generality: Challenges of Feminist Theory and Practice in Work on Woman-Abuse,* 67 N.Y.U. L. REV. 520, 555 (1992). Minow relates one case in which the judge commented on the wife's allegations of spouse abuse, "He may have abused her, but that doesn't necessarily make him a bad father." Martha Minow, *Words and the Door to the Land of Change: Law, Language, and Family Violence,* 43 VAND. L. REV. 1665, 1673 (1990). Cases in which judges award custody of children to fathers who have murdered the children's mothers provide an extreme example of this judicial attitude. *See* Keenan, *supra* note 138, at 414–17.

155. Jaffe explains that children may "witness" the abuse of their mothers in a variety of ways; they may observe the violence directly when they watch their father threaten or hit their mother, they may overhear the violence from another part of the house, or they may observe the results of the violence without hearing or seeing any aggressive act. *See* JAFFE et al., *supra* note 36, at 17. Studies indicate that at least 3.3 million children per year are exposed to parental violence, and that children are present in 41% to 80% of incidents of wife assault. *See id.* at 20.

156. *See id.* at 26 (explaining that the particular harms suffered by a child who witnesses the abuse of his or her mother depend on the child's age, sex, stage of development, role within the family, and other factors). An infant's need for attachment, for example, may go unfulfilled because of the stress the mother experiences from the abuse. *Id.* Infants who witness abuse also have health problems, including low weight, poor eating patterns, sleeping difficulties, and lack of responsiveness to adults. *See id.* at 35, 40. Toddlers frequently have mood-related disorders, such as anxiousness, crying, and sadness. *See id.* at 35. They may show signs of terror, such as yelling, irritable behavior, hiding, shaking, and stuttering, and many regress to earlier developmental stages. *See id.* at 40. Latency-age children model their father's behavior and learn violence as an appropriate way to resolve conflict. *See id.* at 26. When they come to shelters, boys frequently act out, becoming disobedient, defiant, and destructive. *See id.* at 35. Latency-age girls may learn the inevitability of victimization. *See id.* at 26. Young girls who come to shelters appear withdrawn, clingy, and dependent. *See id.* at 35. Practicing at school what they have learned at home may undermine children's social adjustment and academic performance. *See id.* at 26. Many witnessing children live with the shame of the hidden violence in their homes, and their experience undermines their sense of self-esteem and confidence in the future. *See id.* Their father's domination isolates them from peers and extracurricular activities, hindering their social development.

See id. at 26, 27, 49. Children frequently blame themselves for the violence, a tremendous burden for a child to carry. *See id.* at 27. Children remain confused, anxious, and fearful while they await the next violent outburst. *See id.* at 27. As a result, they may spend most of their time at school distracted and inattentive to academic tasks. *See id.* at 27, 50. Their stress also compromises their physical and psychological health. *See id.* at 34–35. Many complain of headaches, tight stomachs, and bite their fingernails or pull their hair, and some become suicidal. *See id.* at 49. Having witnessed violence against their mothers for years, adolescent children may begin to participate or accept violence in their own relationships. *See id.* at 27. Some adolescents escape the violence by running away from home. *See id.* Some adolescents act out their anger and frustration by committing violent crimes, including assaults on their mothers or siblings. *See id.* at 30, 33. Others, particularly girls, attempt to shoulder the responsibility of keeping the family peace and protecting their siblings and mothers. *See id.* at 30–31. Thus, witnessing the abuse of their mothers profoundly affects many children. *See also* Cahn, *supra* note 150, at 1055–59; Sandra A. Graham-Bermann & Alytia A. Levendosky, *Traumatic Stress Symptoms in Children of Battered Women*, 13 J. INTERPERSONAL VIOLENCE 111 (1998); Michael Hershorn & Alan Rosenbaum, *Children of Marital Violence: A Closer Look at the Unintended Victims*, 55 AM. J. ORTHOPSYCHIATRY 260 (1985); George W. Holden & Kathy L. Ritchie, *Linking Extreme Marital Discord, Child Rearing, and Child Behavior Problems: Evidence from Battered Women*, 62 CHILD DEV.. 311 (1991); Johnson, *supra* note 150, at 274–75; Peter Lehmann, *The Development of Posttraumatic Stress Disorder (PTSD) in a Sample of Child Witnesses to Mother Assault*, 12 J. FAM. VIOLENCE 241 (1997); Pagelow, *supra* note 150, at 77; Saunders, *supra* note 42, at 52–53; Alan J. Tomkins et al., *The Plight of Children Who Witness Woman Battering: Psychological Knowledge and Policy Implications*, 18 L. & PSYCHOL. REV. 137 (1994).

157. Approximately half of the men who batter their female partners also abuse their children. *See* Saunders, *supra* note 42, at 51–52. *See also* Lee H. Bowker et al., *On the Relationship Between Wife Beating and Child Abuse,* in FEMINIST PERSPECTIVE ON WIFE ABUSE 165–66 (Kersti Yllo & Michele Bograd eds. 1988); Cahn, *supra* note 150, at 1055–58; Meier, *supra* note 150, at 1308; Dorothy E. Roberts, *Motherhood and Crime*, 79 IOWA L. REV. 95, 111–12 & nn.84–86 (1993); Schneider, *supra* note 154, at 551 n.128, 554. The long-term effects of physical and sexual abuse of children include depression, susceptibility to suicide, anxiety disorders, eating disorders, sexual dysfunction, dissociative disorders, personality disorders, posttraumatic stress disorder (PTSD), substance abuse, and adult psychiatric disorders including psychosis. *See* John Read, *Child Abuse and Psychosis: A Literature Review and Implications for Professional Practice*, 28 PROF. PSYCHOL. 448 (1997).

158. Katz v. Katz, 97 A.D.2d 398, 398 (1983). *See also* OREGON GENDER FAIRNESS REPORT, *supra* note 137, at 50 n.25 (quoting a female judge as stating, "Although the father has an anger problem and has sought minimal help, and while his testimony reflects that he is the epitome of an abuser, that still

does not answer the ultimate question as to what is in the best interests of the child.").

159. *See* Meier, *supra* note 150, at 1309; Schneider, *supra* note 154, at 551–53 & n.135; Perhaps judicial attitudes should not surprise, because mother blaming pervades our society. *See, e.g.,* NANCY CHODOROW, THE REPRODUCTION OF MOTHERING PSYCHOANALYSIS AND THE SOCIOLOGY OF GENDER (1978); DOWD, *supra* note 141, at xiv–xv, 3–15; P. Caplan & I. Hall-McCorquodale, *Mother Blaming in Major Clinical Journals*, 55 AM J. ORTHOPSYCHIATRY 345 (1985); Bernardine Dohrn, *Bad Mothers, Good Mothers, and the State: Children on the Margins*, 2 U. CHI. L. SCH. ROUNDTABLE 1 (1995); Leitch, *supra* note 6, at 167. Martha Fineman argues that society especially stigmatizes and scorns single mothers as deviant. *See* Martha A. Fineman, *Masking Dependency: The Political Role of Family Rhetoric*, 81 VA. L. REV. 2181, 2182, 2190–93, 2206–08 (1995). Some poverty theorists blame single mothers for their families' poverty. *See* BAKER, *supra* note 24, at 348.

160. *See* Mahoney, *supra* note 152, at 37–39; Meier, *supra* note 150, at 1302–03; Schneider, *supra* note 154, at 556. In contrast, most experts understand that a woman's decision to remain in an abusive relationship results from her rational assessment of a variety of factors as well as the psychological correlates of abuse. *See generally* Pamela Choice & Leanne K. Lamke, *A Conceptual Approach to Understanding Abused Women's Stay/Leave Decisions*, 18 J. FAM. ISSUES 290 (1997); Sherry L. Hamby & Bernadette Gray-Little, *Responses to Partner Violence: Moving Away From Deficit Models*, 11 J. FAM. PSYCHOL. 339 (1997); A. J. Z. Henderson et al., *He Loves Me; He Loves Me Not: Attachment and Separation Resolution of Abused Women*, 12 J. FAM. VIOLENCE 169, 170 (1997).

161. *See* Czapanskiy, *supra* note 27, at 257; Meier, *supra* note 150, at 1306.

162. *See* Mahoney, *supra* note 152, at 44. One judge claimed that a battered woman's extensive contacts with a protective shelter showed that "self-interest and excessive liberalism" characterized her environment. Saunders, *supra* note 42, at 56 (citing L. Fredericks, *Minnesota Supreme Court Creates Primary Caretaker Presumption in Child Custody Disputes*, 7 WOMEN'S ADVOC. 1, 2 (1986)).

163. *See* Mahoney, *supra* note 152, at 46; Meier, *supra* note 150, at 1310. *See also* Ostrander v. Ostrander, 541 N.Y.S.2d 630 (N.Y. App. Div. 1989) (awarding custody to father when the battered mother left the children with the father).

164. *See* Mahoney, *supra* note 152, at 46; Meier, *supra* note 150, at 1310; Czapanskiy, *supra* note 27, at 257; Schneider, *supra* note 154, at 557.

165. *See* Meier, *supra* note 150, at 1312–13; Concepcion Silva et al., *Symptoms of Post-Traumatic Stress Disorder in Abused Women in a Primary Care Setting*, 6 J. WOMEN'S HEALTH 543 (1997). Symptoms of PTSD typically result from exposure to extreme trauma, personally or as a witness, or from learning of an unexpected threat to, injury to, or death of someone close. *See* Silva et al., *supra*, at 543. Prolonged exposure to a stressor, regardless of its nature, also can produce symptoms of PTSD. *See id.* at 544.

166. *See* Meier, *supra* note 150, at 1312; Silva et al., *supra* note 165, at 359.

167. *See* Saunders, *supra* note 42, at 54.

168. *See* Hamby & Gray-Little, *supra* note 160, at 339.

169. *See* Meier, *supra* note 150, at 1313.

170. *See Gender and Justice in the Courts: A Report to the Supreme Court of Georgia by the Commission on Gender Bias in the Judicial System*, 8 Ga. St. L. Rev. 539, 589 (1992); Keenan, *supra* note 138, at 424.

171. *See* Massachusetts Gender Bias Report, *supra* note 81, at 69–70; Becker, *supra* note 152, at 24–25. *See generally* Lowenstein, *supra* note 45. Contrary to judicial beliefs, research reveals that allegations of child sexual abuse arise infrequently in custody disputes and that allegations in the divorce context prove unfounded no more frequently than in other contexts. *See* Becker, *supra*, at 25; Nancy Thoennes & Patricia G. Tjaden, *The Extent, Nature, and Validity of Sexual Abuse Allegations in Custody/Visitation Disputes*, 14 Child Abuse & Neglect 151, 155–56, 161 (1990); Jessica Pearson, *Ten Myths About Family Law*, 27 Fam. L.Q. 279, 293–95 (1993). Pearson notes that, "while these allegations may be increasing, they are hardly rampant." Pearson, *supra*, at 294. More specifically, Pearson found that sexual abuse allegations surfaced in only 2% of the 9,000 divorce proceedings that occurred during a six-month period. *See id.* at 294. *See also* Thoennes & Tjaden, *supra*, at 155–56; Meredith Sherman Fahn, *Allegations of Child Sexual Abuse in Custody Disputes: Getting to the Truth of the Matter*, 25 Fam. L.Q. 193, 194, 202 (1991) (rejecting the idea that allegations of child sexual abuse made during custody disputes automatically deserve suspicion). Pearson's results hardly seem surprising in light of other studies. For instance, Bross notes that

the frequency of child sexual abuse is disconcerting . . . . In a 1985 poll, researchers interviewed 2626 [sic] adults from the fifty states. Among this representative sample of Americans eighteen years old or over, twenty-two percent of the women and fifteen percent of the men re- ported being sexually abused as children.

Donald C. Bross, *Terminating the Parent–Child Legal Relationship as a Response to Child Sexual Abuse*, 26 Loy. U. Chi. L.J. 287, 289 (1995) (citing Lois Timinick, *The Times Poll: 22% in Survey Were Child Abuse Victims*, L.A. Times, Aug. 25, 1985, at A1).

172. *See* California Equal Justice Report, *supra* note 137, at 150; Becker, *supra* note 152, at 17; Faller, *supra* note 42, at 430–31.

173. *See* Faller, *supra* note 42, at 430.

174. *See* Massachusetts Gender Bias Report, *supra* note 81, at 69–70; *Florida Gender Bias Report*, *supra* note 81, at 867; *Missouri Task Force*, *supra* note 22, at 513, 567.

175. Although preferences for joint custody and friendly parent provisions dis- advantage all mothers, they severely disadvantage abused mothers *See* Keenan, *supra* note 138, at 424–25.

176. *See* Becker, *supra* note 152, at 26–27. In one case, about the time that the trial court entered its order for unsupervised visitation, the mother moved

with the child to Kentucky. No visitation with the father took place. The trial court then transferred custody from the mother to the father, likely to punish the mother for moving and for noncompliance with the visitation order. Czapanskiy, *supra* note 27, at 268 n.65. Fortunately, the appellate court found the trial court had erred. *See id. See also* Quindlen, *supra* note 27, at 15 (discussing similar cases throughout the United States). *See also Family Violence in Child Custody Statutes, supra* note 149, at 201–02 (arguing the inappropriateness of friendly parent provisions in domestic violence cases).

177. Czapanskiy, *supra* note 27, at 256 (citing GENDER BIAS IN THE COURTS: REPORT OF THE MARYLAND SPECIAL JOINT COMMITTEE ON GENDER BIAS IN THE COURTS 30 (1989)).

178. *See id.* at 268–69 (discussing Hanke v. Hanke, 615 A.2d 1205 (Md. Ct. App. 1992)).

179. *See In re* A.F. v. N.F., 549 N.Y.S.2d 511, 513 (N.Y. App. Div. 1989).

180. *See id.* at 513, 514.

181. *See id.* at 513, 515.

182. *Florida Gender Bias Report, supra* note 81, at 867.

183. *See* SUN & THOMAS, *supra* note 36 (finding that in custody disputes judges followed the recommendations of mental health professionals 90% of the time); Fineman, *supra* note 36, at 740–44. *See also* Saunders, *supra* note 42, at 54. Additionally, social workers harbor suspicions about those who request sole custody. Fineman, *supra*, at 740–44, 766. *See also* JAFFE ET AL., *supra* note 36, at 108.

184. *See* SYLVIA ANN HEWLETT, A LESSER LIFE: THE MYTH OF WOMEN'S LIBERATION IN AMERICA 246–47 (1986); CATHERINE A. MACKINNON, TOWARD A FEMINIST THEORY OF STATE 152–53, 283 n.42 (1989). In the past, the male-dominated psychological profession has marginalized women's concerns, portrayed women as inferior, hysterical human beings, and urged women to happily assume their proper subordinate position to men. Sanity in women often meant little more than proper accommodation to male dominance. *See generally* PHYLLIS CHESLER, WOMEN AND MADNESS (1972). Mental health professionals also historically have blamed mothers for children's developmental problems. *See* Becker, *supra* note 152, at 13; Fineman, *supra* note 36, at 767 n.161; Minow, *supra* note 154, at 1682; Roberts, *supra* note 157, at 110–11 & n.81.

185. *See* Fineman, *supra* note 36, at 734–35.

186. *See id.* at 750–51 & nn.102–04.

187. *See* MASON, *supra* note 137, at 38–64. *See also* HETHERINGTON & KELLY, *supra* note 86, at 134 (noting that the quality, rather than the frequency, of contact between the child and the noncustodial parent determines the child's successful adjustment to divorce). Perhaps this preference for shared parenting relates to the significant control mental health professionals now exercise over custody decision making. Recently men have successfully pushed for more shared parenting. *See* Dan Menzie, Note, *Fathers are Parents Too: Pros and Cons of the New Missouri Domestic Relations Statute,* 57 UMKC L. REV. 963 (1989).

The ability of the mental health profession to retain its decisional control on child issues may depend on its ability to placate these politically powerful males. Thus, the psychological profession's current bias in favor of shared parenting may suggest a continued accommodation to preexisting hierarchy rather than a concern for children's best interests. *See generally* Fineman, *supra* note 36.

188. *See* Fineman, *supra* note 36, at 734–35.

189. *See* HARALAMBIE, *supra* note 43, at 33–34; JAFFE ET AL., *supra* note 36, at 108; Faller, *supra* note 42, at 431; Saunders, *supra* note 42, at 54 (noting that therapists fall prey to the same misunderstandings of battered women's behavior as do judges).

190. Psychiatrists frequently diagnose battered women as paranoid or conclude that battered women suffer from a variety of character disorders. *See* Meier, *supra* note 150, at 1301. *See also* JAFFE ET AL., *supra* note 36, at 71 (noting that mental health professionals have misdiagnosed battered women as schizophrenic or paranoid); Saunders, *supra* note 42, at 54 (warning that battered women's poor performance on psychological tests can lead to misdiagnosis).

191. *See* Meier, *supra* note 150, at 1302 n.19 (citing *Evan Stark, Framing and Reframing Battered Women, in* DOMESTIC VIOLENCE: THE CRIMINAL JUSTICE RESPONSE 287 (Eva Buzawa ed. 1993)). *See also* Saunders, *supra* note 42, at 54 (advising that batterers frequently appear to function well, whereas their partners give an inaccurate appearance of pathology).

192. *See* JAFFE ET AL., *supra* note 36, at 107–08; Mahoney, *supra* note 152, at 47–48.

193. *See* HARALAMBIE, *supra* note 43, at 33–34; Faller, *supra* note 42, at 431.

194. *See* Faller, *supra* note 42, at 431.

195. *See* CALIFORNIA EQUAL JUSTICE REPORT, *supra* note 137, at 155.

196. *See* Stuckey, *supra* note 35, at 1785.

197. One Missouri attorney observed: "Judges and attorneys have difficulty believing sex abuse allegation by women and children and sometimes place children back with abusers. In a recent case, the male guardian ad litem didn't want to believe allegations of sex abuse against the father because he seemed like a nice guy." *Missouri Task Force, supra* note 22, at 568.

198. *See* WEITZMAN, *supra* note 21, at 393–94.

199. Commentators and researchers report that women frequently compromise financial requests in order to retain custody of the children. *See, e.g.,* Becker, *supra* note 152, at 28–29; Fineman, *supra* note 36, at 761; *Florida Gender Bias Report, supra* note 81, at 819–20; Wishik, *supra* note 101, at 101 (finding that a significant number of interviewed women admitted that they bargained away property or support rights in return for child custody).

200. *See* WINNER, *supra* note 54, at 50–51; Richard Neely, *The Primary Caretaker Parent Rule: Child Custody and the Dynamics of Greed,* 3 YALE L. & POL'Y REV. 168 (1984); *Florida Gender Bias Report, supra* note 81, at 819.

201. *See* OREGON GENDER FAIRNESS REPORT, *supra* note 174, at 50.

202. *See id.* at 54.

203. *See generally* MATHER ET AL., *supra* note 2, at 8–42.

204. *See* Lind et al., *supra* note 2, at 972–73, 978–81; Paternoster et al., *supra* note 69, at 167–68; Tom R. Tyler, *Citizen Discontent with Legal Procedures: A Social Science Perspective on Civil Procedure Reform*, 45 AM. J. COMP. L. 871, 891–92 (1997). Tyler labels these concerns "ethicality." Tyler, *supra* note 68, at 113. *See also* Tom R. Tyler, *Multiculturalism and the Willingness of Citizens to Defer to the Legal and Legal Authorities*, 25 L. & SOC. INQUIRY 983 (2000) (noting throughout the importance of respectful treatment to people's perception of procedural justice).

205. *See* Paternoster et al., *supra* note 69, at 168; Tyler, *supra* note 24, at 891–92, 897; Nancy A. Welsh, *Making Deals in Court-Connected Mediation: What's Justice Got to Do With It?*, 79 WASH. U. L.Q. 787, 820, 824–29 (2001).

206. *See* Beck & Sales, *supra* note 4, at 898; Phyllis Gangel-Jacob, *Some Words of Caution About Divorce Mediation*, 23 HOFSTRA L. REV. 825, 826–27 (1995); Ann Kass, *A View from the Bench—The Adversarial Aspects of Divorce*, 4 AM. J. FAM. L. 27, 35 (1990) (quoting a South Carolina judge: "How in the world do you stand it? I find after hearing a few divorce cases, I need to hear a friendly first degree murder case or two to regain my sanity."). Judges experience extreme frustration with contested custody cases. *See* Rudolph J. Gerber, *Recommendation on Domestic Relations Reform*, 32 ARIZ. L. REV. 9, 13–14 (1990).

207. *See generally* WINNER, *supra* note 54.

208. *See, e.g.,* David L. Chambers, *Rethinking the Substantive Rules for Custody Disputes in Divorce*, 83 MICH. L. REV. 477, 477, 568 (1984); Gary Crippen, *Stumbling Beyond Best Interests of the Child: Reexamining Child Custody Standard-Setting in the Wake of Minnesota's Four Year Experiment with the Primary Care-taker Preference*, 74 MINN. L. REV. 427, 432 (1990); Karen Czapanskiy, *Volunteers and Draftees: The Struggle for Parental Equality*, 38 UCLA L. REV. 1415, 1442 (1991); Jacobs, *supra* note 140, at 849 & nn.32–34.

209. *See, e.g.,* COLO. REV. STAT. §14-10-124 (2002).

210. *See, e.g.,* N.Y. DOM. REL. LAW §236(6) (2002).

211. *See, e.g., id.* § 236(B)(5)(d).

212. *See* Galanter & Cahill, *supra* note 2, at 1383–84. When judges order, or the law requires, parties to mediate contested divorce issues, the parties enter a dispute resolution context that does not honor their legal rights. Divorce mediators have no obligation to protect or respect the legal rights of parties, because substantive law does not dictate mediated outcomes. In the words of one mediator:

> How is it that we have come to substitute legal rules for the personal considerations that we have always employed in the past? More importantly, why have we allowed ourselves to be persuaded that it makes any sense to do this? After all, there is really nothing very special about legal rules. In fact, they are based on very abstract principles that have little, if anything, to do with the reality of our individual lives. If we

> had never thought to employ them before, why is it that we must do so now? And why do we think that we would be making a mistake if we did not?

MARLOW, *supra* note 29, at 14. Rather than respect legal rights, the parties, with the assistance of a mediator, negotiate a settlement unconstrained by law. Because of power imbalances between spouses, mediated settlements generally disadvantage women and disrespect women's legal rights, again contributing to problematic results. *See, e.g., Killing Us Softly, supra* note 6.

213. *See* MASSACHUSETTS GENDER BIAS REPORT, *supra* note 81, at 22–23.

214. *See* COLO. REV. STAT. §14-10-127 (2002).

215. *See generally* WINNER, *supra* note 54.

216. *See* Sarat & Felstiner, *supra* note 48, at 764.

217. *See* MATHER ET AL., *supra* note 2, at 31–32, 35–36, 38.

218. *See, e.g.,* Lucy E. White, *Subordination, Rhetorical Survival Skills, and Sunday Shoes: Notes on Hearing of Mrs. G.,* 38 BUFF. L. REV. 1 (1990). *See also* MATHER ET AL., *supra* note 2, at 92.

219. *See* MATHER ET AL., *supra* note 2, at 35, 88, 90, 92, 96–98.

220. *See generally* WINNER, *supra* note 54.

221. *See* MATHER ET AL., *supra* note 2, at 98–99.

222. In their study of Maine and New Hampshire divorce lawyers, Mather et al. found that only divorce specialists, a small percentage of the attorneys they interviewed, considered knowledge of substantive divorce law important. *Id.* at 79–81. Lawyers who do not even know relevant law cannot exhibit respect for legal rights. Mather et al. also found, however, that attorneys sometimes encouraged clients to pursue their legal rights when those clients simply wanted to end the divorce because of guilt, intimation, or exhaustion. *Id.* at 92.

223. SARAT & FELSTINER, *supra* note 54, at 93.

224. *Id.*

225. *See* Russell Korobkin & Chris Guthrie, *Psychology, Economics, and Settlement: A New Look at the Role of the Lawyer,* 76 TEX. L. REV. 77, 122–23 (1997).

226. *See* MATHER ET AL., *supra* note 2, at 75, 114, 121–22 (2001). Sarat and Felstiner's study also confirms how much divorce lawyers prefer settlement. *See* SARAT & FELSTINER, *supra* note 54, at 108–21. *See also* Korobkin & Guthrie, *supra* note 225 (finding evidence that lawyers have an analytical orientation to decision making that facilitates a higher rate of settlement than litigants would achieve on their own); *In re* Marriage of Flynn, 597 N.E.2d 709, 173 (Ill. App. Ct. 1992).

227. *See, e.g.,* William L.F. Felstiner & Austin Sarat, *Enactments of Power: Negotiating Reality and Responsibility in Lawyer–Client Interactions,* 77 CORNELL L. REV. 1447 (1992); Howard S. Erlanger et al., *Participation and Flexibility in Informal Processes: Cautions from the Divorce Context,* 21 L. & SOC'Y REV. 585, 592–94 (1987); Austin Sarat & William L.F. Felstiner, *Law and Strategy in the Divorce Lawyer's Office,* 20 L. & SOC'Y REV. 93, 105 (1986). *See also* David L. Chambers, *25 Divorce Attorneys and 40 Clients in Two Not So Big But Not So Small*

Cities in Massachusetts and California: An Appreciation, 22 L. & Soc. Inquiry 209, 210 (1997) (reviewing Austin Sarat & William L.F. Felstiner, Divorce Lawyers and Their Clients: Power and Meaning in the Legal Process (1995)).

228. *See* Robert H. Mnookin & Lewis Kornhauser, *Bargaining in the Shadow of the Law: The Case of Divorce*, 88 Yale L.J. 950 (1979). *See also* Melvin A. Eisenberg, *Private Ordering Through Negotiation: Dispute-Settlement and Rule-making*, 89 Harv. L. Rev. 637 (1976).

229. *See* Mnookin & Kornhauser, *supra* note 228, at 968–70.

230. *See* Mather et al., *supra* note 2, at 25–30, 80, 81; Felstiner & Sarat, *supra* note 227, at 1497; Austin Sarat & William L.F. Felstiner, *Lawyers and Legal Consciousness: Law Talk in the Divorce Lawyer's Office*, 98 Yale L.J. 1663, 1682–84 (1989). *See generally* Sarat & Felstiner, *supra* note 54; Sarat & Felstiner, *supra* note 48; Sarat & Felstiner, *supra* note 227. Many divorce lawyers do not even consider formal legal knowledge of great importance. Mather et al., *supra*, at 71–72, 79. In his study of divorced spouses, Jacob found that many clients do not frame their cases legalistically and, with the exception of child support guidelines, do not believe the law had much effect on their settlements. *See* Herbert Jacob, *The Elusive Shadow of the Law*, 26 L. & Soc'y Rev. 565, 576–78 (1992). Their lawyers frequently failed to provide them with helpful legal advice, and many clients negotiated their own agreements, using their lawyers more as clerks than as legal professionals. *See id.* at 579–80, 584–85. These studies suggest a far more limited role for law in divorce negotiations than that suggested by Mnookin and Kornhauser. Moreover, these studies are consistent with others that have shown that lawyers in contexts other than divorce frequently settle with little reference to law. *See* Carrie Menkel-Meadow, *Whose Dispute Is It Anyway? A Philosophical and Democratic Defense of Settlement (In Some Cases)*, 83 Geo. L.J. 2663, 2675 (1995).

231. Winner notes that divorce lawyers frequently urge their women clients to accept agreements the women do not want, explaining that the agreements are "for [the client's] own good." Winner, *supra* note 54, at 69, 91. *See also* Melli et al., *supra* note 2, at 1158–59.

232. For instance, Jim came to my office to ask advice. His lawyer refused to pursue equal parenting time for Jim with his two-year-old daughter. The lawyer told Jim that the judge undoubtedly would award the mother sole custody of such a young child. A fight over equal parenting time simply would waste Jim's time and resources. Jim, however, had co-parented his daughter since her birth and remained very invested in her well-being. Moreover, Jim's wife had not allowed him to see his daughter for the past month. If she received sole custody, Jim worried that his relationship with his daughter would end. Jim's parents encouraged him to accept his fate and move on with his life. Despite the advice of his parents and his lawyer, at my urging Jim sought the opinion of another lawyer. She told Jim that the law expressed a preference for shared parenting and for the more cooperative parent. Not only could she guarantee

Jim significant parenting time, he stood a good chance of becoming the primary residential parent if the mother continued to obstruct his visitation rights. Understandably, Jim changed lawyers.

233. *See* WINNER, *supra* note 54, at 91. Sarat and Felstiner studied interactions between divorce lawyers and their clients. Their work provides numerous examples of lawyers who use evasive predictions of what a court will do in order to manipulate clients into acceptance of particular settlements. *See* SARAT & FELSTINER, *supra* note 54, at 124–26. *See also* MATHER ET AL., *supra* note 2, at 99–100. Moreover, lawyers frequently invoke vague "standards" or "rules of thumb" in order to encourage their clients to accept particular settlement provisions. *See* MATHER ET AL., *supra*, at 121–24; Melli et al., *supra* note 2, at 1143–44. "Law" for the client is whatever the lawyer says it is. *See* MATHER ET AL., *supra*, at 96 (noting that the lawyer's personal ideas about appropriate outcomes actually may create the law). The client cannot challenge the lawyer's assertions of knowledge because determinate legal standards do not exist and clients have few resources with which to challenge their lawyers' expertise. *See* MATHER ET AL., *supra*, at 107.

234. Attorney neglect of divorce cases seems rampant. *See* WINNER, *supra* note 54, at 71–92. *See also* MATHER ET AL., *supra* note 2, at 26, 29, 30, 141–42. Several commentators note that many divorce cases are settled in court hallways just minutes before the final hearing. *See generally* Melli et al., *supra* note 2, at 1143. One might think that this settlement behavior equally disadvantages husbands and wives. On closer inspection, this seems unlikely. Generally, husbands have in their possession the income and property that the wife wants transferred to her. Moreover, he is in a much stronger position to resist that transfer than she is to force it. She needs what he has and he, as yet, is under no compunction to give her what she needs. These factors combine with her financial desperation, her attorney's inferior preparation, indeterminate law, prevailing ideologies, and her fear of the impending open conflict to disadvantage her more than her husband.

235. *See* MATHER ET AL., *supra* note 2, at 27–28, 39, 43, 69, 71, 77–78; Jacob, *supra* note 230, at 579–81.

236. *See* SARAT & FELSTINER, *supra* note 54, at 63–83.

237. Mather et al.'s study suggests that lawyers who specialize in divorce are more likely to utilize formal discovery than those who do not. *See* MATHER ET AL., *supra* note 2, at 18–37 (2001). Most lawyers who handle divorce cases, however, do not specialize. *Id.*

238. Many times limited client resources discourage discovery, *id* at 30–31, 39, 53–54, 77, 126, 140, but not always. In Mather et al.'s study, one lawyer who represents wealthy clients stated the following:

Even if it's going to be an agreement, just going through the financials, accounting records, tax records and appraisals and verification of what the assets really are, because there's a major malpractice situation on the hit parade. We just brought two of those cases against other lawyers who really failed. One client received a settlement based on her husband being worth five million, and it turned out he was worth about 27 million. The lawyer didn't do any financial investigation at all and had her settle the case.

Id. at 50–52. Appellate opinions that address petitions to vacate or to set aside property settlements provide numerous examples of the wife's divorce attorney's failure to conduct discovery. *See In re* Marriage of Beck, 404 N.E.2d 972, 974 (Ill. App. Ct. 1980); Beattie v. Beattie, 368 N.E.2d 178, 179–80 (Ill. App. Ct. 1977). In one study of 349 Wisconsin divorce cases, only 90 files contained financial disclosure sheets from both parties, whereas 126 files contained little or no financial information. *See* Melli et al., *supra* note 2, at 1146–47. In particular, lawyers who represent clients with limited financial resources tend to prefer informal settlement processes that do not utilize formal litigation tools such as discovery. *See* MATHER ET AL., *supra* note 2, at 39.

239. *See* Erlanger et al., *supra* note 227, at 592. Lawyers also sometimes delay divorce cases to force clients to accept settlements that lawyers consider reasonable. *See* MATHER ET AL., *supra* note 2, at 101–102.

240. *See* Erlanger et al., *supra* note 227, at 592.

241. *See* Garrison, *supra* note 4, at 685–86.

242. *See* Bryan, *supra* note 8, at 1243–71.

4

SYSTEM CHARACTERISTICS

This chapter assesses whether our current divorce dispute resolution system provides divorce disputants with sufficient voice and participation, ensures decisions based on accurate information, affords a meaningful opportunity for the correction of error, reduces hostilities between the parties, operates efficiently, and processes divorce cases consistently. We turn first to voice and participation.

VOICE

> The right to be heard before being condemned to suffer grievous loss of any kind, even though it may not involve the stigma and hardships of a criminal conviction, is a principle basic to our society.[1]

Parties feel that control over outcomes—or, alternatively, participation and an adequate opportunity to tell their stories—is an important feature in a dispute resolution procedure.[2] This concern runs so deeply that disputants may perceive objectively unjust procedures as fair simply because they provide ample opportunity to speak.[3] Before we explore whether judges and lawyers provide divorce disputants sufficient voice, however, the concept itself requires definition.

The importance people attribute to self-expression reflects their desire for affirmation.[4] When they tell their stories to others, people hope for understanding, acceptance, and inclusion.[5] To fulfill these human needs, a listener ideally should hear the speaker's full story empathically, without edit or reconstruction. Moreover, when a person tells his or her story to a decision maker, he or she expects the actual decision to reflect or respond to the person's expressed concerns. Voice without impact suggests to the speaker that the decision maker did not listen.[6] Ideally, then, the speaker should have an opportunity to tell his or her full story without reconstruction, and the decision reached should address the speaker's concerns.

When we consider whether the current system offers parties sufficient voice, two different types of constraints on voice emerge: one generic, the other gendered. This section begins with voice restrictions that affect all divorce disputants and then turn to an assessment of gendered limitations on voice.

JUDGES AND VOICE

A judge's behavior at trial can influence dramatically a party's perception of voice. Because most judges dislike divorce cases,[7] however, they tend to restrict client voice. Many judges also feel incompetent on family matters. They lack relevant education, they frequently must make decisions that satisfy no one, and they receive little guidance from the highly indeterminate substantive laws that govern custody, visitation, spousal maintenance, and property division. Their discomfort with their abilities and their tasks undoubtedly encourages them to place limitations on testimony and the presentation of evidence.[8] Judges seem particularly hostile to certain issues in divorce cases, such as allegations of child sexual abuse. Their hostility encourages them to limit or refuse to hear evidence from the parent who complains. When a judge refuses to permit a parent to speak or to present evidence of sexual abuse, undoubtedly that parent will feel that the judge has restricted his or her voice.

Many judges believe that parties should resolve family issues privately. Although the parties' resolution of their dispute may seem to maximize client voice, it often has the opposite effect on at least one spouse, usually the wife. As explained more thoroughly later, many wives have difficulty directly confronting their spouses and need a structured and sometimes safe forum in which to tell their stories. Consequently, the judicial mandate to settle privately can compromise disputant voice significantly.

Certainly some judges respect the divorce disputant's need for voice. Yet judges whose hearts and minds reside in the right place often receive little support. Instead, the court tradition in which they function devalues divorce cases and deplores the emotional and psychological issues these cases frequently present. Judicial colleagues and lawyers who handle more prestigious cases may give little credit to a judge who "wastes the court's time" by allowing divorce disputants to tell their stories. In such a culture, even right-minded judges may compromise their values. Consequently, judicial distaste for divorce cases, belief in family privacy, and antipathy to lurid family issues may combine with a hostile court culture to produce insufficient voice for the divorcing couple. This suggests that the system would benefit if judges better understood the importance of disputant voice and if their court culture respected it. Moreover, if judges felt more competent and less hostile to parties, they likely would allow them more voice.

LAWYERS AND VOICE

Lawyers also place significant limitations on client voice. Academic and practice literature encourages divorce lawyers to begin the first client conference by eliciting a client narrative.[9] This same literature also urges lawyers to include clients in the representation process.[10] Many lawyers acknowledge the need to listen to clients, particularly at the first meeting,[11] and typically listen in order to gather necessary information, establish rapport, and to assist in client growth.[12]

The literature on actual lawyer–client interactions, however, depicts the lawyer as dominant and the client as passive.[13] Divorce clients complain that their lawyers fail to include them in decisions. Divorce lawyers themselves admit their reluctance to include their clients in negotiations where decisions get made,[14] particularly when lawyers do not believe that their clients have the emotional capacity to make rational decisions.[15] Felstiner and Sarat's research on divorce describes complex negotiations between the lawyer and the client that ultimately construct their patterns of interaction.[16] During these negotiations, an interdependence between lawyer and client develops because of their need to create a mutually acceptable version of the client's reality.[17] They reconstruct the client's social world through a process of client storytelling and lawyer questioning and interpretation that ultimately, if successful, integrates the lawyer's legal and the client's social worlds.[18]

Sometimes the lawyer and client work well together, making the most of the lawyer's legal and the client's social knowledge.[19] When this occurs, the client has voice and mutual control over the constructed reality. On many more occasions, however, a painful or unsuccessful process suggests lawyer dominance and ineffective client voice.[20] Depending on who controls or contributes to the final version of the client's story, the client may feel either heard or ignored. Moreover, the client's social world rarely remains static during divorce.[21] The lawyer's need to stay in touch with the evolution of the client's world suggests that the mutual construction of the client's story is an ongoing process that provides some client voice throughout representation.[22]

Clients also influence goals, suggesting that their voice affects outcomes.[23] Most of the divorce lawyers whom Felstiner and Sarat studied allowed their clients to formulate goals and saw their own responsibility as merely ensuring the reasonability of them.[24] Seasoned divorce attorneys seem able to look beneath the surface of the client's initial demands and behaviors and to detect more fundamental concerns,[25] implying that these lawyers hear clients at deep levels. Even when lawyers do attempt to manipulate their clients into goals that the clients consider unacceptable, the clients resist and use numerous tactics to make their lawyers listen.[26]

Lawyers and clients in Felstiner and Sarat's study implicitly recognized representation as a joint endeavor, with one party rarely commanding the other.[27] Mather et al. concluded from their study, however, that divorce lawyers exert far more influence over clients than the reverse.[28] Lawyer and client negotiation of goals and reality suggests that divorce clients have some voice with their lawyers; it also suggests, however, the limitations of that voice.

During representation the lawyer almost inevitably will alter the client's story,[29] causing the client to wonder whether the lawyer listened.[30] In order to construct a persuasive story, the lawyer must fit the client's social reality within relevant legal doctrine.[31] Clients have difficulty resisting their lawyers' reconstructions, because lawyers have greater resources and expertise on which to draw,[32] and clients may understand that the lawyers' reconstructions ultimately does serve the clients' best interests.

Practical concerns also encourage lawyers to compromise client voice. Client voice can prove prohibitively costly to the client, particularly those with limited financial resources, and to the lawyer.[33] The lure of settlement also can motivate the lawyer to challenge the client's reality and compromise client voice. Lawyers must confront and alter unrealistic client expectations in order to facilitate settlement.[34] They also frequently must oppose a client's perception of her spouse as unreliable and blameworthy in order to convince the client to negotiate and to trust the spouse to live up to a negotiated settlement.[35] Inevitably, then, some social facts that the client considers important will require exclusion or transformation, which can diminish meaningful client voice.[36]

Other aspects of the lawyer–client relationship hinder client voice. Suspicion as well as interdependence lie at the foundation of the lawyer–client relationship.[37] Clients doubt their lawyers' commitment to them, worry about controlling the content and timing of their lawyers' actions, and wonder whether their busy lawyers have sufficient time to address the idiosyncrasies of their cases. Clients also express concern about their lawyers' divided loyalties, competence, judgment, and personality.[38] Anxiety can discourage candor in the stories that clients tell their lawyers.

Lawyers, too, have concerns that obstruct their ability or willingness to hear their clients. Divorce attorneys fret about their clients' emotionalism,[39] their ambivalence about the impending divorce, their inability to understand what their lawyers tell them, their vindictiveness toward their spouses,[40] their distortion of reality, and their unrealistic expectations.[41] These concerns cause lawyers to deflect, ignore, or respond negatively to some of what their clients say.[42] Yet some divorce lawyers believe that listening to the client's emotional concerns has great importance.[43] Others attempt to control excessive client emotionalism by maintaining a rigidly rational stance that appears callous and disloyal to distraught clients.[44]

Although studies reveal limitations on client voice, they also suggest that divorce attorneys not only do, but must, allow their clients at least some voice during representation. Chambers concludes in his review of Felstiner and Sarat's study that,

> In the end, the reader is left uncertain how much power clients exercise, other than evanescent power over the direction of a conversation. At the end of the last substantive chapter, on resolution through settlement, the clients seem powerless (and seem to feel powerless) in almost every conventional sense; the lawyers control the negotiation with the other side, the clients feel excluded, and the clients' efforts to control "meaning" in the earlier discussions seem to have had only modest effect on the terms of the negotiation the lawyers pursue. The book convincingly demonstrates that during their meetings with their attorneys, clients "resist the power that lawyers seek to exercise" in ways that have not been previously anticipated. Yet, it remains unclear whether the clients would believe that they exercised power in any way that was meaningful to them.[45]

Consistent with Chambers' insight, divorce clients continue to complain about inattentiveness, insensitivity, and neglect by their lawyers, suggesting their frustration with insufficient voice.[46] The consistency and pervasiveness of these complaints suggest that lawyers and the family law system would benefit if legal procedures encouraged communication between lawyers and clients[47] as well as client participation. This is not to suggest, however, that adequate voice necessarily requires client autonomy in decision making: Certainly some clients will want their lawyers to pursue goals their lawyers consider immoral or unnecessarily destructive. I do not think that lawyers can or should blindly defer to their clients' demands,[48] particularly in divorce cases, where destructive emotions run high and the issues have great importance. A lawyer can, however, provide a client with meaningful voice short of decisional autonomy.

GENDERED CONSTRAINTS ON VOICE

In addition to the generic restrictions on voice experienced by both men and women, women face additional practical, social, and psychological obstacles to adequate voice.[49]

FINANCIAL DISPARITIES

As the U.S. Supreme Court has noted, "the right to be heard would be, in many cases, of little avail if it did not comprehend the right to be heard by counsel."[50] Yet the financial dependency of wives on husbands[51] restricts women's access to independent legal representation.[52] Husbands characteristically control the marital financial resources and restrict the wife's access to them during divorce.[53] Judges rarely award temporary maintenance[54] or attorney fees[55] that might allow a wife independent representation. Wives who seek independent legal representation often cannot find it, because lawyers understand that wives frequently cannot pay. Consequently, many wives proceed without legal representation[56] or agree to joint representation by lawyers their husbands have chosen.[57]

Even if both spouses can afford attorneys, frequently the wife must hire a less expensive and less competent lawyer.[58] Wives who initially can afford to hire lawyers may run out of funds during the lengthy divorce process.[59] Limited financial resources leave wives vulnerable to numerous adversarial tactics that prolong the divorce process and increase their expenses.[60] Husbands' attorneys may delay, file frivolous motions, and fail to comply with discovery requests.[61] Husbands themselves may foil discovery and conceal assets.[62] On the streets, attorneys call this common tactic "starving her out."[63] When women clients can no longer pay, lawyers sometimes abandon them or provide inadequate representation.[64]

A wife's inadequate financial resources may prevent her or her attorney from participating in a manner that effectively promotes her interests.[65] Because husbands generally control the marital financial resources, sometimes conceal assets,[66] or deliberately misrepresent the value of these assets,[67] the wife frequently must conduct expensive discovery. If she cannot afford discovery, she will lack the information she needs to effectively express her interests during negotiation or at trial.[68] Many wives simply cannot afford discovery.[69] And, if the wife's attorney attempts discovery, the courts often do not enforce the request.[70] Without adequate tools to detect and present one's interests, voice frequently becomes mute.

Once the parties identify the marital assets, they must retain appraisers or financial consultants to value them. Expert services add expenses that the wife can ill-afford.[71] Moreover, courts rarely award adequate expert fees in divorce cases.[72] Even if the wife can afford to employ some experts, the husband often can hire more convincing experts with better credentials. Without adequate expert assistance, the wife has difficulty determining and voicing her interests.

ROLE ALLOCATIONS

A wife's caretaking responsibilities within the family also can limit her ability to express her concerns at divorce. Despite the increase in egalitarian sex role attitudes, wives still retain primary responsibility for homemaking and child rearing.[73] Her socialization as a caregiver and the validation that she receives from her husband and children, and from society, for behavior that conforms to unspoken expectations of self-sacrifice[74] secure her acceptance of these roles. The importance the wife places on these roles encourages her to place greater value on custody of the children than does her husband.[75] A custody loss not only would unacceptably alter her relationship with the children, it would deeply violate her sense of self.[76] A mother about to divorce, then, may feel compelled to limit her financial requests if her husband threatens a custody dispute.[77] She also may limit her voice on custody and visitation arrangements out of fear of losing custody altogether.[78] The wife's meager financial resources and biased legal decision makers can make her fear even more salient, for she knows that she cannot, and that he can, hire necessary attorneys and experts.[79] Winner tells Cyndi's particularly disturbing story:

> Cyndi, a working mother from New York said the court papers were filled with falsehoods about her ability as a mother, which Cyndi had to defend herself against. She knew that in reality her husband did not want custody, because he had expressed little desire to care for the children. The father's real goal was to get out of paying child support. If he obtained custody, Cyndi, as the noncustodial parent, would be legally responsible for paying child support. Cyndi's husband and his lawyer convinced the judge through false statements that she was not as good a mother as he was a father. The judge believed him and Cyndi lost custody. But not too long afterward, and unknown to the court, her ex-husband sent the kids to live with her. Cyndi is still paying her husband child support, even though she is now the de facto custodial parent. She told me she would rather keep her kids, even if it means paying child support too, because they mean more to her than anything. She fears having to go back to court to reopen the custody dispute, but adds that the current situation is also hard for her. If she does something to displease her ex-husband she knows that he can wrench the children away at any time, as their lawful custodial parent.[80]

INTANGIBLE RESOURCE DISPARITIES

Many psychological factors or socialized tendencies cause wives significant problems with adequate voice compared to husbands.[81] These intangible resource disparities between men and women in general, and between husbands and wives in particular, prove important. Lawyers negotiate many divorce settlements for their clients and arguably insulate women who can afford their services from the consequences of intangible resource disparities. However, as noted earlier, many wives lack the financial resources to hire lawyers. These wives must express their interests directly to their husbands in hopes of being heard. Moreover, as discussed earlier, many lawyers represent wives poorly, allow or encourage their clients to negotiate directly with their husbands, or serve merely as clerks who shepherd through the courts an agreement reached privately by the husband and wife. Consequently, even when lawyers represent wives, intangible resource disparities frequently have a direct impact on the ability of wives to express their interests effectively. Moreover, when a lawyer does negotiate competently for a wife, the wife's gendered tendencies may interfere with the lawyer's ability to secure the wife's permission to advocate strongly for her interests. Finally, increasing numbers of wives and husbands proceed pro se or participate in mediation without representation. In these informal settings, they negotiate directly with one another, and financial dependency, as well as gendered tendencies, bear immediately on the adequacy of the wife's voice.[82]

NAIVE TRUST

Many wives naively trust their husbands,[83] their lawyers, and the legal system during the divorce process.[84] The wife's trust of her husband may encourage her to assume that she does not need her own lawyer to protect her interests and that her husband will treat her fairly at divorce.[85] Some wives agree to representation by attorneys that their husbands or their husbands' lawyers have chosen.[86] Other perceive discovery as unnecessary, because they trust their husbands to define accurately, to value fairly, and even to divide appropriately, the marital assets.[87] Naive trust dulls the wife's perception of her need for independent voice and representation.

While many couples today exhibit egalitarian attitudes about marriage, the traditional division of labor within the family seems quite intractable.[88] Certainly more wives than ever now participate in the work force and share the burden of providing for the family.[89] Yet husbands exercise greater control over marital decision making than wives, particularly important financial decisions.[90] The husband's authority over financial issues encourages the wife to accept his definition and valuation of the marital property. She may naively fail to recognize her need for expert verification in order to adequately express and protect her interests, particularly if she lacks the resources to hire that expert.[91]

The wife's trust in the justice of the legal system and in the integrity of her lawyer also discourages her from exercising the vigilance needed to protect her interests. As Winner notes,

> Women . . . are more likely [than men] to regard the system idealistically, believing perhaps too literally in the image of the blindfolded lady holding up the scales of justice. It is little wonder that so many women made poorer by their divorces use the same words to describe this misplaced trust in the system, saying, "I was so naive—I was a babe in the woods."[92]

Moreover, when a wife finally understands that her husband is indifferent to her needs, that the judge harbors bias against her, or that her lawyer has unjustly or incompetently compromised her case, she becomes frightened and disheartened. The brutality of the transition from the mindset of the family to that of law and the market can stun and confuse her,[93] leaving her ill-equipped to assertively voice her interests during divorce negotiations or at trial. Some wives seem so stunned by their attorneys' claims that the law provides no more than the meager offers before them that they acquiesce without question or contest.[94]

THE ETHIC OF CARE

Many have written about women's ethic of care, their distinctive orientation toward moral issues.[95] The literature suggests that women tend to care more for others than for themselves,[96] whereas men exhibit more individualistic tendencies.[97] In the family, where women are socially conditioned to perform as caretakers,[98] this tendency becomes more pronounced.[99]

Although care for others and attendance to relationships has great value, this orientation may create voice problems for wives. Negotiation, mediation, and trial contexts assume that two self-interested individuals will voice and pursue their individual interests,[100] an assumption contrary to women's orientation. Moreover, as noted before, a husband's threat to contest custody may weaken severely the voice of a care-oriented wife.[101] Wives' relational orientation also encourages them to focus on the emotional issues in divorce, sometimes to the exclusion of financial concerns.[102] Husbands, on the other hand, tend to treat the divorce more as a business transaction[103] that necessitates assertive, self-interested financial negotiations. Winner relates:

"Being nice" to her husband during the divorce was the main concern of Rae Logan, Director of the State Bond Commission in Louisiana. Logan concedes: "I was so concerned about being nice. He got the Fiat, the savings account, and the girlfriend. I got the bills, the furniture, and the children. It was my fault. I was so concerned with maintaining his image. I was concerned with not being seen as the stereotypical "'hysterical' divorcee." Many women, to their own disadvantage, are simply not culturally geared to think about money at the time of divorce.[104]

STATUS

Status significantly influences the adequacy of voice, because people grant authority to high status persons,[105] as well as defer to the opinions of, and succumb, knowingly or unconsciously, to the influence of high status persons.[106] Income, education, occupational rank, and sex determine an individual's status.[107] During divorce proceedings, husbands tend to have higher status than their wives,[108] encouraging others, including attorneys, judges, mediators, and wives, to defer to them. Moreover, women's lower status relative to men makes women easier to influence than men and promotes their greater tendency to conform[109]—troublesome traits in negotiations that demand assertiveness.

SELF-ESTEEM

People with high self-esteem more effectively voice their concerns and negotiate better outcomes than do those with low self-esteem.[110] High self-esteem also leaves one less vulnerable to the influence of others.[111] In contrast, low self-esteem can inhibit bargaining ability and encourage acceptance of unfavorable settlements.[112] For a variety of reasons, many women have low self-esteem,[113] and women have lower self-esteem than do men.[114] Divorce exacerbates the disparity in self-esteem between men and women, because the loss of marital status depresses the wife's self-esteem more than it does the husband's.[115] Divorcing wives with low self-esteem may become vulnerable to their husbands' or their attorneys' attempts to influence them, diminishing their voice and making it more likely that they will accept poor offers.[116]

DEPRESSION

Depression has a devastating impact on a person's ability to assertively voice their interests and negotiate effectively,[117] and truly depressed persons predictably fare poorly in negotiations.[118] Generally women suffer far more from depression than do men.[119] Married couples exhibit an even greater difference in depression between men and women.[120] At divorce, the wife's acquisition of unfamiliar roles (primary breadwinner, single parent), her loss of the valued role of wife, and her predictable financial problems enhance the likelihood of her depression.[121]

EXPECTATIONS

People who negotiate with higher expectations tend to obtain more than people with lower expectations.[122] Women expect less than men for their contributions.[123] At divorce, wives may have difficulty voicing objectively reasonable requests, consequently obtaining a smaller share of the marital assets than do their husbands.[124]

ASSERTIVE BARGAINING TACTICS

Competitive bargaining over scarce marital resources[125] normally induces competitive negotiation tactics.[126] A reluctance to assertively counter such tactics can disadvantage a party. Several factors discourage women from using assertive conflict resolution styles in divorce negotiations.[127] In the early 1970s, Matina Horner found that women were inhibited in achievement-oriented behavior.[128] Women saw their feminine sex role identity as inconsistent with displays of competence, independence, competition, intellectual acumen, and leadership.[129] They feared that engagement in such displays risked social rejection, loss of femininity, and personal or social destruction.[130] Many had high ability and cared about achievement;[131] nevertheless, even when they knew their success necessitated competitive behavior, they hesitated to behave in that fashion.[132] Their greatest hesitation occurred when they competed with men[133] or when important males, particularly husbands or intimates, or parents, disapproved of their achievement-oriented behavior.[134]

Although Horner conducted this research over 30 years ago and women's worlds undoubtedly have changed since then, more recent research suggests the continuing viability of Horner's findings. Susan Pollak and Carol Gilligan found that a greater percentage of women than men associate violence with competitive success.[135] Other research confirms that men as well as women feel threatened when women dominate in an achievement situation.[136] Taken together, these findings suggest that women tend to avoid competition and to perform beneath their abilities in competitive situations, particularly when they compete with males to whom they closely relate.

Research indicates that women, in fact, tend to employ weak, indirect tactics, whereas men tend to use strong, direct tactics.[137]

Women also exhibit greater reluctance than men to behave competitively in situations in which competition meets with disapproval.[138] A wife's assertive demands in divorce negotiations often meet with her husband's, and sometimes with her attorney's, disapproval. She often then abandons those demands.[139]

When couples resolve marital conflicts, wives tend to accommodate, compromise, and facilitate more than their husbands.[140] Moreover, a study of distressed married couples suggests that wives have more difficulty asserting themselves in conversations with their husbands than they do in conversations with other men.[141] Spouses inevitably bring their marital conflict resolution styles to the divorce negotiation table,[142] compromising the wife's ability to voice and protect her interests.[143]

THE SPECIAL CASE OF THE ABUSED SPOUSE

Many wives suffer physical abuse, emotional abuse, or both from their husbands,[144] and a high percentage of divorcing wives have experienced domestic violence.[145] Abused wives face nearly insurmountable problems expressing their interests effectively during divorce.

Typically, abusive husbands establish and enforce stringent rules that govern their wives' and their children's behavior.[146] These rules demand that the wife focus exclusively and continually on fulfillment of the abuser's needs, however he defines them. Abused wives frequently internalize these rules.[147] Moreover, to avoid the violence that results if they challenge or break these rules,[148] many battered women routinely comply with the batterer's articulated or anticipated demands.[149] At divorce, a woman who believes that she has survived by fulfillment of the batterer's needs and by compliance with his rules may have extreme difficulty in identifying and voicing her own interests.[150]

The risk of violence escalates when the abused wife attempts to break the abuser's control when she leaves him.[151] She may sense this heightened danger[152] and hesitate to voice any requests for property or maintenance that will ruffle his feathers—trading, in her mind, her life for their assets.[153] Additionally, batterers frequently isolate their victims from family and friends,[154] depriving their wives of the emotional support they might need to assert themselves. Many abused wives also are averse to risk, feel guilty about fracturing the family,[155] suffer low self-esteem[156] and depression,[157] have low expectations,[158] feel terror,[159] have difficulty concentrating,[160] and frequently are passive.[161] Finally, battered wives simply may lack the financial knowledge necessary to accurately assess their financial needs and develop realistic financial demands. Each of these factors severely compromises a battered wife's ability to adequately voice her concerns.[162]

Because of this, abused women typically need a lawyer's assistance to identify and express their interests. Many abused wives, however, cannot afford legal counsel.[163] Abusive husbands typically exercise extreme financial control,[164] leaving their wives without the funds they need to hire attorneys. Moreover, the abuser likely has compromised his victim's work performance and participation, making her a less than desirable employee.[165] Even after separation, she may have difficulty locating employment and earning the funds she needs to hire a lawyer.[166]

If a battered woman can afford an attorney, her attorney may not comprehend her interests.[167] Many abused wives resist identifying themselves as abused.[168] An uneducated lawyer may not discover the abuse[169] and may misapprehend and misrepresent her needs. If a wife does reveal abuse, many lawyers do not listen or minimize the importance of the violence.[170] Even lawyers who listen to and believe their clients frequently fail to bring the abuse to the court's attention.[171]

If a judge does not know that a wife has experienced abuse, he or she also may misunderstand the wife's communications and fail to detect the wife's and the children's financial and safety needs. Even when judges hear that violence has occurred, they commonly disbelieve what they have heard or minimize its importance.[172] Simply put, abused wives encounter significant difficultly with voice in the face of ignorant and biased lawyers and judges.

An abused mother's fear of losing custody also may dampen her willingness to voice her financial concerns[173] or assertively pursue a custody and visitation arrangement that offers her and the children sufficient protection.[174] Mothers frequently leave their batterers in order to protect their children.[175] Their abusive husbands, however, commonly threaten to take the children if their wives leave them.[176] At divorce, a battered mother most likely anticipates and fears a custody dispute. Many batterers do pursue child custody as a way to perpetuate control over their victims.[177] The many factors noted earlier that compromise her case for custody lend credence to her fear and induce her to limit her voice.[178]

If a battered wife and her abusive husband settle their divorce dispute through mediation, meaningful voice seems even less likely.[179] In close proximity with her abuser and without the shield of a lawyer, an abused wife may revert to survival patterns and defer to her abuser's spoken or unspoken wishes. Or, she deliberately may constrain her voice in order to avoid additional violence. Mediators claim that they can balance power, perhaps by meeting separately with each spouse. The extreme power disparities between an abused wife and her violent husband, however, defy balancing[180] and ensure the wife's inadequate voice. Moreover, many mediators who claim knowledge about and sensitivity to domestic violence exhibit the same bias against battered women as judges, lawyers, and mental health professionals.[181]

The numerous practical, social, and psychological constraints on women's voice illustrate the legal system's extreme procedural inadequacy. Inadequate voice also links directly to poor outcomes.[182] If the system hinders women's ability to identify, investigate, and effectively pursue their concerns, one can anticipate the poor outcomes for women and their dependent children noted at the beginning of this book. We turn next to an assessment of whether accurate information currently informs divorce decisions.

ACCURATE INFORMATION

To ensure quality outcomes, the public wants accurate information to inform decision making.[183] We already have explored many factors that compromise information accuracy. The generic and gendered constraints on voice we just reviewed substantially limit the ability of parties to access and present accurate information to decision makers. Lawyers far too frequently fail to conduct discovery, and when they do, party and lawyer refusal to cooperate and judicial reluctance to enforce discovery requests prevent the acquisition of needed information. The common phenomenon of uninformed settlement on the courthouse steps[184] suggests that limited information, at best, informs these settlements.[185] Parties themselves conceal and distort information. One can only speculate on the information pro se parties acquire before settlement or litigation. And, even when parties do offer accurate information, uneducated or biased decision makers do not use that information to make quality decisions. Rather, as we have seen, ignorance and bias taint that information and result in poor and sometimes outrageous decisions.

Judges can appoint independent evaluators in custody disputes to counter the incomplete information presented by parties. As we have seen, however, many of these evaluators lack competence, perform poorly, and exhibit bias on the relevant issues. And judges themselves far too frequently refuse to accept evidence that they find distasteful.

This brief summary reiterates what we already know: Divorce decisions get made on the basis of inaccurate information and, predictably, these decisions lack quality. It also suggests that procedural reforms should facilitate the acquisition of information without significant cost, should constrain decision maker bias, and should mitigate decision maker incompetence. The link between this procedural goal and substantive justice seems obvious. Informed, unbiased, and educated decision makers promise better outcomes than those currently reached. We next explore system efficiency.

SYSTEM EFFICIENCY

Legal authorities recognize that a dispute resolution system should provide parties with a timely and affordable opportunity to resolve their disputes.[186] State legislatures, and more recently the federal government, deplore the inefficiency of the legal system generally.[187] Yet efficiency concerns seem particularly acute in divorce cases. Clients complain vehemently about legal fees.[188] Fear of costs leads more and more parties to proceed without legal representation.[189] Lawyers, too, fret about the cost of divorce[190] and recognize that many, particularly women, cannot afford their services.[191]

Congested court dockets delay case resolution, and divorce cases make a significant contribution. Estimates indicate that divorce cases account for 25% to 50% of all state court civil dockets.[192] Sometimes years pass between the filing and the final resolution of a divorce case, and judges themselves blame divorce cases for their overloaded civil dockets.[193] For all concerned, inefficiency in the family law system has reached crisis proportions.[194]

Some of the expense and delay associated with divorce undoubtedly results from the sheer number of divorce cases filed in our courts. Yet, as we have seen, parties and lawyers resolve at least 90% of divorce cases through settlement or default rather than judicial decree, suggesting that factors other than crowded dockets affect delay.

It should not by now be a surprise that clients themselves contribute to system inefficiency. Some cases proceed slowly because a party cannot identify what goals to pursue.[195] Some clients change their minds midstream,[196] and others seem more concerned with revenge than quick resolution.[197] Unrealistic expectations[198] and emotionalism[199] also inhibit settlement. One party may deliberately stall resolution in order to force the financially dependent spouse into an unfair outcome. And, some clients fail to cooperate with their lawyers.[200] No matter how well-intended, a lawyer cannot complete a financial affidavit or respond to a discovery request until the client provides relevant information.

Attorneys also cause delay. Clients complain that attorneys neglect cases for substantial periods of time. Some lawyers employ tactics that generate hostilities between parties that in turn inhibit early settlement.[201] Lawyers, as well as clients, sometimes promote delay to gain a negotiation advantage[202] or to acquire time to bring unrealistic clients into line.[203] Other attorneys deliberately draw out the divorce process because they realize that protracted disputes generate larger fees.[204]

Although this book focuses on procedure, indeterminate laws and inconsistent judicial decisions contribute significantly to delay and costs, because they encourage litigation and hinder settlement.[205] Unpredictable outcomes provide no check on a party's expectations, and the possibility of success in litigation continues to entice,[206] particularly clients with financial resources. Protracted settlement negotiations occur because lawyers cannot use predictable outcomes to confirm their client's rights and encourage agreement.[207] Even clients may balk at settlements when their lawyers cannot use law and precedent to convince them that the settlement reflects their rights. Although legislatures may never implement more determinate property distribution, spousal maintenance, and child custody laws, we can encourage sophisticated actors to render more consistent decisions.

This discussion also suggests that procedural reforms should encourage early and informed settlements, require lawyers and clients to share the information necessary for quality settlements, adjust unrealistic lawyer and client expectations, intercept destructive lawyer and client tactics, and reserve trial to those cases that require it.

PRO SE ACTIONS

As noted earlier, growing numbers of parties represent themselves in divorce,[208] particularly, but not always,[209] those who lack the resources to hire counsel.[210] By 1995 in California, for example, pro se parties brought 65% of California divorces,[211] and more recent data suggest that self-representation occurs in 75% of these cases.[212] Presumably pro se divorces cost parties less than those with legal representation. And some evidence suggests that pro se divorce cases conclude faster[213] and produce at least as much party satisfaction with their divorce decrees and the legal process than others that involve attorneys.[214] Although pro se divorces might seem more efficient for parties than represented divorces, to the extent that we seek to reduce court congestion, we also must consider their impact on the courts.

Pro se parties who settle their cases consume little judicial time, and most of them do seem to settle.[215] They do, however, consume substantial amounts of time of, sometimes hostile,[216] court personnel[217] straining further an already stressed system. Depending on the judge, pro se parties who do litigate can consume large amounts of judicial time.

Courts generally differ in the way they treat pro se litigants.[218] Some judges accord self-represented litigants no special treatment,[219] whereas others feel obligated to assist a disadvantaged pro se party.[220] A legally unsophisticated pro se party who attempts to introduce irrelevant evidence at trial, for instance, requires the judge to explain why he or she cannot allow admission or to admit unnecessary evidence the judge does not want to hear.[221] One judge to whom I spoke believed that most judges err on the side of admission, in order to placate the pro se litigant or to avoid a lengthy and sometimes futile explanation of a technical legal concept. Pro se settlement might clear some judicial time, but pro se litigation frequently does the opposite. This suggests that procedural reform should systematically address the efficiency concerns raised by pro se litigants.

A final concern needs mention. For many reasons, legal actors express a systemic preference for settlement. As one commentator notes and cautions,

> Allowing men and women to enter enforceable divorce contracts recognizes their rights-bearing citizenship, honors their autonomy, and places them on equal legal footing with one another. Moreover, the parties themselves generally prefer settlement to adjudication, believing rightly or wrongly, that an agreement reached through negotiation will better reflect their private preferences than would an adjudicated result. Liberal theory maintains that, unless private preferences severely compromise important state interests, the state should not interfere. Feminist theorists also observe that honoring women's freedom to contract is a step away from patriarchy, which historically considered women unsuited for autonomous decisionmaking.
>
> Practical arguments also seem to favor settlement. Settlement, some claim, promotes the efficient resolution of divorce disputes, lowering the costs of divorce for disputants and for the legal system. Proponents also argue that settlement produces results superior to those generated by adjudication. Parties, they claim, possess more information than courts and thus can make better decisions. Disputants can incorporate a wider range of values and interests than courts, generating agreements more responsive to individual needs and interests than judicial orders. Divorcing husbands and wives can "enhance their personhood" through respectful negotiations, rather than demean one another in the dehumanizing process of adjudication. Moreover, by compromising or trading off their interests, spouses can avoid the destructive winner-take-all results sometimes produced by adjudication. Finally, proponents claim that negotiated settlements generate greater party satisfaction and compliance than do judicial orders, an attractive argument in a system currently riddled with dissatisfaction and noncompliance.[222]

Court efficiency supports this conventional wisdom. Although lawyer-brokered settlements do not guarantee cost and time savings to parties, they do alleviate court congestion. Pro se settlements may provide parties a cheaper and faster route to divorce, as well as lighten court dockets. Pro se settlements seem particularly attractive for simple cases that do not raise issues of property distribution, spousal maintenance, or child custody or visitation.[223]

In all cases that do involve property and support issues, however, settlements reached with or without the assistance of lawyers raise substantive justice concerns. Because settlement resolves approximately 95% of divorce cases, settlement accounts for most of the dysfunctional outcomes noted at the beginning of this book. Presumably pro se parties, particularly women, will experience the same or worse pressures to accept unfair settlements[224] as those represented by lawyers.[225] And, although represented parties may have some idea of their legal rights, pro se parties may have no such knowledge.[226] If only one party has representation, which occurs in at least 30% of cases,[227] the pro se party may rely on deliberately misleading information provided by the attorney.[228] One study indicates that pro se parties do not pursue temporary orders,[229] even though temporary maintenance might allow the financially dependent spouse to withstand the negotiation process and secure a decent settlement. Likewise, pro se parties less frequently request spousal maintenance than represented parties.[230]

We have no idea how children fare in pro se divorce, and we only can imagine the difficulties a battered wife would have in negotiations with her abusive husband.[231] We simply cannot encourage settlement, whether reached in represented or pro se divorce, for efficiency reasons, unless we also provide a mechanism to monitor quality. Our concern for short-term efficiencies cannot obscure the long-term social and economic costs caused by poor settlements.

HOSTILITY REDUCTION

Research does not strongly indicate that people perceive hostility reduction as an important component of procedural justice.[232] Most of the rhetoric about the importance of hostility reduction comes, instead, from mediation proponents.[233] Moreover, hostility reduction cannot take priority over other important goals. A dominant husband might respond angrily to an order to pay spousal maintenance, but his dependent wife's financial security must take priority. Denial of an abusive spouse's request for custody might anger that parent, yet the child's safety must take priority. Nevertheless, hostility reduction is included here as a procedural goal primarily because continued hostility between divorced parents can compromise their children's well-being.[234] Acrimonious and protracted divorce also implicates efficiency concerns and can generate long-lasting bitterness.

What about divorce generates hostility? Understandably divorce itself generates myriad emotions, including anger. Divorce threatens identity, fractures dreams, and jeopardizes financial security and relationships with children. Divorce can shred the entire social fabric of a person's life. Many people, understandably, react with a degree of hostility.[235] Yet some parties exhibit dysfunctional levels of hostility and seem hell-bent on punishment of the other spouse.[236] If their lawyers cannot control them, these parties behave in ways that inevitably provoke the anger of their spouses.

Although parties themselves sometimes bear responsibility for unnecessary hostility, legal actors and procedures also make a contribution. Popular myth offers divorce lawyers who encourage hostile contests.[237] Judges believe that divorce lawyers behave aggressively, distrust one another, pick apart the bones of their opponents, create false issues, and drive divorcing parties apart emotionally and psychologically.[238] Some attorneys and judges hold unnecessary adversarial tactics responsible for violence committed by divorced men against ex-spouses, divorce lawyers, and judges.[239]

Certain lawyer tactics undoubtedly create or exacerbate hostility between divorce parties. Behaviors we noted earlier, such as disrespectful treatment of the opposing spouse or lawyer, overly zealous empathy with a client, failure to respond to routine discovery requests, threats, deliberate concealment of assets, creation of false issues, and lying provide but a few examples.[240] Attorneys who advise their clients not to pay temporary support in order to gain a settlement advantage predictably cause the wife to resent her husband. Anger simmers, and she may retaliate by restriction of the husband's access to the children. Her actions, in turn, anger him and tempt him to treat her even more harshly. Crowded dockets, because they prevent timely resolution, invite the use of adversarial tactics to force advantageous settlement.

Although some lawyers use tactics that foster hostilities, research and common sense suggest that not all lawyers engage in these tactics. Researchers find that many divorce attorneys behave in a hyper-rational and detached manner in order to compensate for their clients' emotionalism.[241] Lawyers also attempt to diffuse client anger in order to promote settlement.[242] Consequently, although some lawyers undoubtedly employ tactics that generate hostility, lawyers alone cannot bear the total responsibility for anger between ex-spouses.

Indeterminate divorce laws also encourage anger, because they reward parties who employ adversarial tactics. If the law indicated the inevitability of a particular result, for example, attorneys and clients would have less motivation to delay. In contrast, indeterminate law encourages delay because it inspires the hope of securing a better result.[243] Indeterminacy also fails to provide clear standards for attorneys and parties to employ in negotiation. Instead, spousal maintenance, property distribution, and child custody remain open for sometimes heated argument.[244] Judges themselves inadvertently provoke hostilities, because they frequently render inconsistent decisions. Different judges grant like parties different awards. Worse, the same judge frequently grants like parties different awards.[245] Just as indeterminate law promotes contentious negotiations, so too does judicial inconsistency.[246]

Judicial disrespect for divorce disputants and their rights also encourages hostilities. One Utah judge told a wife to "get down on [your] hands and knees and pray about what [you are] doing."[247] This judge then awarded custody of the children to the husband, because he disapproved of the wife's desire to work full-time. He told her that she now could "go to the big city, work full-time, and see what it's like."[248] Disrespectful judicial treatment threatens the individual's self-worth and generates anger. It also invites the other party to ridicule and disrespect that spouse. Judicial restriction of voice or participation also exacerbates the anger and pain caused by divorce.

Adversarial trials, particularly of child issues,[249] that competitively pit one spouse against the other can exacerbate hostilities.[250] Typically parents retain experts who compete with one another to denigrate and distort the other parent's relationship with the child.[251] Parents themselves vie to gather negative information about their spouses. Feelings of betrayal replace those of trust. Personal facts expose parents to public ridicule. Parties endure hostile cross-examinations. Anger results, and preexisting anger solidifies.[252]

Unfair results generate anger.[253] A caretaking parent who loses custody to a spouse who spent little time with the child undoubtedly experiences anger. A mother who lives in poverty with her children while her ex-husband enjoys the fruits of joint marital labors undoubtedly experiences anger.[254] A 60-year-old traditional homemaker of 30 years forced to abandon her lifelong middle-class lifestyle undoubtedly experiences anger.[255] Noncompliance also fuels postdivorce anger.[256] Unpaid support places many women and dependent children in jeopardy and understandably precipitates hostilities. A caring father whose ex-wife denies him visitation with his child understandably feels anger.

This suggests that, in order to reduce postdivorce hostilities reforms should intercept and discourage adversarial tactics, encourage respectful judicial treatment, de-emphasize adversarial trial of custody issues, offer more predictable and better outcomes, and encourage compliance.

PROCEDURAL CONSISTENCY

Consistent procedures treat similar people similarly across time.[257] Parties assess procedural consistency by comparison of their current treatment to their previous experiences, to their expectations of the treatment they should receive, and to what they think others have experienced, especially those close to them.[258]

For many citizens, divorce provides their only exposure to legal procedures. They have no previous experience that informs their assessment of procedural consistency. Those parties with experience in other legal disputes, however, will compare their earlier exposure to their divorce encounter.[259] Many aspects of the divorce reality we already have explored suggest that the procedural experiences of divorce disputants will vary greatly from those they encountered in previous legal contexts. Less respectful treatment, bias, and voice restrictions provide a few examples.

Divorce parties' complaints indicate that decision makers, lawyers and judges alike, do not treat them in ways that fulfill their expectations. Clients claim that lawyers do not listen, neglect cases, tell clients they cannot achieve what clients want, exhibit bias, treat them and their rights with disrespect, and charge too much for their services. Regardless of whether these complaints have merit, they do indicate that lawyers fail to fulfill client expectations of lawyer treatment. Little wonder that many divorce clients seem disillusioned and ambivalent about their experiences with their lawyers.

We already have seen that judges, too, frequently behave inconsistently with parties' expectations. Parties seem shocked that judges treat them and their rights with disrespect and sometimes exhibit outright hostility to their cases. Judicial bias shocks parties, as does judicial restriction of voice. Judges chide parties for their failure to settle, and they refuse to accept distasteful evidence. The reaction of divorce parties to their treatment by judges clearly indicates that judges frequently fail to treat them as they expected.

Most people know others who have divorced. A party then can compare the experiences of others with their own to assess procedural consistency. Lawyers note procedural inconsistencies within the system,[260] and many people find their procedural expectations violated in divorce. If a party's experience proves consistent with the previous negative experience of a friend, perhaps no threat to procedural consistency exists. This seems a particularly unsatisfactory justification, however, for the continuation of current defective practices. Although a system can gain some acceptance if it processes all disputes in a similar manner, certainly that practice itself first must have some merit.

Other factors might influence parties' perception of procedural consistency. If a friend obtained a hearing in a small claims court within three months of filing, a divorce disputant unrealistically may expect his divorce to conclude within that time period. If a party obtained temporary maintenance early in a previous divorce proceeding, she unrealistically may expect temporary maintenance early in a subsequent action. If the lawyer for a party's sister conducted extensive formal discovery that uncovered hidden marital assets, that party may expect extensive discovery in her own divorce proceeding. This suggests that attention to procedural consistency, and parties' expectations of treatment, would increase procedural justice perceptions.

Although the focus here is on procedure, it must be acknowledged that "outcome" consistency also affects peoples' judgment about the legitimacy of a legal system. People expect a just legal system to produce consistent outcomes.[261] People in like circumstances should receive like awards. As noted earlier, outcomes produced in divorce cases vary wildly. Some traditional homemakers in long-term marriages receive permanent spousal maintenance; others, whose husbands earn equivalent amounts, do not. Courts sometimes divide marital property equally between spouses, and some make unequal awards that usually favor husbands. Sometimes the parent with the closer bond to the child receives custody, and sometimes the parent who abused the child receives custody.

Lawyers themselves warn their clients to settle to avoid the arbitrary nature of judges and litigation.[262] The dizzying array of inconsistent results leads the public,[263] and many divorce attorneys, to conclude that the system operates arbitrarily, divorced from the rule of law and the demand of rational consistency.[264] Attention, then, to substantive as well as procedural consistency seems advisable.

THE OPPORTUNITY TO CORRECT DECISIONAL ERRORS

Procedural justice next requires an opportunity to correct decisional errors.[265] Finality certainly has its virtues. It allows disputants to turn their attention and resources elsewhere. Divorce disputants, and their children in particular, need to restore psychological and emotional equilibrium. State interference in private lives must end. Too much flexibility and fluidity lead only to instability, injustice, and ultimately threaten the rule of law.[266] Yet bad decisions sometimes get made and deserve correction. The current family law system fails to provide any meaningful opportunity to correct error.

Generally, divorce decisions get made in one of four ways: (a) the parties litigate contested issues, and the court enters a final judgment; (b) the respondent never answers the petition or fails to comply with discovery requests,[267] and the court enters a default judgment;[268] (c) the parties or lawyers introduce a settlement agreement at final hearing for judicial approval and incorporation into the final judgment of dissolution; or (d) prior to marriage the parties enter an agreement that governs the support and property issues at divorce. As noted earlier, approximately 90% of divorce cases fit into the last three categories.[269] Consequently, we must explore the opportunity to correct settlement and default errors, as well as judicial mistakes.

TRIAL COURT ERROR

If a party thinks a judge erred at trial, states generally provide that party with an opportunity to request that the trial court reconsider its opinion.[270] Given judicial distaste for divorce cases and docket pressures, any attempt to convince a judge to rehear a disputed issue likely will meet with defeat and close that avenue for correction. A disgruntled party, of course, may appeal a trial judge's decision to a higher court. Appellate judges apply an abuse of discretion standard that is highly deferential to trial courts[271] and that limits the appellate court's authority to find error.[272] Moreover, the ambiguity of divorce law makes it difficult for an appellate court to find a clear abuse of discretion.[273] Consider, for instance, the following situation: Assume that state custody law prohibits a judge from making a custody decision based on the parent's sex. The trial judge, however, deep in his heart believes that women make better custodial parents than men. He ignores the father's superior parenting and places the child with the mother. To avoid reversal on appeal, our judge need only justify his opinion by reference to any permissible custody criteria. The appellate court has no grounds to overturn, provided the record contains minimal facts to support the judge's opinion.[274] Only when a judge baldly exposes the error of his thinking does the appellate court have grounds for reversal.[275] Even then, many appellate courts simply return the case to the original judge for further proceedings,[276] making it possible for the trial judge to justify the outcome he wants using the proper criteria.[277]

Wisdom from the streets of divorce practice necessitates success at trial, because appeal frequently proves futile.[278] Attorneys, who know the low probability of success, advise clients against appeal. And most parties, particularly women,[279] lack the financial and emotional resources to maintain an appeal.[280] In most cases, then, the availability of appeal provides only minimal opportunity to correct judicial error.[281]

DEFAULT JUDGMENTS

If the court enters a default judgment, the respondent can seek to have that judgment set aside. Two rules generally apply. First, all states have rules that allow for relief from judgments generally, and they apply to default judgments.[282] Second, default rules themselves also specify the procedures that parties must follow to allow courts to set aside default judgments for good cause shown.[283] Consistent with these rules, case law indicates that the following provide common grounds to set aside a default judgment of dissolution: (a) noncompliance with statutory procedures for default,[284] (b) lack of personal jurisdiction over the respondent,[285] (c) lack of subject matter jurisdiction over the specific issues in the case,[286] (d) excusable neglect by the respondent[287] or the respondent's attorney,[288] and (e) various forms of fraud.[289] The judges to whom I have spoken, however, as well as my research, indicate the rarity of petitions to set-aside default dissolution of marriage judgments and their limited utility as an error correction method.

SETTLEMENT ERRORS

When parties enter into a divorce settlement agreement, any correction of error proves unlikely. The two opportunities to correct error that exist at final hearing prove illusory. First, most jurisdictions impose a duty on the judge to review the agreement for fairness or lack of unconscionability.[290] Judicial frustration with overcrowded dockets,[291] deference to family privacy, and distaste for divorce cases,[292] as well as a systemic preference for private settlement,[293] encourage judges to accept agreements without question. A judge typically will ask the parties whether they freely and voluntarily entered into the agreement and whether they consider it fair.[294] Coached by their lawyers, parties answer yes. As one lawyer explained to his divorce client,

> An agreement is totally creative between the two of you. The two of you can agree to anything you want to, as long as it's not illegal. The judge is going to say fine, and it can be as lopsided as you want to make it. The judge will say fine if you both think it's fair and both of you agree to it.[295]

Judges simply do not exercise their authority to review the substance of settlement agreements.[296] This first opportunity to correct settlement error currently does not exist.

Second, a party can challenge the enforceability of an unfair settlement agreement at final hearing. Limited resources severely restrict many parties from pursuit of a costly trial on enforceability. For those who do challenge, however, court rhetoric seems receptive. Many courts reason that the state should limit the parties' freedom to contract at divorce because of the important public policy issues at stake. The state, they maintain, should guard against fraud, duress, and undue influence in the making,[297] and against unconscionability in the substance[298] of agreements.[299] Despite their lofty rhetoric, courts demonstrate extreme reluctance to find objectively unfair agreements unenforceable.[300] For most, this opportunity to correct error evaporates at trial.[301]

If a party fails to challenge an agreement at final hearing or introduces an agreement in a default proceeding,[302] the trial court incorporates the agreement into its final judgment of dissolution. Subsequent challenges to the agreement's enforceability have created confusion in many jurisdictions.[303] Once the agreement becomes part of a final judgment, the question arises whether the law of contract enforceability or the rules on relief from judgment should govern.[304] Regardless of how states approach this dilemma, however, judges remain reluctant to reconsider the terms to which the parties ostensibly have agreed. One troubling example of trial court reluctance to set aside settlements follows.

In July of 1999, Arvin was hospitalized after he fell and broke his hip.[305] During the hospitalization he suffered a mini-stroke.[306] Arvin returned home in September, and on October 21, his wife, Victoria, filed for divorce.[307]

On December 3, Victoria requested Arvin's doctor to apply for Arvin's placement in a nursing home, because Arvin required a lot of care. On December 22, Arvin and Victoria entered a separation agreement that assigned essentially all of the marital property to Victoria. Two days after he signed the agreement, Arvin and Victoria went to see Arvin's doctor. Arvin complained that, for about a week, he had left-sided weakness, three or four falls per day, and some slurred speech. The physician admitted Arvin to the hospital and found that Arvin had suffered a recent stroke. He also concluded that Arvin had, for quite some time, suffered from dementia. Five days later, the trial court incorporated the separation agreement into the final judgment of dissolution.[308]

Six months later, after his release from the hospital and his admission to a nursing home, an attorney hired by Arvin's son from another marriage filed a motion for relief from judgment that sought to set aside the dissolution of marriage decree.[309] Arvin alleged that, at the time he signed the property settlement agreement, he suffered from a legal disability and duress and lacked independent counsel, that Victoria had unduly influenced him to sign the agreement, and that Victoria had perpetrated fraud on him and the court. Victoria claimed that Arvin did not suffer from a disability when he signed the agreement, that she and Arvin voluntarily chose representation by the same attorney, and that Arvin had dictated the agreement's terms. Despite the compelling nature of the husband's arguments and evidence, the trial court refused the relief the husband requested without a hearing.[310] Arvin appealed. The appellate court acknowledged that the public policy of Indiana favors separation agreements,[311] but found that the trial court abused its discretion because it failed to consider Arvin's evidence and it used an improper legal standard.[312]

A party can, as Arvin did, appeal a trial court's refusal to vacate a settlement agreement, whether or not it is incorporated into a decree. Contrary to the outcome in Arvin's case, however, appellate courts generally frown on these challenges, negating the utility of this avenue for error correction.[313]

Once again, the link between procedure and substance emerges. Because settlement contributes substantially to the financial impoverishment of divorced women and children,[314] the opportunity to correct settlement error has important substantive as well as procedural implications. Below I use the law of the state of Illinois to highlight the impact that deficiencies in error correction have on substantive results for women. These examples come from appellate opinions, but only parties with sufficient financial and emotional resources can afford to appeal a trial court's refusal to vacate an agreement, and most wives lack these resources.[315] The following decisions, then, suggest only the tip of an iceberg. The cases also illustrate many other procedural concerns raised throughout this book, such as how gender constraints on voice, bias, and inaccurate information influence settlement results.

THE ILLINOIS EXAMPLE

The law of the state of Illinois illustrates how trial and appellate courts typically address petitions to vacate divorce settlements. State policy favors divorce settlements, and Illinois courts presume the validity of agreements.[316] An Illinois statute declares that a court may not set aside or vacate a divorce settlement unless it finds the agreement unconscionable.[317] In making this determination, the court employs a concept of unconscionability taken from Illinois commercial law.[318] Unconscionability requires an absence of meaningful choice on the part of one party, together with contract terms unreasonably favorable to the other party.[319] Only an extremely one-sided or oppressive agreement, one "which no man, not under delusion, would make, on the one hand, and which no fair and honest man would accept, on the other,"[320] fulfills this criteria.

The Illinois courts use a two-part test to determine unconscionability. They inquire into (a) the conditions under which the parties entered the agreement, and (b) the economic circumstances produced by the agreement.[321] Courts examine claims of duress, coercion,[322] and fraud[323] under the first prong of the unconscionability test. The party who challenges an agreement must establish their unconscionability claim by clear and convincing evidence[324] that indicates an absence of meaningful choice.[325] Of course, parties have difficulty fulfilling this standard.[326] Judicial application of Illinois' unconscionability doctrine undermines error correction.[327]

We turn now to one case described in detail and then to shorter discussions of other representative cases. The facts in the first case come from the appellate opinion, from interviews with the wife and her second attorney, and from the transcript of the hearing on the wife's motion to vacate the settlement agreement.[328]

Doris married Virgil in 1956 in Waterloo, Illinois.[329] Virgil had an eighth-grade education; Doris had graduated from high school.[330] The couple had two adult children[331] at the time of divorce. Throughout the marriage, Virgil worked as a self-employed farmer.[332] During the marriage, Doris completed several college accounting courses.[333] At the time of divorce, the Harrisonville Telephone Company employed her as an accountant at an annual salary of $26,400.[334]

Doris and Virgil had experienced marital troubles for years.[335] Virgil dominated Doris, and according to Doris' second attorney, Virgil emotionally abused her.[336] At the divorce hearing, Doris testified that during their marriage Virgil's mental cruelty had kept her nervous and upset.[337] The judge granted the divorce on grounds of "extreme and repeated mental cruelty."[338]

Doris worked during most of the marriage, routinely turning her paycheck over to Virgil who invested all extra funds in the family farm and other enterprises.[339] Doris even gave Virgil the inheritance she received from her parents to invest in the farm.[340] Virgil made all important financial decisions in the family. He did tell Doris what he intended to do, but he did not seek her advice or permission.[341] In 1982, after 26 years of marriage, Doris told Virgil she wanted a divorce.[342] She was age 46, and Virgil was age 49.[343]

Virgil proposed that they see the same local attorney.[344] Doris replied that she wanted her own attorney, but Virgil persuaded her that one attorney would keep legal fees to a minimum.[345] The attorney to whom Virgil took Doris had represented Virgil in several commercial transactions.[346] Moreover, after the divorce, Virgil and the attorney maintained a business relationship, buying and selling land together.[347]

Virgil and Doris met the attorney at his office on a Saturday morning.[348] During their conference, Virgil and Doris agreed that Virgil should retain the property necessary to continue farming and that Doris should receive a cash settlement.[349] Virgil and Doris disagreed, however, about how much money Doris should receive.[350] Virgil valued the marital estate at $315,000.[351]

The $315,000 value stands in stark contrast to the values indicated on financial statements prepared by Virgil and Doris during their marriage.[352] One financial statement prepared two years before the settlement negotiations indicated a net worth of $764,045.[353] A second statement prepared only six months before the settlement conference indicated a net worth of $618,000.[354] When the parties prepared these statements, the only property values Doris knew came from what Virgil told her, or what he told the bank officer to put down on the statement.[355] Virgil and Doris submitted these statements to local banks, that in turn granted Virgil and Doris the farming loans they requested.[356]

Despite glaring discrepancies between Virgil's representations of net worth on the financial statements and those he made during negotiations, no one obtained an independent appraisal before settlement.[357] Accustomed to Virgil's authority, Doris did not even contest Virgil's estimates.[358] She did, however, object to Virgil's failure to include in the marital estate a one-third interest that the couple jointly owned in a farming corporation.[359] She also objected to the exclusion of approximately $37,000 in promissory notes that the corporation owed to Virgil,[360] because the farming corporation gave these promissory notes to Virgil in return for funds loaned to the corporation from Virgil and Doris's joint checking account.[361] Doris claimed that Virgil told her that she had no rights in the farming corporation or the promissory notes.[362] The attorney, Mr. Crowder, advised Doris that these assets had no value anyway.[363] No one investigated Doris' rights in the farming corporation, nor appraised its value.[364] Doris suggested that she would like the settlement agreement to contain a paragraph that protected her rights in the promissory notes if the corporation paid them in the future.[365] Throughout the conference, Doris thought the lawyer represented her and Virgil,[366] and she expected the lawyer to tell her if the agreement did not protect her entitlements under the law.[367]

During the conference Doris initially offered to accept 40% of the marital assets, or $126,000.[368] Virgil resisted, saying he would pay only $50,000.[369] The lawyer told them both that a court likely would make a 50/50 distribution of the marital assets.[370] Moreover, the lawyer told Virgil that the law entitled Doris to more than $50,000.[371] Virgil then offered Doris $60,000.[372] Doris insisted on $100,000.[373] Virgil countered with $75,000.[374]

Throughout the conference, Doris admitted her distress and depression.[375] As the negotiations proceeded, she felt as though all of her years of labor[376] and her substantial financial contributions counted for little in the end.[377] Stunned and betrayed,[378] she "could not believe that everything was so one-sided."[379] By the time Virgil made his final offer of $75,000, Doris felt resigned.[380] She still tried to get him to agree to more, but he refused.[381] Doris accepted the $75,000 without interest,[382] even though Virgil would pay the $75,000 over a six- to seven-year period.[383]

Doris and Virgil returned home.[384] Over the weekend, Doris claimed that Virgil continued to pressure her to accept his terms.[385] Early on Monday, the attorney called and said that he had prepared the agreement for their signatures.[386] On Monday evening, the parties returned to the attorney's office and met with another attorney who actually had prepared the settlement agreement.[387]

Doris remained distraught; her sense of betrayal persisted as well as her depression. She felt numb.[388] The new attorney explained that she would receive a cash settlement and that the parties would execute deeds to property and transfer titles to automobiles.[389] The lawyer told Virgil and Doris to look over the agreement and that he would answer any questions; he did not go through the agreement and explain the meaning of each paragraph.[390] The attorney never told Doris that she forever relinquished her rights to spousal maintenance in the agreement.[391]

This attorney testified at trial that he provided no explanation of the document and that he represented neither party.[392] Doris signed the agreement.[393] From beginning to end, the second conference took no more than 20 minutes.[394] When asked why Doris signed the agreement, Doris's new attorney explained that Doris's distraught state, her naive trust in the lawyer, and her accommodation to Virgil's dominance influenced her acquiescence.[395] Doris also reported that she trusted the lawyer.[396] The agreement did not contain the paragraph that Doris had requested on the promissory notes.

Under the agreement, Doris received a 1979 Mercury automobile, miscellaneous items of personal property, and $75,000, which Virgil had to pay in installments with no interest—approximately 24% of the value that Virgil placed on the marital assets.[397] Virgil received $240,000 in farm property and equipment and various items of personal property—approximately 76% of the marital estate.[398] Virgil also received a one-third interest in the farming corporation and $37,900 in promissory notes.[399] Both Doris and Virgil waived their respective rights to spousal maintenance.[400] Doris's new lawyer insisted that "Virgil made out like a bandit."[401]

Afterward, Doris told a niece who worked for a lawyer about the agreement, and the niece protested the unfair terms.[402] Doris sought the advice of a second lawyer, who agreed with the niece.[403] The new attorney represented Doris at the trial in which she asked the court to set aside the agreement.[404] The attorney that allegedly had represented both parties during the negotiations represented Virgil at the trial and on appeal.[405] He justified his representation of Virgil by claiming to have performed as a mediator and not a lawyer during the negotiations.[406] Doris claimed she had never heard of mediation, nor did the attorney ever mention mediation.[407] The trial court refused to set aside the agreement, and Doris appealed.[408]

Was the agreement unconscionable? The appellate court did not believe so.[409] First, the appellate court omitted or reconstructed many of Doris's experiences. Rather than recognize Virgil's dominance, the court implied that Doris was at least Virgil's equal because she had taken some college courses and she worked as an accountant.[410] The court made no mention of Doris' financial contributions to the marriage. Neither did the court acknowledge that the attorney who allegedly represented both Virgil and Doris had represented Virgil in commercial transactions, represented Virgil at trial, and also represented Virgil on appeal. The court obscured the inequity of the property distribution by noting that Doris received $75,000 in cash, while declining to mention that Virgil received $240,000, or 76% of the marital estate.[411] Finally, the court never acknowledged Doris' emotional state during the negotiations. Rather, it spoke of offers and counteroffers, depicting Doris as an assertive negotiator and implying that she had no need for an attorney's advocacy.

On appeal, Doris claimed that Virgil's misrepresentation of the value of the marital assets, her lack of representation by independent counsel, and the haste with which the agreement was contrived created sufficiently questionable conditions to fulfill the first prong of the unconscionability test.[412] Regarding Virgil's misrepresentation, the appellate court found that the trial court did not abuse its discretion when it rejected the expert testimony and found that the husband did not misrepresent the value of the marital estate.[413] The appellate court seemed to impute negligence to Doris for her failure to discover the actual value of the marital estate and to investigate her rights in the farming corporation and promissory notes—a theme found in several other cases. It never considered the possibility that preexisting marital patterns, as well as Doris's mental state, lack of independent knowledge, and reliance on the attorney substantially inhibited her voice and her ability to protect herself. Moreover, the court implicitly condoned Virgil's misstatements and hard bargaining tactics, which, even if suitable between competitors in the marketplace, should have no place in negotiations between spouses.

Regarding Doris's lack of independent counsel, the court found it enough that the attorney had informed her that a court would most likely award her half of the marital assets.[414] The court seemed oblivious to both the self-serving nature of the lawyer's testimony and its questionable veracity. Even if the lawyer did inform Doris, she needed more than information to protect herself. The court imputed to her a fictitious equality with her husband; ignored her inexperience, socialization, and emotional condition; and condoned a lawyer's clearly improper behavior.

Regarding Doris's claim that the agreement was hastily contrived and not a product of her free will, the court found the 20 minutes that Doris had to review the agreement sufficient.[415] Additionally, the court stated that Doris "chose" to devote only 20 minutes to a review of the agreement, implicitly attributing haste and negligence to her.[416] The court concluded that the conditions under which Doris entered the agreement did not support a finding that Doris had satisfied the first prong of the unconscionability standard.[417]

Turning to the second prong, the court noted that unequal distribution does not itself establish unconscionability.[418] It observed that Doris's salary of $26,400 and her $75,000 property distribution did not "leave her destitute" and concluded that the agreement was not one-sided enough to be unconscionable.[419]

Courts typically look with disfavor on financially dependent wives for "choosing" to forgo legal representation.[420] Elaine had been married to Joseph for 24 years when Joseph sought a divorce.[421] Elaine worked at K-Mart, earning approximately $5,500 to $6,000 per year.[422] Joseph worked as a self-employed farmer, earning approximately $10,000 per year.[423] The couple had four minor children.[424] Before and during the divorce Elaine suffered from mental problems.[425]

Joseph took Elaine to the office of his attorney, Mr. Johnson.[426] Johnson prepared a property settlement agreement in which Elaine received no spousal maintenance, approximately 25% ($25,000) of the marital assets, custody of the four minor children, and child support in a smaller amount than recommended by the county bar association.[427] Johnson then called another attorney, Mr. Bird, to come to his office to represent Elaine.[428] Elaine had never met nor talked to Bird before he appeared at Johnson's office.[429] When he arrived, Bird reviewed the settlement agreement with Elaine and inquired whether she had sufficient composure to act as the plaintiff in the divorce proceeding.[430] Bird spent no time alone with Elaine until the following day, when he walked with her from Johnson's office to the courthouse for the divorce hearing.[431] The judge granted the divorce and incorporated the parties' settlement in his final order.[432]

Elaine's extreme anxiety over the divorce led her to check herself into a hospital, where the doctors diagnosed her with anxiety neurosis as a result of the divorce.[433] She regained her composure three weeks after the divorce and requested that the court vacate the final judgment, alleging among other things that she lacked the benefit of private counsel during the divorce negotiations.[434] The trial court denied her petition, and Elaine appealed.[435] In upholding the trial court, the appellate court noted that, during the divorce negotiations, Elaine had not wanted an independent attorney.[436] The court apparently gathered this information from the self-serving testimony of Johnson, Joseph's attorney.[437] The court concluded that Elaine had made a knowing decision to forgo independent representation.[438]

Courts also minimize wives' complaints of anxiety, depression, and mental distress, commonly noting that divorce always causes stress.[439] In Elaine's case, she alleged that her emotional condition during divorce negotiations impaired her capacity to contract.[440] Although the severity of her condition led her to admit herself to a local hospital immediately following the divorce, the appellate court credited the trial court's finding that Elaine, although obviously upset during the divorce proceedings, was no more upset and nervous than normal.[441] The trial court also noted that Elaine's mental illness was not particularly acute.[442] Unsurprisingly, Elaine fared no better with this argument than with her argument regarding independent legal counsel.

As noted earlier, divorce attorneys typically coach their clients about how to respond to the routine pattern of questions at the final divorce hearing. Emotionally impaired people still can give rehearsed answers to the anticipated questions, but when faced with claims of duress or coercion, courts point to this coached testimony and impute actual understanding and willing assent to wives.[443] To return once more to Elaine's case, she claimed that her mental condition impaired her ability to understand the agreement's terms.[444] In response, the appellate court referred to Elaine's trial testimony and quipped, "If she said that she understood, she understood."[445]

Courts sometimes misconstrue a wife's equivocal testimony as her willing acquiescence to a settlement.[446] At the age of 66, Mary Ann filed for divorce from her husband, George, a 54-year-old music professor.[447] Mary

Ann had poor health and little likelihood of employment.[448] The agreement her attorney urged her to enter provided no maintenance;[449] instead, it allotted her 62% of the marital assets, including half of George's retirement account.[450] Because of her age, Mary Ann could immediately remove her portion of George's pension and draw from a lifelong annuity that would generate an annual income of $8,400.[451] The appellate court never indicated the value of the remaining assets or the amount of George's income.[452] At final hearing, Mary Ann testified about the settlement, and the trial court incorporated the settlement into the final judgment of dissolution.[453] Soon after the court entered judgment, Mary Ann, proceeding pro se, filed a petition that asked the court to vacate the agreement.[454] She argued that her attorney had coerced her into acceptance[455] and that the agreement was unconscionable because it provided no maintenance.[456] The trial court denied her petition, and Mary Ann appealed.[457]

In addressing Mary Ann's claim of unconscionability, the appellate court quoted her trial testimony to illustrate that Mary Ann knew that the agreement provided no maintenance and that she willingly acquiesced to the agreement's terms.[458] First, the court offered a colloquy between Mary Ann and her attorney, Mr. Bickley:

> [Bickley] Are you willing then to waive maintenance in return for a higher percentage of the proceeds to be acquired by the sale of the assets of this particular marital property?
>
> [Mary Ann] I'm just—I'm trying to do math in my head and I'm not that good at it. So, I'm waiving maintenance for all time, no matter what happens to me or what my physical condition is?
>
> [Bickley] That's correct. Once you waive maintenance—
>
> [Mary Ann] For the sake of eight per cent being given to me as opposed to being given to my husband?
>
> [Bickley] You are in effect being given between eight and ten per cent more of the assets of this estate than you would be entitled to under the current law.
>
> [Mary Ann] Otherwise I get fifty per cent? Is that—
>
> [Bickley] You get fifty per cent.
>
> [Mary Ann] Yes.[459]

The trial judge then explained to Mary Ann that the marital assets need not be divided equally, but that the court would consider the ability of each spouse to accumulate additional assets in the future as well as what assets Mary Ann would need to live comfortably without maintenance.[460] Bickley then made another attempt to elicit appropriate responses from Mary Ann:

[Bickley] Well, the question that is presently pending before the Court, is do you understand now . . . that if you waive maintenance today, you can never come before this Court or any other court and ask for an imposition of maintenance for you, do you understand that?

[Mary Ann] Yes, I understand that. It's just such a big thing to understand to say yes, and say yes, and I agree, I'll do it. I'll never come back again, you know, no matter what my situation is.

[Bickley] Well, that is why we are here in court . . . .

[Mary Ann] Yes.

[Bickley] We are here to get a dissolution of marriage.

[Mary Ann] Yes.

[Bickley] And to reach an accord with respect to all of the property rights between the parties.

[Mary Ann] All right.

[Bickley] Do you understand that?

[Mary Ann] I do understand that.[461]

The appellate court then quoted Mary Ann's responses to the questions of George's attorney, Mr. Kuhs:

[Kuhs] Do you feel that this is a fair settlement of this case under the circumstances?

[Mary Ann] A fair settlement? Is my answer going to determine anything that is going to happen here?

THE COURT: Do you feel that it is fair and equitable? Are you satisfied with it? Was there any force or coercion used upon you to enter into this agreement?

[Mary Ann] No. It seems like the best we can do under the circumstances.

THE COURT: Under the circumstances do you feel that it is fair and equitable?

[Kuhs] No one has threatened you or coerced you to sign this?

[Mary Ann] No one has threatened me.

[Kuhs] You are not under the influence of alcohol or any other medication or drugs today, are you?

[Mary Ann] Nothing at all.

[Kuhs] Thank you.[462]

Finally, the appellate court turned to an exchange with Mary Ann at the conclusion of the hearing:

[Mary Ann] May I ask a question? Was the subject of my health brought up?

THE COURT: Well, I would assume it was brought up in negotiations.

[Mary Ann] Was it?

[Bickley] Anything further?

[Kuhs] Thank you, your Honor.

THE COURT: You're welcome. Good luck.[463]

What the appellate court perceived as Mary Ann's knowing acquiescence was probably the strongest protest the 66-year-old homemaker could
muster.[464] The appellate court added insult by concluding, "the fact that
Mary Ann has since changed her mind should not render the settlement
invalid."[465]

Courts minimize the duress mothers experience when threatened with
a loss of custody.[466] For instance, in August 1994, Yolanda left her husband,
Jeffrey, after nearly 20 years of marriage.[467] She took their three youngest
sons with her to the couple's summer home, while the older two boys
stayed with their father.[468] Jeffrey worked as a hospital administrator, earning
approximately $150,000 per year. Yolanda had not worked outside the home
during the marriage.[469] The court soon ordered Jeffrey to pay to Yolanda
$2,400 per month for unallocated family support.[470]

Sometime within the first year after separation, Yolanda decided to
move to Michigan with her three youngest sons.[471] On August 28, 1995,
Jeffrey filed an emergency petition that requested the court to enjoin Yolanda
from permanent removal of the boys to Michigan.[472] The court scheduled
a hearing for three days later.[473] On the date of the hearing, Jeffrey and his
lawyer and Yolanda and her attorney appeared at the court.[474] For two hours
they all negotiated in the hallway outside the courtroom.[475] Apparently no
one had conducted discovery before negotiations.[476] At her attorney's urging,
Yolanda orally agreed to accept what appears to be between 17% and
23% of the marital assets[477] and three years of minimal and nonmodifiable
rehabilitative spousal maintenance,[478] in return for custody of her three
youngest sons.[479] Rather than argue the merits of Jeffrey's emergency petition,
at the hearing Jeffrey, Yolanda, and their lawyers presented the terms of an
oral settlement agreement to the trial court.[480] On the basis of the testimony,
the judge agreed to enter judgment on October 5, 1995.[481]

On October 5, Yolanda appeared in court with her new lawyer, Mr.
Holden.[482] Holden requested a continuance, but the court declined and
entered judgment.[483] On November 5, Yolanda filed a motion to vacate the
judgment, arguing, among other things, that she suffered from duress during
negotiations because of her extreme fear of losing her children.[484] Yolanda's
fear seems credible because she already had lost her two older sons to Jeffrey,
the court might have disapproved of her removal of the three youngest sons
to Michigan, she only had three days' notice of the emergency hearing, and
she had minimal financial resources with which to fight Jeffrey.[485] Moreover,
the unfair financial terms to which she agreed suggested that her fear impaired

her ability to exercise her free will—she felt she had no other choice.[486] The trial court, however, denied Yolanda's motion to vacate, and the appellate court affirmed.[487] In addressing Yolanda's duress argument, the appellate court stated the following:

> Wife bears the burden of showing duress by presenting clear and convincing evidence that she was bereft of the quality of mind necessary to make a contract. While wife's fear that she may lose custody of her children no doubt caused her anxiety, we do not recognize this as a factor impairing her ability to exercise her free will and make a meaningful choice when the record reflects that she agreed to negotiations, took part in the negotiations and then presented the substance of these negotiations, under oath, to the trial court. Many spouses may experience anxiety when appearing in court because of a petition to dissolve a marriage and this anxiety is no doubt heightened when one fears she may lose custody of her children; however, this factor, without more, does not clearly and convincingly demonstrate that one lacked the ability to make a voluntary decision.[488]

Wives who allege that their attorneys coerced them into signing a poor agreement[489] or inadequately represented them get caught in a battle with their former attorneys.[490] A wife may claim, for instance, that when she signed the agreement she did not know that the law entitled her to half of the marital assets. Her former counsel, however, in order to protect him or herself, likely will testify that he or she advised the wife of her right to half of the marital assets. Courts routinely find that the wife knew whatever the lawyer claims to have told her.[491] Likewise, trial courts impute negligence to the wife when her attorney fails to conduct discovery[492] or fails to detect and correct errors in the final settlement provisions.[493]

Trial courts regularly ignore the pleas of wives who have been badly represented by lawyers chosen either by their husbands or by their husbands' attorneys.[494] For instance, after several months of marital discord and talk of divorce, Lawrence informed his wife, Janice, that he had an appointment with an attorney.[495] At the meeting, the attorney persuaded Janice to sign a handwritten letter addressed to another attorney whom Janice did not know.[496] The letter, which requested that the attorney represent Janice, specified the settlement terms that Janice allegedly wanted the court to include in its decree.[497] At no time did Janice meet with or discuss her case with this attorney.[498] Nevertheless, this attorney appeared at the final hearing without Janice and advised the court that he represented her.[499] He testified that he did not know whether Janice knew what property was included in the marital estate when she signed her letter.[500] He further testified that the husband's attorney and the husband himself gave him the only information he had regarding the alleged oral property agreement.[501] The husband paid the attorney's fees.[502] On August 29, the court entered final judgment, incorporating the terms of the supposed oral property agreement.[503] Janice had no knowledge of the final hearing or of the final decree.[504]

Lawrence and Janice continued living together until September 6, when Lawrence threw her out of the house and apparently refused to allow her to visit their minor daughter.[505] At the beginning of October, Janice consulted an attorney about visitation with her child, and for the first time she learned of the divorce decree.[506] The trial court denied Janice's petition to vacate, but fortunately, Janice had sufficient resources to take her case to a more sympathetic appellate court that reversed the decision and remanded.[507]

Courts find unrepresented and naive wives negligent for failing to conduct discovery, and subsequently deny their claims of fraud or misrepresentation.[508] For instance, when Victoria married Albert, he was an experienced and successful businessman.[509] Their marriage lasted 19 years before Albert's dissatisfaction with Victoria's budding business career led him to file for divorce.[510] The year before he sought a divorce, Albert listed his net worth on a credit application at $2,071,500.[511] That same year, Victoria earned $16,000 from her business.[512]

Albert informed Victoria that he had retained an attorney to represent him in the divorce and suggested that Victoria do the same.[513] The attorney Albert chose was a friend of Albert and Victoria who previously had represented them both.[514] According to the appellate court, Victoria "refused" Albert's advice to obtain independent counsel.[515] When Albert and Victoria first met with Albert's attorney, the attorney informed Victoria that he represented Albert and that she should retain separate counsel.[516] Again, Victoria "refused."[517]

Albert's attorney prepared a separation agreement in which Victoria and Albert acknowledged that each had disclosed fully their respective incomes and assets, and that each knew of the other's property.[518] The agreement provided Victoria with $24,000 in cash, $93,000 in her business's assets, her $12,000 individual retirement account, and maintenance of $2,180.56 per month for six years.[519] At the divorce hearing, the court questioned Victoria about her lack of representation.[520] Victoria replied that she had chosen to proceed pro se.[521] She also indicated her satisfaction with the agreement.[522] The court incorporated the agreement in the final judgment of divorce.[523]

Four months later, Victoria consulted an attorney and petitioned the court to vacate the agreement.[524] She claimed that Albert had failed to disclose, among other items, a $72,480 profit-sharing plan and a $45,000 business interest.[525] The trial court granted her petition to vacate, but the appellate court reversed.[526] Crucial to its holding was Victoria's failure to discover the assets that Albert had not disclosed.[527] The court stated: "The fact that Victoria could have discovered information about Albert's financial status through her own investigation or by hiring an attorney diminishes her claim of detrimental reliance on Albert's alleged misrepresentations."[528] The appellate court then upheld the trial court's order that Albert pay a large portion of Victoria's attorneys' fees, noting that Victoria lacked the financial ability to pay them herself.[529] In justifying its position, the court stated,

> The record in the present case evinces a great financial disparity between the parties. As part of the divorce settlement agreement, Albert agreed to pay Victoria a $24,000 lump sum to set up housekeeping and $2,180.56 a month for 72 months. Victoria became aware that she had a financial problem a few months after she moved into her one bedroom apartment after the divorce since "every penny was being spent just to pay rent and electric bills and phone bills." Victoria expected to receive an inheritance of $20,000 to $25,000. In the meantime, the record shows that as of February 19, 1991, Victoria had only $1,000 in her personal bank account and $800 in her business account besides her Individual Retirement Accounts valued at $12,000. On the other hand, Albert maintained a high standard of living which has not changed since his divorce from Victoria. His admitted net worth including real estate, personal property, marital property and what he considered as non-marital property exceeds a million dollars.[530]

As illustrated here, courts do not consider highly skewed property distributions one-sided enough to be unconscionable.[531] Sharon and James, for instance, had been married for 14 years when James sought a divorce.[532] Sharon signed a property settlement agreement that the trial court incorporated into its final judgment.[533] Sharon later petitioned the court to vacate the property settlement provisions, alleging that James had coerced her into the agreement and that the terms of the agreement were so one-sided as to be unconscionable.[534] According to James's figures, he received 71% of the marital assets.[535] Sharon argued that he received closer to 78%.[536] The trial court found the agreement unconscionable, but the appellate court reversed, stating "we find that the division of the marital property in the Agreement in the present case does not *remotely rise* to the level of unconscionability."[537] Court application of Illinois law thus illustrates that the opportunity to correct settlement error rarely exists.

PREMARITAL AGREEMENTS

With growing frequency[538] parties enter premarital agreements that, if enforceable, govern support and property issues at divorce. Most of these agreements seek to protect the financial resources of the wealthier spouse from claims under divorce law by the economically inferior spouse.[539] Many states determine the enforceability of premarital agreements under common law concepts of procedural fairness[540] as well as unconscionability standards similar to those applied to settlement agreements.[541] Variation exists in the time at which the unconscionability review should occur. Some states assess unconscionability at the time of execution, others at the time of divorce.[542] Moreover, common law states vary greatly in the authority they grant to courts to reject unfair agreements.[543] Despite this variation, no reason exists to think that courts will use this standard to refuse enforcement of unfair premarital agreements any more frequently or eagerly than inequitable separation agreements.[544] Correction of error seems unlikely.

Moreover, increasingly, states have adopted the Uniform Premarital Agreement Act (UPAA).[545] The UPAA provides even less opportunity to correct error than the common law unconscionability standard.[546] A party may avoid enforcement of a premarital agreement only if he or she can prove that he or she did not execute the agreement voluntarily, or that the agreement was unconscionable when executed.[547] An agreement that seemed fair at the inception of a lengthy marriage, however, can result in grave injustice at the time of divorce.[548] The UPAA's focus on the time of execution severely restricts the error correction function of the unconscionability standard. Moreover, to escape enforcement on the grounds of unconscionability, a challenger also must prove that he or she did not receive a fair and reasonable disclosure of the property or financial obligations of the other party before execution, that he or she did not waive the right to disclosure, and that he or she did not have, or reasonably could not have had, adequate knowledge of the other's property or obligations.[549] A finding of unconscionability under the UPAA, then, proves even less likely than under common law principles.

A Colorado court provides the usual justification for judicial deference to premarital, as opposed to settlement, agreements.

> A marital agreement is an agreement either between prospective spouses made in contemplation of marriage or between present spouses, but only if signed by both parties prior to the filing of an action for dissolution of marriage or for legal separation. In contrast, a separation agreement promotes the amicable settlement of disputes between the parties to a marriage attendant upon their separation or dissolution of their marriage.
>
> The two types of agreement are subject to different standards of review. A marital agreement is enforceable unless it was executed involuntarily or there was not a fair and reasonable disclosure of the property of financial obligations involved. In contrast a separation agreement is enforceable unless it is found to be unconscionable.
>
> The conscionability standard applicable to separation agreements is different because of the public policy concern for safeguarding the interests of a spouse whose consent to the agreement may have been

obtained under more emotionally stressful circumstances, especially if that spouse is unrepresented by counsel.

Thus, before a court incorporates property division provisions of a separation agreement into a dissolution decree, it should first review the provisions for fraud, overreaching, concealment of assets, or sharp dealing not consistent with the obligations of marital partners to deal fairly with each other, and then look at the economic circumstances of the parties which result from the agreement, including a determination whether under the totality of the circumstances the property disposition is fair, just and reasonable.[550]

Although the Colorado court acknowledges that certain pressures might produce an unfair *settlement* agreement, the court takes no note of the numerous circumstances that produce unfair *premarital* agreements. The strength of a party's desire to marry may inhibit rational bargaining behavior.[551] Many times one party presents the agreement to the other immediately before the wedding, along with the threat of marriage cancellation if the other refuses to sign.[552] One party might sign, because hesitation might pose a subtle threat to the relationship if the other interprets the reluctance as a lack of commitment, a lack of confidence in the relationship, or a suspicion about the other party's motives.[553] Many people at entry to marriage know little about marital property and support laws and may relinquish important rights through ignorance.[554] Most believe, in spite of statistics to the contrary, that their marriages will last forever. They may not comprehend the importance of the premarital agreement that anticipates divorce.[555] Gender constraints on voice make hard bargaining in the context of love particularly difficult for women.[556]

As the Colorado court further illustrates, the UPAA justifies greater deference to premarital than to settlement agreements on the untested presumption that parties about to enter marriage more likely will act in a self-interested manner than those who face divorce. To the contrary, as one commentator aptly notes,

Arguably, parties contemplating divorce have more reason to act in a self-protective, self-interested, "rational" manner than do parties contemplating marriage. In short the greater enforceability afforded premarital agreements by the U.P.A.A., as contrasted with the [Uniform Marital Dissolution Act]'s approach to separation agreements, has little in logic or policy to recommend it.[557]

In the end, the legal principles that currently address the enforceability of premarital agreements pose a threat to error correction and to substantive justice at least as grave as the unconscionability standard for divorce settlements. Many commentators express concern about the substantive justice issues raised by blind legal deference to premarital agreements[558] and find it unsurprising that women, far more frequently than men, challenge them.[559]

In summary, the lack of any meaningful opportunity to correct decisional error in divorce cases compromises substantive as well as procedural justice. Although the cases indicate that the lack of opportunity to correct error falls most heavily on women,[560] this deficiency can affect men as well. The foregoing discussion does suggest that procedures should promote fair agreements at the outset; that trial judges should look with suspicion, rather than deference, at settlement or premarital agreements that threaten the well-being of the financially dependent spouse and, usually, the children; and that appellate judges should not defer to trial court judges who enter decrees that economically disadvantage dependent spouses.

NOTES

1. Joint Anti-Fascists Refugee Comm. v. McGrath, 341 U.S. 123, 168 (1951) (concurring opinion). *See also* Homer v. Richmond, 292 F.2d 719 (D.C. Cir. 1961).

2. *See, e.g.,* Robert Folger, *Distributive and Procedural Justice: Combined Impact of "Voice" and Peer Opinions on Responses to Inequity,* 35 J. PERSONALITY & SOC. PSYCHOL. 108, 115 (1977) (concluding that participant voice directly influenced perceptions of outcome fairness); Pauline Houlden et al., *Preferences for Modes of Dispute Resolution as a Function of Process and Decision Control,* 14 J. EXPERIMENTAL SOC. PSYCHOL. 13 (1978) (noting that control over the presentation of evidence has more value to parties than decisional control); Stephen LaTour, *Determinants of Participant and Observer Satisfaction With Adversary and Inquisitorial Modes of Adjudication,* 36 J. PERSONALITY & SOC. PSYCHOL. 1531, 1532 (1978) (concluding that the opportunity to present evidence proves an important factor in a party's evaluation of adjudication); E. Allan Lind et al., *Decision Control and Process Control on Procedural Fairness Judgments,* 13 J. APPLIED SOC. PSYCHOL. 338, 340 (1983) (finding that high disputant process control resulted in judgments of greater procedural fairness regardless of whether the procedure resulted in a binding result); E. Allan Lind et al., *Reactions to Procedural Models for Adjudicative Conflict Resolution,* 22 J. CONFLICT RESOL. (1978) (noting the superiority of procedures that required participation to those that did not); Raymond Paternoster et al., *Do Fair Procedures Matter? The Effect of Procedural Justice on Spouse Assault,* 31 L. & SOC'Y REV. 163, 167 (1997); Tom R. Tyler, *What Is Procedural Justice?: Criteria Used by Citizens to Assess the Fairness of Legal Procedures,* 22 L. & SOC'Y REV. 103, 111 (1988) (hereinafter *What Is Procedural Justice?*) (finding the opportunity to be heard a necessary component of procedural justice); Tom R. Tyler et al., *Influence of Voice on Satisfaction With Leaders: Exploring the Meaning of Process Control,* 48 J. PERSONALITY & SOC. PSYCHOL. 72, 74 (1985) (finding that an individual's increased ability to submit evidence and to control its presentation resulted in better procedural justice perceptions than conditions of low decisional control); Tom R. Tyler,

Conditions Leading to Value-Expressive Effects in Judgments of Procedural Justice: A Test of Four Models, 52 J. Personality & Soc. Psychol. 333, 338 (1987) (hereinafter *Value-Expressive Effects*) (noting that opportunities to speak, more than actual control over decisions, influences citizens' views about procedural fairness); Nancy A. Welsh, *Making Deals in Court-Connected Mediation: What's Justice Got to Do With It?,* 79 Wash. U. L.Q. 787, 820 (2001). *See also, e.g.,* Ralph Cavanagh & Austin Sarat, *Thinking About Courts: Toward and Beyond a Jurisprudence of Judicial Competence,* 14 L. & Soc'y Rev. 371, 378, 380 (1980) (noting that judicial competence requires affording interested parties a meaningful opportunity to be heard); Paul G. Chevigny, *Fairness and Participation,* 64 N.Y.U. L. Rev. 1211, 1216–18 (1989) (reviewing Allan Lind & Tom R. Tyler, The Social Psychology of Procedural Justice (1988)); Lon Fuller, *The Forms and Limits of Adjudication,* 92 Harv. L. Rev. 353, 365 (1978) (claiming that the more party participation, the more adjudication approaches its optimum expression); Gerald Turkel, *Legitimation, Authority, and Consensus Formation,* 8 Int'l J. Soc. L. 19, 22–23 (1980) (discussing how communication between officials and those they govern legitimates authority); David B. Wexler & Bruce J. Winick, *Therapeutic Jurisprudence as a New Approach to Mental Health Law Policy Analysis and Research,* 45 Miami L. Rev. 979, 989 (1991) (noting the importance of voice to procedural justice perceptions).

3. *See* Tom R. Tyler & K. McGraw, *Ideology and Interpretation of Personal Experience: Procedural Justice and Political Quiescence,* 42 J. Soc. Issues 115 (1986).

4. *See* Donald N. Bersoff, *Judicial Deference to Nonlegal Decisionmakers: Imposing Simplistic Solutions on Problems of Cognitive Complexity in Mental Disability Law,* 46 SMU L. Rev. 329, 365 & n.184 (1992) (citing numerous studies confirming this point).

5. *See* Paternoster et al., *supra* note 2, at 167; Welsh, *supra* note 2, at 820, 824–29.

6. Research confirms that disputants must believe that decision makers considered their views before disputants conclude that they had sufficient voice. *See* Bersoff, *supra* note 4, at 367; Paternoster et al., *supra* note 2, at 167; *Value-Expressive Effects, supra* note 2, at 339. *See also* Welsh, *supra,* at 820.

7. *See, e.g.,* Gary Skoloff & Robert J. Levy, *Custody Doctrines and Custody Practice: A Divorce Practitioner's View,* 36 Fam. L.Q. 79, 82 (2002).

8. *See* Lynn Mather et al., Divorce Lawyers at Work: Varieties of Professionalism in Practice 120 (2001) (noting one judge's refusal to hear evidence of the wife's adultery, despite its legal relevance).

9. *See* David A. Binder & Susan C. Price, Legal Interviewing and Counseling: A Client-Centered Approach 53–58 (1977); Peggy Maisel & Lesley Greenbaum, Introduction to Law and Legal Skills 5 (2001); James H. Feldman, *That First Contact Is Crucial—Have Your Ducks in a Row,* 12 Fam. Advoc. 6, 6 (1990). *See also* Christopher P. Gilkerson, *Theoretics of Practice: The Integration of Progressive Thought and Action: Poverty Law Narratives: The Critical Practice and Theory of Receiving and Translating Client Stories,* 43 Hastings L.J. 861, 905–08 (1992) (describing how poverty lawyers should solicit their clients' narratives).

10. *See* Binny Miller, *Give Them Back Their Lives: Recognizing Client Narrative in Case Theory*, 93 MICH. L. REV. 485 (1994); Robert D. Dinerstein, *Client-Centered Counseling: Reappraisal and Refinement*, 32 ARIZ. L. REV. 501 (1990).

11. *See* MATHER ET AL., *supra* note 8, at 20; John Griffiths, *What Do Dutch Lawyers Actually Do in Divorce Cases?*, 20 L. & SOC'Y REV. 135, 151–52 (1986) (noting that most divorce lawyers begin a first meeting with clients by allowing the client to tell his or her story in his or her own way).

12. *See* MATHER ET AL., *supra* note 8, at 67–68.

13. *See* Dinerstein, *supra* note 10, at 504, 506; William L.F. Felstiner & Austin Sarat, *Enactments of Power: Negotiating Reality and Responsibility in Lawyer–Client Interactions*, 77 CORNELL L. REV. 1447, 1451–54 (1992); Griffiths, *supra* note 11, at 151, 155 (observing that lawyers typically control the course of the discussion with clients and that clients tend to respond passively to the legal, and assertively to the social, aspects of the divorce). Felstiner and Sarat also suggest, however, that the image of lawyer dominance presented in existing literature varies when lawyers represent corporate, long-term, or wealthy clients. Felstiner & Sarat, *supra*, at 1451–54. For a more thorough review of the literature on lawyer–client relationships, see *id.* & nn.6–33.

14. *See* Judith Ryan, *Mediator Strategies for Lawyers: The Four-Party Settlement Conference*, 30 FAM. & CONCILIATION CT. REV. 364, 364 (1992). *But see* Griffiths, *supra* note 11, at 156 (noting that Dutch lawyers advise their clients but also give them great freedom to work out their own solutions).

15. *See* MATHER ET AL., *supra* note 8, at 91–92.

16. Felstiner and Sarat's research on divorce has some limitations. *See* David L. Chambers, *25 Divorce Attorneys and 40 Clients in Two Not So Big But Not So Small Cities in Massachusetts and California: An Appreciation*, 22 L. & SOC. INQUIRY 209, 215–26 (1997) (reviewing AUSTIN SARAT & WILLIAM L.F. FELSTINER, DIVORCE LAWYERS AND THEIR CLIENTS: POWER AND MEANING IN THE LEGAL PROCESS (1995)). *See also* Skoloff & Levy, *supra* note 7, at 93–97. More recent work by Mather et al., however, confirms the validity of many of Felstiner and Sarat's observations. *See* MATHER ET AL., *supra* note 8.

17. *See* Austin Sarat & William L.F. Felstiner, *Law and Social Relations: Vocabularies of Motive in Lawyer/Client Interaction*, 22 L. & SOC'Y REV. 737, 740 (1988) (noting how the lawyer's reaction to the client shapes the client's perceptions and how the client's story channels the lawyer's professional behavior).

18. *See* Felstiner & Sarat, *supra* note 13, at 1454–55. *See also* Gilkerson, *supra* note 9, at 897–89, 902–03.

19. Felstiner & Sarat, *supra* note 13, at 1460.

20. *See* MATHER ET AL., *supra* note 8, at 107 (noting that, on balance, the lawyer's influence usually dominates). In Griffith's study of Dutch divorce lawyers, he found that lawyers and clients frequently experience two different divorces: lawyers tend to focus on the legal divorce, whereas clients focus on the social and emotional divorce. Griffiths, *supra* note 11, at 155. Griffiths also noted that clients repeatedly attempted to persuade their lawyers that the other party was to blame for the divorce. The lawyers, however, typically did not react or positively discouraged such efforts.

21. *See* Felstiner & Sarat, *supra* note 13, at 1460.

22. Felstiner and Sarat note that "[t]he nature of client communications means that lawyers must continually sift through and evaluate the social world presented by the client in order to reconstruct a picture of the world that they can effectively use in promoting the client's interests." *Id.* at 1462.

23. Some divorce attorneys pursue whatever goals the client wants, *see* MATHER ET AL., *supra* note 8, at 50, 87, 88, but most attempt to adjust what the lawyers perceive as unrealistic demands. *See id.* at 87–109.

24. *See id.* at 94–105; Felstiner & Sarat, *supra* note 13, at 1459; Griffiths, *supra* note 11, at 156–57 (finding much the same in a study of Dutch divorce lawyers).

25. *See* Felstiner & Sarat, *supra* note 13, at 1463. *See also* David Luban, *Paternalism and the Legal Professional*, 1981 WIS. L. REV. 454, 454.

26. *See* MATHER ET AL., *supra* note 8, at 90, 107; Felstiner & Sarat, *supra* note 13, at 1466.

27. *See* Felstiner & Sarat, *supra* note 13, at 1468.

28. *See* MATHER ET AL., *supra* note 8, at 107.

29. *See* Gilkerson, *supra* note 9, at 903–05; Clark D. Cunningham, *Representation as Text: Towards an Ethnography of Legal Discourse, The Lawyer as Translator*, 77 CORNELL L. REV. 1298, 1366 (1992).

30. Divorce lawyers typically urge their clients to focus on pragmatic issues, *See* MATHER ET AL., *supra* note 8, at 91, whereas clients, particularly women, remain more concerned about emotions. *See id.* at 91 (2001). *See also* Griffiths, *supra* note 11, at 155. If the lawyer adequately explains why he or she must alter the client's story, however, the client may not react negatively to the reconstruction.

31. *See* Felstiner & Sarat, *supra* note 13, at 1459; Miller, *supra* note 10. Sometimes this can be a painful process. A mother, for instance, may have to permit her attorney to reconstruct her story in a way that seems foreign to her sense of self in order to avoid prejudicing her request for custody before a gender-biased judge. *See also* Anthony V. Alfieri, *Disabled Clients, Disabling Lawyers*, 43 HASTINGS L.J. 769, 822–26 (1992) (describing this phenomenon in disability law); Gilkerson, *supra* note 9, at 880–81.

32. *See* MATHER ET AL., *supra* note 8, at 107. Sarat and Felstiner note that divorce clients generally begin their conversations with their lawyers with an attempt to explain the failure of their marriages. Most lawyers avoid participation in the client's attempts at rationalization and exculpation by remaining unresponsive or by changing the subject. When the conversation turns to current problems and the legal process, lawyers become more interactive, frequently challenging their client's characterizations and explanations. When the lawyer–client dialogue focuses on future concerns, however, lawyers listen to their client's feelings about the divorce, claim knowledge of similar reactions by other clients, suggest interpretations of the client's reality, and urge clients to refrain from letting their emotions dictate their behavior. Relying on the lawyer's expertise, clients frequently acquiesce in the lawyer's interpretation of reality and acknowledge the validity of the lawyer's advice. *See* Sarat & Felstiner, *supra* note 17. The researchers, however, also make clear that client

acquiescence is peppered with moments of client resistance to lawyer authority. *Id.* at 766–67. *See also* MATHER ET AL., *supra* note 8, at 90, 107; Gilkerson, *supra* note 9, at 905. Griffith's study of Dutch lawyers reveals how lawyers deliberately control client choices. Dutch lawyers saw their primary role as a facilitator of a "reasonable divorce." Griffiths, *supra* note 11, at 169–71. When their clients attempted to pursue unreasonable goals, the lawyers employed numerous tactics to achieve what they perceived as reasonable settlements. *Id.* at 171–72. Some lawyers manipulated their clients by selective transmission of the law, *id.* at 159–62, deliberately keeping some clients uninformed altogether. *Id.* at 160, 164. Many lawyers attempted to persuade their clients by reference to norms other than law, such as the children's need to maintain contact with both parents. *Id.* at 162, 171. Most of the lawyers did all they could to minimize conflict between spouses, usually by refusing to take an adversarial stance, *id.* at 164–65, and by remaining neutral in the face of client attempts to disparage the other party. *Id.* at 166. Some even threatened to withdraw if their clients refused to be reasonable. *Id.* at 171–72. Clients have few resources with which to resist these pressures and manipulations. *See also* MATHER ET AL., *supra*, at 96–105 (noting that many divorce lawyers use similar tactics to control clients).

33. *See* MATHER ET AL., *supra* note 8, at 25–30; Dinerstein, *supra* note 10, at 578.

34. *See* MATHER ET AL., *supra* note 8, at 96–106.

35. *See* Griffiths, *supra* note 11, at 166; Sarat & Felstiner, *supra* note 17, at 765. *See also* HUBERT J. O'GORMAN, LAWYERS AND MATRIMONIAL CASES: A STUDY OF INFORMAL PRESSURE IN PRIVATE PROFESSIONAL PRACTICE 84–86 (1963).

36. This particular phenomenon led Griffiths to comment that "lawyer and client are busy with two different divorces: the lawyer with a legal divorce, the client with a social and emotional one." Griffiths, *supra* note 11, at 155.

37. *See* Robert A. Burt, *Conflict and Trust Between Attorney and Client*, 69 GEO. L.J. 1015, 1019–20 (1981). *See also* Dinerstein, *supra* note 10, at 574–75.

38. *See* Felstiner & Sarat, *supra* note 13, at 1455–56.

39. *See* MATHER ET AL., *supra* note 8, at 31, 68–69, 92.

40. The emphasis clients place on blaming their spouses puts lawyers in a difficult position. As Sarat and Felstiner note,

> If they were to join with clients in the project of reconstructing the marriage failure and the moral standing of spouses, they would be dragged into a domain that is, in principle, irrelevant to no-fault divorce, wastes time, and is in fact beyond their expertise. On the other hand, if they directly challenge client characterizations, or dismiss them as legally irrelevant, they risk alienating their clients or deepening client mistrust. Thus, most of the time lawyers remain silent in the face of client attacks on their spouses. They refuse to explore the past and to participate in the construction of a shared version of the social history of the marriage. When they do interpret behavior they limit themselves to conduct that is directly relevant to the legal process of divorce, and they stress

circumstances and situations that produce common responses rather than intentions or dispositions unique to particular individuals. In this way they deflect what is, for many clients, a strong desire to achieve some moral vindication, even in a no-fault world.

Sarat & Felstiner, *supra* note 17, at 764. The end result of the lawyer's refusal to support the client's search for vindication may be a dissatisfied client who does not feel that the lawyer understood or empathized with him or her. *Id.* at 765.

41. *See* KENNETH KRESSEL, THE PROCESS OF DIVORCE: HOW PROFESSIONALS AND COUPLES NEGOTIATE SETTLEMENTS 140 (1985); MATHER ET AL., *supra* note 8, at 50, 93–107; O'GORMAN, *supra* note 35, at 82–86; Felstiner & Sarat, *supra* note 13, at 1456.

42. *See* MATHER ET AL., *supra* note 8, at 98–99. Lawyers also may advance the divorce slowly in order to allow the client time to process emotions that interfere with the negotiation process. *See id.* at 101–02; Marygold S. Melli et al., *The Process of Negotiation: An Exploratory Investigation in the Context of No-Fault Divorce*, 40 RUTGERS L. REV. 1133, 1152 (1988). This deliberate, well-motivated tactic, however, may provide another source of client dissatisfaction. Moreover, the claims of some lawyers that delay serves their client's best interest might amount to little more than a self-serving excuse for inattentiveness.

43. *See* MATHER ET AL., *supra* note 8, at 20, 23–25. Even three decades ago, divorce lawyers expressed this concern. O'Gorman quotes one divorce lawyer: "You have to let them get if off their chest. Let them talk to you. When they blow off about their troubles long enough, they feel better; and sometimes they are better able to see what can be done . . . . That's where a lawyer can help; by letting them talk." O'GORMAN, *supra* note 35, at 86.

44. *See* Felstiner & Sarat, *supra* note 13, at 1456.

45. Chambers, *supra* note 16, at 227.

46. *See* Andrew Schepard, *The Evolving Judicial Role in Child Custody Disputes: From Fault Finder to Conflict Manager to Differential Case Management*, 22 U. ARK. LITTLE ROCK L. REV. 395, 409–10 & n.42 (2000); Gail Diane Cox, *Excessive Fees Are Attacked Across the Board*, NAT'L L.J., Nov. 4, 1996, at A1, A22 (noting that a California legal fee dispute arbitrator believes that fee disputes generally stem from poor communication between the lawyer and the client). *See generally* KAREN WINNER, DIVORCED FROM JUSTICE: THE ABUSE OF WOMEN AND CHILDREN BY DIVORCE LAWYERS AND JUDGES (1996).

47. *See* Dinerstein, *supra* note 10, at 549–50 (noting that client participation enhances the likelihood of client satisfaction).

48. *See* William H. Simon, *Homo Psychologicus: Notes on a New Legal Formalism*, 32 STAN. L. REV. 487 (1980), William H. Simon, *Ethical Discretion in Lawyering*, 101 HARV. L. REV. 1083, and Thomas L. Shaffer, *Legal Ethics and the Good Client*, 36 CATH. U.L. REV. 319 (1987) for arguments that favor limitations on client autonomy. *See* Dinerstein, *supra* note 10, for a thoughtful discussion of the conflict between advocates for and opponents of client autonomy.

49. The limitations on women's voice noted here mimic in many ways the cultural injustice experienced by women in our society. As Becker explains,

> Cultural injustice is rooted in social patterns of representation, interpretation, and communication. Examples include cultural domination (being subjected to patterns of interpretation and communication that are associated with another culture and are alien and/or hostile to one's own); nonrecognition (being rendered invisible by means of the authoritative representational, communicative, and interpretative practices of one's culture); and disrespect (being routinely maligned or disparaged in stereotypic public cultural representations and/or in everyday life interactions).

Mary Becker, *Patriarchy and Inequality: Towards a Substantive Feminism*, 1999 U. Chi. Legal F. 21, 44.

50. Powell v. Alabama, 287 U.S. 45, 68 (1932).

51. See Penelope Eileen Bryan, *Women's Freedom to Contract at Divorce: A Mask for Contextual Coercion*, 47 Buff. L. Rev. 1153, 1172–73 (1999) for an explanation of wives' financial dependency on their husbands.

52. Many note that the wife's relative lack of financial resources hampers her ability to pay attorneys' fees. *See, e.g.,* Terry Arendell, Mothers and Divorce: Legal Economic and Social Dilemmas 12 (1986); *Report of the Florida Supreme Court Gender Bias Study Commission*, 42 Fla. L. Rev. 803, 808–11 (1990) (hereinafter *Florida Gender Bias Report*); *Report of the Missouri Task Force on Gender and Justice*, 58 Mo. L. Rev. 485, 528–30 (1993) (hereinafter *Missouri Gender Bias Report*).

53. The husband's authority or power over financial matters stems from his individual possession of resources, such as wages and prestige, that are given value in the world outside the family. *See* Phillip Blumstein & Pepper Schwartz, American Couples 52–93 (1983). *See also* Susan Moller Okin, Justice, Gender and the Family 156–59 (1989); June Carbone, From Partners to Parents 12 (2000). *See generally* Bryan, *supra* note 51, at 1173–91.

54. *See* Report of the Gender Bias Study of the Supreme Judicial Court, Commonwealth of Massachusetts 12 (1989) (hereinafter Massachusetts Gender Bias Report); Karen Czapanskiy, *Domestic Violence, the Family, and the Lawyering Process: Lessons From Studies on Gender Bias in the Courts*, 27 Fam. L.Q. 247, 250 n.11 (1993); *Florida Gender Bias Report*, *supra* note 52, at 887–88; *Missouri Gender Bias Report*, *supra* note 52, at 550–51.

55. *See* Massachusetts Gender Bias Report, *supra* note 54, at 21; Czapanskiy, *supra* note 54, at 250 n.11; *Florida Gender Bias Report*, *supra* note 52, at 808–11; Marsha Garrison, *Equitable Distribution in New York: Results and Reform: Good Intentions Gone Awry: The Impact of New York's Equitable Distribution Law on Divorce Outcomes*, 57 Brook. L. Rev. 621, 712 (1991); *Missouri Gender Bias Report*, *supra* note 52, at 531–34 (noting that many attorneys admitted their reluctance to represent women in divorce proceedings because they knew they would not get paid); Lynn Hecht Schafran, *Gender and Justice: Florida and the Nation*, 42 Fla. L. Rev. 181, 187–88 (1990).

56. *See* Massachusetts Gender Bias Report, *supra* note 54, at 20; Winner, *supra* note 46, at xviii–xxxix; Czapanskiy, *supra* note 54, at 250 n.11; *In re* Marriage of Broday, 628 N.E.2d 790 (Ill. App. Ct. 1993).

57. *See In re* Marriage of Brandt, 489 N.E.2d 902 (Ill. App. Ct. 1986). Judges, however, typically hold wives without funds responsible for "choosing" to proceed pro se and refuse to vacate allegedly unfair agreements. *See, e.g., Broday*, 628 N.E.2d at 795–96. Courts also presume that wives receive adequate independent representation from attorneys their husbands have chosen for them. *See, e.g., Brandt*, 489 N.E.2d 902.

58. *See* Penelope E. Bryan, *Reclaiming Professionalism: The Lawyer's Role in Divorce Mediation*, 28 Fam. L.Q. 177, 177–88 (1994); *Florida Gender Bias Report, supra* note 52, at 810. Many lawyers, particularly good and expensive lawyers, admit that they prefer to represent husbands because husbands can pay their fees. Winner states,

> The man who controls the family's money—and his wife's share—is in a position financially and legally to overpower his spouse in the divorce proceeding. In 1991 Barbara L. Paltrow, President of the Nassau County Women's Bar Association, described the prototypical case in a letter to her peers: "He had access to high priced legal talent from the start, access to lawyers who knew how to use the system to great and often unfair advantage. The wife, on the other hand, quickly discovered that most lawyers would not represent her on the promise of getting paid, eventually, from family resources controlled by the husband. In order to have any representation these women had to exhaust their life savings, if they had any, and borrow to the hilt from family or friends. Even this was rarely enough to pay for the protracted litigation forced upon them."

Winner, *supra* note 46, at 13.

59. *See Florida Gender Bias Report, supra* note 52, at 808–09; *Missouri Gender Bias Report, supra* note 52, at 535.

60. One seasoned family law attorney put it this way:

> The inability of the economically dependent spouse to participate on equal footing in litigation in the areas of domestic relations . . . creates bias in my opinion in favor of men and against women and runs to all areas, all issues in domestic relations. The party with the control of the finances literally has such a significant advantage in my opinion that they cannot only control the litigation but also wind up with a great advantage on every issue and I think if played right can succeed in almost every issue. We see this more and more.

Missouri Gender Bias Report, supra note 52, at 530.

61. *See* Winner, *supra* note 46, at 66–70. Winner tells of Charlotte Bogart, who in 1981 at the age of 58, separated from her husband, Donald, after a 26-year marriage. During the marriage, Donald had beaten Charlotte, breaking her leg and injuring her shoulder on separate occasions. Donald's lawyer requested

bifurcation of the divorce from the maintenance and property issues. Charlotte had to change lawyers during the divorce. Her former lawyer wrote her new lawyer a letter warning of Donald's lawyer's threats to delay the ultimate settlement for years. The judge granted the divorce in 1988, retaining jurisdiction over the remaining property and support issues. Once the divorce was final, Donald, who had control over the $1 million marital estate, lost all motivation to settle the remaining issues. Thirteen years later, at the age of 71, Charlotte finally gave up her fight and accepted her ex-husband's settlement offer. She had paid over $100,000 in attorney fees during her 13-year struggle for justice. *See id.* at 66–69. Many times divorce cases are settled before the parties exchange basic financial information. In their study of 349 Wisconsin divorce cases, Melli et al. found that only 90 case files contained mandatory financial disclosure sheets from both parties; 126 case files contained little or no financial information. See Melli et al., *supra* note 42, at 1146–47.

62. *See* Massachusetts Gender Bias Report, *supra* note 54, at 21; Lenore J. Weitzman, The Divorce Revolution: The Unexpected Consequences for Women and Children in America 342–43 (1985) (noting that some men delay a bonus, commission, or raise until after the divorce, minimizing the income available for child support or spousal maintenance).

63. *See* Weitzman, *supra* note 62; *Florida Gender Bias Report, supra* note 52, at 810; *Missouri Gender Bias Report, supra* note 52, at 535. As Winner notes: "In divorce court, some lawyers use so-called scorched earth tactics against wives in a campaign to wear them down and starve them out. They attempt to outspend the wife by legally obstructing the proceedings and delaying an agreement until she finally runs out of money and patience and gives up." Winner, *supra* note 46, at 58. Cases challenging settlement agreements frequently reflect the circumstances that Winner describes and that courts largely ignore. *See generally* Bryan, *supra* note 58, at 177–88.

64. *See* Winner, *supra* note 46, at xix, 13. Winner tells Ginger's story:

> Barkley [Ginger's brother] related how his sister's first attorney had walked off the case. Her siblings had sunk more than $30,000 into legal fees for the lawyer to defend their sister's rights in court, only to see him withdraw from the proceeding after his bill climbed to $70,000. He had already threatened to quit unless he got more money, so one of Ginger's sisters, a retired school teacher, had borrowed $23,000 on her credit cards to pay him to continue representing Ginger. They had also signed a promissory note. Despite these payments, the attorney dropped Ginger's case four months later. He had the judge's permission to do so.

> *Id.* at 17. *See also Florida Gender Bias Report, supra* note 52, at 809. As an alternative to abandonment, a lawyer may insist that the client sign a confession of judgment or a promissory note that can later serve as the basis for the lawyer's lien on the client's property, sometimes the marital home. *See* Winner, *supra*, at 85–88.

65. *See* Wisconsin Equal Justice Task Final Report 237–38 (1991) (hereinafter Wisconsin Equal Justice Report); *Missouri Gender Bias Report, supra* note 52, at 528–30.

66. *See* Patricia Phillips, Divorce: A Woman's Guide to Getting a Fair Share 94, 101–09 (1995); Winner, *supra* note 46, at 64–65. *See also* In re Marriage of Palacios, 656 N.E.2d 107, *appeal denied,* 662 N.E.2d 427 (Ill. App. Ct. 1995) (finding that husband concealed $5.38 million in lottery winnings from his wife); *In re* Marriage of Frederick, 578 N.E.2d 612 (Ill. App. Ct. 1991); Ridgway v. Ridgway, 497 N.E.2d 126 (Ill. App. Ct. 1986); *In re* Marriage of Broday, 628 N.E.2d 790 (Ill. App. Ct. 1993); Bellow v. Bellow, 352 N.E.2d 427 (Ill. App. Ct. 1976).

67. *See* Massachusetts Gender Bias Report, *supra* note 54, at 21. *See generally* In re Marriage of Brandt, 489 N.E.2d 902 (Ill. App. Ct. 1986).

68. *See, e.g.,* Massachusetts Gender Bias Report, *supra* note 54, at 22–23; Okin, *supra* note 53, at 152; *Florida Gender Bias Report, supra* note 52, at 810; Melli et al., *supra* note 42, at 1146–47. *See also* Donald J. MacDougall, *Negotiated Settlement of Family Disputes, in* The Resolution of Family Conflict: Comparative Legal Perspectives 26, 34 (John M. Eekelaar & Sanford N. Katz eds. 1984) (discussing the importance of information to effective negotiation). Cases that challenge settlement agreements abound with examples of wives' and their attorneys' failure to conduct discovery. Typically, courts either perceive the wife's or her attorney's failure to conduct discovery as the product of the wife's negligence. *See, e.g., Broday,* 628 N.E.2d 790. They fail to acknowledge that the wife's meager financial resources may compromise her ability to discover. For instance, in *Broday,* the court cites the wife's negligence to discover in denying her later claim of concealment or misrepresentation by her husband. *See id.*

69. *See* Massachusetts Gender Bias Report, *supra* note 54, at 22–23; *Missouri Gender Bias Report, supra* note 52, at 531. In many cases where the wife attempts to vacate a previous divorce judgment that incorporated a property settlement agreement, the lack of discovery by the wife's lawyer is apparent. *See In re* Marriage of Steadman, 670 N.E.2d 1146 (Ill. App. Ct. 1996); *Broday,* 628 N.E.2d 790; *In re* Marriage of Foster, 451 N.E.2d 915 (Ill. App. Ct. 1983). *See also* Melli et al., *supra* note 42, at 1146–47. One must assume either that all of these lawyers are incompetent, that their clients lacked the resources with which to pursue discovery, or both.

70. *See* Massachusetts Gender Bias Report, *supra* note 54, at 22–23.

71. Winner writes,

> Husbands usually control the money supply at the end of the marriage. If a woman's husband chooses to conceal assets, the discovery process can be dragged out for years, her lawyer charging fees every step of the way, in the effort to collect and assess financial information from her husband and his lawyers . . . . For many women, the process of discovery is much like cutting off an arm to save a finger. Commissioning experts

> to track down assets is a major expense. And the financial information the lawyer obtains from the husband and his attorneys doesn't necessarily help women in the courtroom, because the information often isn't reliable. Perjury is a major problem in divorce court.

WINNER, *supra* note 46, at 40–41. *See also Florida Gender Bias Report, supra* note 52, at 810.

72. *See* MASSACHUSETTS GENDER BIAS REPORT, *supra* note 54, at 21.

73. *See* Karen S. Peterson, *"Market Work," Yes; Housework, Hah!*, USA TODAY, Mar. 13, 2002, 2002 WL 4721686 (citing a 2002 study by the University of Michigan Institute for Social Research in which the researchers found that men perform housework approximately 16 hours per week, whereas wives spend approximately 27 hours per week at such tasks).

74. *See generally* PHYLLIS CHESLER, MOTHERS ON TRIAL: THE BATTLE FOR CHILDREN AND CUSTODY (1987).

75. In her study of the California divorce courts, Weitzman found that 96% of the divorced women, compared to 57% of the divorced men, reported that they wanted custody of their children. Only 38% of the divorced men, however, spoke of custody with their lawyers, and only 13% requested custody in their divorce petition. Weitzman concludes that most divorcing fathers do not have a serious interest in custody, whereas most divorcing mothers do. WEITZMAN, *supra* note 62, at 243–44. Others found a similar discrepancy between what type of custody fathers said they wanted and what custody they actually requested. *See* Robert H. Mnookin et al., *Private Ordering Revisited: What Custodial Arrangements are Parents Negotiating?*, in DIVORCE REFORM AT THE CROSSROADS 37, 72 (Stephen D. Sugarman & Herma Hill Kay eds. 1985).

76. *See* CHESLER, *supra* note 74, at 334–38; *Missouri Gender Bias Report, supra* note 52, at 536; Dorothy E. Roberts, *Motherhood and Crime*, 79 IOWA L. REV. 95, 96–98 (1993). Moreover, divorced mothers without custody face social stigmatization. Because most people believe that the law favors mother custody and that all good mothers want custody, what kind of a mother could she possibly be if she lost or voluntarily relinquished custody? *See* CHESLER, *supra*, at 176–82.

77. *See* MASSACHUSETTS GENDER BIAS REPORT, *supra* note 54, at 25 (noting that in divorce mediation women bargain away their economic rights in order to retain custody of the children); WINNER, *supra* note 46, at 50–51; *Florida Gender Bias Report, supra* note 52, at 819–20; Phyllis Gangel-Jacob, *Some Words of Caution About Divorce Mediation*, 23 HOFSTRA L. REV. 825, 832–33 (1995) (noting that fathers frequently use custody as a bargaining chip); Richard Neely, *The Primary Caretaker Parent Rule: Child Custody and the Dynamics of Greed*, 3 YALE L. & POL'Y REV. 168 (1984).

78. *See* Daniel G. Saunders, *Child Custody Decisions in Families Experiencing Woman Abuse*, 39 SOC. WORK 51, 56 (1994) (noting that a battered mother's fear of looking bad in a sole custody trial may encourage her to agree to a dangerous joint custody arrangement).

79. Experienced lawyers recognize that the wife's limited financial resources compromise her interests on all divorce issues. *See Missouri Gender Bias Report, supra* note 52, at 530.

80. WINNER, *supra* note 46, at 63–64. In its most extreme form, the wife's training and socialization as caregiver have led some women to relinquish custody in order to protect their children from a custody battle.

81. *See* Penelope E. Bryan, *Killing Us Softly: Divorce Mediation and the Politics of Power,* 40 BUFF. L. REV. 441 (1992); Bryan, *supra* note 51, at 1180–91. In addition, the law itself speaks with a male voice that often fails to capture or allow expression of women's voices and concerns. *See, e.g., id.* at 1191–1219; Martha Fineman, *Dominant Discourse, Professional Language, and Legal Change in Child Custody Decisionmaking,* 101 HARV. L. REV. 727 (1988); Lucinda M. Finley, *Breaking Women's Silence in Law: The Dilemma of the Gendered Nature of Legal Reasoning,* 64 NOTRE DAME L. REV. 886, 889 (1989).

82. Mediators claim they can balance the power between husbands and wives during mediation and thus prevent lopsided agreements. On closer examination, however, this claim proves false. See Bryan, *supra* note 81, for an explanation of why mediators do not and cannot compensate for the power imbalances between husbands and wives. Moreover, even when lawyers represent wives in mediation, power imbalances between spouses can still severely disadvantage wives. *See* Bryan, *supra* note 58, at 193. The Massachusetts' Gender Bias Report reveals that mediation disadvantages women on financial as well as child issues. MASSACHUSETTS GENDER BIAS REPORT, *supra* note 54, at 23–27.

83. The wife's financial dependency on her husband helps explain her naive trust of him. Because of the dependent person's psychological need to perceive her benefactor as benevolent, dependency tends to breed naive trust. Becker explains that our patriarchal culture discourages the recognition of conflicts of interest between men and women generally:

> In a patriarchal culture, there is a strong tendency to deny conflicts of interest between women and men despite obvious inequalities in the allocation of responsibilities and scarce resources. For example, Arlie Hochschild has documented the tendency of working parents to deny inequality in their marriages, despite the fact that women in the families she studied worked the equivalent of an extra month a year. Because women and men live together in intimate relationships as parents and children or husbands and wives, we are reluctant to admit conflicts of interest. And it is easy to deny conflicts of interest because patriarchy justifies inequalities and injustices, even violence, in terms of women's choices and defects: if women get what they choose or deserve, we need not worry about conflicts of interest nor that mostly male decisionmakers divide the pie.

Becker, *supra* note 49, at 21. Becker's insights make it easier to understand why women may not perceive the conflict between their interests and the interests of their "soon-to-be" ex-husbands.

84. *See* ARENDELL, *supra* note 52, at 9.

85. *See In re* Marriage of Broday, 628 N.E.2d 790, 795 (Ill. App. Ct. 1993).

86. *See In re* Marriage of Beck, 404 N.E.2d 790, 795 (Ill. App. Ct. 1980); Beattie v. Beattie, 368 N.E.2d 178, 179–80 (Ill. App. Ct. 1977).

87. *See generally* Bryan, *supra* note 51, at 1243–70.

88. *See, e.g.,* NANCY E. DOWD, IN DEFENSE OF SINGLE-PARENT FAMILIES 33 (1997); MARTHA ALBERTSON FINEMAN, THE NEUTERED MOTHER, THE SEXUAL FAMILY AND OTHER TWENTIETH CENTURY TRAGEDIES 164 (1995); Karen Czapanskiy, *Volunteers and Draftees: The Struggle for Parental Equality,* 38 UCLA L. REV. 1415, 1415–16, 1435, 1451–53 & n.125 (1991). Pateman traces the historical evolution of women's domestic service within the family and concludes that being a woman (wife) means providing services for and at the command of a man (husband). *See* CAROLE PATEMAN, THE SEXUAL CONTRACT 116–28 (1988).

89. *See* Czapanskiy, *supra* note 88, at 1415 & n.1, 1451–53, & n.124.

90. *See, e.g.,* BLUMSTEIN & SCHWARTZ, *supra* note 53, at 53–59, 62–65; Bryan, *supra* note 81, at 481–87.

91. *See, e.g., In re* Marriage of Broday, 628 N.E.2d 790, 795 (Ill. App. Ct. 1993).

92. WINNER, *supra* note 46, at 12.

93. Regan explains the dichotomy between the family and the market as follows:

> In this dichotomy, the family represents the sphere of life characterized by relationships of mutuality and care, in which individuals are willing to forego their own advantage for the sake of others with whom they share largely ineluctable bonds. The interdependence of family members' lives creates the prospect that individuals within a family may sometimes be subject to obligations that cannot wholly be described as voluntarily chosen. By contrast, the market ostensibly is the realm of the sovereign individual, animated by self-interest, who surrenders her freedom only to the degree that she has consented to do so. Individuals in the market thus relate as strangers, whose ties to one another are deliberately forged as well as broken, and whose obligations to each other are best characterized as contractual.

> Milton C. Regan, Jr., *Spouses and Strangers: Divorce Obligations and Property Rhetoric,* 82 GEO. L.J. 2303, 2306 (1994). *See also* DAVID L. KIRP ET AL., GENDER JUSTICE 179 (1986) (noting the difference between family and marketplace norms).

94. *See, e.g., In re* Marriage of Brandt, 489 N.E.2d 902 (Ill. App. Ct. 1986).

95. *See* CAROL GILLIGAN, IN A DIFFERENT VOICE: PSYCHOLOGICAL THEORY AND WOMEN'S DEVELOPMENT (1982) (spawning debate about the existence and the origin of women's care orientation).

96. Gilligan explains,

> In analyzing women's thinking about what constitutes care and what connection means, I noted women's difficulty in including themselves among the people for whom they considered it moral to care. The inclusion of self is genuinely problematic not only for women but

also for society in general. Self-inclusion on the part of women challenges the conventional understanding of feminine goodness by severing the link between care and self-sacrifice; in addition, the inclusion of women challenges the interpretive categories of the Western tradition, calling into question descriptions of human nature and holding up to scrutiny the meaning of "relationship," "love," "morality," and "self."

Carol Gilligan, *Prologue: Adolescent Development Reconsidered*, in Mapping the Moral Domain vii, xxx–xxxi (Carol Gilligan et al. eds. 1988). *See also* Gilligan, *supra* note 95; Kathryn Abrams, *Choice, Dependence, and the Reinvigoration of the Traditional Family*, 73 Ind. L.J. 517, 522 (1998) (noting that women's relational orientation may inhibit their bargaining power with men); Trina Grillo, *The Mediation Alternative: Process Dangers for Women*, 100 Yale L.J. 1545, 1601 (1991). The tendency of wives to discount the importance of their own needs may be particularly acute in violent marriages. *See* Angela Browne, When Battered Women Kill 78–79 (1987); Karla Fischer et al., *The Culture of Battering and the Role of Mediation in Domestic Violence Cases*, 46 SMU L. Rev. 2117, 2162 (1993).

97. *See* Gilligan, *supra* note 95. Many explain that the industrial revolution removed fathers from the home, leaving mothers as the primary caregivers. This division of family labor encouraged men to focus on individual ambition and achievement, minimizing the importance of fatherhood to men. David Blankenship, Fatherless America: Confronting Our Most Urgent Social Problem 15 (1995).

98. *See, e.g.,* Herma Hill Kay, *Beyond No-Fault: New Directions in Divorce Reform*, in Divorce Reform at the Crossroads 6, 30 (Stephen D. Sugarman & Herma Hill Kay eds. 1990).

99. Williams argues that the market requires the husband to perform as an ideal worker with few family responsibilities. In order for husbands to meet this market requirement, wives assume the domestic responsibilities. *See* Joan Williams, *Is Coverture Dead? Beyond a New Theory of Alimony*, 82 Geo. L.J. 2227, 2235–41 (1994).

100. *See* Robert H. Mnookin, *Divorce Bargaining: The Limits on Private Ordering*, in The Resolution of Family Conflict: Comparative Legal Perspectives 364, 367–68 (John M. Eekelaar & Sanford N. Katz eds. 1984).

101. *See* Bryan, *supra* note 51, at 1178–80 & nn.110–13.

102. *See* Bryan, *supra* note 81, at 488–90 & n.203. *See also* Mather et al., *supra* note 8, at 91.

103. *See* Mather et al., *supra* note 8, at 91; Winner, *supra* note 46, at 23, 57.

104. Winner, *supra* note 46, at 12. *See also* Isolina Ricci, *Mediator's Notebook: Reflections on Promoting Equal Empowerment and Entitlements for Women*, J. Divorce, Spring–Summer 1985, at 49.

105. *See* Alice H. Eagly, *Gender and Social Influence: A Social Psychological Analysis*, 38 Am. Psychol. 971 (1983). *See also* John Scanzoni, Sexual Bargaining: Power Politics in the American Marriage 82–83 (2d ed. 1982).

106. *See generally* Joseph Berger & Morris Zelditch, Jr., *Artifacts and Challenges: A Comment on Lee and Ofshe*, 46 Soc. Psychol. Q. 59 (1983); Eagly, *supra* note 105; Gerald W. McDonald, *Family Power: The Assessment of a Decade of Theory and Research, 1970–1979*, 42 J. Marriage & Fam. 841 (1980); Charlan Jeanne Nemeth, *Reflections on the Dialogue Between Status and Style: Influence Processes of Social Control and Social Change*, 46 Soc. Psychol. Q. 70 (1983); Aysan Tuzlak & James C. Moore, Jr., *Status, Demeanor and Influence: An Empirical Reassessment*, 47 Soc. Psychol. Q. 178 (1984).

107. *See* Bryan, *supra* note 81, at 458–63.

108. *See id.* for an explanation of status disparities between men and women, particularly between husbands and wives.

109. *See id.* at 462.

110. *See* John F. Stolte, *Self-Efficacy: Sources and Consequences in Negotiation Networks*, 119 J. Soc. Psychol. 69 (1983). *See also* John Scanzoni & Maximiliane Szinovacz, Family Decision-Making: A Developmental Sex Role Model 31 (1980).

111. *See, e.g.*, Steven J. Sherman, *Internal–External Control and Its Relationships to Attitude Change Under Different Social Influence Techniques*, 26 J. Personality & Soc. Psychol. 23 (1972); David Vern Stimpson, *The Influence of Commitment and Self-Esteem on Susceptibility to Persuasion*, 80 J. Soc. Psychol. 189 (1970).

112. "Diminished feelings of self-worth may inhibit the ability to bargain constructively and effectively, or worse, produce an abject acceptance of almost any terms dictated by the other." Kressel, *supra* note 41, at 83. Kressel speaks of the low self-esteem of the spouse whose husband or wife seeks the divorce. *See id.* No reason exists, however, to suspect that low self-esteem attributable to this cause has greater effect on negotiating ability than low self-esteem attributable to other causes.

113. *See* Bryan, *supra* note 81, at 472–74 for an explanation of women's low self-esteem.

114. *See, e.g.*, Jon W. Hoelter, *Factorial Invariance and Self-Esteem: Reassessing Race and Sex Differences*, 61 Soc. Forces 834 (1983); Sharron Koffman & Hilary M. Lips, *Sex Differences in Self-Esteem and Performance Expectancies in Married Couples*, 8 Soc. Behav. & Personality 57 (1980). *But see* Marlene Mackie, *The Domestication of Self: Gender Comparisons of Self-Imagery and Self-Esteem*, 46 Soc. Psychol. Q. 343 (1983) (finding no self-esteem differences between husbands and wives).

115. *See, e.g.*, William A. Barry, *Marriage Research and Conflict: An Integrative Review*, 73 Psychol. Bull. 41 (1970); Anne Statham Macke et al., *Housewives' Self-Esteem and Their Husbands' Success: The Myth of Vicarious Involvement*, 41 J. Marriage & Fam. 51 (1979) (finding that housewives' self-esteem is related to perceived marital success); Mackie, *supra* note 114, at 346. As one author notes "becoming a man's wife is still the major means through which most women can find a recognized social identity." *See* Pateman, *supra* note 88, at 132. Loss of that valued identity can lead to lowered self-esteem.

116. *See* Bryan, *supra* note 81, at 472 & n.125.

117. *See id.* at 466–71.

118. *See id. See also* Bryan, *supra* note 58, at 177–88, 199–200 (providing an example of how depression affects negotiation competence).

119. Rosenfield notes that the differences between depression in men and women are "found across cultures, over time, in different age groups, in rural as well as urban areas, and in treated as well as untreated populations. Researchers estimate that women have as much as twice the rate of distress and depression as men." Sarah Rosenfield, *The Effects of Women's Employment: Personal Control and Sex Differences in Mental Health*, 30 J. HEALTH & SOC. BEHAV. 77, 77 (1989). For an explanation of why women are more prone to depression than men, *see* Bryan, *supra* note 81, at 467–68.

120. *See* Rosenfield, *supra* note 119, at 77.

121. *See* Bryan, *supra* note 81, at 469–70.

122. *See* DONALD G. GIFFORD, LEGAL NEGOTIATIONS: THEORY AND APPLICATIONS 99 (1989) (citations omitted); DEAN G. PRUITT, NEGOTIATION BEHAVIOR 26 (1981) (citing John G. Holmes et al., *The Effects of Prenegotiation Expectations on the Distributive Bargaining Process*, 7 J. EXPERIMENTAL SOC. PSYCHOL. 582–99 (1971)); Donald L. Harnett et al., *Personality, Bargaining Style and Payoff in Bilateral Monopoly Bargaining Among European Managers*, 36 SOCIOMETRY 325, 342 (1973).

123. *See* Bryan, *supra* note 81, at 475–77, for an explanation of why women expect less than men. *See also* John T. Jost, *An Experimental Replication of the Depressed-Entitlement Effect Among Women*, 21 PSYCHOL. WOMEN Q. 387 (1997).

124. *See* Bryan, *supra* note 51, at 1243–70 & nn.430–647 for several examples. *See also* Bryan, *supra* note 58, at 177–88.

125. Conflict theorists acknowledge the competitive nature of bargaining over scarce resources. *See, e.g.*, KENNETH E. BOULDING, CONFLICT AND DEFENSE: A GENERAL THEORY 4–5 (1962); MORTON DEUTSCH, THE RESOLUTION OF CONFLICT 20–25 (1973).

126. *See* Morton Deutsch, *Conflict and Its Resolution*, 7 Nat'l Tech. Info. Service Technical Rep. No. 1 (Oct. 1, 1965); Barbara J. Lonsdorf, *Coercion: A Factor Affecting Women's Inferior Financial Outcome in Divorce*, 3 AM J. FAM. L. 281, 288 (1989). *See, e.g.*, June Starr & Barbara Yngvesson, *Scarcity and Disputing: Zeroing-In on Compromise Decisions*, 2 AM. ETHNOLOGIST 553 (1975).

127. *See* WINNER, *supra* note 46, at 12, 23, 57; Bryan, *supra* note 81, at 477–81; Elizabeth G. Anderson, *Women and Contracts: No New Deal*, 88 MICH. L. REV. 1792, 1807 (1990) (reviewing CAROLE PATEMAN, THE SEXUAL CONTRACT (1988)) (noting that their traditional socialization makes it difficult for Western women to conceive of themselves as aggressive, self-seeking bargainers). *See also* Carol M. Rose, *Women and Property: Gaining and Losing Ground*, 78 VA. L. REV. 421 (1992) (finding that women's greater "taste for cooperation" than men's disadvantages women in negotiations). Moreover, Rose persuasively argues that the simple perception of others that women have a greater "taste for cooperation" than men can disadvantage women in negotiations. *Id.*

128. *See* Matina S. Horner, *Toward an Understanding of Achievement-Related Conflicts in Women*, 28 J. Soc. Issues 157, 173 (1972).

129. *See id.* at 171. Becker notes that our patriarchal culture recognizes "real women" as "dependent, vulnerable, pliant, weak, supportive, nurturing, intuitive, emotional, and empathetic." Becker, *supra* note 49, at 27.

130. *See* Horner, *supra* note 128, at 162.

131. *See* Bryan, *supra* note 81, at 479 & n.161.

132. *See* Horner, *supra* note 128, at 171. The negative consequences anticipated by these women seem quite reasonable when one considers that women's popularity is adversely affected by aggressive, assertive behavior. *See* Edward K. Sadalla et al., *Dominance and Heterosexual Attraction*, 52 J. Personality & Soc. Psychol. 730, 731–34 (1987). Additionally, women's recent advances have precipitated a powerful backlash. *See generally* Susan Faludi, Backlash: The Undeclared War Against American Women (1991).

133. *See* Horner, *supra* note 128, at 173.

134. *See id.* at 168–69. Horner's original research has received criticism on methodological grounds and has proven difficult to replicate. *See, e.g.*, Adeline Levine & Janice Crumrine, *Women and the Fear of Success: A Problem in Replication*, 80 Am. J. Soc. 964, 969–71 (1975) (finding no sex differences in fear of success imagery); Belle Rose Ragins & Eric Sundstrom, *Gender and Power in Organizations: A Longitudinal Perspective*, 105 Psychol. Bull. 51, 71 (1989). More recent research, however, lends support to Horner's original conclusions. *See* Bryan, *supra* note 51, at nn.126–28 and accompanying text.

135. *See* Susan Pollak & Carol Gilligan, *Images of Violence in Thematic Apperception Test Stories*, 42 J. Personality & Soc. Psychol. 159, 163 (1982). This research, like Horner's, has been criticized. *See* Cynthia J. Benton et al., *Is Hostility Linked With Affiliation Among Males and With Achievement Among Females? A Critique of Pollak and Gilligan*, 45 J. Personality & Soc. Psychol. 1167 (1983). *See generally* Bernard Weiner et al., *Compounding the Errors: A Reply to Pollak and Gilligan*, 45 J. Personality & Soc. Psychol. 1176 (1983) (criticizing Pollak and Gilligan's study). A more recent study that replicates Pollak and Gilligan's findings, however, suggests that the unwelcome message brought by Pollak and Gilligan's work, rather than faulty methodology, explains the controversy. *See* Vicki S. Helgeson & Don J. Sharpsteen, *Perceptions of Danger in Achievement and Affiliation Situations: An Extension of the Pollak and Gilligan Versus Benton et al. Debate*, 53 J. Personality & Soc. Psychol. 727 (1987) (citing Susan Pollak & Carol Gilligan, *Killing the Messenger*, 48 J. Personality & Soc. Psychol. 374 (1985)).

136. *See* Helgeson & Sharpsteen, *supra* note 135, at 732.

137. *See generally* Gloria Cowan et al., *The Effects of Target, Age and Gender on Use of Power Strategies*, 47 J. Personality & Soc. Psychol. 1391 (1984); Toni Falbo & Letitia Anne Peplau, *Power Strategies in Intimate Relationships*, 38 J. Personality & Soc. Psychol. 618 (1980); Judith A. Howard et al., *Sex, Power and Influence Tactics in Intimate Relationships*, 51 J. Personality & Soc. Psychol. 102 (1986). *See also* Carol Watson, *Gender Versus Power as a*

Predictor of Negotiation Behavior and Outcomes, 10 NEGOTIATION J. 117 (1994) (finding that power and gender influence negotiation behavior and outcomes).

138. *See* Sheryle Whitcher Alagna, *Sex Role Identity, Peer Evaluation of Competition, and the Responses of Women and Men in a Competitive Situation*, 43 J. PERSONALITY & SOC. PSYCHOL. 546, 553 (1982). *See also* KRESSEL, *supra* note 41, at 52–53; Ricci, *supra* note 104, at 53.

139. As Isolina Ricci notes,

> When [the wife] does develop a utilitarian parenting or financial plan, the husband might call her "cold," "calculating" or "selfish." Without interventions, these attributional labels may be taken to heart rather than identified as a part of the husband's bargaining tactics, and the wife may pull back and revise her plan to gain his approval.

Ricci, *supra* note 104, at 53.

140. *See* Leonard H. Chusmir & Joan Mills, *Gender Differences in Conflict Resolution Styles of Managers: At Work and At Home*, 20 SEX ROLES 149, 151 (1989).

141. *See* Anne K. McCarrick et al., *Gender Differences in Competition and Dominance During Married Couples Group Therapy*, 44 SOC. PSYCHOL. Q. 164 (1981).

142. *See* Bryan, *supra* note 81, at, 453 n.37.

143. During the investigation of gender bias in the Massachusetts courts, Barbara Hauser, a director of the Family Service Clinic at Middlesex Probate Court, testified,

> At times it appears that the court and its personnel have a limited appreciation about the inequality in ability of parties to bargain effectively at the time of marital separation. Women in these times often feel less adequate than men in areas of articulating their needs and wishes, forcefulness in negotiating, and economic stability. Furthermore, women often have a wish to resolve conflict through communication and mediation rather than taking a more adversarial posture, and it is thus important that these differences be recognized rather than overlooked in any form of divorce proceedings.

MASSACHUSETTS GENDER BIAS REPORT, *supra* note 54, at 25.

144. *See* Martha R. Mahoney, *Legal Images of Battered Women: Redefining the Issue of Separation*, 90 MICH. L. REV. 1, 10–11 (1991). Some estimate spousal abuse occurs in at least one fourth to one third of marriages. *See* MURRAY A. STRAUSS ET AL., BEHIND CLOSED DOORS: VIOLENCE IN THE AMERICAN FAMILY 32 (1980); Mary Ann Dutton, *Understanding Women's Responses to Domestic Violence: A Redefinition of Battered Woman Syndrome*, 21 HOFSTRA L. REV. 1191, 1210 (1993); Murray A. Straus & Richard J. Gelles, *How Violent Are American Families? Estimates from the National Family Violence Resurvey and Other Studies*, *in* PHYSICAL VIOLENCE IN AMERICAN FAMILIES: RISK FACTORS AND ADAPTATIONS TO VIOLENCE IN 8,145 FAMILIES 110 (Murray A. Strauss & Richard J. Gelles eds. 1990). Others estimate spousal abuse occurs in one half to two thirds of all marriages. *See Florida Gender Bias Report*, *supra* note 52, at 848

& n.225; Laurie Woods, *Litigation on Behalf of Battered Women*, 7 WOMEN'S RTS. L. REP. 39, 41 (1981). Repeated severe violence occurs in 1 of 14 marriages. *See* PETER G. JAFFE ET AL., CHILDREN OF BATTERED WOMEN 19 (1990). Some criticize Straus and Gelles' findings for underestimating the incidence of marital violence. *See* Fischer et al., *supra* note 96, at 2124–25 & n.44, 2137 & n.97.

145. *See* Fischer et al., *supra* note 96, at 2142; Linda K. Girdner, *Custody Mediation in the United States: Empowerment or Social Control?*, 3 CANADIAN J. WOMEN & L. 134, 138 n.19 (1989) (noting studies in which 50% to 75% of the women gave physical violence as a reason for marital separation); Joan S. Meier, *Notes From the Underground: Integrating Psychological and Legal Perspectives on Domestic Violence in Theory and Practice*, 21 HOFSTRA L. REV. 1295, 1304 & n.24 (1993) (finding that approximately two thirds of divorced or separated women report violence in their former relationships) (citing Irene Frieze & Angela Browne, *Violence in Marriage, in* FAMILY VIOLENCE 177–80 (Lloyd Ohlin & Michael Tonry eds. 1989)); Murray A. Straus, *Foreword*, PARTNER VIOLENCE: A COMPREHENSIVE REVIEW OF 20 YEARS OF RESEARCH v, vi (Jana L. Jasinski & Linda M. Williams eds. 1998) (noting studies that demonstrated that domestic violence was a factor in 40% of divorces); Joan Zorza, *Recognizing and Protecting the Privacy and Confidentiality Needs of Battered Women*, 29 FAM. L.Q. 273 (1995) (noting that although divorced and separated women comprise only 10% of all American women, they represent 75% of all battered women and report being battered 14 times as often as women still living with partners) (citing Caroline WOLF HARLOW, U.S. DEP'T OF JUSTICE, FEMALE VICTIMS OF VIOLENT CRIME 5 (Jan. 1991)).

146. *See* Fischer et al., *supra* note 96, at 2126–29.

147. *See id.* at 2129–30; Mildred Daley Pagelow, *Justice for Victims of Spouse Abuse in Divorce and Child Custody Cases*, 8 VIOLENCE & VICTIMS 69, 74 (1993); *Florida Gender Bias Report*, *supra* note 52, at 851.

148. *See* Fischer et al., *supra* note 96, at 2131–37.

149. *See* Dutton, *supra* note 144, at 1227.

150. *See* Mary E. Becker, *Double Binds Facing Mothers in Abusive Families: Social Support Systems, Custody Outcomes, and Liability for Acts of Others*, 2 U. CHI. L. SCH. ROUNDTABLE 13, 18 (1995); Pagelow, *supra* note 147, at 74.

151. *See* Glenda Kaufman Kantor & Jana L. Jasinski, *Dynamics and Risk Factors in Partner Violence, in* PARTNER VIOLENCE: A COMPREHENSIVE REVIEW OF 20 YEARS OF RESEARCH 1, 33 (Jana L. Jasinski & Linda M. Williams eds. 1998); Catherine F. Klein & Leslye E. Orloff, *Providing Legal Protection for Battered Women: An Analysis of State Statutes and Case Law*, 21 HOFSTRA L. REV. 801, 815–16 (1993); Mahoney, *supra* note 144, at 5–7, 65–68 (naming this phenomenon "separation assault"). The abuser may direct the violence at his wife, her children, or her family. As Pagelow notes,

When a battering victim takes the first steps toward freedom, the abuse frequently escalates to deadly intensity. An abused woman may be most at risk of femicide when she leaves or when it becomes clear to her spouse that she will be leaving for good. The most common type of retaliation is against the woman herself, stalked and killed by "obsessive" mates; other times it results in murder–suicide. Murder–suicide most frequently occurs between husband and wife, and is almost always perpetrated by the male who first kills his wife, girlfriend, or estranged partner. Batterers also murder or attempt to murder their own children for revenge when victims try to get away, and occasionally they also carry out their threats against their wives' families.

Pagelow, *supra* note 147, at 72. *See also* Fischer et al., *supra* note 96, at 2138–39.

152. *See* Pagelow, *supra* note 147, at 71–72. Sometimes for years before their wives' departure, abusive husbands threaten their victims that any attempt to leave will be met with violence toward them, their children, or their families. *See id.* at 72 (1993). *See also* Dutton, *supra* note 144, at 1232.

153. *See* Dutton, *supra* note 144, at 1232; Pagelow, *supra* note 147, at 74.

154. *See* Jaffe et al., *supra* note 144, at 23, 26; Susan Schechter, Women and Male Violence: The Visions and Struggles of the Battered Women's Movement 219–44 (1982); Fischer et al., *supra* note 96, at 2132; Pagelow, *supra* note 147, at 70 (describing a systematic pattern of withdrawal from relations with family and friends).

155. *See* Becker, *supra* note 150, at 18 (noting that battered women frequently learn from religious training or from their families of origin that they are responsible for the quality of the marriage and for keeping the family together).

156. *See* Jaffe et al., *supra* note 144, at 23; Massachusetts Gender Bias Report, *supra* note 54, at 83; Lenore E. Walker, The Battered Woman 32 (1979); Dutton, *supra* note 144, at 1218–19, 1221; Roberta L. Valente, *Addressing Domestic Violence: The Role of the Family Law Practitioner*, 29 Fam. L.Q. 187, 191 (1995).

157. *See* Dutton, *supra* note 144, at 1216, 1221.

158. *See id.* at 1218–19.

159. *See id.* at 1221.

160. *See id.*

161. *See generally* Lenore E. Walker, The Battered Woman Syndrome (1984); Walker, *supra* note 156; Pamela Choice & Leanne K. Lamke, *A Conceptual Approach to Understanding Abused Women's Stay/Leave Decisions*, 18 J. Fam. Issues 290 (1997); Desmond Ellis, *Marital Conflict Mediation and Post-Separation Wife Abuse*, 8 L. & Ineq. J. 317, 331 (1990); Sherry L. Hamby & Bernadette Gray-Little, *Responses to Partner Violence: Moving Away from Deficit Models*, 11 J. Fam. Psychol. 339, 340 (1997); Linda R. Keenan, *Note, Domestic Violence and Custody Litigation: The Need for Statutory Reform*, 13 Hofstra L. Rev. 407, 418 (1985). Many battered women, however, also rebel and resist the batterer's pervasive control. *See* Fischer et al., *supra* note 96, at 2133–37. Moreover, many scholars and researchers persuasively argue that passivity is only one of many symptoms that battered women may exhibit. *See, e.g.*, Hamby & Gray-Little, *supra*, at 340–41, 347–49; Mahoney, *supra* note 144.

162. *See* Bryan, *supra* note 81, at 457–81.

163. *See* Czapanskiy, *supra* note 54, at 250 & n.11.

164. *See* WALKER, *supra* note 156, at 129–44; Fischer et al., *supra* note 96, at 2121 & n.17; Valente, *supra* note 156, at 189.

165. As Zorza notes,

> Working is effectively foreclosed to many battered women because abusers often sabotage their efforts to get to their jobs or continue to abuse them while they are at work. Seventy-four percent of battered women who work report that they are harassed on the job by their abusers. Abusive men cause over half of working battered women to be late for work at least sixty days a year, and over half to miss at least thirty-six full days of work annually. Twenty percent of all employed battered women lose their jobs because their abusers so harass them on the telephone or in person at work.

Zorza, *supra* note 145, at 277. *See also* Keenan, *supra* note 161, at 426; Valente, *supra* note 156, at 189.

166. A study of protective order petitions filed in a Pennsylvania county during 1990 revealed that 45% of the petitioners were unemployed and that their personal income averaged only $535 per month. *See* Edward W. Gondolf et al., *Court Response to Petitions for Civil Protection Orders*, 9 J. INTERPERSONAL VIOLENCE 503, 508 (1994). Moreover, the judges hearing the protective order petitions minimally granted the financial relief the petitioners requested. *See id.* at 510–12. *See also* Czapanskiy, *supra* note 54, at 253 & n.16.

167. *See The Family Violence Project of the National Council of Juvenile and Family Court Judges, Family Violence in Child Custody Statutes: An Analysis of State Codes and Legal Practice*, 29 FAM. L.Q. 197, 212–14 (1995) (hereinafter *The Family Violence Project*) (noting the inadequate legal representation frequently provided to domestic violence victims); Valente, *supra* note 156, at 187, 190.

168. *See* Fischer et al., *supra* note 96, at 2139–41; Mahoney, *supra* note 144, at 8 n.29; Martha Minow, *Words and the Door to the Land of Change: Law, Language, and Family Violence*, 43 VAND. L. REV. 1665, 1686 (1990); Pagelow, *supra* note 147, at 70, 76; Elizabeth M. Schneider, *Particularity and Generality: Challenges of Feminist Theory and Practice in Work on Woman-Abuse*, 67 N.Y.U. L. REV. 520, 530 (1992); Valente, *supra* note 156, at 187.

169. *See The Family Violence Project*, *supra* note 167, at 212 (noting that lawyers fail to identify domestic violence victims); Klein & Orloff, *supra* note 151, at 814; (acknowledging that few lawyers attempt to determine whether their clients have suffered domestic violence).

170. *See* Czapanskiy, *supra* note 54, at 257.

171. *See id.; The Family Violence Project*, *supra* note 167, at 213–14.

172. A recent deskbook for judges actually encourages judges to approach wives' claims of abuse suspiciously and to honor a father's visitation rights despite the father's abuse of the mother. Martha Albertson Fineman, *Domestic Violence, Custody, and Visitation*, 36 FAM. L.Q. 211, 217–22 (2002) (commenting on NATIONAL INTERDISCIPLINARY COLLOQUIUM ON CHILD CUSTODY, LEGAL AND

Mental Health Perspectives on Child Custody Law: A Deskbook for Judges (Robert J. Levy ed. 1998).

173. *See* Fischer et al., *supra* note 96, at 2160; Keenan, *supra* note 161, at 413, 423–24; Mahoney, *supra* note 144, at 43–48; Pagelow, *supra* note 147, at 74. The battered wife also may return to the batterer in order to avoid the risk of losing custody.

174. *See* Saunders, *supra* note 78, at 56 (noting that a battered mother's fear of looking bad in a sole custody trial may encourage her to agree to a dangerous joint custody arrangement).

175. *See, e.g., id.* at 54.

176. *See* Jaffe et al., *supra* note 144, at 107; Becker, *supra* note 150, at 28; Keenan, *supra* note 161, at 422–23.

177. *See* Czapanskiy, *supra* note 54, at 257; Fischer et al., *supra* note 96, at 2159–60; Mahoney, *supra* note 144, at 43–44; Meier, *supra* note 144, at 1308 n.40; Pagelow, *supra* note 147, at 74; Schneider, *supra* note 168, at 555.

178. *See* Mahoney, *supra* note 144, at 44 n.199 (discussing studies confirming high percentages of custody awards to fathers who battered their wives). *See also* Chesler, *supra* note 74, at 79 tab. 6 (finding that 59% of the fathers in study who won custody in litigation had abused their wives and that 50% of the fathers who obtained custody through private negotiations had abused their wives).

179. *See* Connie J. A. Beck & Bruce D. Sales, *A Critical Reappraisal of Divorce Mediation Research and Policy*, 6 Psychol. Pub. Pol'y & L. 989, 996–98 (2000); Andree G. Gagnon, *Ending Mandatory Divorce Mediation for Battered Women*, 15 Harv. Women's L.J. 272 (1992); Gangel-Jacob, *supra* note 77, at 834–35; Fischer et al., *supra* note 96, at 2118, 2165–71; Dianne Post, *Mediation Can Make Bad Worse*, Nat'l L. J., June 8, 1992, at 15; Ellis, *supra* note 161, at 327–39; Lisa G. Lerman, *Mediation of Wife Abuse Cases: The Adverse Impact of Informal Dispute Resolution on Women*, 7 Harv. Women's L.J. 57 (1984).

180. Many commentators reveal the problems battered wives confront in divorce mediation. *See* Massachusetts Gender Bias Report, *supra* note 54, at 94; Bryan, *supra* note 58, at 203–05; Fischer et al., *supra* note 96; Gagnon, *supra* note 179; Barbara J. Hart, *Gentle Jeopardy: The Further Endangerment of Battered Women and Children in Custody Mediation*, 7 Mediation Q. 317 (1990); Keenan, *supra* note 161, at 437–38; Saunders, *supra* note 78, at 55. Gerencser provides one example:

A recent family mediation began with the father shouting, "Do you know what I'd do if my son ever came home with an earring? I'd cut off his ear." He was responding to the mother's request that he stop berating their son. This outburst was no surprise. In a pre-mediation screening questionnaire, the mother said the father had abused her. Although she wanted to try mediation, she was unsure whether she could participate on an equal basis with the father. As the mediation progressed, the mother willingly acquiesced to the father's visitation demands in his presence. However, she said privately that she did not want him near her or their children, and that she had agreed to his demands only because she was afraid of him. The mediation ended in an impasse, with no reported mention of the father's abusive history or the mother's fear of further abuse based on her conduct at the mediation.

Alison E. Gerencser, *Family Mediation: Screening for Domestic Abuse*, 23 FLA. ST. U.L. REV. 43, 43 (1995). Gerencser does believe that some battered spouses can successfully mediate, but she also recommends that states provide sophisticated procedures for screening for domestic violence and exemptions from mediation for battered women. *See id.* at 55–60. Consider also one battered woman's experience in mediation:

> In court-ordered mediation we were told to cooperate and communicate in regards to the children. He took this one step further and used this to continue to harass me. . . . On the way home from our last mediation session of which we were told to ride to and from together—cooperation as they say—he got extremely agitated over something that I said in mediation. I had made the mistake of feeling safe enough to say how I really felt. [I thought] this would help the mediator to see what a mess I was really living in. I did not know about power and control at that time. . . . I dropped him off at his mother's house and he threw the papers the mediator gave us—these were contracts—and cussed me out later that evening around midnight. He broke into our apartment and started going through my things. He said he was looking for evidence that I was having an affair. This was his reason for our marriage to be ending, nothing about the abuse. When I realized there was something wrong in my apartment, I got up to investigate. He then struggled with me, slapping me and kicking me. He threw me to the floor and screamed at me that he was going to have me one last time. I was raped at knife point that night while my children were in the next room. Mediation is extremely dangerous when domestic violence is evident. If people who are ending relationships had equal power and could communicate, they would not need mediation. In cases where there is domestic violence, this never occurs. Mediation is set up with the idea that reasonable rational people will be participating in it.

WISCONSIN EQUAL JUSTICE REPORT, *supra* note 65, at 210.

181. The Colorado Women's Bar Association invited me to participate on a panel addressing mediation in divorce cases that involve domestic violence. One of the panelists was a woman lawyer–mediator who advocated mediation for dissolution of violent marriages and who claimed great sensitivity to domestic violence issues. In a spontaneous burst of candor, however, she stated that "violence was a two-way street," clearly implying to all present that the responsibility for the violence lay equally at the feet of the violent husband and the abused wife. The audience emitted a gasp of disbelief. This woman exposed what I frequently find; mediators talk a good game, but they often lack the knowledge and the ability to address domestic violence issues in divorce mediation.

182. *See* Joan M. Krauskopf & Sharon Burgess Seiling, *A Pilot Study on Marital Power as an Influence in Division of Pension Benefits at Divorce of Long Term Marriages*, 1996 J. Dispute Resol. 169 (finding that power imbalances between wives and husbands led to wives receiving fewer pension benefits than the law allowed).

183. *See, e.g.,* Paternoster et al., *supra* note 2, at 167–68; Tom R. Tyler, Why People Obey the Law (1990); *What Is Procedural Justice?*, *supra* note 2, at 106, 112–13, 126–27 (1988).

184. *See* Melli et al., *supra* note 42, at 1143, 1155–56.

185. *See id.* at 1146–47. Appellate opinions that address petitions to vacate settlement agreements provide numerous examples of the lack of discovery by the wife's divorce attorney. *See, e.g., In re* Marriage of Steadman, 670 N.E.2d 1146 (Ill. App. Ct. 1996); *In re* Marriage of Broday, 628 N.E.2d 790 (Ill. App. Ct. 1993); *In re* Marriage of Foster, 451 N.E.2d 915 (Ill. App. Ct. 1983); *In re* Marriage of Beck, 404 N.E.2d 972, 974 (Ill. App. Ct. 1980); Beattie v. Beattie, 368 N.E.2d 178, 179–80 (Ill. App. Ct. 1977). One assumes either that these lawyers lacked competence or that their clients lacked the resources to pursue discovery. Moreover, in one study of 349 Wisconsin divorces cases, only 90 files contained financial disclosure sheets from both parties, whereas 126 files contained little or not financial information. Melli et al., *supra* note 42, at 1146–47. *See* Bryan, *supra* note 58, at 177–88 (relating a story of a lawyer's failure to conduct discovery that led to an inequitable settlement).

186. *See* Tom R. Tyler, *Citizen Discontent With Legal Procedures: A Social Science Perspective on Civil Procedure Reform*, 45 Am. J. Comp. L. 871, 876 (1997). *See also* E. Allan Lind et al., *In the Eye of the Beholder: Tort Litigants' Evaluation of Their Experiences in the Civil Justice System*, 24 L. & Soc'y Rev. 953, 955 (1990) (noting that policy makers frequently assume that litigation costs and delay contribute to public dissatisfaction with the civil justice system). Results obtained by Lind et al., however, indicate that objective measures of costs and delay have significantly less effect on tort litigants' perceptions of procedural justice than other process variables and the subjective assessments of costs and delay formed by parties' expectations. *Id.* at 969–72, 982–84.

187. *See, e.g.,* Jon O. Newman, *Rethinking Fairness: Perspectives on the Litigation Process*, 94 Yale L.J. 1643, 1644 (1985). *But see* Samuel R. Gross & Kent D. Syverud, *Don't Try: Civil Jury Verdicts in a System Geared to Settlement*, 44 UCLA L. Rev. 1, 61–64 (1996) (arguing that less costly civil trials with more predictable results might encourage litigants to try rather than settle cases, ultimately increasing system costs).

188. *See* Kressel, *supra* note 41, at 156. Media reports validate client concern about the cost of divorce. For instance, the New Jersey Supreme Court appointed a special committee to investigate whether attorneys charged family law litigants excessive legal fees. At their final public hearing, the committee listened to a tearful Diane Terhune explain how she had spent most of a $290,000 inheritance on an eight-year court battle with her ex-husband over child support. Cox, *supra* note 46. Those who deal routinely with claims of excessive legal fees note that these disputes most frequently occur in family law cases.

Some attribute the high rate of complaint about fees to the emotional context of divorce cases. Joel Mark, a Los Angeles attorney who has served as a California state bar fee dispute arbitrator since 1984, states that "[o]ne literally sees letters saying, 'I don't care what it costs, you have to nail him—or her.' . . . And then when it's sorted out, and often these are people with limited funds, the client may resent the fee—especially if the outcome of the case disappointed them." Cox, *supra* note 46, at A1. Mark believes that most complaints about fees result from poor lawyer–client communication, with fees serving as a lightning rod for client dissatisfaction. *Id. See also* Rudolph J. Gerber, *Recommendation on Domestic Relations Reform,* 32 ARIZ. L. REV. 9, 11 (1990).

189. *See* Robert B. Yegge, *Divorce Litigants Without Lawyers,* 28 FAM. L.Q. 407, 408–09 (1994). In 1992 the National Center for State Courts studied 16 urban jurisdictions. In each jurisdiction, lawyers represented both parties in no more than 50% of the cases. A smaller 1990 study in Maricopa County, Arizona, found that both parties in 52% of divorce cases proceeded without lawyers. *Id.*

190. *See* Melli et al., *supra* note 42, at 1155–56; Yegge, *supra* note 189, at 408–09.

191. *See, e.g.,* Skoloff & Levy, *supra* note 7, at 83–84. Lawyers sometimes demand that clients secure their legal fees with mortgages on their marital homes. *See* Peter A. Joy, *Making Ethics Opinions Meaningful: Toward More Effective Regulation of Lawyer's Conduct,* 15 GEO. J. LEGAL ETHICS 313, 356 n.248 (2002).

192. *See* Gerber, *supra* note 188, at 10; Laurie C. Kadoch, *Five Degrees of Separation: A Response to Judge Sheldon's The Sleepwalker's Tour of Divorce Law,* 49 ME. L. REV. 321, 331 (1997); Kenneth J. Rigby, *Alternative Dispute Resolution,* 44 LA. L. REV. 1725, 1726 (1984); Catherine J. Ross, *The Failure of Fragmentation: The Promise of a System of Unified Family Courts,* 33 REV. JUR. U.I.P.R. 311, 313 (1999); Tyler, *supra* note 186, at 878. As Ross notes,

> Nearly all disputes that reach courts are heard at the state trial court level, where each year higher proportions of cases involve family problems. In the last few years, according to conservative estimates, domestic relations cases alone made up between 25 percent and 30 percent of all state court civil dockets. The National Center for State Courts emphasizes that domestic relations cases are the "largest and fastest growing segment of state court civil caseloads." Between 1984 and 1995 the number of domestic relations cases jumped by 70 percent, so that in 1995, state court trial courts heard approximately 4.9 million cases involving domestic relations. The National Center defines domestic relations cases as including divorce, child support and custody, domestic violence, paternity, interstate child support, and adoption.

Ross, *supra,* at 313 (citations omitted).

193. *See* Ross, *supra* note 192, at 313. *See also* Beck & Sales, *supra* note 179, at 889–90.

194. *See generally* Gerber, *supra* note 188, at 9–11; Ross, *supra* note 192, at 316.

195. *See, e.g.,* Beck & Sales, *supra* note 179, at 990.

196. *See, e.g., id.*

197. *See, e.g., id.*

198. *See* KRESSEL, *supra* note 41, at 144 (noting that lawyers recognize that unrealistic client expectations significantly impede settlement); MATHER ET AL., *supra* note 8, at 93–107. *See also* Beck & Sales, *supra* note 179, at 990.

199. *See* KRESSEL, *supra* note 41, at 47 (noting that divorce lawyers complain that client irrationality impedes settlement); MATHER ET AL., *supra* note 8, at 92. Early in the divorce process, for instance, clients frequently feel insecure about themselves and their parenting roles. Their frequent attempts to prove their competence as a person and fitness as a parent can impede negotiations. *See* KRESSEL, *supra*, at 42.

200. *See* MATHER ET AL., *supra* note 8, at 90, 107.

201. *See* Chambers, *supra* note 16, at 209–10, 212–13 (noting one wife's anger with an underhanded tactic employed by her husband's attorney that made her reluctant to settle). Some lawyers believe that their advocacy role requires adversity. *See* KRESSEL, *supra* note 41, at 48–49.

202. *See Missouri Gender Bias Report, supra* note 52, at 534 (noting that an award of fees for the dependent spouse's attorney would provide an incentive for the economically advantaged spouse to settle quickly). Strategic bargaining, of course, occurs across the spectrum of civil cases. *See* Gross & Syverud, *supra* note 187, at 52 ("litigants conceal or distort information to impress their opponents, demand things they do not want in order to get other concessions that they do, and play chicken with the opposition in order to get paid to avoid trials that nobody wants.").

203. *See* Mather et al., *supra* note 8, at 101–02.

204. *See* John Elson, *Divorce Bar Needs an Added Level of Checks*, NAT'L L.J., June 20, 1994, at A19–20; Ray Simon, *Gross Profits? An Introduction to a Program on Legal Fees*, 22 HOFSTRA L. REV. 625, 627 n.17 (1994) (referring to comments by Professor John Elson at Northwestern University Law School).

205. *See* Gary Crippen, *The Abundance of Family Law Appeals: Too Much of a Good Thing?*, 26 FAM. L.Q. 85, 101 (1992).

206. Gross and Syverud note, however, that enhanced predictability of civil trial outcomes might encourage litigants to try rather than settle cases, ultimately increasing system costs. Gross & Syverud, *supra* note 187, at 61–64. In a predictable system a spouse who faces an objectively unfair settlement offer, for instance, may more readily pursue litigation to secure a more favorable outcome. Because of the importance of quality outcomes in divorce, however, I cannot see this possibility as problematic. I also suspect that, once spouses truly understood that trial increases the cost of divorce without substantive advantage and that frivolous litigation invites sanctions, litigation would decline.

207. *See* Gross & Syverud, *supra* note 187, at 51 ("Every theory of bargaining assumes that a negotiated settlement is determined, at least in part, by the parties' predictions of the outcome of the case if it did go to trial.").

208. *See* Yegge, *supra* note 189, at 408–09. In 1992, the National Center for State Courts studied 16 urban jurisdictions. In each jurisdiction lawyers represented both parties in no more than 50% of the cases. *Id.* In a smaller 1990 study in Maricopa County, Arizona, researchers found that 90% of divorce cases involved at least one self-represented party, and 52% involved self-representation by both parties. *See* Bruce D. Sales, et al., *Is Self-Representation a Reasonable Alternative to Attorney Representation in Divorce Cases?*, 37 St. Louis U. L.J. 553, 594 (1993).

209. *See* Sales et al., *supra* note 208, at 594.

210. *See* Frances L. Harrison et al., *California's Family Law Facilitator Program: A New Paradigm for the Courts*, 2 J. Center for Families, Children & Cts. 61, 61, 76 (2000); Sales et al., *supra* note 208, at 554, 561, 590, 594; Yegge, *supra* note 189, at 409.

211. *See* Harrison et al., *supra* note 210, at 61.

212. *See id.*

213. *See* Yegge, *supra* note 189, at 409–10.

214. *See* Sales et al., *supra* note 208, at 576–83; Yegge, *supra* note 189, at 410.

215. *See* Yegge, *supra* note 189, at 410.

216. *See* Russell Engler, *And Justice for All—Including the Unrepresented Poor: Revisiting the Roles of the Judges, Mediators, and Clerks*, 67 Fordham L. Rev. 1987, 1997–98 (1999).

217. *See* Harrison et al., *supra* note 210, at 61–70, 74–75; Sales et al., *supra* note 208, at 557–58; Yegge, *supra* note 189, at 413–14. *See also* Engler, *supra* note 216, at 2012.

218. *See* Sales et al., *supra* note 208, at 558.

219. *See* Engler, *supra* note 216, at 1988–89.

220. *See* Mather et al., *supra* note 8, at 44; Sales et al., *supra* note 208, at 558.

221. *See* Engler, *supra* note 216, at 2013.

222. Bryan, *supra* note 51, at 1153–56.

223. Parties indicate that simplicity influences their decision to proceed pro se. *See* Sales et al., *supra* note 208, at 554, 561, 590, 598–99.

224. *See* Bryan, *supra* note 51, at 1172–1234 for an explanation of the barriers women face to fair settlements.

225. *See id.* at 1234–70.

226. *See* Engler, *supra* note 216, at 1988–89.

227. *See id.* at 2049. *See also* Mather et al., *supra* note 8, at 77 (noting that Maine and New Hampshire divorce attorneys report that they face unrepresented parties in approximately half of their cases).

228. *See* Engler, *supra* note 216, at 2006.

229. Parties indicate that simplicity influences their decision to proceed pro se. *See* Yegge, *supra* note 189, at 410.

230. *See id.*

231. *See* Bryan, *supra* note 51, at 1219–34.

232. *See* Susan S. Silbey, *The Emperor's New Clothes: Mediation Mythology and Markets*, 2002 J. DISP. RESOL. 171, 173 (noting that little evidence supports that humans generally prefer harmony over conflict or contest).

233. *See, e.g.*, Jessica Pearson & Nancy Thoennes, *Custody Mediation in Denver: Short and Longer Term Effects, in* THE RESOLUTION OF FAMILY CONFLICT: COMPARATIVE LEGAL PERSPECTIVES 248, 256 (John M. Eekelaar & Sanford N. Katz eds. 1984); Joshua D. Rosenberg, *In Defense of Mediation*, 33 ARIZ. L. REV. 467, 472 (1991). *See generally* Silbey, *supra* note 232, at 176.

234. *See* Joan B. Kelly, *Psychological and Legal Interventions for Parents and Children in Custody and Access Disputes: Current Research and Practice*, 10 VA. J. SOC. POL'Y & L. 129, 131 (2002); Daniel A. Krauss & Bruce D. Sales, *Legal Standards, Expertise, and Experts in the Resolution of Contested Custody Cases*, 6 PSYCHOL. PUB. POL'Y & L. 843, 856–57 (2000); Andrew Schepard, *Parental Conflict Prevention Programs and the United Family Court: A Public Health Perspective*, 32 FAM. L.Q. 95, 103–05 (1998).

235. *See* Janet R. Johnston, *Building Multidisciplinary Professional Partnerships with the Court on Behalf of High-Conflict Divorcing Families and Their Children: Who Needs What Kind of Help?*, 22 U. ARK. LITTLE ROCK L. REV. 453, 456 (2000).

236. *See generally* Beck & Sales, *supra* note 179, at 990, 1021–29 (explaining various sources of hostility between spouses, including interactive patterns).

237. *See, e.g., id.* at 113–14 (2000); Gerber, *supra* note 188, at 11–12; William Rich, *The Role of Lawyers: Beyond Advocacy*, 1980 B.Y.U. L. REV. 767, 782.

238. *See* Anne Kass, *A View from the Bench—The Adversarial Aspects of Divorce*, 4 AM. J. FAM. L. 27, 29–30 (1990) (noting that the linear communication model used by lawyers and the cognitive dissonance of lawyers contribute to divorce hostilities).

239. *See* Joan M. Cheever & Joanne Naiman, *The Deadly Practice of Divorce: Lately Divorced Men Have Been Taking Aim in Court*, 15 NAT'L L.J. 1 (1992) (within the last nine months of 1992 seven men, distraught over divorce proceedings, killed two lawyers, three ex-wives, and two relatives and wounded three judges, three lawyers, three sheriff's deputies, and two court personnel). Note, however, that research suggests that subsequent violence against a battered spouse is less likely when she avoids contact with her tormentor and when she is represented by a traditional lawyer advocate. *See* Ellis, *supra* note 161, at 318.

240. *See* MATHER ET AL., *supra* note 8, at 49–50, 87, 88; WINNER, *supra* note 46, at 57–70. *See also* Johnston, *supra* note 235, at 460.

241. *See* MATHER ET AL., *supra* note 8, at 32, 35–36, 68–69, 92; Felstiner & Sarat, *supra* note 13, at 1456; Griffiths, *supra* note 11, at 152.

242. *See* MATHER ET AL., *supra* note 8, at 92; Beck & Sales, *supra* note 179, at 1014–16; Griffiths, *supra* note 11, at 166; Austin Sarat & William L.F. Felstiner, *Lawyers and Legal Consciousness: Law Talk in the Divorce Lawyer's Office*, 98 YALE L.J. 1545, 1669 n.39 (1989); Austin Sarat & William L.F. Felstiner, *Law and Strategy in the Divorce Lawyer's Office*, 20 L. & SOC'Y REV. 93 (1986). *See also* KRESSEL, *supra* note 41, at 161 (noting that divorce lawyers far more frequently encourage their clients to be cooperative than

competitive); Garon et al., *supra* note 44, at 184 (noting a shift in the role of family law lawyers from gladiators to problem-solvers).

243. Krauss and Sales note,

> Additionally, the inexact [best interests of the child] standard has been criticized for promoting various strategic behaviors by the negotiating parties that increase the costs of bargaining and that are antithetical to honest negotiation, including the following: dishonestly pretending to desire certain custodial arrangements so that they can receive concessions from the other party, threatening to move away or out of state with the child, inventing stories of sexual and physical abuse and neglect, and creating stories of moral unfitness of the other party. These behaviors are likely to occur in any bargaining context but are likely to be especially prominent and effective when it is not clear what will occur if a negotiated settlement is unreachable.

> Krauss & Sales, *supra* note 234, at 860–61.

244. *See* KRESSEL, *supra* note 41, at 49–51.

245. *See id.* at 50.

246. *See id.* at 50, 163.

247. *See* WINNER, *supra* note 46, at 134.

248. *See id.*

249. *See* Gerber, *supra* note 188, at 17; Schepard, *supra* note 46, at 410–11. *See also* Kelly, *supra* note 234, at 131–32.

250. *See* Beck & Sales, *supra* note 179, at 1013.

251. *See* Johnston, *supra* note 235, at 461–62.

252. *See id.* at 460.

253. *See* MATHER ET AL., *supra* note 8, at 22, 115–16; Gangel-Jacob, *supra* note 77, at 827 (noting that fair financial resolutions diffuse emotionalism). For numerous examples of anger spawned by unfair results, see WINNER, *supra* note 46.

254. *See* Sally Burnett Sharp, *Fairness Standards and Separation Agreements: A Word of Caution on Contractual Freedom*, 132 U. PA. L. REV. 1399, 1406–07 (1984). Weitzman discovered that the divorced parents who seemed to maintain the best postdivorce relationships had approximately equal financial situations. WEITZMAN, *supra* note 62, at 192.

255. *See* WEITZMAN, *supra* note 62, at 346 (noting that longer-married older housewives suffer the greatest financial hardships after divorce and exhibit the most anger). In the words of a 62-year-old woman, "I'm still very bitter about losing everything. . . . it still eats at me to hear about my husband's lifestyle and vacations when I have to count every dollar . . . and I worry a lot about my future—about money and medical bills and all that." *Id.* at 347.

256. *See* Beck & Sales, *supra* note 179, at 1026.

257. *See What Is Procedural Justice?*, *supra* note 2, at 105 (referring to G.S. Leventhal, *What Should Be Done with Equity Theory*, in SOCIAL EXCHANGE: ADVANCES IN THEORY AND RESEARCH 43 (K. J. Gergen, M.S. Greenberg & R. H. Weiss

eds. 1980)). Leventhal refers to procedural consistency as similarity of treatment and similarity of outcome. *Id.* The discussion in this section, however, addresses only similarity of treatment.

258. *See* Paternoster et al., *supra* note 2, at 167–68; *What Is Procedural Justice?*, *supra* note 2, at 107, 113. Research that explores the relative importance of the different procedural justice criteria suggests that, in many contexts, people consider consistency among the most important of criteria. *See* J. Greenberg, *Reactions to Procedural Justice in Payment Distributions: Do the Means Justify the Ends?*, 72 J. Applied Psychol. 55 (1986); E. Barrett-Howard & Tom R. Tyler, *Procedural Justice as a Criterion in Allocation Decisions*, 50 J. Personality & Soc. Psychol. 296 (1986).

259. Tyler notes that when parties assess procedural consistency, they compare their current treatment with experiences they or others have had in the past. *What Is Procedural Justice?*, *supra* note 2, at 107.

260. *See* Mather et al., *supra* note 8, at 60.

261. As Baker notes, "[t]he doctrine of political responsibility demands 'articulate consistency.' This consistency is not easily satisfied by arguments of policy, but is satisfied by arguments of principle which provide 'distribution consistency from one case to the next.'" Livingston Baker, *Dworkin's Rights Thesis: Implications for the Relationship Between the Legal Order and the Moral Order*, 1980 B.Y.U. L. Rev. 837, 839 (citing Ronald Dworkin, Taking Rights Seriously 87 (1977)). *See also* Ronald Dworkin, Taking Rights Seriously 113 (1977) ("The gravitational force of precedent may be explained by appeal, not to the wisdom of enforcing enactments, but to the fairness of treating like cases alike.").

262. *See* Austin Sarat & William L.F. Felstiner, Divorce Lawyers and Their Clients: Power and Meaning in the Legal Process 130 (1995); Chambers, *supra* note 16, at 212–13.

263. *See* Lenard Marlow, Divorce and the Myth of Lawyers 34–37 (1992).

264. A legitimate legal system need not always produce consistent results. Certainly the public will tolerate some deviation from the ideal. Yet, in a democratic country, if a legal system consistently operates arbitrarily and outside the procedures and substantive norms the public has authorized, it lacks political legitimacy.

　　Nor must a legitimate legal system always produce consistent results if doing so sacrifices higher values. For instance, for decades family members were immune from lawsuits against one another. Consistency of outcome would dictate a continuation of that immunity. However, Dworkin's concept of integrity, an internal coherence in law with fundamental principles, eventually trumped and brought lawsuits between family members more into line with lawsuits generally. *See* Ronald Dworkin, Law's Empire 219–220, 225–58 (1986). Unless higher values intercede, however, treating like cases alike remains a legitimating factor.

265. *See* Paternoster et al., *supra* note 2, at 167–68; *What Is Procedural Justice?*, *supra* note 2, at 113. *See also* Lawrence M. Friedman, Total Justice 81 (1985).

266. *See* Judith Resnik, *Tiers*, 57 S. Cal. L. Rev. 837, 855 (1984).

267. *See, e.g., In re* Marriage of Massey, 732 P.2d 1341 (Mont. 1987); Whitworth v. Whitworth, 878 S.W.2d 479 (Mo. Ct. App. 1994).

268. Some states, however, disfavor default judgments in divorce cases because of the state interest in the welfare of the parties. *See, e.g.,* Comstock v. Comstock, 91 S.W.3d 174 (Mo. Ct. App. 2002); Reed v. Reed, 48 S.W.3d 634, 639 (Mo. Ct. App. 2001). Although default remains available, a respondent can more easily set aside the default. *See, e.g., Reed, supra.*

269. Settlement and default resolve approximately 90% to 95% of divorce cases. *See, e.g.,* Marc Galanter, *Why the "Haves" Come Out Ahead: Speculations on the Limits of Legal Change,* 9 L. & Soc'y Rev 95, 108 (1974); Robert J. Levy, *Comment on the Pearson-Thoennes Study and on Mediation,* 17 Fam. L. Q. 525, 530 (1983) (noting that 85% to 90% of divorce cases settle); Melli et al., *supra* note 42, at 1142 (finding that 217 of 349 Wisconsin divorce cases settled); Mnookin, *supra* note 100, at 364, 364 (observing that the vast majority of divorce cases are resolved by negotiation). *See also* Sally Burnett Sharp, *Semantics as Jurisprudence: The Elevation of Form Over Substance in the Treatment of Separation Agreements in North Carolina,* 69 N.C. L. Rev. 319, 320 & n.4 (1991). The rate of settlement for divorce cases mimics the rate for civil cases generally. *See* Marc Galanter, *Reading the Landscape of Disputes: What We Know and Don't Know (and Think We Know) About Our Allegedly Contentious and Litigious Society,* 31 UCLA L. Rev. 4, 27 (1983).

270. *See, e.g.,* Colo. Rule Civ. Proc. 59 (2004).

271. *See Missouri Gender Bias Report, supra* note 52, at 540; Crippen, *supra* note 205, at 88–90.

272. The Washington Supreme Court, for instance, stated that, "[i]n matters dealing with the welfare of children, trial courts are given broad discretion. A trial court's disposition of the case involving rights of custody and visitation will not be disturbed on appeal unless the court manifestly abused its discretion." *In re* Marriage of Calalquinto, 669 P.2d 886, 887 (Wash. 1983).

273. *See* Crippen, *supra* note 205, at 88–90. The deference appellate courts give to trial courts may vary from issue to issue. An appellate court may be more comfortable overturning a trial court's determination of subject matter or personal jurisdiction than its distribution of property.

274. In *In re* Marriage of Clarke, 671 P.2d 1334 (Colo. Ct. App. 1983), the mother had temporary custody of a son for two years before final hearing. *Id.* at 1335. The Colorado custody statute provides: "In considering a proposed custodian, the court shall not presume that any person is better able to serve the best interests of the child because of that person's sex." *Id.* Nevertheless, the trial judge expressed his belief that "most young people in trouble . . . have not had a meaningful relationship with their fathers . . . I think it is very important for every boy to have a 'meaningful relationship' with his father . . . I cannot help but take that into consideration." *Id.* He awarded custody of the then four-year-old son to the father, despite the court-appointed custody investigator's recommendation that the mother receive custody. *Id.* The appellate court upheld the trial court, because allegedly "ample" evidence indicated that the trial judge considered other relevant statutory provisions. *Id.* The other

evidence consisted of the father's expert, who recommended custody to the father, the father's strong family ties, the father's ability to provide more parental time, and the father's farm environment that the court concluded would particularly benefit the four-year-old child. *Id.*

275. As the Washington Supreme Court candidly stated,

> In reviewing the entire record before us, we cannot tell what standards of law the trial court followed in reaching its decision on visitation rights. While the findings and conclusions of law suggest the homosexuality of the father was not the determining factor the unfortunate and unnecessary references by the trial court to homosexuality generally indicate the contrary.

> *In re* Marriage of Calalquinto, 669 P.2d 886, 888 (Wash. 1983). *See also id.* at 889–90 (Justice Stafford concurring in part and dissenting in part).

276. *E.g., id.* at 888.

277. Remand to the original judge also raises questions of impartiality. As Resnik explains,

> [A] judge who has listened to a trial, thought about the testimony, and written findings of fact and conclusions of law cannot comfortably be characterized as having no views about that case, when it is returned upon remand. . . . The theory is that the judge, as a long term incumbent of the judicial role, has the capacity to think anew. . . . But social scientists have taught us that our controls over cognitive capacities are limited. . . . We construct "schema" and "scripts" to aid us in digesting information, and it is not so clear that we can will away the views held. In short, while prejudgment is always a danger, the problem seems particularly acute when someone has already undertaken the responsibility to judge.

> Judith Resnik, *On the Bias: Feminist Reconsiderations of the Aspirations for Our Judges*, 61 S. CAL. L. REV. 1877, 1903 (1988).

278. *See* Crippen, *supra* note 205, at 91.

279. An attorney responding to the Florida Gender Bias Commission captured the reality of many women at the end of the divorce proceeding:

> [I]t's just a simple reality. You run into situations in the representations specifically of women who generally don't have the purse strings and by the end of the divorce they have run out of money, they have run out of credit worthiness, they have run out of every possible relative or friend [from whom] they could borrow money in pursuing the litigation itself . . . .

> *Florida Gender Bias Report,* *supra* note 52, at 810–11.

280. *See Missouri Gender Bias Report, supra* note 52, at 539–40.

281. Many trial court decisions may seem open to correction of error because of their susceptibility to modification. A substantial change in circumstances

sometimes results in revision of a child or spousal support award as well as custody arrangements. Modification, however, does not create an opportunity to correct poor or erroneous initial decisions. It offers only an occasion, usually much later in time, to alter the original decision because circumstances have changed, not because the original decision lacked merit.

282. *See, e.g., In re* Marriage of Holley, 659 N.E.2d 581, 583 (Ind. Ct. App. 1995); *In re* Marriage of Sullivan, No. C7-99-1367, 2000 U.S. App. WL 168732 (D. Minn. Feb. 15, 2000); *In re* Marriage of Dooley, 15 S.W.3d 747 (Mo. Ct. App. 2000). *See generally* Fed. Rule Civ. Proc., 55(c) & 60, 28 U.S.C.A. Federal Rule 60, which many states have adopted, provides for relief from judgments for the following reasons: (a) mistake, inadvertence, surprise, or excusable neglect; (b) newly discovered evidence which by due diligence could not have been discovered in time to move for a new trial; (c) fraud, misrepresentation, or other misconduct of an adverse party; (d) the judgment is void; (e) the judgment has been satisfied, released, or discharged, or a previous judgment on which it is based has been reversed or otherwise vacated, or it is no longer equitable that the judgment should have prospective application; or (f) any other reason that justifies relief from the operation of the judgment.

283. *See, e.g.,* Reed v. Reed, 48 S.W.3d 634 (Mo. Ct. App. 2001); *In re* Marriage of Mikesell, 850 P.2d 294 (Mont. 1993). *See generally* Fed. Rule Civ. Proc., 55(c), 28 U.S.C.A. (2002).

284. *See, e.g., In re* Marriage of Canine, No. 01-1357, 2002 WL 1973877 (Iowa Ct. App. 2002).

285. *See, e.g.,* Laney v. Laney, 487 So. 2d 1109 (Fla. Dist. Ct. App. 1986); *In re* Marriage of Hoover, 732 N.E.2d 145 (Ill. App. Ct. 2000); *In re* Marriage of Dooley, 15 S.W.3d 747 (Mo. Ct. App. 2000).

286. *See, e.g.,* Warfield v. Warfield, 661 So. 2d 924 (Fla. Dist. Ct. App. 1995); *In re* Dooley, 15 S.W.3d 747.

287. *See, e.g., In re* Marriage of Canine, No. 01-1357, 2002 WL 1973877; Reed v. Reed, 48 S.W.3d 634 (Mo. Ct. App. 2001).

288. *See, e.g., In re* Marriage of Holley, 659 N.E.2d 581 (Ind. Ct. App. 1995); *In re* Marriage of Sullivan, 2000 WL 168732 (Minn. Ct. App. 2000) (unpublished opinion).

289. *See, e.g.,* Corrigan v. Corrigan, 184 So. 2d 664 (Fla. Dist. Ct. App. 1966). *See also* Jason Pasto, *Attacking the Judgment of Divorce that Incorporates a Marital Settlement Agreement,* 11 J. Contemp. Legal Issues 185, 186–88 (2000).

290. *See* Engler, *supra* note 216, at 2019; Sharp, *supra* note 269, at 322 & n.14.

291. *See* Engler, *supra* note 216, at 2020.

292. *See* Bryan, *supra* note 51, at 1238 & n.405.

293. *See id* at 1153–56.

294. *See, e.g.,* Kadoch, *supra* note 192, at 328–33. In the words of one trial judge,

> If they know what they're doing, even if it is out of line, then it is not my job to change their decision. I'll inquire to make sure they know what they are doing. I have to let them know what their options are.

But I won't usually change it. I don't know if I have ever changed an amount set by a couple.

Melli et al., *supra* note 42, at 1145.

295. *See* SARAT & FELSTINER, *supra* note 262, at 121–22.

296. *See., e.g.*, Engler, *supra* note 216, at 1988–89; Robert H. Mnookin & Louis Kornhauser, *Bargaining in the Shadow of the Law: The Case of Divorce*, 88 YALE L.J. 950, 951 & n.2 (1975); Sharp, *supra* note 254, at 1408–10, 1443–44, 1448–49; Jana B. Singer, *The Privatization of Family Law*, 1992 WIS. L. REV. 1443, 1474–75. Courts, unsurprisingly, seem particularly reluctant to alter custody and visitation agreements reached by the parties. Sally Burnett Sharp, *Modification of Agreement-Based Custody Decrees: Unitary or Dual Standard?*, 68 VA. L. REV. 1263, 1264 (1982).

297. *See* Sharp, *supra* note 269, at 329 n.50. Sharp argues that these concepts do not capture the full range of bargaining tactics that contaminate the negotiation process at divorce, Sharp, *supra* note 254, at 1424–41, particularly false promises of reconciliation, *id.* at 1434–36, and threats to pursue custody. *Id.* at 1437–40.

298. *See, e.g.*, McIntosh v. McIntosh, 328 S.E.2d 600, 602 (N.C. Ct. App. 1985) (citing cases in which courts have thrown a "cloak of protection" around divorce agreements in order to ensure their fairness). Sharp argues, however, that fairness standards do not protect against unfair settlement agreements. Sharp, *supra* note 254, at 1442–51.

299. New York law notes: "In view of the fiduciary relationship existing between spouses, separation agreements are more closely scrutinized by courts than ordinary contracts and may be set aside upon the demonstration of good cause, such as mistake, fraud, duress or overreaching." Manes v. Manes & Ressa, 277 A.D.2d 359, 361 (N.Y. Ct. App. 2000).

300. *See* Bryan, *supra* note 51, at 1240–70; Lou McPhail, Comment, *Divorce—Alimony, Allowances, and Disposition of Property—Abuse of Discretion—The Unconscionable Stipulated Divorce Agreement and Rule 60(b)(vi): What About the Children*, 72 N. DAK. L. REV. 1099, 1106–07 (1996) (commenting on Crawford v. Crawford, 524 N.W.2d 833 (N.D. 1994), in which the North Dakota Supreme Court found a stipulated agreement unconscionable); Sharp, *supra* note 269, at 329 n.50. *See also* Sharp, *supra* note 254, at 1443–45; Crupi v. Crupi, 784 So. 2d 611, 613 (Fla. Ct. App. 2001); Broer v. Hellerman, 770 N.Y.S. 2d 212, 214 (N.Y. App.Div. 2003) ("However, judicial review of separation agreements is generally limited to encourage spouses to resolve issues on their own and a reviewing court should not set aside the terms of an agreement which simply reflects unwise bargaining."); McDowell v. McDowell, 301 S.E.2d 729, 732 (N.C. Ct. App. 1983) ("However, as courts do not make contracts, we are not permitted to inquire into whether the contract was good or bad, wise or foolish.").

301. If a trial court vacates an agreement, trial will likely follow. Court concern over crowded dockets, judicial dislike of divorce cases, and strongly worded statutes favoring divorce settlements provide ample incentive for trial courts

to deny petitions to vacate, many times without allowing an evidentiary hearing. *See In re* Marriage of Hoppe, 580 N.E.2d 1186 (Ill. App. Ct. 1991); *In re* Marriage of Burch, 563 N.E.2d 1049 (Ill. App. Ct. 1990); *In re* Marriage of Beck, 404 N.E.2d 972 (Ill. App. Ct. 1980); Dendrinos v. Dendrinos, 374 N.E.2d 1016 (Ill. App. Ct. 1978). Because dependent wives bring most challenges, gender bias provides additional inducement.

302. *See* Pasto, *supra* note 289.

303. *See* Sharp, *supra* note 269, at 320.

304. *See* Pasto, *supra* note 289, at 185. Evidently, other countries experience the same confusion. *See* Sharp, *supra* note 254, at 1411–14; Marie-Therese Meulders-Klein, *Financial Agreements on Divorce and the Freedom of Contract in Continental Europe, in* THE RESOLUTION OF FAMILY CONFLICT: COMPARATIVE LEGAL PERSPECTIVES 297, 303 (John M. Eekelaar & Sanford N. Katz eds. 1984).

305. Rothschild v. Devos, 757 N.E.2d 219, 220 (Ind. Ct. App. 2001).

306. *Id.* at 220–21.

307. *Id.* at 221.

308. *Id.*

309. *Id.*

310. *Id.*

311. *Id.* at 223.

312. *Id.* at 223–24.

313. *See* Bryan, *supra* note 51, at 1239–70.

314. *See* Gail Frommer Brod, *Premarital Agreements and Gender Justice*, 6 YALE J. L. & FEMINISM 229, 240–49, 151–52 (1994) (arguing that premarital agreements disadvantage wives at divorce); Bryan, *supra* note 51 (explaining why and illustrating how divorce settlement agreements disadvantage women); Katharine B. Silbaugh, *Marriage Contracts and the Family Economy*, 93 Nw. U. L. REV. 65, 128–29 (1998) (acknowledging that a premarital agreement that results in a lower standard of living for wife and mother inevitably affects her child's welfare).

315. The costs of appeal provide a substantial impediment for economically dependent spouses. *See Florida Gender Bias Report, supra* note 52, at 810–11; *Missouri Gender Bias Report, supra* note 52, at 539.

316. *See, e.g., In re* Marriage of Gorman, 671 N.E.2d 819, 825 (Ill. App. Ct. 1996); *In re* Marriage of Gidlund, 614 N.E.2d 315, 317 (Ill. App. Ct. 1993); *In re* Marriage of Riedy, 474 N.E.2d 28, 30 (Ill. App. Ct. 1985); Bickson v. Bickson, 183 N.E.2d 16 (Ill. App. Ct. 1962).

317. This standard is set forth in the Illinois Marriage and Dissolution of Marriage Act, which provides,

> The terms of the separation agreement, except those providing for the support, custody and visitation of children, are binding upon the court unless it finds, after considering the economic circumstances of the parties and any other relevant evidence produced by the parties, on their own motion or on request of the court, that the separation agreement is unconscionable.

40 ILL. COMP. STAT. ANN. 502(b) (West 1992). If a spouse challenges a separation agreement by invocation of a civil procedure rule that provides for relief from final judgments, the courts commonly employ contract principles to determine the agreement's enforceability. *See, e.g.,* McPhail, *supra* note 300, at 1105–06 (commenting on Galloway v. Galloway, 281 N.W.2d 804 (N.D. 1979)).

318. *See, e.g., In re* Marriage of Kloster, 469 N.E.2d 381, 385 (Ill. App. Ct. 1984); *In re* Marriage of Foster, 451 N.E.2d 915, 918 (Ill. App. Ct. 1983). Occasionally an appellate court will note that unconscionability also protects against "overreaching, concealment of assets, and sharp dealing not consistent with the obligations of marital partners to deal fairly with each other." *In re* Marriage of Carlson, 428 N.E.2d 1005, 1010 (Ill. App. Ct. 1981) (citations omitted). In the vast majority of cases, however, courts omit any reference to this obligation.

319. *See, e.g., In re* Marriage of Johnson, 790 N.E.2d 91, 95 (Ill. App. Ct. 2003); *In re* Gorman, 671 N.E.2d at 826; *In re* Marriage of Broday, 628 N.E.2d 790 (Ill. App. Ct. 1993); *In re* Carlson, 428 N.E.2d at 1010.

320. *See In re* Marriage of Gurin, 571 N.E.2d 857, 864 (Ill. App. Ct. 1991) (quoting *In re* Carlson, 428 N.E.2d at 1010 (Ill. App. Ct. 1981). *See also, e.g., In re* Kloster, 469 N.E.2d at 385; *In re* Foster, 451 N.E.2d at 919; *In re* Carlson, 428 N.E.2d at 1010. Many states have a strong policy favoring divorce settlements. *See, e.g.,* Egedi v. Egedi, 88 Cal. App. 4th 17, 22 (Cal. Ct. App. 2001); Cross v. Cross, 290 A.D.2d 920, 921–22 (N.Y. App. Div. 2002); Damone v. Damone, 782 A.2d 1208, 1214 (Vt. 2001), and do not allow courts to lightly set them aside. *Egedi,* 88 Cal. App. 4th at 22; *Cross,* 290 A.D.2d at 921–22; *Damone,* 782 A.2d at 1214. For instance, in New York a court may set aside a marital settlement agreement for unconscionability. Unconscionability, however, requires that agreement be so unfair that no person in his or her senses and not under delusion would accept it. The inequality must be so strong and manifest as to shock the conscience and confound the judgment of any person of common sense. *See* Giustiniani v. Giustiniani, 278 A.D.2d 609, 610–11 (N.Y. App. Div. 2000).

321. *See In re* Gorman, 671 N.E.2d at 826; *In re* Foster, 451 N.E.2d at 919.

322. Illinois courts define duress as,

The imposition, oppression, undue influence or the taking of undue advantage of the stress of another whereby one is deprived of the exercise of his free will. The person asserting duress has the burden of proving, by clear and convincing evidence, that he was bereft of the quality of mind essential to the making of the contract.

In re Marriage of Hamm-Smith, 633 N.E.2d 225, 230 (Ill. App. Ct. 1994) (citations omitted).

323. Illinois courts define fraud as follows:

For a misrepresentation to constitute fraud, it must consist of a material false statement which is known to be false by the party making it, made to induce the other party to act in reliance on the truth of the statement, and actually acted upon by that other party.

In re Marriage of Held, 392 N.E.2d 169, 172–73 (Ill. App. Ct. 1979) (citation omitted). *See also In re* Marriage of Palacios, 656 N.E.2d 107, 111 (Ill. App. Ct. 1995).

324. *See In re* Marriage of Goldberg, 668 N.E.2d 1104, 1107 (Ill. App. Ct. 1996) (explaining that a claim of fraud requires clear and convincing evidence that the defendant intentionally misstated or concealed a material fact that he had a duty to disclose and on which the plaintiff detrimentally relied); *In re* Gorman, 671 N.E.2d at 826 ("The person asserting coercion bears the burden of proving it by clear and convincing evidence."); *In re* Broday, 628 N.E.2d 790; *In re* Carlson, 428 N.E.2d 1005; Beattie v. Beattie, 368 N.E.2d 178, 182 (Ill. App. Ct. 1977) (stating that party seeking to set aside a divorce settlement must prove by "clear and convincing evidence that the agreement was entered as the result of coercion, fraud or duress, or is contrary to public policy or morals.").

325. *See In re* Carlson, 428 N.E.2d at 1010.

326. *See* Sharp, *supra* note 254, at 1405 (observing that judicial application of contract doctrine does not provide adequate safeguards against unfair results or procedures).

327. Professor Sharp also explains why the doctrine of confidential relationship also provides insufficient protection from unfair settlement agreements. *Id.* at 1414–22.

328. *See In re* Marriage of Brandt, 489 N.E.2d 902 (Ill. App. Ct. 1986).

329. *See id.*; Report of Proceedings (Dec. 19, 1983), (Doris Brandt) at 2, *In re* Marriage of Brandt, 489 N.E.2d 902 (Ill. App. Ct. 1986) [hereinafter Doris Brandt Proceedings 1983].

330. *See Brandt*, 489 N.E.2d at 903.

331. *See* Doris Brandt Proceedings 1983, *supra* note 329, at 2. One child was 24 and the other was 19 at the time of the hearing. *See id.*

332. *See id.*

333. *See Brandt*, 489 N.E.2d at 903.

334. *See id.* at 903, 906.

335. Evidently Doris had attempted to leave the marriage nine years before the ultimate separation. *See* Doris Brandt Proceedings 1983, *supra* note 329, at 53.

336. Telephone Interview with Doris's second attorney (Mar. 7, 1997).

337. *See* Doris Brandt Proceedings 1983, *supra* note 329, at 2–3.

338. *See id.* at 3. Too much, however, should not be made of Doris's testimony or the judge's findings. Doris gave no specific instances of Virgil's mental cruelty, the trial court accepted her limited testimony as sufficient to establish grounds for divorce, and Illinois did not allow no-fault divorce in 1983 when the divorce occurred.

339. Telephone Interview with Doris Brandt (Mar. 10, 1997).

340. *Id.*

341. *Id.*

342. *Id.*

343. *See* Doris Brandt Proceedings 1983, *supra* note 329, at 2.

344. Telephone Interview with Doris Brandt (Mar. 10, 1997).

345. *Id.*

346. Telephone Interview with Doris's new attorney (Mar. 7, 1997).

347. *Id.*

348. *See* Report of Proceedings (Apr. 10, 1984), (Virgil Brandt) at 5, *In re* Marriage of Brandt, 489 N.E.2d 902 (Ill. App. Ct. 1986) [hereinafter Virgil Brandt Proceedings 1984].

349. *See id.* at 12.

350. See Report of Proceedings (1984), (Doris Brandt) at 30, *In re* Marriage of Brandt, 489 N.E.2d 902 (Ill. App. Ct. 1986) [hereinafter Doris Brandt Proceedings 1984].

351. *See* Virgil Brandt Proceedings 1984, *supra* note 348, at 15. Doris describes the process of reaching the $315,000 value as follows.

Q. Could you tell the Court what happened in Mr. Crowder's office that day?

A. Virgil and I were on one side of the table, and Mr. Crowder on the other. . . . The two of them went through, and I was listening, went through the acreage, real estate, the amounts, the values, the approximate value of the cattle on hand, what they figured was a fair value of the house, and the indebtedness was taken from that figure, and we came up with something like $305,000.00 or $315,000.00.

Q. When you say you are listening—

A. Virgil was basically doing the valuing, and Mr. Crowder was doing the writing, as I remember, and from time to time they would make comments to me about it.

Q. Did you express any opinion as to value?

A. I am not a realtor, I had no idea. I assumed Mr. Crowder was representing both of us, and if he thought I wasn't getting a fair shake, he would open his mouth or say differently.

Doris Brandt Proceedings 1984, *supra* note 350, at 30.

352. *See id.*

353. *See* Virgil Brandt Proceedings 1984, *supra* note 348, at 11.

354. *See id.* at 6. Virgil also testified that this financial statement omitted an $80,000 debt. *See id.* at 7. This reduced the value of the marital property to $538,000.

355. *See* Doris Brandt Proceedings 1984, *supra* note 350, at 32. At trial Doris explained how the couple arrived at the figures in the financial statements. *Id.* at 31–33. At trial Virgil tried to make it seem as though Doris knew as much as he did about the value of the farm property, machinery, and crops. *See* Virgil Brandt Proceedings 1984, *supra* note 348, at 7–12. In this author's opinion, his testimony is evasive and unconvincing.

356. *See id.* at 8, 11.

357. At trial Doris' expert appraiser valued the land owned jointly by Virgil and Doris at $275,000 and the land owned by the farming corporation at $664,000. *See* Report of Proceedings (Apr. 10, 1984), (Kelly G. Martin) at 25–27, *In re* Marriage of Brandt, 489 N.E.2d 902 (Ill. App. Ct. 1986). Virgil (and Doris) owned a one-third interest in the farming corporation, making the value of Virgil and Doris' portion $225,000, according to Doris's expert. The farming corporation owed Virgil and Doris approximately $39,000. *See* Virgil Brandt Proceedings 1984, *supra* note 348, at 13–14, 17; Doris Brandt Proceedings 1984, *supra* note 350, at 33. The parties stipulated that the farming equipment was worth between $73,000 and $78,000. *See* Report of Proceedings (Apr. 10, 1984), (Floyd Crowder) at 96, *In re* Marriage of Brandt, 489 N.E.2d 902 (Ill. App. Ct. 1986) [hereinafter Floyd Crowder Proceedings April 1984]. The livestock apparently was valued at approximately $10,000. *See* Doris Brandt Proceedings 1984, *supra* note 350, at 36. Adding these figures together, the marital estate approached $619,000—surprisingly close to the amount on the most recent financial statement. If this estimate is accurate, Doris received 12% of the marital assets, whereas Virgil received 88%. Virgil's experts, however, testified that the real estate was worth substantially less. *See* Floyd Crowder Proceedings April 1984, *supra*, at 103–06, 130. Moreover, Virgil testified that the jointly owned property was burdened with $178,000 of debt and that his portion of the farming corporation was burdened with $187,000 of debt. Using Doris's expert's evaluation of the property and Virgil's testimony about debt as accurate, the net value of the marital estate would approximate $254,000. At trial Virgil himself testified that during negotiations in Crowder's office a net value of $247,000, rather than $305,000, was placed on the marital property. *See* Virgil Brandt Proceedings 1984, *supra* note 348, at 12–13. Even using this lower figure, Doris would have received only 30% of the marital assets, whereas Virgil would have received 70%. Virgil, however, is the only person who testified that the amount agreed to during negotiations was only $247,000. Crowder testified that the notes that he kept during negotiation indicated the parties had agreed that the value of the marital estate was $410,000. *See* Floyd Crowder Proceedings April 1984, *supra*. Crowder also indicated that this figure was mistaken, because it failed to reflect a $37,500 house debt. Later Crowder indicates that the $315,000 value placed on the marital estate during negotiations should have been reduced by an outstanding debt, presumably the house debt referred to earlier. See Floyd Crowder Proceedings April 1984, *supra*, at 79. Using Crowder's figures, the value placed on the marital estate during negotiations was somewhere between $372,500 and $277,500. Doris also testified that a value of between $305,000 and $315,000 was placed on the marital assets during negotiations. *See* Doris Brandt Proceedings 1984, *supra*, at 30.

358. Later, at trial, both Virgil's and Doris' experts testified that the value of the marital estate exceeded $315,000.

359. Virgil and Doris owned approximately 217 acres, *See* Virgil Brandt Proceedings 1984, *supra* note 348, at 3–4. The farming corporation owned approximately

767 acres. *See id.* at 3. The Brandts owned a one-third interest in the farming corporation.

360. Also excluded from the marital estate was Doris Brandt's pension plan with the Harrisonville Telephone Company. *See* Doris Brandt Proceedings 1984, *supra* note 350, at 35. The record contains no indication of the value of Doris's pension plan, nor does it mention whether Virgil had any pension plan. In 1987, many states did not consider individual pensions plans marital property.

361. *See id.* at 33.

362. Telephone Interview with Doris Brandt (Mar. 10, 1997). At trial Virgil denied telling Doris she had no rights in the corporation; rather, he claimed that he only told her that the corporation was worthless. *See* Virgil Brandt Proceedings 1984, *supra* note 348, at 12, 18–19.

363. Telephone Interview with Doris Brandt (Mar. 10, 1997). The attorney, Crowder, testified at trial that Virgil, not Crowder, indicated that the farming corporation was worthless. *See* Floyd Crowder Proceedings Apr. 1984, *supra* note 357, at 72.

364. The trial transcript did not contain this information.

365. At trial Virgil admitted that during the settlement conference he and Doris discussed the money they had put into the farming corporation and that Doris indicated she would like her share. According to Virgil, he told Doris that if he ever got his money out of the corporation, he'd be glad to give her her share. That understanding, Virgil admitted, was never put into the agreement. *See* Virgil Brandt Proceedings 1984, *supra* note 348, at 17–18.

366. When asked during the hearing whether the lawyer was representing him during the settlement conference, Virgil replied, "I think he was representing both of us." *See id.* at 21.

367. Telephone Interview with Doris Brandt (Mar. 10, 1997). *See also* Doris Brandt Proceedings 1984, *supra* note 350, at 30.

368. *See* Doris Brandt Proceedings 1984, *supra* note 350, at 37.

369. *See id.* at 37.

370. *See id.* at 48. Why Doris asked for only 40% of the marital assets rather than the 50% the lawyer indicated she was entitled to remains unknown.

371. *See id.* at 48.

372. *See id.*

373. *See id.* at 47.

374. *See id.* at 48.

375. Telephone Interview with Doris's new attorney (Mar. 7, 1997).

376. In addition to her economic and caretaking contributions to the marriage, Doris explained that she took one week of her two-week vacation each year to help plant the crops. She took the other week to help harvest the crops. Telephone Interview with Doris Brandt (Mar. 10, 1997).

377. *Id.*

378. *Id.* Doris further explained that Virgil laid claim even to small items that had personal significance only to her, like a set of silver given to Doris by co-

workers. At one point Virgil demanded that he be given the truck and that the younger daughter, away at college, be given the automobile, leaving Doris without a vehicle. The lawyer told him that Doris had to have a car. *Id.*

379. *Id.* Doris' words echo those of a divorced woman in Weitzman's study on the California divorce courts: "It's horrible when you have to face how little you are worth—what a low value the society places on all those years of your life ...." WEITZMAN, *supra* note 62, at 173. Another woman in the same study commented,

> I figured it out. After ten years of marriage I got $200 a month for five years. That comes out to $1,100 for each year of marriage. That means I was his 60-hour-a-week servant for $100 a month. Just about slave labor . . . housekeeper, nurse, chauffeur, mother. And prostitute—that's what I felt like. . . . It's an insult.

WEITZMAN, *supra*, at 173.

380. Telephone Interview with Doris Brandt (Mar. 10, 1997).

381. When questioned at trial about why she finally accepted the $75,000, Doris replied, "I felt we had been there all day. He is a very insistent person, and I felt I wasn't going to get any further with him." Doris Brandt Proceedings 1984, *supra* note 350, at 37.

382. Doris's lawyer questioned her about why she had not demanded interest:

> Q. Was there a discussion as to interest?
>
> A. Yes, he wouldn't pay that, so I went along with the fact if he wouldn't, he wouldn't.
>
> Q. Did you receive any advice about the payment of interest or what you were entitled to?
>
> A. Mr. Crowder had brought it up in the conversation, yes, but Virgil wouldn't buy it.
>
> Q. Why did you accept these figures at no interest rate?
>
> A. I felt that Mr. Crowder was representing me as well as Virgil. If he thought I deserved it, he would have forced the issue. And like I said a few sentences ago, I didn't think I was going to get any further. Virgil wouldn't and that was it.
>
> Q. What led you to believe you wouldn't get any further with Virgil?
>
> A. He is a very headstrong man with his own mind. I had lived with him enough years to know he doesn't change his mind.

Id. at 38.

383. *See* Floyd Crowder Proceedings April 1984, *supra* note 357, at 88.

384. *See* Doris Brandt Proceedings 1984, *supra* note 350, at 38.

385. The following colloquy occurred between Doris and her attorney:

> Q. Any pressure between the 25th and 27th?
>
> A. Yes, there was.
>
> Q. Could you explain that?

A. A lot of conversation, strong language, no physical abuse.

Q. How would you characterize the strong language? Explain that.

A. Loud conversations and very—He was very determined to get his way. He was just quite a talker.

Q. Did you feel you had any choice?

A. No, I did not feel I had any choice.

Id. at 43.

386. *See id.*
387. *See* Virgil Brandt Proceedings 1984, *supra* note 348, at 20.
388. Telephone Interview with Doris Brandt (Mar. 10, 1997).
389. *In re* Marriage of Brandt, 489 N.E.2d 902, 906 (Ill. App. Ct. 1986).
390. *See* Virgil Brandt Proceedings 1984, *supra* note 348, at 20–21; Doris Brandt Proceedings 1984, *supra* note 350, at 35; Report of Proceedings (Aug. 7, 1984), (Arlie Traughber) at 60, *In re* Marriage of Brandt, 489 N.E.2d 902 (Ill. App. Ct. 1986) [hereinafter Arlie Traughber Proceedings 1984].
391. *See* Doris Brandt Proceedings 1984, *supra* note 350, at 35.
392. *See* Arlie Traughber Proceedings 1984, *supra* note 390, at 61.
393. *See* Doris Brandt Proceedings 1984, *supra* note 350, at 50.
394. *See id.*
395. Telephone Interview with Doris's new attorney (Mar. 7, 1997).
396. *See id.*; Doris Brandt Proceedings 1984, *supra* note 350, at 30, 38.
397. At trial both parties introduced expert appraisals of the value of the couple's jointly owned property and the farming corporation. Virgil also introduced evidence of the debt on the jointly owned property and the farming corporation. None of these appraisals reflect the net values placed on the financial statements.
398. *See In re* Marriage of Brandt, 489 N.E.2d 902, 903–04 (Ill. App. Ct. 1986).
399. *See id.*
400. *See id.* at 903.
401. Telephone Interview with Doris's new attorney (Mar. 7, 1997).
402. Telephone Interview with Doris Brandt (Mar. 10, 1997).
403. *See id.*
404. Telephone Interview with Doris's new attorney (Mar. 7, 1997).
405. *See id.*
406. *See id.*
407. Telephone Interview with Doris Brandt (Mar. 10, 1997).
408. *See In re* Marriage of Brandt, 489 N.E.2d 902, 903 (Ill. App. Ct. 1986).
409. *See id.* at 906.
410. *See id.* at 903.
411. *See id.*
412. *See id.* at 904.
413. *See id.*
414. *See id.* at 905.
415. *See id.* at 905–06.

416. Joan Williams explains how choice rhetoric frequently is used in family law to deny structural patterns of inequality between men and women. Women are perceived as equal—they simply make different choices than men might make. *See* Williams, *supra* note 99, at 2241. Women "choose," for instance, to marginalize their careers in order to fulfill caregiving responsibilities, or women "choose" to remain unemployed during marriage. *See id.* at 2241 & n.62. Williams argues that this distorted version of equality distinctly disadvantages women at divorce. *See id.* at 2241. *See also* Mary E. O'Connell, *Alimony After No-Fault: A Practice in Search of a Theory*, 23 New Eng. L. Rev. 437, 500 (1988).
417. *See Brandt*, 489 N.E.2d at 906.
418. *See id.*
419. *See id.*
420. *See, e.g., In re* Marriage of Broday, 628 N.E.2d 790 (Ill. App. Ct. 1983).
421. *See* Beattie v. Beattie, 368 N.E.2d 178, 180 (Ill. App. Ct. 1977).
422. *See id.* at 184.
423. *See id.* at 180, 184.
424. *See id.* at 180.
425. *See id.* at 181.
426. *See id.* at 180.
427. *See id.*
428. *See id.*
429. *See id.*
430. *See id.* at 181.
431. *See* Beattie v. Beattie, 368 N.E.2d 178 (Ill. App. Ct. 1977).
432. *See id.* at 179.
433. *See id.* at 181.
434. *See id.* at 179.
435. *See id.*
436. *See id.* at 182.
437. *See id.*
438. *See id.*
439. *See, e.g., In re* Marriage of Flynn, 597 N.E.2d 709, 713 (Ill. App. Ct. 1992). *But see In re* Marriage of Frey, 630 N.E.2d 466, 466–70 (Ill. App. Ct. 1994) (considering the wife's emotional distress in upholding a trial court's finding of unconscionability).
440. *See Beattie*, 368 N.E.2d at 182. More than 60 Illinois cases were researched in preparing this discussion. In some of them, husbands challenged settlements. Interestingly, in these cases no court ever mentioned that husbands "normally" are emotionally upset at divorce.
441. *See id.* at 183.
442. *See id.*
443. *See, e.g.,* Crawford v. Crawford, 350 N.E.2d 103 (Ill. App. Ct. 1976) (reversing the trial court's denial of wife's petition to vacate); Byrne v. Byrne, 643 N.Y.S.2d 659 (N.Y. App. Div. 1996) (finding the wife had "unequivocally

agreed" to the terms of a stipulation that concededly contained several concessions regarding the husband's financial obligations). If an attorney reads a
settlement's terms into the record in open court and competent attorneys
represent both parties, New York courts are reluctant to vacate the agreement.
See, e.g., Burkart v. Burkart, 582 N.Y.S.2d 783 (N.Y. App. Div. 1992);
Zioncheck v. Zioncheck, 470 N.Y.S.2d 950 (N.Y. App. Div. 1984).

444. *See Beattie,* 368 N.E.2d at 182.

445. *See id.* at 183. *See also In re* Marriage of Steadman, 670 N.E.2d 1146, 1151
(Ill. App. Ct. 1996).

446. *See In re* Marriage of Flynn, 597 N.E.2d 709 (Ill. App. Ct. 1992).

447. *See id.* at 710, 713.

448. *See id.* at 713.

449. *See id.*

450. *See id.*

451. *See id.*

452. *See id.*

453. *See id.* at 711–12.

454. *See id.* at 712.

455. *See id.* at 713.

456. *See In re* Marriage of Flynn, 597 N.E.2d 709, 712–13 (Ill. App. Ct. 1992).

457. *See id.* at 712.

458. *See id.* at 711–12.

459. *See id.* at 711.

460. *See id.*

461. *See id.*

462. *See id.* at 712.

463. *See id.*

464. Pateman writes,

> Civil mastery requires agreement from the subordinate and numerous
> stories are spun in which slaves and women in chains contract and
> consent to their subjection. In the famous pornographic story, The story
> of O, in which O, a woman, is imprisoned and used sexually by her
> captors, she is always asked before each assault and violation whether
> or not she consents. Men exercise their masculine capacity for political
> creativity by generating political relationships of subordination
> through contract.

PATEMAN, *supra* note 88, at 186–87.

465. *Flynn,* 597 N.E.2d at 714. *See also* Bryan, *supra* note 58, at 177–88; *In re*
Marriage of Steadman, 670 N.E.2d 1146 (Ill. App. Ct. 1996); Crawford v.
Crawford, 350 N.E.2d 103 (Ill. App. Ct. 1976) (reversing the trial court's
denial of the wife's petition to vacate).

466. *See, e.g., In re* Marriage of Hoppe, 580 N.E.2d 1186 (Ill. App. Ct. 1991)
(reversing and remanding the trial court's denial of the wife's petition to
vacate). *But see In re* Marriage of Carlson, 428 N.E.2d 1005, 1011 (Ill. App.

Ct. 1981) (considering the husband's threat to take custody of the children one important factor in finding the agreement unconscionable).

467. *See Steadman,* 670 N.E.2d at 1148.
468. *See id.*
469. *See id.*
470. *See id.*
471. *See id.*
472. *See id.*
473. *See id.*
474. *See id.*
475. *See id.*
476. *See id.*
477. *In re* Marriage of Steadman, 670 N.E.2d 1146, 1149 (Ill. App. Ct. 1996).
478. *See id.* at 1151–52.
479. *See id.*
480. *See id.* at 1148.
481. *See id.* at 1149.
482. *See id.*
483. *See id.*
484. *See id.* at 1149, 1151–52.
485. *See id.* at 148.
486. At the settlement hearing, Yolanda testified as follows:

> MR. KOZLOWSKI [Counsel for Wife]: And that's the agreement we worked out today in the hall, and we will reduce it to writing with the joint custody [agreement], and you're satisfied with that?
>
> THE WITNESS [Wife]: I have no choice.
>
> THE COURT: Well, ma'am, I want you to understand that you do have a choice. We can sit down right now and have a formal hearing and the parties can present evidence on both sides and call any witnesses that you want and the Court will make a decision.
>
> THE WITNESS: Okay
>
> THE COURT: The question is, is this your agreement?
>
> THE WITNESS: At this time, yes, sir.

Id. at 1149.
487. *See In re* Marriage of Steadman, 670 N.E.2d 1146, 1148 (Ill. App. Ct. 1996).
488. *See id.* at 1151–52 (citations omitted).
489. An occasional variation on this theme arises when the wife alleges that the trial court coerced her into a bad agreement by exerting pressure to settle before a hearing. For instance, in Cantamessa v. Cantamessa, 565 N.Y.S.2d 895 (N.Y. App. Div. 1991), on the day of final hearing, the judge encouraged the parties to settle and consulted with the parties and their attorneys during negotiations. At the court's urging, the wife finally entered into an agreement.

The wife testified that she understood the settlement's terms, she had sufficient time to discuss the settlement with her attorney, and that she was satisfied with the agreement and with her attorney's representation. The court then incorporated the stipulated settlement into the final judgment of dissolution. The wife subsequently petitioned to vacate the settlement agreement. The appellate court acknowledged that the property the husband retained had substantially more value than that retained by the wife and that the agreement was "improvident." *Id.* at 897. The court also noted that considerable conflict surrounded the value of the husband's ownership interest in his business, implying that discovery had yet to resolve this question despite over four years of litigation. The appellate court, however, did not recognize that this wife likely experienced what many wives experience at divorce: the refusal of the more powerful husband to comply with discovery requests, the failure of the wife's attorneys to conduct adequate discovery before negotiations "on the courthouse steps," the capitulation of the wife to the overpowering nature of the husband, his attorney, and the judge in pressured negotiations just before trial, and the wife's ultimate inability to resist pressures to enter an "improvident" agreement. Rather, the court found the wife's claims of emotional stress and unsettled mental state unpersuasive grounds to set aside the stipulation, particularly when the agreement was "freely" entered into the record—thus, no coercion. Similarly, although the agreement was admittedly "improvident," the court found it was not one-sided enough to support a finding of unconscionability. *Id.*

490. *See, e.g., In re* Marriage of Foster, 451 N.E.2d 915, 917 (Ill. App. Ct. 1983).

491. *See, e.g.,* Bryan, *supra* note 58, at 177–88; *See In re* Marriage of Brandt, 489 N.E.2d 902, 902–05 (Ill. App. Ct. 1986); *In re Foster,* 451 N.E.2d at 917.

492. In a peculiar twist on this theme, one appellate court found the wife's attorney's failure to determine the status of the marital property unproblematic because an "unequivocal evaluation by the petitioner's [wife's] attorney would have been unwarranted." *In re Foster,* 451 N.E.2d at 918.

493. *See In re Steadman,* 670 N.E.2d at 1153. In Boyle v. Burkich, 665 N.Y.S.2d 104 (N.Y. App. Div. 1997), the wife and husband participated in mediation. The couple's contract with the mediator stipulated that the mediator would assist the couple in developing a consensual settlement agreement, that the mediator would not provide legal advice, that the mediator would act as a neutral facilitator, and that the husband and wife should retain independent counsel. During the mediation the wife discovered that the husband was having an affair with the mediator's daughter. When the wife brought this to the mediator's attention and challenged her neutrality, the mediator told the wife to leave the daughter "out of it." The wife then proceeded with the mediation and ultimately entered a separation agreement. When the wife took the mediated agreement to her lawyer, the lawyer told the wife nothing could be done about the mediator's lack of neutrality and the agreement's seemingly unfair terms. The agreement was incorporated into the final judgment of dissolution. The wife subsequently sought to vacate the agreement, alleging that the husband and the mediator had acted in concert to fraudulently

prevent full disclosure of the husband's assets and income. In upholding the trial court's refusal to vacate the agreement, the appellate court emphasized that the wife had reasonable opportunity to confer with her attorney before entering the agreement. No mention was made of the attorney's representations to the wife that nothing could be done about the terms of the mediated agreement or of the attorney's failure to challenge that agreement. Telephone Interview with James W. Cooper, wife's appellate counsel (Nov. 9, 1998).

494. *See In re* Marriage of Beck, 404 N.E.2d 972 (Ill. App. Ct. 1980) (reversing trial court's decision in favor of wife).

495. *See id.* at 973.

496. *See id.*

497. *See id.*

498. *See id.*

499. *See id.* at 973–74.

500. *See id.* at 974.

501. *See id.*

502. *See id.*

503. *See id.* at 973.

504. *See id.* at 975.

505. *See id.* at 974.

506. *See id.*

507. *See id.* at 974, 976.

508. *See, e.g.*, Berman v. Berman, 629 N.Y.S.2d 82 (N.Y. App. Div. 1995) (explaining that the wife sought damages for the husband's fraudulent undervaluation of property during settlement negotiations; court found unpersuasive the wife's statement that she relied on the husband's statement of net worth because the agreement stipulated that both parties voluntarily restricted discovery and the wife knew about at least one of the disputed pieces of property).

509. *See In re* Marriage of Broday, 628 N.E.2d 790, 793 (Ill. App. Ct. 1993).

510. *See id.* at 793–94.

511. *See id.* at 793.

512. *See id.*

513. *See id.*

514. *See id.*

515. *See id.*

516. *See id.* at 794.

517. *See id.*

518. *See id.*

519. *In re* Marriage of Broday, 628 N.E.2d 790, 794 (Ill. App. Ct. 1993).

520. *See id.*

521. *See id.*

522. *See id.*

523. *See id.*

524. *See id.*

525. *See id.*

526. *See id.* at 793.

527. *See id.* at 795.
528. *Id.*
529. *See id.* at 798.
530. *See id.* at 797.
531. *See In re* Marriage of Steadman, 670 N.E.2d 1146, 1152–53 (Ill. App. Ct. 1996) (noting that after 19 years of marriage and five children, the wife received between 17% and 24% of the marital assets and only short-term and minimal spousal maintenance); *In re* Marriage of Foster, 451 N.E.2d 915, 919 (Ill. App. Ct. 1983) (Kasserman, J., dissenting) (noting that the husband received at least $100,000 more than the wife); *In re* Marriage of Beck, 404 N.E.2d 972, 975 (Ill. App. Ct. 1980) (discussing that the trial court characterized the settlement as a "bad deal," yet denied the wife's petition to vacate); Beattie v. Beattie, 368 N.E.2d 178, 183 (Ill. App. Ct. 1977).
532. *See In re* Marriage of Gorman, 671 N.E.2d 819, 821 (Ill. App. Ct. 1996).
533. *See id.*
534. *See id.* at 822.
535. *See id.* at 826.
536. *See id.*
537. *Id.* at 827 (emphasis added).
538. Marston notes,

> More couples are writing prenuptial agreements than ever before. One report estimates that the number of prenuptial agreements tripled between 1978 and 1988 and has steadily increased ever since. Of marrying couples, approximately 5 percent (about 50,000) sign prenuptials each year. Furthermore, an estimated 20 percent of remarriages feature a prenuptial agreement.

Allison A. Marston, *Planning for Love: The Politics of Prenuptial Agreements*, 49 Stan. L. Rev. 887, 891 (1997). *See also* Brod, *supra* note 314, at 231.
539. *See* Brod, *supra* note 314, at 234–40 & n.15; Silbaugh, *supra* note 314, at 134.
540. *See* Brod, *supra* note 314, at 254. Procedural fairness considers (a) the circumstances under which the parties negotiated and executed the agreement, (b) the voluntary nature of the agreement, and (c) the parties' knowledge of the rights, and their value, affected by the agreement. *Id.* at 254–59. *See also* Silbaugh, *supra* note 314, at 74 (noting that procedural fairness varies from state to state, but recognizing common themes such as full disclosure of assets, independent legal counsel, disclosure of rights waived, and sufficient time to review before marriage).
541. *See* Barbara Ann Atwood, *Ten Years Later: Lingering Concerns about the Uniform Premarital Agreement Act*, 19 J. Legis. 127, 135–41 (1993). *See also* Brod, *supra* note 314, at 259–62; Silbaugh, *supra* note 314, at 75. Pennsylvania law, however, requires only full and fair disclosure and prohibits any substantive review for fairness. *See* Atwood, *supra*, at 140. *See* Simeone v. Simeone, 581 A.2d 162 (Pa. 1990).
542. *See* Atwood, *supra* note 541, at 138–41.

543. *See id.*

544. *See generally* Singer, *supra* note 296, at 1475.

545. *See* Atwood, *supra* note 541, at 127–28; Dennis I. Belcher & Laura O. Pomeroy, *For Richer, For Poorer: Strategies for Premarital Agreements*, 12 PROB. & PROP. 54, 56 (1998); Brian Bix, *Bargaining in the Shadow of Love: The Enforcement of Premarital Agreements and How We Think About Marriage*, 40 WM. & MARY L. REV. 145, 154 & n.34 (1998) (noting that approximately half of the states have adopted the Act).

546. *See* Atwood, *supra* note 541, at 128–29, 141–49, 151–53; Bix, *supra* note 545, at 154–56; Brod, *supra* note 314, at 253, 275–79; Laura Weinrib, *Reconstructing Family: Constructive Trust at Relational Dissolution*, 37 HARV. C.R.-C.L. L. REV. 207, 222–23 (2002). *See also* S. Christine Mercing, Comment, *The Uniform Premarital Agreement Act: Survey of Its Impact in Texas and Across the Nation*, 42 BAYLOR L. REV. 825, 826–27 (1990) (noting that the adoption of the Uniform Premarital Agreement Act in Texas seems to make enforcement easier than under preexisting law); Marsh v. Marsh, 949 S.W.2d 734, 738 (Tex. Ct. App. 1997) (noting that Texas, in 1993, amended its statute to eliminate common law defenses to premarital agreements).

547. *See* Atwood, *supra* note 541, at 143; Belcher & Pomeroy, *supra* note 545, at 56–58.

548. *See* J. Thomas Oldham, *Premarital Contracts Are Now Enforceable, Unless . . . ,* 21 HOUS. L. REV. 757, 775–76 (1984).

549. *See* Atwood, *supra* note 541, at 143–44. The only other relief from unfair premarital agreements provided in the Act concerns spousal maintenance. If an agreement results in a party's eligibility for support under a public assistance program, a court may require the other party to provide support to the extent necessary to avoid that eligibility. *Id.* at 144.

550. *In re* Marriage of Bisque, 31 P.3d 175, 177–78 (Colo. Ct. App. 2001) (citations omitted). *But see* Mercing, *supra* note 546, at 827–28 (noting that Texas statutes treat marital and premarital agreement identically for enforcement purposes). *Compare* Marsh v. Marsh, 949 S.W.2d 734, 739 (Tex. Ct. App. 1997) (noting that the party who challenges the enforceability of the premarital agreement has the burden to prove involuntariness or unconscionability) *with* Pletcher v. Goetz, 9 S.W.3d 442, 445 (Tex. Ct. App. 1999) (noting that the party who challenges the enforceability of a settlement agreement has the burden to prove involuntariness or unconscionability); Blonstein v. Blonstein, 831 S.W.2d 468, 472 (Tex. Ct. App. 1992) (noting that the party who challenges the enforceability of a settlement agreement has the burden to prove involuntariness or unconscionability).

551. *See* Atwood, *supra* note 541, at 134.

552. *See* Bix, *supra* note 545, at 186; Marston, *supra* note 538, at 912 & n.187.

553. *See* Atwood, *supra* note 541, at 134–35.

554. *See* Atwood, *supra* note 541, at 135; Bix, *supra* note 545, at 195.

555. *See* Atwood, *supra* note 541, at 135; Bix, *supra* note 545, at 193–95.

556. See Bryan, *supra* note 51, for an explanation of why women enter unfair settlement agreements. Many of the factors Bryan presents in this article

undoubtedly inhibit women's ability to obtain fair premarital agreements. Brod notes,

> The court opinions after Posner that reconsidered the law of premarital agreements assert four common themes. One them focuses on the achievement by women of formal, legal equality as a justification for enforcing premarital agreements between men and women as equal, contracting partners. A second theme vaguely refers to women's changed social status (without convincing evidence of women's actual equality) as a justification for enforcing premarital agreements. The third theme emphasizes the widespread entry of women into the labor market (while ignoring sex discrimination in employment) as a reason for treating women as needing less protection from premarital agreements. Finally, the fourth theme treats the protective stance of the law as a manifestation of archaic paternalism. Courts elaborating these four themes erroneously focused on women's de jure equality while ignoring their de facto inequality. It seems that some judges were ignorant of women's actual, continued, economic and social inequality (particularly in the labor market), while others may have been unsympathetic to women or hostile to gender equality.

Brod, *supra* note 314, at 265–66. *See also* Abrams, *supra* note 96, at 521–22 (noting that the greater social and economic pressure to marry placed on women as opposed to men and women's socially conditioned relational orientation may inhibit women's premarital bargaining power); Marston, *supra* note 538, at 911–13.

557. *See* Atwood, *supra* note 541, at 152.
558. *See, e.g.,* Atwood, *supra* note 541; Brod, *supra* note 314. *See also* Silbaugh, *supra* note 314.
559. *See* Atwood, *supra* note 541, at 133 & n.29. In 1992, 39 reported cases contained challenges to premarital agreements at divorce. In 33 of these cases, wives brought the challenge. *Id.* at 133 n.29.
560. *See* Judith T. Younger, *Marriage, Divorce, and the Family: A Cautionary Tale,* 21 Hofstra L. Rev. 1367, 1374–75 (1993) (noting that women and children have fared poorly in the movement toward state endorsement of private settlements in divorce).

III

PROCEDURAL SOLUTIONS

Before the discussion of procedural reforms, I want to reemphasize the inevitable interdependence of procedure and substance. Reforms that fulfill identified procedural justice criteria also affect substantive outcomes. For example, a better educated judiciary offers decision makers with greater authority and less bias, and these expert and neutral decision makers should produce better substantive results. Early mandatory disclosure increases system efficiency and also levels the negotiation field on which parties make substantive deals. Consequently, before we consider reforms, I will briefly revisit what procedural and substantive goals those reforms should promote.

As discussed earlier, procedural reforms should offer expert and unbiased decision makers who treat parties and their rights with respect. Decisions should rest on accurate information, and a meaningful opportunity for error correction must exist. Parties should have adequate participation and voice in the process. Reforms should reduce disputant hostilities and resolve disputes efficiently.

Procedural reforms also must anticipate their inevitable effect on substantive outcomes. The reforms offered here attempt to promote the functionality of postdivorce families. As noted earlier, the financial deprivation experienced by women and children of divorce significantly impairs their postdivorce functionality. Moreover, insensitive and destructive custody arrangements severely compromise children. We cannot continue, for instance, to award custody to a parent who has sexually abused a child. Consequently, to promote better financial and custody outcomes, the procedural changes here attempt to level the playing field between parties as they negotiate or litigate divorce outcomes. Each procedural reform offered anticipates its substantive effect.

Legal reform, however, has its limits. Although procedures can promote better outcomes, many postdivorce families inevitably will lack the financial resources to adequately provide for their children. Private dissolution laws cannot transfer public funds to those families who lack adequate resources. Consequently, the reforms offered may have limited impact on financial results for poor families. Our inability to reach all families, however, should not prevent us from doing what we can for others. Moreover, although the offered procedures may not improve the financial circumstances of poor families, these families still will benefit from enhanced procedural justice and better custody decisions.

5

A SPECIALIZED COURT
WITH UNIQUE PROCEDURES

A description of and justification for a specialized divorce court with unique procedures follow, but first a compelling question deserves an answer: Why should courts remain the resolution mechanism of choice for divorce disputes? Courts, argue many, should confine themselves to doing what they do well,[1] otherwise they raise the specter of illegitimacy.[2] And are not courts particularly ill-suited to resolve emotional disputes between related parties,[3] particularly when many parents must maintain a relationship for the benefit of the children?[4] Surely the poor past performance of courts emphasized throughout this book militates against their continued authority over divorce cases. Moreover, should not the parties, rather than the state, have the final say in ordering their postdivorce lives, particularly the aspects pertaining to child custody and visitation? Why is private settlement or mediation not the answer?

First we must question whether courts truly lack competence in disputes between related parties. Those who challenge court competence make two main arguments. The first, in order to resolve disputes between related parties, courts must legalize matters considered inappropriate for law. A legally framed dispute may not capture the "real" problem in the relationship.[5] Law singles out only specific incidents and artificially constricts the reality of a complex relationship of long duration. Courts, then, are ill-equipped to determine the source of the problem.[6] The second objection assumes that the related parties ideally should continue and that litigation will destroy their relationship.[7]

Neither objection carries much weight in divorces that do not involve children. All states now offer some form of no-fault divorce,[8] and judges and legislatures discourage fault-based divorce.[9] The question of who caused the relationship's failure rarely has relevance,[10] and judges need not delve into a complex relationship history to determine the source of the couple's problems.[11] Dissolution of these marriages involves only the distribution of marital resources, an issue that judges have the theoretical competence to resolve.[12] Moreover, unless they truly desire otherwise, these parties need to end, not continue, their relationship.

Many jurisdictions, however, still find fault relevant to claims for spousal maintenance.[13] A husband may contest his wife's right to spousal maintenance based on her adultery. She, then, may contend that she committed adultery only because of his sexual desertion or infidelity. These circumstances might require a court to unravel a complex relationship history. The premise that courts "necessarily" lack competence to resolve such issues, however, seems suspect. Certainly we consider courts competent to sort through other equally complex factual issues involving relationships and fault, such as ongoing commercial relations, breach of fiduciary duty, domestic violence, and child abuse and neglect.

The relationship nature of divorce, then, does not necessarily disqualify courts in cases that involve only financial issues. Nevertheless, many other factors mentioned earlier, such as ignorance and bias, have induced judges to perform poorly and to frequently sacrifice both procedural and substantive justice. Poor past performance, however, does not mean that judges cannot correct the error of their ways. The specialized court recommended here offers them that opportunity.[14]

Divorces that involve children present different issues of court competence. In such cases, children benefit when their parents maintain a civil postdivorce relationship, and the best interests standard frequently requires courts to unravel complex and interdependent relationship histories. Often, the anticipation of, preparation for, and the experience of traditional litigation temporarily and sometimes permanently exacerbate hostilities between divorcing parents and fracture their fragile relationships.[15] The adversarial nature of custody litigation, unequal parental resources, and inept or dueling experts frequently make it more rather than less difficult for judges to unravel relationship histories and make quality decisions. The other system shortcomings mentioned earlier, such as ignorance and bias, strain procedural justice and produce poor results at trial. To temper these negative effects and to enhance the competence of divorce courts on child issues, this section offers a "court" that blends administrative, inquisitorial, and adjudicative models.[16] In sum, although the arguments against court competence in divorce cases may have some merit, the specialized court offered here attempts to address these concerns.

A defense of courts as decision makers also prompts the question "compared to what?" Critics offer private ordering, such as lawyer-negotiated settlements or mediation, as better alternatives. Private ordering of divorce disputes, however, has not alleviated the system's procedural and substantive shortcomings. As noted earlier, many lawyers severely compromise procedural justice when they restrict client voice, treat their clients and their rights disrespectfully, lack expertise and authority, exhibit bias, waste resources, and breed hostilities.

I again remind that parties privately resolve most cases. Accountability for poor outcomes falls more heavily on private ordering[17] than on poor judicial performance.[18] An effective dispute resolution system, then, cannot blindly sanction private settlement. It must anticipate and shape lawyer and disputant behavior in a manner that fosters procedural and substantive justice. The blended system offered here attempts to do just that.

The divorce mediation experiment, as a particular form of private ordering, has outlived its utility.[19] At mediation's inception, proponents promised that it would fulfill many procedural and substantive justice criteria better than courts.[20] Specifically, they argued, and continue to argue, that mediation enhances disputant voice,[21] lessens disputant hostility,[22] honors family privacy,[23] promotes the adjustment of children, costs less,[24] and generates better results.[25] Few of these claims, however, withstand close scrutiny.[26] Parties may talk more in mediation than when lawyers or judges process their disputes, but the voices of the less powerful have little effect.[27] Mediations performed without formal discovery lead to inequitable results.[28] No valid research[29] establishes that mediation results in less hostility between divorced parties than does resolution through litigation or lawyer negotiation.[30] Nor does mediation necessarily conserve resources.[31] Moreover, children of divorce do not fare better when their parents use mediation rather than lawyer negotiation or litigation to resolve their divorce dispute.[32]

Critics of mediation continue to argue that mediation systematically disadvantages the less powerful[33] and poses substantial risks for abused wives.[34] Although mediation may honor family privacy, it does so at the expense of substantive fairness[35] and respect for legal rights.[36] And, finally, little reason exists to believe that the parties themselves prefer mediation to more formal procedures.[37]

Many of mediation's shortcomings, as noted, also rear their heads in divorce disputes resolved by lawyers and judges. Frustration with the current state of affairs, however, should not drive us to uncritically implement seriously flawed alternatives that exacerbate procedural and substantive deficiencies. The reforms proposed here offer an alternative to private ordering that encourages lawyers, judges, and disputants to enhance procedural and substantive justice.

The blended court proposed here has other valuable functions. Trials make public some of the more complex and difficult issues that arise in divorce cases, promoting public awareness and encouraging needed action.[38] The trial of Dr. Elizabeth Morgan, for example, has done much to fuel public debate about, and expose judicial insensitivity to, child sexual abuse.[39] Likewise, publication of legal decisions that reveal judicial bias on financial issues can inspire outrage.[40] In contrast, private ordering substantially limits exposure. Although the system must remain sensitive to privacy concerns, exposure can promote reforms that enhance substantive and/or procedural justice.

Judges simply must try some cases. Attempts at private ordering sometimes do, and should, fail. Not all parties make fair financial offers. Some parents insist on destructive custody arrangements. Under such circumstances, the state must exercise its authority and impose a just result.

Historically, divorce law has evolved from the dialogue, sometimes heated, between state courts and legislatures.[41] Individual cases present unique fact patterns that reveal the need to alter existing law. Courts also provide a forum in which the less powerful, who lack the resources to lobby legislators, can voice their grievances.[42] In their courtrooms, judges gain insights about the law's shortcomings that elude legislators. Because substantive law must remain responsive to the social conditions it governs, this corrective function of courts proves particularly important in divorce law, where social realities change with dizzying speed.[43] Although judges have not always altered or applied law in a manner that satisfies substantive justice, specially trained and experienced judges can promote a more sensitive evolution of law.

The symbolic and coercive authority of a judge sometimes can encourage a disputant to take seriously an obligation to an ex-spouse or a child. I recall one father who refused to stop smoking in the presence of his asthmatic son. His ex-wife and his son's doctors explained that his smoking jeopardized his son's health, but nothing fazed the father. The son experienced a severe asthmatic attack after visitation with his father, requiring the son's hospitalization. Frustrated, the mother petitioned the court to terminate the father's visitation rights. After listening to the mother, the boy's sister, the physicians, and the father, the judge turned to the father and sternly told him that he must never again smoke in his son's presence. Violation of the order would result in contempt and jail. To the mother's knowledge (and relief), the chastised father never again smoked in his son's presence.

And, finally, a judge's respectful and empathetic treatment of parties fulfills their dignity concerns[44] and can encourage a reduction in hostilities.[45] For all of the above reasons, then, courts, particularly in the form proposed here, remain an essential component of an effective divorce dispute resolution system.

DESCRIPTION AND JUSTIFICATION OF A SPECIALIZED COURT

The specialized court retains many of the typical characteristics of trial courts of general jurisdiction. Personnel, however, take on new roles, and procedures vary substantially. This section does not describe this court in exhaustive detail, but focuses instead on the types of reforms needed to enhance procedural and substantive justice.

SEPARATION

Specialized divorce courts should stand separate from other trial courts of general jurisdiction.[46] The services rendered, the data collected, the procedural rules, and the training and duties of court personnel differ from those of other trial courts. To promote efficiency, avoid confusion, and ensure successful goal fulfillment, the family court system must have its own judges, magistrates, administrative personnel, and court staff, as well as its own facilities.

Separation allows the creation of a new court culture. Judges and other family court personnel must break with old ideas about how courts function and immerse themselves in a different philosophy and mode of operation.[47] Removal from the powerful influence of dysfunctional traditions[48] enhances their ability to create and sustain a new court culture.[49]

Separation promotes clarification and fulfillment of goals. With clear and adequately justified goals, all court personnel more easily can understand and appreciate the importance of their contributions to the overall mission.[50] A sense of shared mission helps personnel to sustain their motivation.

Separation from other trial courts, however, cannot result in a second-class court system with poor facilities, understaffed programs, and underpaid personnel. States must offer a system that inspires public respect and that produces quality outcomes. A court system that resolves issues of such importance to us all deserves no less. At a minimum, states must provide facilities and technical support equivalent to those provided to traditionally elite trial courts. Court personnel must receive adequate compensation, earning at least the same pay and benefits as other trial court personnel.[51]

Adequate compensation enhances status and attracts and retains the high quality personnel[52] necessary for the success of the specialized court.

JURISDICTION

Much of the current literature on family court reform speaks of unified courts. Proponents advocate a court with jurisdiction over issues of juvenile delinquency, dependency and neglect, criminal prosecutions for domestic violence, divorce, and other related issues.[53] Significant problems exist in all of the distinct legal areas that unified family courts place under one courthouse roof. Courts mismanage dependency and neglect as well as juvenile and divorce cases. Although proponents believe that unified courts offer comprehensive services to families and increase efficiency, I doubt that simply assigning all of these issues to one court ensures that the court will operate in a procedurally and substantively just manner. Consequently, a unified court is not proposed here. I deliberately limited the task to the design and justification of a court system that addresses only divorce and closely related issues. Perhaps this more modest endeavor will facilitate rational consideration of more complex structures.[54]

The proposed specialized court has jurisdiction over the dissolution of formal marriages;[55] the dissolution of common law marriages; the validity and enforceability of cohabitation, antenuptial, and separation contracts; requests for formal separation; custody, visitation, and child support disputes that arise outside of marriage[56] or outside a divorce proceeding; and requests for modification or enforcement of existing support or custody orders.

SELECTION AND RETENTION OF JUDGES

To ensure their actual and perceived neutrality,[57] the system must insulate judges as much as possible from campaigns for and against them by special interest groups during the appointment and retention process.[58] Consequently, a judicial nominating commission, rather than the electorate, chooses judicial candidates. The state supreme court appoints an equal number of members from both political parties,[59] and the commission's composition must reflect a broad cross-section of the community the court serves.[60] The commission, for instance, might include lawyers with and without expertise in family law, child advocates, representatives from the women's and fathers' rights movements, and experts from relevant disciplines. Ethnic and gender diversity must exist. The representation of divergent views and interests avoids the actual or perceived domination of the judicial selection process by particular interest groups.[61]

A broadly diverse commission also inhibits the ability of membership coalitions to capture the appointments process.[62] Domination by any particular group would defeat many of the benefits of specialization and taint the legitimacy of the court. The commission recommends judicial candidates to the governor for actual appointment.

The commission searches for candidates who exhibit appropriate judicial temperament and a genuine interest in and commitment to family issues. Experience in family law practice, or other relevant specialized knowledge, proves an important consideration.[63] We can hope, but must not presume, that such individuals will exhibit sensitivity to and respect for divorce disputants and their children. Their commitment and knowledge also will encourage their adherence to the goals of the new court system. Commissioners must approach with caution those who might seek to process their own personal problems in their courtrooms or those who might invite perceptions of bias. For instance, the commission should not consider candidates who have verifiable histories of family violence. Even if such individuals had the capacity to render fair and unbiased decisions in cases similar to their own, they would compromise respected authority and invite public suspicion of judicial bias. The commission should not automatically exclude candidates with previous judicial experience, but it should screen such candidates carefully to ensure their willingness and ability to entertain and implement new ideas about divorce courts and disputes.

During a judge's tenure, the court administrator collects data on the judge's performance. The administrator limits data collection to judicial behaviors related to procedural and substantive justice. Surveys ask the parties and attorneys who appear before a judge whether the judge appeared knowledgeable and impartial and treated them and their rights with respect. Surveys also ask whether parties believe they had sufficient voice or participation in the proceedings before the judge. Court personnel collect data on case characteristics and judicial awards to determine whether the decisions made by each judge reflect quality and consistent results. Even in cases that settle, court staff survey the parties' procedural and substantive assessment of their overall divorce experience in order to identify weaknesses embedded in the divorce process. At all times, each judge has access to accumulated data in order to alter his or her behavior as needed. Judicial data remains confidential until judicial review.

At the end of each year, the chief judge reviews the performance of each judge based on collected data and informed by the concerns raised throughout this book.[64] The chief judge identifies deficiencies and strengths in performance and discusses these issues with the particular judge. At this conference, the individual judge can, of course, correct any misperceptions the data might reflect. At the end of the five-year appointment period, the judicial commission may extend a judge's term for an additional five years on the basis of performance.

The chief judge makes retention recommendations with specific factual findings based on a judge's yearly reviews. The commission uses this recommendation, as well as the data collected during the judge's term, to make its final retention decision. A dissatisfied judge can request reconsideration by the commission.

This internal review poses some dangers, especially if the position of chief judge rotates yearly among the judges, as is recommend later. In an attempt to avoid future criticism of his or her own performance, the chief judge might feel reluctant to criticize a judicial colleague who, at some point in the future, will become the reviewing chief judge. However, the yearly judicial review strives not so much to criticize as to make certain that judges know their strengths and weaknesses and can optimize their performance. Moreover, even if internal review by interdependent actors does promote less than candid feedback, the independent retention review by outside parties at the end of five years of service helps to ensure retention of only those judges who perform in accordance with system goals.

The position of chief judge rotates yearly through a maximum of five judges. The commission reviews each chief judge's performance each year. This external review of the chief judge helps minimize the potential weaknesses of the largely internal review process set out earlier. Because chief judges will want to appear as competent as their colleagues, the external review encourages them to evaluate their colleagues as candidly as the commission reviews them.

Outside review of the chief judge also protects against internal bias or unfairness in the retention process. If a judge receives a poor evaluation from a biased chief judge, when that judge serves as chief judge the commission's independent review provides an opportunity to intercept that bias. Judges serve in divisions of five in order to ensure that each has the opportunity for one outside review before the commission makes a final retention decision.

I propose this selection and retention process for several reasons.[65] First, it provides a balance between judicial independence[66] and judicial accountability.[67] Accountability counsels against life tenure.[68] On the other hand, independence recommends that we not subject judicial selection or retention to popular vote. Special interest groups currently campaign— with alarming effectiveness—against retention of judges who decide cases contrary to their wishes.[69] Divorce judges in particular operate in a context rife with controversy and dominated by special interest groups. These groups undoubtedly will watch closely, and voice dissatisfaction with, particular judicial decisions. Campaign ads sponsored by interest groups often state that judges base decisions on personal opinions rather than law, impugning judicial integrity.[70] The attention the media itself directs to judges who make controversial decisions makes judges particularly vulnerable.[71] If the state provides retention by election, judges simply could not ignore their vulnerability to political attack,[72] and that vulnerability undoubtedly would influence their decisions.[73]

Many note with alarm the increasing cost of judicial selection and retention elections.[74] Campaign demands force judges to accept political contributions from the very individuals who appear before them as parties and attorneys.[75] Gratitude for election support might tempt a judge to shape an opinion to accommodate a major contributor.[76] Even if a judge resists that temptation, the spectacle of elections and the suspicion that contributions will shape decisions threaten the integrity of the court and invite disrespect for court authority.[77]

The recent case of *Republican Party of Minnesota v. White*[78] offers to make state judicial selection and retention elections more unseemly. In *White*, the U.S. Supreme Court invalidated a state law that prohibited candidates for judicial office from announcing their views on disputed legal or political issues.[79] The majority opinion emphasized that the law impermissibly restricted content-based political speech.[80] Consequently, judges now can campaign by stating their views on controversial issues, which in turn suggests that judges have prejudged cases they will be called on to impartially decide. Chemerinsky notes, "Certainly, it is distressing to think of judicial candidates appealing to voters with commercials stating their opposition to abortion rights or their desire to impose the death penalty. But the simple reality is that judicial elections make judges and judicial candidates into politicians."[81] In our specialized court, one might imagine a judicial candidate who seeks selection or retention by appealing to interest groups by announcing his or her views on the importance of fathers to children or on the importance of maternal nurture to children. In a court that so desperately needs the legitimating cloak of impartiality, the possibility of these types of campaign statements pose too great a risk.[82] Better to have a nominating commission make inquiries into a particular candidate's views during the appointment and retention processes than to expose judges to public ridicule.[83]

Quality decisions and court integrity require judicial insulation from popular caprice, self-interested wealthy contributors, and unseemly campaigns.[84] The point is not to silence interest groups or aggrieved individuals, for their vigilance may spark needed awareness and constructive debate. The point only is to create a selection and retention process that facilitates independent and quality judicial decision making.[85] Although appointment does not guarantee a judiciary free from special interest pressures, it does provide an appropriate balance between independence and accountability.[86]

Retention reviews informed by articulated goals provide for judicial accountability and encourage judicial acceptance and pursuit of identified goals. Objective assessment of judicial effectiveness on procedural and substantive grounds encourages continued support for innovative reform.[87] Moreover, when a judge experiences review by others, he or she might develop more empathy for those whom he or she in turn must judge. Empathy can encourage more respectful judicial treatment of divorce disputants.[88]

Certainly review might prove unpopular among judicial candidates. Yet all states subject all judges to some type of review or retention process.[89] The review and retention process recommended here seems more fair, rational, and dignified than the retention elections required of most state judges.

Judges in the specialized court commit to a minimum of five years of exclusive service. Continuity of service enhances procedural justice, because judges will increase their respected authority through the acquisition of expertise.[90] When disputants return to the court to resolve postdivorce disputes, their appearance before the same judge increases procedural consistency. Extended and exclusive service also enhances substantive justice, because judges will acquire the experience and knowledge necessary for quality decisions, and the judge most knowledgeable about the case will preside until its closure.[91] The same judge also will preside over postdivorce disputes, which assures that the judge with the greatest historical knowledge will make relevant decisions.[92]

EDUCATION AND TRAINING

Once chosen, judges undergo specialized education and training.[93] Education must provide a thorough grounding in the relevant substantive law. No matter how progressive and sensitive the substantive law, as we have seen, an uneducated or unwilling judiciary readily can thwart its purposes.[94] Consequently, education must promote formal legal competence.

Training exposes judges to procedural justice requirements and explains their importance. Judges must, for instance, understand the necessity of participation and voice and respectful treatment of disputants.[95] They must understand as well the importance of the quality, as well as the consistency, of outcomes.

Judges also must receive information pertinent to the social worlds into which they intrude.[96] To mention but a few educational priorities, judges must learn to curb their biases and realistically assess the financial vulnerability of postdivorce families.[97] They must receive accurate information about the financial needs of divorced families and the ability of custodial parents to generate income while they care for children. Judges also must learn about the psychology of divorce for adults and children, with particular emphasis on the developmental needs of children and on what custody and visitation arrangements might best address those needs.[98] Judges must accept the frequency of family violence and learn to identify the symptoms and effects of adult and child abuse. Educators must provide judges with the most current information on the effectiveness of different intervention strategies and the potential risks of future violence. Experts should instruct judges on the newest and most valid research on difficult issues, such as the likelihood of false allegations of child sexual abuse. States should update training at least once a year to keep judges current on research developments.[99] Research updates are essential, because our understanding in these areas keeps changing as research becomes more sophisticated and the social conditions of families evolve.[100]

In addition to initial training, judges attend bi-weekly conferences with their judicial colleagues, and sometimes with multidisciplinary teams. These conferences provide a forum for judges to discuss difficult cases, to secure the advice and insight of their colleagues, and to ease the burden and isolation of judging.[101] When considered appropriate, judges include experts from other disciplines, such as medicine, psychology, sociology and economics. Not only can these conferences help a judge to wisely resolve an individual case, they also can promote consistency of outcomes among judges.[102] Finally, the conference strengthens the culture of the court through dialogue that reinforces articulated goals.[103]

Several system goals necessitate judicial training. Knowledgeable judges should generate higher quality decisions,[104] decreasing the dysfunctionality of postdivorce families. A judge, for instance, who understands that wife beating affects children and that the likelihood of repeated violence increases at divorce, will not impose a joint custody arrangement on a violent family.[105] Similarly, a judge who knows that custodial parents of young children generally do not earn what adults without children earn and that children need their parents immediately after divorce, likely will award spousal maintenance to the custodial parent, provided the other spouse has adequate income. In addition, lawyers who represent clients in specialized courts tend to develop the specialized knowledge the court demands.[106] A more sophisticated bar also contributes to better outcomes.

Knowledgeable judges also enhance procedural justice. A judge who understands the psychological, emotional, and financial agony of divorce will find it easier to treat parties with respect even when they act in ways the judge finds irrational or offensive. The authority of judges and lawyers who have acquired a level of expertise also will command greater respect from divorce disputants. Knowledge also helps to curb bias in the bench and bar. Knowledgeable and experienced judges generally operate more efficiently.[107] Judicial training, thus, enhances both procedural and substantive justice, which in turn encourages compliance.[108]

The benefits of judicial training presuppose the accuracy of the information judges receive. This assumption is somewhat troublesome. Whereas education on the applicable law raises little controversy, the use of social science research in law has a checkered history. To mention but a few problems: (a) psychologists for centuries miscomprehended and discriminated against women;[109] (b) social scientists sometimes shape their research topics and designs in order to secure funding, and funding agencies frequently have their own agendas; (c) researchers sometimes conduct poorly designed studies, and a few actually inaccurately report their results; (d) policy makers frequently use flawed research to support social policies consistent with their own interests; and (e) some issues do not lend themselves easily to empirical investigation.[110] Some feminists, for instance, harbor suspicions about the recent plethora of studies that investigate, and allegedly confirm, the importance of fathers to children. Legal actors initially accepted Dr. Richard Gardner's now discredited opinions regarding the falsity of child sexual abuse allegations.[111] Many have challenged Lenore Weitzman's findings on the dire economic consequences of divorce for women and children. Lenore Walker's pioneering work on the battered woman syndrome today seems outdated.[112] As the social realities of families evolve and our knowledge about the condition of families deepens, we undoubtedly will recognize that we initially misunderstood some issues. Precisely because of the provisional state of some of our knowledge about families, judicial training must include the potential pitfalls of heavy and uncritical reliance on social science research.[113]

The benefits of judicial training also assume the applicability of the information judges receive to the cases they resolve. The use of social science research to help decide specific cases is problematic if not properly tempered. Statistics speak in aggregates that ignore individual differences: most battered women look like this, children of divorce suffer these specific problems, treatment for men who batter women usually fails, and so on. A particular individual might well defy general norms. Educators must caution judges about these limitations.

Despite its shortcoming, social science research has its place in judicial training. In some areas, such as child custody and visitation, we have no other acceptable basis for decision making than the best information we have,[114] coupled with a thorough understanding of a particular family's circumstances. We can justify, and expect respect for, a decision based on "the best information we have," tailored to the particular family's circumstances. We cannot, however, defend, or expect respect for, a decision based on the "gut reaction," naiveté, or bias of a particular decision maker.

Moreover, a decision that comports with our best knowledge at the moment need not constrain future decisions if our knowledge changes. Judicial training, then, not only can improve the quality of decision making, it provides a ready mechanism for the evolution and continued legitimacy of law in a rapidly changing area.

DUTIES

Judges in the specialized court have duties similar to those in other civil courts. Judges hear pretrial motions, challenges to sanctions, requests for temporary restraining orders, and petitions to vacate settlement or antenuptial agreements. They participate in pretrial conferences and preside over all contested proceedings. To facilitate error correction and to promote their own legitimacy, in all instances judges explain the decisions they reach.[115]

Judges also preside over all final hearings, even those in which the parties offer a preapproved agreement. Sensitive judicial participation at final hearing reinforces the solemnity of the occasion and encourages parents and spouses to part with civility. I am reminded of a particular hearing. The spouses had not spoken to one another for several months, channeling all communication through their respective attorneys. The couple had settled their differences through negotiation, and their attorneys stood to introduce the agreement into evidence. The judge received the agreement, and the attorneys began their perfunctory questions. When the wife's attorney asked her whether she considered the marriage irretrievably broken, the wife's tears resisted control. She broke down and told the court that after 15 years of marriage her husband had left her for another woman. She still loved him and did not understand why they had to divorce. To my pleasant surprise, the judge spoke quietly and respectfully to her. He acknowledged her pain, expressed his appreciation for the difficulty of ending a marriage, and told her to take whatever time she needed to compose herself. She cried hard for a moment or two and then regained her composure. Asked again by her attorney whether she considered the marriage irretrievably broken, she replied in a steadier voice that she did. The husband's attorney then turned to his client and asked if he believed the marriage irretrievably broken. The husband turned to his wife rather than the judge and told her that he genuinely regretted hurting her and the children, that he still treasured many of their years together, that he was grateful for the support she had given him over the years, and that he had the greatest respect for her as a mother. He then turned to the court and stated that the marriage was irretrievably broken. The court thanked the husband for his consideration of his wife and solemnly entered an order granting the divorce. This ritual had a strong effect on the wife. Although she remained upset, her entire demeanor changed. She quieted, sat up a little straighter, and held herself with dignity. Certainly, not every final hearing will proceed in this manner. Yet the judge's sensitivity and respect for the parties helped them toward a civil closure.

We now know that most couples present settlement agreements for judicial approval at final hearings and that judges pay only cursory attention to these agreements before their incorporation into final judgments. We also know that many settlement and antenuptial agreements result in the dysfunctional financial and custody arrangements we strive to correct. Consequently, judges must review all settlement and antenuptial agreements for substantive fairness at final hearing.[116]

This suggestion, admittedly, flies in the face of conventional wisdom. Some undoubtedly will argue that existing contract doctrine, coupled with protective provisions in divorce laws, provides sufficient protection against unfair agreements. The previous section on error correction that scrutinizes divorce settlements refutes this argument.[117] Others quake at the suspected cost of review. I, as do others,[118] find this argument unconvincing. Certainly meaningful, as opposed to perfunctory, review requires more judicial time and a corresponding increase in state expenditures. The social and financial costs that poor agreements systematically impose on the state, however, far exceed the cost of review. Moreover, many believe that grossly unfair or inadequate settlement agreements simply promote costly postdivorce litigation.[119]

Procedural mechanisms exist to minimize the judicial time devoted to settlement review. Later I propose a dispute assessment conference early in the divorce. This conference intercepts the negotiation process in several ways that encourage better settlements and that expedite judicial review. The sophistication that lawyers develop in specialized courts encourages better initial settlements and lessens the need for judicial review. Two weeks before final hearing, the parties also must submit their negotiated agreement and their explanation of its provisions. Mandatory standardized forms related to financial and child issues as well as mandatory financial affidavits must accompany the agreement.[120] If parties who have settled fail to provide this information, the judge cannot grant the divorce.

To expedite proceedings, a judicial assistance program reviews all case files as well as settlement agreements before final hearing. Staff extract, to the extent possible, information the court will need to resolve the case or to evaluate a settlement. Staff also locate and retain necessary expert assistance whenever a judge so requests. Judicial review at final hearing concentrates primarily on those agreements that court staff find suspect.[121] Judges, however, have the authority to refuse agreements that they independently find lacking.

A second objection to judicial scrutiny claims that no reliable standards exist against which to measure the wisdom of a particular agreement.[122] Certainly the indeterminate nature of most of divorce law, as well as inconsistent judicial decisions, bolster this argument. Current legal standards, however, do provide substantial guidance for review. Maintenance standards make suspect an agreement that provides no spousal maintenance for a 55-year-old wife in a 25-year marriage whose husband's income substantially exceeds hers. Likewise, the law suggests a maintenance award for a custodial mother of two young children whose husband's income substantially exceeds hers. Child support that falls short of the state's guidelines mandates intervention. Property distributions raise suspicion when an unequal or equal property distribution disadvantages the financially dependent spouse. Custody law triggers concern when an agreement provides for joint custody in a divorce that contains allegations of domestic violence. That settlement agreements frequently fail to reflect these expectations hardly establishes the law's inadequacy as a standard for review, particularly by educated court staff and judges.[123]

A final objection to judicial review claims that respect for individual autonomy and freedom of contract trump the state's interest in fair agreements.[124] Our earlier exploration in chapter 2 of the social and financial costs incurred by the state suggests the speciousness of this claim. Moreover, the coercive context that produces unfair agreements does not respect private autonomy; rather, it severely curtails the meaningful choice of less powerful spouses.[125] Judicial review ultimately threatens only the autonomy of those who successfully coerce their unwitting or disadvantaged spouses into unfair agreements,[126] an autonomy that does not warrant respect,[127] particularly in the divorce context. And, finally, unfair agreements also threaten state legitimacy, which depends on the substantive justice expected of courts.

Judicial review of settlement and antenuptial agreements offers the procedural advantage of error correction. Review also can enhance party participation or voice. In the proposed specialized court, if a judge finds an agreement unacceptable, he or she can refuse the divorce and can require the parties to renegotiate. To the extent that the unfair agreement results from one party's inadequate voice, judicial rejection reinforces the disadvantaged party's voice during renegotiation. The interception of unfair agreements also contributes significantly to substantive justice. Not only can the court reject unfair agreements, the prospect of judicial rejection encourages spouses to enter agreements likely to meet with judicial approval. The encouragement to settle fairly because of anticipated review also promotes early settlement and efficiency. Delay and adversarial tactics that currently lead to unfair agreements lose their appeal when parties can anticipate judicial rejection of those very agreements.

Where no agreement exists, or when the parties cannot renegotiate an agreement that the court finds acceptable, a contested hearing before the court follows. In this forum, judges behave more like administrative law than traditional trial court judges.[128] Administrative judges carry the responsibility to develop a full and fair record, particularly when confronted with an unrepresented party.[129] If a witness's testimony fails to address a question the judge wants answered, the judge should ask the question. If a lawyer fails to introduce important evidence, the judge asks the lawyer to present such evidence. If an absent witness seems critical to an informed decision, the judge requests counsel to subpoena that witness, or the judge issues his or her own subpoena. If the court needs advice from an independent expert, the court appoints such an expert.[130]

Contrary to the understanding of many state judges, judicial activism fits within long-established common-law tradition and reflects a trend in modern procedure.[131] The benefits of judicial participation led Cappelletti and Garth to note: "It is now generally accepted that the use of a more active judge can be an aid, not a hindrance, to a basically adversarial system of justice."[132]

Procedural justice provides ample support for judicial activism. Judges must shed their robes of passivity to ensure that accurate and complete information informs their decisions. Judicial activism assists parties who lack the requisite knowledge or resources for effective representation, in effect offering them meaningful participation or voice. A judge who demands a full and complete record shows respect for the parties and their legal rights. A judge who demands adequate information might, of course, slow the divorce process. On the other hand, substantive justice concerns justify a delay that ensures better decisions. And judicial participation does level the playing field between parties, making a significant contribution to better outcomes.

CONCERNS ABOUT SPECIALIZATION

Although much commends the specialization recommended here, objections do exist. Some argue that, in order for judges to render the highest quality decisions, they must interpret and apply the law in light of broad and coherent principles about procedural and substantive fairness.[133] Judges learn about these overarching principles through sensitive application of relevant precedent and from exposure to "the (horizontal) consistency of principle across the range of the legal standards the community now enforces."[134] A judge confined to law in one area will have greater difficulty than more generalist colleagues in determining the overarching principles that should guide his or her interpretation and application of law in any particular case.[135] In this way, specialized judges can hinder the development of procedural and substantive fairness in their particular areas of specialization.[136] More simply stated by Revesz: "This testing and retesting of legal principles in varied factual contexts, . . . undoubtedly improves the quality of decision making. First, it expands the landscape from which the judge draws insight."[137]

I raise three main objections to this contention. First, today divorce judges typically serve in trial courts of general jurisdiction and rotate in and out of the family division. Over time they hear a broad spectrum of cases. If the above argument holds true, this exposure should hone their sense of procedural and substantive fairness, which, in turn, should appear in their behavior and decisions in divorce cases. As this book amply illustrates, this hypothetical ideal has not materialized.[138] Judges do not behave consistently with general procedural justice norms. Moreover, the importation of conventions of fairness from other areas of law have resulted in less rather than more substantive justice. For example, as we have seen, judicial application of contract concepts to separation and antenuptial agreements produce unjust results.

Likewise, generalist judges acknowledge the value of professional degrees and the enhanced earning capacity that one spouse acquires during the marriage. They steadfastly refuse, however, to conceptualize these resources as "property" available for distribution at divorce, because professional degrees lack the traditional characteristics of "property."[139] This literal adherence to traditional property law lacks sensitivity to the divorce context, where the degree may represent the sole marital asset acquired over years of joint effort and sacrifice.

Jurisprudential norms like formal equality that pervade other areas of law also produce injustice for families in which such equality rarely exists.[140] Reliance on concepts from other areas of law has stifled judicial sensitivity and has obscured the necessity to shape norms that provide procedural and substantive justice to all family members—exactly, in essence, what this book attempts.

Some might argue that the doctrinal inconsistency between divorce and other laws that I recognize as appropriate would compromise law's legitimacy. They fail to comprehend, however, that consistent production of procedural and substantive justice, not doctrinal rigidity, promotes legitimacy. Certainly law is no stranger to legal concepts that vary in meaning from one context to another. Moreover, if, in their quest to develop divorce-sensitive doctrine, specialized courts stray too far from immutable legal doctrine, generalist appellate courts can correct the error of their ways.[141] Legislative override provides another corrective mechanism.

Second, the restricted jurisdiction described here provides ample diversity and complexity. Judges in our specialized court experience many areas of law from which they can draw insights. Divorce cases raise constitutional issues.[142] Property distribution frequently interfaces with corporate and partnership law.[143] Bankruptcy[144] and tax[145] law affect spousal maintenance and property distribution. Federal statutes frequently have an impact on the distribution of pension plans.[146] Property distribution can generate conflict of law issues. Custody cases involve complex jurisdictional[147] and full faith and credit, or comity, concerns. Spousal maintenance decisions require economic projections by specialists. Quality custody and visitation decisions require knowledge from multiple disciplines. Presumably, enough complexity and crossover exists in divorce law alone to expand judicial insight.[148]

Third, limits exist on what generalist courts can do well.[149] The poor procedural and substantive performance of generalist judges in divorce cases strongly suggest that current courts have overstepped those limits. Generalist judges consistently fail to understand how their decisions affect individual family members and society at large. Their lack of specialization has hindered the sensitivity to context necessary to render decisions true to procedural and substantive justice.[150] Moreover, their participation in other types of "more valuable" cases provides a disincentive for them to develop that sensitivity. Judges do not need, then, a vision of justice borne from broad exposure. Rather they need a deeper and more accurate understanding of the worlds and individuals before them.

The Court of Appeals for the Federal Circuit (CAFC) illustrates how specialization can promote sensitivity. The CAFC exercises exclusive jurisdiction over patent appeals from the U.S. district courts and the Patent Trademark Office.[151] Congress created this specialized appellate court in 1982 with the hope that its exclusive appellate jurisdiction would lead to unity and stability in patent law.[152] Unity and stability, reasoned Congress, in turn would facilitate technological growth, industrial innovation, and business planning. Despite initial predictions of failure, Dreyfuss argues that the CAFC has successfully fulfilled its intended mission, largely because of a developed sensitivity to the dynamics of invention.[153] The CAFC has taken that sensitivity and used it to weave the conceptual strands of patent law into a coherent tapestry.[154] Now more stable and uniform patent law encourages technological advances and innovations. This example suggests that specialized divorce courts also could blend sensitivity to context with responsive legal doctrine.

Despite its promising development, however, Dreyfuss also argues that CAFC's restricted jurisdiction has hampered somewhat the court's success. She explains,

> Patent law constitutes only a small part of competition law, and the system that patent law creates to promote innovation is only one of the many ways in which innovation is facilitated in the legal system.

If the CAFC is told to encourage invention, but is permitted to see only a small part of the matrix into which patent cases fit, it is likely that it will misconceive the role that patent law plays in the larger scheme. It will over-emphasize the need to reward inventors because that is the only tool with which it can further the legislative goal of promoting innovation. Conversely, it will undervalue the interest of competitors because it will not have the occasion to consider the role that vigorous competition plays in encouraging invention. Just as we saw that the different strands of patent law could not be knit together until a single court had the power to deal with all patent cases, it may be that competition law cannot coalesce properly until one court has the power to deal with all of the elements that it encompasses.[155]

In the end Dreyfuss advocates expansion of the CAFC's jurisdiction to encompass other competition issues.[156] More generalization, thus, becomes the cure for specialization's shortcomings, and we seem to have come full circle.

The court proposed here, however, does not pose the problem that Dreyfuss detects. The state policy advocated here promotes the optimal functionality of the postdivorce family. Whereas patent law captures only one segment of competition law, divorce law addresses a whole unto itself. No other area of law has responsibility for the functionality of postdivorce families. Our court then, in contrast to CAFC, need not fit its doctrine into a broader area of law to maximize its central goal.

Once acquired, however, the very expertise that promotes judicial sensitivity can result in sloppy and rigid decision making. Specialized courts tend to generate more consistent opinions than their generalized counterparts. Although procedural and substantive justice recommends this consistency, too much of a good thing can create new problems. For instance, a judge who has experienced the truth of allegations of child sexual abuse in case after case may come to believe the truth of all allegations of child sexual abuse. This assumption, borne of experience, might result in injustice in a case of false allegations. The specialized court, however, addresses this possibility. The updated training that judges receive each year challenges judicial minds to remain open. Biweekly conferences with colleagues and other experts encourages judges to discuss real or hypothetical cases. The insights they receive discourages rigidity and intercepts developing biases.[157] Judicial evaluation also encourages judges to pay individual attention to individual cases. The operation of this specialized court, then, attempts to mitigate the development of judicial rigidity.

The inability to attract superior judicial candidates provides another objection to specialized courts. Boredom borne of repetition, low status, and the stress and exhaustion associated with a steady diet of difficult cases arguably make service on the specialized court unattractive to the best legal talent. Posner argues, for instance, that the repetitive work performed by specialized judges fails to attract individuals with superior intellects.[158] As Judge Plager observes, however, this claim represents only Judge Posner's personal opinion and lacks verification of any sort.[159] A limited spectrum of cases that develops expertise might prove more attractive to individuals with truly superior intellects than a broader range of cases that overwhelms and breeds insensitivity and incompetence. Posner himself admits that judges likely can avoid vocational monotony if their specialized jurisdiction extends over a cluster of related issues.[160]

As we have seen, the issues that arise in divorce cases offer enough diversity and complexity to ward off vocational monotony. Moreover, the specialized court's jurisdiction extends over a cluster of closely related issues. Service in a well-organized system that performs a mission of grave social importance also mitigates the impact of the repetitive nature of the judicial docket.[161] Finally, some of the boredom that generalist judges experience in response to divorce cases stems from their failure to appreciate the complexity and significance of divorce issues.[162] Initial and continuing judicial education helps our more specialized brethren to avoid this type of boredom. The specialized judicial universe offered here, in essence, contains issues as complex and varied as the legal and social worlds of the parties and their children. The demands of judicial competence offer challenges to the best legal minds.

Although boredom borne of repetition in the proposed specialized court seems highly unlikely, the most qualified candidates might balk at the stress and exhaustion attributable to a steady diet of difficult social and financial issues. The opportunity for collaboration during biweekly conferences, however, reduces the stress and isolation experienced in more traditional courts. Some of the stress judges experience in these cases undoubtedly stems from ignorance and inability, in an adversarial context, to decipher conflicting expert, parental, and witness testimony. Judicial education presumably mitigates the stress related to ignorance. And custody evaluation teams will remove most custody cases from the adversarial context and provide judges with the expert and neutral information they need for quality decision making. The chief judge also has a reduced or nonexistent caseload for an entire year, which provides relief from continual exposure to an emotionally compelling area. Month-long vacations also help judges to maintain their emotional equilibrium. Other administrative and staff assistance protect against judicial exhaustion from case overload. And, finally, the stress of current legal practice might well make a specialized judicial appointment far more attractive than in earlier years.

A final objection to the specialized court arises in Dreyfuss's historical review of specialized federal courts. She notes that specialized federal courts have had difficulty gaining acceptance when they exercise jurisdiction over areas that lack social consensus. We can anticipate, for instance, that a specialized environmental court might fail, because we lack social consensus on many environmental issues.[163] Such a court would make only controversial decisions, with no ability to replenish its legitimacy by deciding less controversial issues. Moreover, the court's highly conspicuous opinions would make it a ready target for those who disagree with its decisions.[164]

Certainly the specialized court proposed here will make decisions in an area where little consensus exists. A court-sponsored public education program, however, encourages public acceptance and respect by educating the community about the specialized court. This education program explains how the court functions as well as its goals. Lay and legal constituents also learn of the specialized training all court personnel receive. Moreover, this book attempts to promote more public consensus by exposing the systemic and social costs attributable to divorce and making alleviation of those costs the court's primary mission. The procedural justice built into this court system provides strong protection for the legitimacy of the substantive decisions that emerge. Finally, a data collection and court evaluation program designs instruments and collects data on all key court employees for purposes of evaluation and retention. Personnel also design and implement the research necessary to evaluate the court procedures and programs consistent with the goals articulated throughout this book. These precautions ensure adherence to goals and serve to protect the court's legitimacy even when a judge makes a controversial decision. Even skeptics recognize that structural and operational differences can make some specialized courts more effective than others.[165]

In conclusion, the court offered here anticipates and attempts to ameliorate many of the problems commonly associated with specialization, creating, hopefully, a viable alternative to today's chaos.

NOTES

1. *See* Ralph Cavanagh & Austin Sarat, *Thinking About Courts: Toward and Beyond a Jurisprudence of Judicial Competence*, 14 L. & Soc'y Rev. 371, 372, 375 (1980).

2. *See* Owen Fiss, *The Supreme Court, 1978 Term Foreword: The Forms of Justice*, 93 Harv. L. Rev. 1, 44–45 (1979).

3. *See* Cavanagh & Sarat, *supra* note 1, at 375–76, 394–95 (noting that court critics challenge the competence of courts to effectively resolve disputes between people involved in ongoing social relations).

4. *See* Cavanagh & Sarat, *supra* note 1, at 384–85 (noting that the need to declare a winner and the inability of courts to unravel causation militate against adjudication in lawsuits involving long-term interdependent relationships); Lon Fuller, *The Forms and Limits of Adjudication*, 92 Harv. L. Rev. 353, 371 (1978) (arguing that law's commitment to reasoned argument makes disputes that involve human relations inappropriate grist for legal decision making).

But see Cavanagh & Sarat, *supra*, at 385–86 (suggesting that courts have more competence than many maintain, that the ability of courts to promote private ordering is, perhaps, more important than their adjudicative function, and that disagreement with substantive results actually fuels most court criticism).

5. *See generally* Susan S. Silbey, *The Emperor's New Clothes: Mediation Mythology and Markets*, 2002 J. Disp. Resol. 171, 176.

6. *See* Cavanagh & Sarat, *supra* note 1, at 395–96.

7. *See id.*; Rudolph J. Gerber, *Recommendation on Domestic Relations Reform*, 32 Ariz. L. Rev. 9, 11–12 (1990).

8. *See* Linda D. Elrod & Robert G. Spector, *A Review of the Year in Family Law: State Courts React to Troxel*, 35 Fam. L.Q. 577, 619 chart 4 (2002).

9. *See, e.g.*, Husband D. v. Wife D., 383 A.2d 302, 306 (Del. Fam. Ct. 1977).

10. Some jurisdictions continue to offer fault-based grounds for divorce alongside their no-fault option. *See* Elrod & Spector, *supra* note 8, at 619 chart 4. Fault-based divorce, however, frequently involves proof problems, making it difficult for parties to pursue. *See* Walter Wadlington & Raymond C. O'Brien, Domestic Relations: Cases and Materials 304–05 (2002). Perhaps more importantly, many judges strongly disfavor fault-based divorces and may retaliate against the spouse who pursues one.

11. Although most states require a judge to make an affirmative finding of irretrievable breakdown or irreconcilable differences before granting a divorce, in practice judges require only that the parties answer affirmatively their attorneys' perfunctory question about the breakdown of the marriage. An uncontested divorce proceeding rarely takes longer than five to six minutes. *See* Cavanagh & Sarat, *supra* note 1, at 398 & n.10.

12. The distribution of marital resources is much akin to an award of contract or tort damages or to the dissolution of a business partnership, tasks commonly performed by courts. *See* Cavanagh & Sarat, *supra* note 1, at 395.

13. *See* Elrod & Spector, *supra* note 8, at 616 chart 1.

14. Cavanagh and Sarat note that court critics frequently underestimate the ability of courts to respond to social demands by altering structures and procedures. Cavanagh & Sarat, *supra* note 1, at 373, 376.

15. *See* Gerber, *supra* note 7, at 11–12.

16. Professor Melton hinted at the wisdom of a blended procedure in his broad ranging discussion of future directions for family courts. Gary B. Melton, *Children, Families, and the Courts in the Twenty-First Century*, 66 So. Cal. L. Rev. 1993, 2026, 2035, 2041 (1993). *See also* Henrik H.H. Andrup, *Divorce Proceedings: Ends and Means*, in The Resolution of Family Conflict: Comparative Legal Perspectives 163, 175–76 (John M. Eekelaar & Sanford N. Katz eds. 1984) (recommending, without so stating, a blended procedure).

17. *See* Penelope Eileen Bryan, *Women's Freedom to Contract at Divorce: A Mask for Contextual Coercion*, 47 Buff. L. Rev. 1153 (1999).

18. The inconsistent and unpredictable court decisions that permeate divorce cases, however, do compromise the ability of lawyers and disputants to negotiate quality settlements.

19. I make this claim in the face of numerous state statutes that mandate mediation in disputed child custody cases. *See* Daniel A. Krauss & Bruce D. Sales, *Legal Standards, Expertise, and Experts in the Resolution of Contested Custody Cases*, 6 PSYCHOL. PUB. POL'Y & L. 843, 849 (2000) (noting that, as of 1992, 33 states require mediation in child custody disputes). *See also* Jana B. Singer, *The Privatization of Family Law*, 1992 WIS. L. REV. 1443 for a wide-ranging and thoughtful critique of the general trend toward private ordering in family law, in particular the tendency that private ordering has to exacerbate gender inequalities. *Id.* at 1540–49.

20. *See, e.g.*, Penelope E. Bryan, *Killing Us Softly: Divorce Mediation and the Politics of Power*, 40 BUFF. L. REV. 441, 441 n.1 (1992); Krauss & Sales, *supra* note 19, at 849. *See generally* Silbey, *supra* note 5, at 173–74; Singer, *supra* note 19, at 1497–1508.

21. *See, e.g.*, Joshua D. Rosenberg, *In Defense of Mediation*, 33 ARIZ. L. REV. 467, 472 (1991).

22. *See, e.g.*, Jessica Pearson & Nancy Thoennes, *Custody Mediation in Denver: Short and Longer Term Effects*, in THE RESOLUTION OF FAMILY CONFLICT: COMPARATIVE LEGAL PERSPECTIVES 248, 256 (John M. Eekelaar & Sanford N. Katz eds. 1984); Rosenberg, *supra* note 21, at 472.

23. *See, e.g.*, Rosenberg, *supra* note 21, at 473.

24. *See, e.g., id.* at 472.

25. *See* Carrie Menkel-Meadow, *Whose Dispute Is It Anyway?: A Philosophical and Democratic Defense of Settlement (In Some Cases)*, 83 GEO. L.J. 2663, 2687–88 (1995).

26. *See* Connie J.A. Beck & Bruce Sales, *A Critical Reappraisal of Divorce Mediation Research and Policy*, 6 PSYCHOL. PUB. POL'Y & L. 989 (2000); Silbey, *supra* note 5, at 173–74. *See also* MAUREEN BAKER, CANADIAN FAMILY POLICIES: CROSS-NATIONAL COMPARISONS 302 (1995); Russell Engler, *And Justice for All—Including the Unrepresented Poor: Revisiting the Roles of the Judges, Mediators, and Clerks*, 67 FORDHAM L. REV. 1987, 2007–11 (1999) (noting some of the problems mediation presents for pro se parties); Krauss & Sales, *supra* note 19, at 849; Tom R. Tyler, *Citizen Discontent with Legal Procedures: A Social Science Perspective on Civil Procedure Reform*, 45 AM. J. COMP. L. 871, 879–81 (1997). Hensler notes that proponents have become reluctant to authorize or support evaluative studies on alternative dispute resolution (ADR). She has argued that their personal stakes in ADR account for their aversion to research that might produce unfavorable results. *See* Deborah R. Hensler, *ADR Research at the Crossroads*, 2000 J. DISP. RESOL. 71.

27. *See, e.g.*, Penelope Eileen Bryan, *Reclaiming Professionalism: The Lawyer's Role in Divorce Mediation*, 28 FAM. L.Q. 177, 177–207 (1994); Bryan, *supra* note 20; Silbey, *supra* note 5, at 173.

28. *See, e.g.*, Bryan, *supra* note 27, at 177–88; Phyllis Gangel-Jacob, *Some Words of Caution About Divorce Mediation*, 23 HOFSTRA L. REV. 825, 831 (1995) (noting that fair settlements demand the full and fair financial disclosure that mediation lacks); Boyd v. Boyd, 67 S.W.3d 398, 403–04 (Tex. Ct. App. 2002)

(mediation conducted before formal discovery and husband failed to disclose $230,000 bonus).

29. *See, e.g.,* Desmond Ellis, *Marital Conflict Mediation and Post-Separation Wife Abuse,* 8 L. & INEQ. J. 317, 325–27 (1990) (criticizing the methodology used in the Denver Mediation Study by Pearson and Thoennes); Robert J. Levy, *Comment on the Pearson-Thoennes Study and on Mediation,* 17 FAM. L.Q. 525 (1983) (criticizing the methodology used in the Denver Mediation Study by Pearson and Thoennes).

30. *See* Beck & Sales, *supra* note 26, at 1021–29; Joan B. Kelly et al., *Mediated and Adversarial Divorce: Initial Findings from a Longitudinal Study, in* DIVORCE MEDIATION: THEORY AND PRACTICE 435, 465–66, 472 (Jay Folberg & Ann Milne eds. 1988). Kelly also found no significant difference in hostilities between parties who mediated or litigated two years postdivorce. JOAN B. KELLY, MEDIATED AND ADVERSARIAL DIVORCE RESOLUTION PROCESSES: AN ANALYSIS OF POST-DIVORCE OUTCOMES: FINAL REPORT PREPARED FOR THE FUND FOR RESEARCH IN DISPUTE RESOLUTION 20 (1990).

31. *See, e.g.,* KENNETH KRESSEL, THE PROCESS OF DIVORCE: HOW PROFESSIONALS AND COUPLES NEGOTIATE SETTLEMENTS 189 (1985) (noting that divorce mediation results in only modest time and cost savings for the disputants); Ellis, *supra* note 29, at 323; Tyler, *supra* note 26, at 881. *But see* Jessica Pearson, *The Equity of Mediated Divorce Agreements,* 9 MEDIATION Q. 179, 193 (1991).

32. For instance, no study that compares mediation to litigation of child custody issues indicates a better postdivorce adjustment of children whose parents mediated their disputes. *See* Krauss & Sales, *supra* note 19, at 858.

33. *See* Bryan, *supra* note 27; Bryan, *supra* note 20; Trina Grillo, *The Mediation Alternative: Process Dangers for Women,* 100 YALE L.J. 1545, 1601 (1991); Christopher Honeyman, *Patterns of Bias in Mediation,* 1985 J. DISPUTE RESOL. 141; M. Laurie Leitch, *The Politics of Compromise: A Feminist Perspective on Mediation,* 14/15 MEDIATION Q. 163, 167 (1986–1987); Silbey, *supra* note 5, at 173. *See also* Engler, *supra* note 26, at 2007–11 (noting the problems pro se parties encounter in mediation).

34. *See* Beck & Sales, *supra* note 26, at 996–98; Ellis, *supra* note 29, at 327–39; Karla Fischer et al., *The Culture of Battering and the Role of Mediation in Domestic Violence Cases,* 46 S.M.U. L. REV. 2117, 2118, 2165–71 (1993); Andree G. Gagnon, *Ending Mandatory Divorce Mediation for Battered Women,* 15 HARV. WOMEN'S L.J. 272 (1992); Gangel-Jacob, *supra* note 28, at 834–35; Barbara Hart, *Gentle Jeopardy: The Further Endangerment of Battered Women and Children in Custody Mediation,* 7 MEDIATION Q. 317 (1990); Lisa G. Lerman, *Mediation of Wife Abuse Cases: The Adverse Impact of Informal Dispute Resolution on Women,* 7 HARV. WOMEN'S L.J. 57 (1984); Dianne Post, *Mediation Can Make Bad Worse,* NAT'L L. J. June 8, 1992, at 15.

35. *See* Junda Woo, *Mediation Seen as Being Biased Against Women,* WALL ST. J., Aug. 4, 1992, at B1. As Nolan-Haley notes,

Under prevailing criteria, mediation is evaluated generally in terms of self-determination, participant satisfaction, and efficiency. As applied to court mediation, these criteria may be useful indicators for evaluating process, but are less helpful when evaluating outcome. These criteria tell us only that litigants were doing something, that they felt good about it, and that dockets were cleared as a result. They tell us little about whether litigants actually knew what they were doing or why they were doing it. Thus, these criteria tell us little about justice in court mediation.

Jacqueline M. Nolan-Haley, *Court Mediation and the Search for Justice Through Law*, 74 WASH. U. L.Q. 47, 85–86 (1996). *See also* Bryan, *supra* note 27, at 177–207; Bryan, *supra* note 20; Gangel-Jacob, *supra* note 28, at 832–33 (expressing concern that custody mediation contributes to the use of custody threats to financially and emotionally batter caretaking mothers); Silbey, *supra* note 5, at 173.

36. *See, e.g.*, Bryan, *supra* note 20, at 505–08; Gangel-Jacob, *supra* note 28, at 829–31 (voicing concern that mediation may not sufficiently honor legal rights); Nolan-Haley, *supra* note 35, at 74–79; Laurie Woods, *Mediation: A Backlash to Women's Progress on Family Law Issues*, 19 CLEARINGHOUSE REV. 431, 435–36 (1985).

37. *See* Beck & Sales, *supra* note 26, at 1029–41 (discussing the methodological weaknesses in studies that indicate greater satisfaction for parties who participate in mediation as opposed to litigation); Deborah R. Hensler, *Suppose It's Not True: Challenging Mediation Ideology*, 2002 J. DISP. RESOL. 81, 92 (2002) (concluding, after a review, that empirical research does not provide strong support for the proposition that civil disputants prefer mediation to adversarial litigation and adjudication); Larry Heuer & Steven Penrod, *Procedural Preference as a Function of Conflict Intensity*, 51 J. PERSONALITY & SOC. PSYCHOL. 700 (1986) (finding that parties in high and low intensity conflicts preferred adversarial adjudication to other procedural options); E. Allan Lind et al., *In the Eye of the Beholder: Tort Litigants' Evaluations of Their Experiences in the Civil Justice System*, 24 L. & SOC'Y REV. 953, 978–81 (1990) (finding that parties in tort cases rated trial, as opposed to bilateral settlement, higher on procedural justice); Silbey, *supra* note 5, at 174.

38. *See generally* Helen Hershkoff, *State Courts and the "Passive Virtues": Rethinking the Judicial Function*, 114 HARV. L. REV. 1833, 1939 (2001); David Luban, *Settlements and the Erosion of the Public Realm*, 83 GEO. L.J. 2619 (1995). *See also* Ellen R. Jordan, *Specialized Courts: A Choice?*, 76 NW. U. L. REV. 745, 755 (1981) (arguing that private arbitration may be inappropriate in disputes implicating public interests, raising issues of public accountability, or requiring comparison with other cases to ensure equal treatment). *But see* Menkel-Meadow, *supra* note 25, at 2683–85 (arguing that sometimes the secrecy surrounding settlement can be justified).

39. *See, e.g.*, John Elson, *A Hard Case of Contempt; Elizabeth Morgan: Mother Courage or a Paranoid Liar*, TIME, Sept. 18, 1989, at 66; John E. Smith, *Dr. Morgan Walks, Beneficiary of Limit on Jailing for Civil Contempt*, WASH. TIMES, Sept. 26, 1989, at A1. Concern with judicial mishandling of custody cases involving child sexual abuse recently led the National Organization for Women

(NOW) to offer a judicial training program. *See* David E. Rovella, *Sex-Abuse Charge in Custody Fights Perplexes Courts: New NOW Curriculum Gives Judges Guidance, But Fathers' Groups are Wary,* NAT'L L.J., Nov. 11, 1996, at A1, A20. *See also* Carol S. Bruch, *Parental Alienation Syndrome and Parental Alienation: Getting It Wrong in Child Custody Cases,* 35 FAM. L.Q. 527 (2001).

40. *See* Bryan, *supra* note 17, at 1239–70.

41. *See* Emily Field Van Tassel, *Book Review: Judicial Patriarchy and Republican Family Law,* 74 GEO. L.J. 1553, 1562–65 (1986) (reviewing MICHAEL GROSSBERG, GOVERNING THE HEARTH: LAW AND THE FAMILY IN NINETEENTH-CENTURY AMERICA 1985)). *See also* BAKER, *supra* note 26, at 346 (noting judicial influence in the development of family law).

42. Men, for instance, hold most of the elected positions in state legislatures. *See* Mary Becker, *Patriarchy and Inequality: Towards a Substantive Feminism,* 1999 U. CHI. LEGAL F. 21, 62 n.202 (citing Howe Verhovek, Record for Women in Washington Legislature, N.Y. TIMES, Feb. 4, 1999, at A18 (reporting that women now constitute 40.8% of the Washington state legislature, but only 7.9% of the Alabama state legislature)). Women, understandably, have difficulty advocating legislation favorable to women before the very men the legislation will disadvantage. Although courts have proven just as insensitive to women's concerns as legislatures, judicial training and education can help eliminate this insensitivity.

43. As Resnik explains,

> Adjudication is one instance of governmental deployment of power that has the potential for genuine contextualism, for taking seriously the needs of the individuals affected by decisions and shaping decisions accordingly. Precisely because adjudication is socially embedded, it can be fluid and responsive. If we are able to reconceive the judicial role, we may well help those empowered to judge to use their powers in a way which we respect.

Judith Resnik, *On the Bias: Feminist Reconsiderations of the Aspirations for Our Judges,* 61 S. CAL. L. REV. 1877, 1909 (1988). *See also* Hershkoff, *supra* note 38, at 1939.

44. The dignity function of courts seems particularly important to disputants' perception of procedural fairness. For instance, Lind et al. found that tort litigants actually preferred litigation or arbitration, as opposed to settlement, largely because of the dignity function of the more formal procedures. Lind et al., *supra* note 37, at 958, 960–61, 965–67, 972.

45. One deskbook for judges notes the following:

> We don't believe that judges can cure spouses' hatred. But judges have a chance and an opportunity to lessen the hatred and the impact that hatred has on the dissolution proceeding and the spouses' post-dissolution relationships. How can the judge have such a powerful impact on such volatile emotions? It is precisely because the judge remains above the fray, tolerant, sympathetic, refusing to take sides,

identifying with the needs and the pain of both spouses and their children, nonjudgmental, able to talk with each spouse with understanding and warmth and to both of them together if the need should arise, able to put the spouses' fear in context with the many other similar cases the judge has seen and decided. It is because of all these qualities—qualities that together add up to wisdom from the spouses' viewpoint—that permit the judge to be influential. It is remarkable how frequently (but, unfortunately, not universally) in our experience a judge's dispassionate but warm approach to the spouses makes a difference in the flow of the dispute, the post-dissolution relationships of the parents and the comfort of the children.

Herma Hill Kay, *No-Fault Divorce and Child Custody: Chilling out the Gender Wars*, 36 FAM. L.Q. 27, 46 (2002) (citing NATIONAL INTERDISCIPLINARY COLLOQUIUM ON CHILD CUSTODY, LEGAL AND MENTAL HEALTH PERSPECTIVES ON CHILD CUSTODY LAW: A DESK BOOK FOR JUDGES §1:2, at 5 (1998)).

46. The recommendations made anticipate at least moderately urban courts. Rural areas with less dense populations and fewer court resources undoubtedly must make adjustments. Even these areas, however, should attempt to separate the location and the operation of the specialized court from trial courts of general jurisdiction.

47. *See* Jack Arbuthnot, *Court's Perceived Obstacles to Establishing Divorce Education Programs*, 40 FAM. CT. REV. 371, 379 (2002) (describing judicial resistance to innovations).

48. In his study of the Circuit Court of Cook County, Illinois, Jacob observed the difficulty involved in the implementation of innovative changes in a preexisting court system. Herbert Jacob, *The Governance of Trial Judges*, 31 L. & SOC'Y REV. 3, 24–29 (1997). Jacob also found that in the Circuit Court of Cook County, the least experienced and least qualified judges worked in high-volume courts and that the presiding judge assigned the best qualified and most experienced judges to big civil cases and other high-profile cases that often involved middle-class business clients represented by middle- and upper-status law firms. *Id.* at 26–27. Jacob concludes that high-volume courts do not naturally occur, but rather result from a conscious decision to assign particular courts relatively few judges so that more judges become available for "important" cases. *Id.* at 27. The incentives that produce this allocation of judicial resources makes meaningful change within the existing system unlikely. Building a separate court from the ground up seems a more feasible option.

49. For instance, some report that some judges do not mind handling family law matters but feel pressured by their peers to express their dislike of such matters. *Report of the Missouri Task Force on Gender and Justice*, 58 MO. L. REV. 485, 538 (1993) (hereinafter *Missouri Gender Bias Report*). *See also* Catherine J. Ross, *The Failure of Fragmentation: The Promise of a System of Unified Family Courts*, 33 REV. JUR. U.I.P.R. 311, 311 (1999) (noting that the traditional legal system disfavors courts that hear child and family cases).

50. *See generally* Engler, *supra* note 26, at 2027–41.

51. I personally believe that court personnel should receive preferential treatment in terms of facilities, resources, pay, and benefits because of the importance of the services they provide and the need to maintain the morale of those dealing daily with difficult and emotionally draining social issues. However, because states historically have devalued family courts, I suspect the best that I can hope for is equal treatment.

52. *See* Richard L. Revesz, *Specialized Courts and the Administrative Lawmaking System*, 138 Pa. L. Rev. 1111, 1154–55 & n.174 (1990).

53. *See, e.g.,* Frederick P. Aucamp, *A Family Court for Virginia*, 13 U. Rich. L. Rev. 885 (1979); Patricia G. Barnes, *It May Take a Village . . . Or a Specialized Court to Address Family Problems*, 82 A.B.A. J. 22 (1996); Anne H. Geraghty & Wallace J. Mlyniec, *Unified Family Courts: Tempering Enthusiasm with Caution*, 40 Fam. Ct. Rev. 435, 435–36 (2002). *See also* Linda D. Elrod, *Reforming the System to Protect Children in High Conflict Custody Cases*, 28 Wm. Mitchell L. Rev. 495, 519–21 (2001). Some advocate increasing other family support services in order to decrease the caseload of family and juvenile courts. The success of this strategy, however, seems unlikely within the foreseeable future. *See* Melton, *supra* note 16, at 2000–2002 & n.40.

54. *See* Geraghty & Mlyniec, *supra* note 53 (raising doubts about the wisdom and efficacy of unified family courts).

55. The dissolution of a formal legal marriage, of course, can also raise tangential issues such as the enforceability of prenuptial agreements or the validity of the marriage.

56. In this context the court likely would need to address paternity issues as well.

57. In her discussion of specialized federal courts, Dreyfuss notes that perceptions of partiality, whether or not deserved, significantly compromised the success of some courts. Rochelle Cooper Dreyfuss, *Specialized Adjudication*, 1990 BYU L. Rev. 377.

58. Many commentators who debate the merits of specialized courts in other contexts note that advocacy by special interest groups can compromise the judicial appointments process. *See* Dreyfuss, *supra* note 57, at 379–80; Jordan, *supra* note 38, at 748.

59. I recommend political balance on the nominating commission because politics seem less likely to affect the choices of bipartisan, as opposed to politically imbalanced, commissions. *See* Malia Reddick, *Merit Selection: A Review of the Social Scientific Literature*, 106 Dick. L. Rev. 729, 733 (2002).

60. States have made notable gains in the representation of women and minorities on judicial nominating commissions, with some states offering far more diversity than others. *See* Reddick, *supra* note 59, at 730–32.

61. *See* Revesz, *supra* note 52, at 1148–50.

62. *See id.* at 1149–50. *See also* Reddick, *supra* note 59, at 733 (referring to "logrolling": when "individual commissioners or groups of commissions agree to support one another's nominees").

63. In Australia's specialized family court, a candidate for judicial appointment must establish "by reason of training, experience and personality, he is a suitable

person to deal with matters of family law." Frank Bates, *The Role of the Expert in Judicial Divorce Procedures, in* The Resolution of Family Conflict: Comparative Legal Perspectives 123, 123 (John M. Eekelaar & Sanford N. Katz eds. 1984).

64. All judges, of course, also must conform their behavior to the Code of Judicial Conduct. Data collection for purposes of yearly review, however, is confined here to judicial behavior related to procedural justice criteria.

65. Behrens and Silverman present a convincing case for the superiority of judicial appointment rather than election. *See* Mark A. Behrens & Cary Silverman, *The Case for Adopting Appointive Judicial Selection Systems for State Court Judges,* 11 Cornell J. L. & Pub. Pol'y 273 (2002). *See* James J. Alfini & Jarrett Gable, *The Role of the Organized Bar in State Judicial Selection Reform: The Year 2000 Standards,* 106 Dick. L. Rev. 683 (2002) for an explanation of the American Bar Association's 2000 proposal on Standards on State Judicial Selection.

66. In the first instance, judicial independence serves to protect the judiciary from undue influence exerted by the legislative or executive branch of the government. *See* John A. Ferejohn & Larry D. Kramer, *Independent Judges, Dependent Judiciary: Institutionalizing Judicial Restraint,* 77 N.Y.U. L. Rev. 962, 965–68 (2002). Second, independence seeks to protect judges from efforts of the people to overpower them. *Id.* at 969. As Ferejohn and Kramer note: "Separating the judiciary from the other branches of government means little if judges are then subjected directly to the very same pressures that caused us to mistrust executive and legislative influence in the first place." *Id.* Judicial elections pose a serious threat to independence because of interest group pressures. *Id.* Ferejohn and Kramer comment,

> The distinction between majoritarian pressures and corruption nevertheless matters because, as Madison saw, majoritarian pressures are vastly more threatening to judicial independence, and because these pressures can also find expression outside the political branches (through the media, for example). The principle of judicial independence calls for hindering political pressure of every kind, from any source, if they would interfere with a well-functioning judiciary by distorting its decisionmaking process.

Id. at 969–70.

67. *See id.* at 974–75 (noting what most believe to be the irreconcilable tension between judicial independence and accountability). *See also* Elizabeth A. Larkin, *Judicial Selection Methods: Judicial Independence and Popular Democracy,* 79 Denv. U. L. Rev. 65, 65 (2001) (recognizing the tension between judicial independence and accountability).

68. Ferejohn and Kramer query,

> Judges have friends and financial interests and ideologies; they have loves and hates and passions and prejudices just like the rest of us. So what do we do when our independent judges let these sorts of influences guide their actions in the courtroom? If independence means freedom

from oversight by other departments of government and by voters, how do we prevent judges from ignoring or misapplying the law for their own inappropriate reasons?

Ferejohn & Kramer, *supra* note 66, at 973. See also Saikrishna B. Prakash, *America's Aristocracy*, 109 YALE L.J. 541, 568–82 (1999) (reviewing MARK TUSHNET, TAKING THE CONSTITUTION AWAY FROM THE COURTS (1999)) for practical and theoretical arguments against life tenure for federal judges.

69. *See* Erwin Chemerinsky, *Comment: Evaluating Judicial Candidates*, 61 S. CAL. L. REV. 1985, 1986–87 (1988); Frances Kahn Zemans, *The Accountable Judge: Guardian of Judicial Independence*, 72 S. CAL. L. REV. 625, 627, 648–49 (1999) (describing the election defeat of Tennessee Supreme Court Justice Penny White that resulted from her concurring opinion in a death penalty case). *See also id.* at 651–53 (describing the activism of several interest groups in judicial elections). Zemans illustrates the difficulties that state judges face:

> While riding his bicycle in the "wrong" Chicago neighborhood, an African-American boy was brutally beaten and left brain damaged. Three offenders were apprehended, tried, and convicted. After sentencing the primary perpetrator to eight years in prison, the judge accepted a plea from two accomplices in exchange for a sentence of probation and community service. The primary perpetrator then returned to court to seek a reduction in his sentence. The Cook County judge refused, finding that "he planned the attack, led the attack and finished the attack upon a defenseless 13-year-old boy." Supporters of the convicted felon reacted strongly, including shouting "Down with 242"—the judge's number on the ballot in the retention election just eleven days away—and circulating leaflets with the judge's name and "Vote NO" printed on them. "Think about the impact of this kind of campaign on the administration of justice," stated the presiding judge of the criminal courts; "every judge would potentially be held hostage by disgruntled litigants." Such fears are not without some merit.

Zemans, *supra*, at 639–40. *See also* Behrens & Silverman, *supra* note 65, at 275; John Gibeaut, *Taking Aim*, A.B.A. J., Nov. 1996, at 50 (describing several successful campaigns by interest groups to oust judges who issued decisions with which they disapproved). Judges maintain that they are not above criticism, but protest these attacks because they disregard the context of the case, the judge's overall record on a particular issue, or both. *Id.* at 51. In August 1996, the American Bar Association (ABA) appointed the Commission on Separation of Powers and Judicial Independence to study how political criticism affects judicial independence. *Id.* Republican presidential candidate Bob Dole called for the impeachment of federal Judge Harold Baer, Jr. of the U.S. District Court for the Southern District of New York after Judge Baer suppressed the introduction at trial of 80 pounds of cocaine and heroin seized from a drug-trafficking suspect. Democrats followed suit. Judge Baer actually reversed himself after President Clinton's press secretary hinted that Baer should resign. *Id.* This type of pressure on the federal judiciary, whose judges enjoy life tenure, puts in bold relief the need to provide some protection for state judges in the proposed specialized court. Indeed, some note that state court judges seem particularly vulnerable to political moods because of the sheer number of politically controversial cases they handle and because states subject their retention to popular vote. *Id.* at 52–53.

It appears that the public may have better sense than politicians. In an ABA-conducted poll, 84% of the respondents indicated that they thought it unreasonable for a president or a member of Congress to try to influence a federal judge's decision during a case, and 83% thought it inappropriate to use judicial decisions in political campaigns. *Id.* at 52.

70. *See* Molly McDonough, *Money and the Bench*, 42 A.B.A. J. E-Report 3 (Nov. 2002); Joseph R. Grodin, *Developing a Consensus of Constraint: A Judge's Perspective on Judicial Retention Elections*, 61 S. Cal. L. Rev. 1969, 1980–81 (1988). *See also* Larkin, *supra* note 67, at 69 (noting that judicial legitimacy depends, in part, on the public's perception that judges make fair and impartial decisions based on the merits of a case).

71. *See* Zemans, *supra* note 69, at 638–39 (describing a Chicago Tribune columnist's several-year campaign against Chief Justice Heiple of the Illinois Supreme Court because of the justice's controversial decision in the (in)famous Baby Richard case).

72. *See* Grodin, *supra* note 70, at 1979–80.

73. *See* Paul J. DeMuniz, *Politicizing State Judicial Elections: A Threat to Judicial Independence*, 38 Willamette L. Rev. 367, 389 (2002) (noting that the politicization of the death penalty issue has affected state court behavior, resulting in lower reversal rates following judicial campaigns).

74. *See* Kathryn Abrams, *Some Realism About Electoralism: Rethinking Judicial Campaign Finance*, 72 S. Cal. L. Rev. 505 (1999); Alfini & Gable, *supra* note 65, at 683–84; Behrens & Silverman, *supra* note 65, at 274–75; Terry Carter, *Footing the Bill for Judicial Campaigns: North Carolina Enacts Law for Public Financing of Judicial Election*, 40 A.B.A.J. E-Report 1 (Oct. 18, 2002) (noting that during the 2000 election cycle state supreme court candidates raised more than $45.6 million, a 61% increase over 1998 elections); Erwin Chemerinsky, *Preserving an Independent Judiciary: The Need for Contribution and Expenditure Limits in Judicial Elections*, 74 Chi.-Kent L. Rev. 133, 135–39 (1998); Grodin, *supra* note 70, at 1981; McDonough, *supra* note 70 (noting that four Ohio supreme court candidates in 2002 raised a record $5.5 million in campaign funds and that estimates predicted that third parties and the candidates would spend $8 to $10 million by election day).

75. *See* Abrams, *supra* note 74, at 516–17; Bernard Boland, *Shopping for Judges at Wal-Mart?*, 59 Bench & Bar Minn. 24 (Dec. 2002); Grodin, *supra* note 70, at 1981.

76. *See* Abrams, *supra* note 74, at 516–17 (reviewing the rather shocking story of the Pennzoil litigation).

77. *See* Chemerinsky, *supra* note 74, at 138; Grodin, *supra* note 70, at 1981–82; McDonough, *supra* note 70 (noting the concern of ABA President Alfred P. Carlton, Jr.). A poll of Pennsylvania citizens, for example, indicated that 88%

of respondents believed that large contributions to judicial campaigns at least sometimes influence judicial decisions. *See* Andrew Crompton, Comment, *Pennsylvanian's Should Adopt a Merit Selection System for State Appellate Court Judges*, 106 DICK. L. REV. 755, 758 (2002). *See also* Behrens & Silverman, *supra* note 65, at 276 (noting a recent national poll that found that 81% of Americans believe that campaign contributions and politics influence judges). With prompting from the American Bar Association, judges and lawyers in many states now seek ways to mitigate the problems of judicial elections. North Carolina, for instance, recently passed a law to provide public funding for judicial election campaigns. *See* Carter, *supra* note 74. Although this is a step in the right direction, candidates can opt out of public funding, *id.*, and public funding does not insulate a judicial candidate from attack by media or interest groups.

78. 122 S. Ct. 2528 (2002).

79. *See* Erwin Chemerinsky, *Judicial Elections and The First Amendment*, 38 TRIAL 78, 78 (Nov. 2002).

80. *Id.*

81. *Id.* at 81. *See also* DeMuniz, *supra* note 73, at 389 (noting that judicial candidates now "criticize court rulings or opponents and . . . either imply or explicitly state how they would rule in cases raising hot button issues in order to gain campaign support").

82. *See* Alfini & Gable, *supra* note 65, at 683–84 (noting that judicial elections ultimately threaten public confidence in unbiased decisions); Reddick, *supra* note 59, at 744–45 (noting that judicial elections compromise the appearance of an independent and impartial judiciary).

83. *See* Chemerinsky, *supra* note 69, at 1989–92; Grodin, *supra* note 70, at 1983.

84. *See* Abrams, *supra* note 74, at 524–34 (reviewing possibilities for minimizing the negative effects of judicial elections and concluding that times have changed sufficiently to revisit their continued desirability). *See also* Chemerinsky, *supra* note 69 (strongly favoring the abolition of judicial elections in all states).

85. Ferejohn and Kramer note,

> Judicial independence seeks first and foremost to foster a decisionmaking process in which cases are decided on the basis of reasons that an existing legal cultures recognizes as appropriate. To use a rough heuristic device, judicial independence seeks to ensure that cases are decided for reasons that can be offered publicly in a brief or oral argument, and not for reasons that, if offered publicly as a basis for decision, would be deemed unethical, improper, or irrelevant.

> Ferejohn & Kramer, *supra* note 66, at 972.

86. Ferejohn and Kramer argue for a balance between independence and accountability:

> Many commentators see these concerns for judicial accountability as inescapably in conflict with the goals of judicial independence: The

only way to make judges accountable for their decisions is to control them in ways that intrude on their independence. But this mischaracterizes the problem, and we think that framing the issue differently dissolves any apparent contradiction. Neither judicial independence nor judicial accountability are ends in and of themselves. Both are means toward the construction of a satisfactory process for adjudication. As we have seen, this means a process that is appropriately "legal" in its nature: one in which decisions are made for appropriately legal sorts of reasons, without regard for considerations that law considers extraneous or immaterial. As we have also seen, however, it means a process that is subject to legitimate democratic control over differences in the range of outcomes procurable within the confines of legal analysis: a process in which judges cannot deviate too far from popular political understandings for reasons unconstrained but not excluded by law. Not surprisingly, these joint and several allegiances to law and democracy—with their joint and several objectives of procedural rectitude, legal impartiality, and democratic accountability—necessitate a complex institutional design. Searching for the right system, we mix and match in different ways and to different degrees various arrangements—some protecting the independence of judges, others making them accountable—in the effort to construct a properly balanced judiciary. Finding the right mix surely is not easy, but complexity is not the same as contradiction.

Ferejohn & Kramer, *supra* note 66, at 972. The retention process offered here strives to achieve the balanced complexity that Ferejohn and Kramer advocate.

87. *See* Arbuthnot, *supra* note 47, at 379.

88. *See* Resnik, *supra* note 43, at 1935.

89. All states already have selection and retention processes in place. Thirty-two states currently use partisan or nonpartisan elections for judicial selection. *See* Behrens & Silverman, *supra* note 65, at 277. Currently 41 states subject at least some of their judges to electoral review. *See* Chemerinsky, *supra* note 79. Alterations to these established methods might prove politically difficult. *See* Stephen Shapiro, *The Judiciary in the United States: A Search for Fairness, Independence, and Competence*, 14 Geo. J. Legal Ethics 667, 673–74 (2001) (noting voter resistance and state constitutional constraints). Alternatively, a state could create an administrative agency with appointed judges that exercised exclusive jurisdiction over the issues noted here.

90. *See* Elrod, *supra* note 53, at 524 (recommending three-year terms for family court judges, partially because of the acquisition of judicial expertise).

91. Lawyers and judges believe that family law cases benefit from judicial continuity. *See Missouri Gender Bias Report*, *supra* note 49, at 541.

92. Returning to the same judge also can mean perpetuation of an initial error if a judge cannot maintain an open mind. However, the specialized training judges receive, the bi-yearly updates on current research, their bi-weekly conferences with one another and with others from different disciplines, and their yearly reviews minimize this potential problem.

93. Many others also argue that family court judges need specialized training. *See, e.g.*, LENORE J. WEITZMAN, THE DIVORCE REVOLUTION: THE UNEXPECTED SOCIAL AND ECONOMIC CONSEQUENCES FOR WOMEN AND CHILDREN IN AMERICA 396–98 (1985); Elrod, *supra* note 53, at 523–25; Janet R. Johnston, *Building Multidisciplinary Professional Partnerships with the Court on Behalf of High-Conflict Divorcing Families and Their Children: Who Needs What Kind of Help?*, 22 U. ARK. LITTLE ROCK L. REV. 453, 459 (2000); Herma Hill Kay, *Beyond No-Fault: New Directions in Divorce Reform, in* DIVORCE REFORM AT THE CROSSROADS 39–40 (Stephen D. Sugarman & Herman Hill Kay eds. 1990).

94. *See, e.g.*, MARTHA ALBERTSON FINEMAN, THE NEUTERED MOTHER, THE SEXUAL FAMILY, AND OTHER TWENTIETH CENTURY TRAGEDIES 17 (1995).

95. As Becker notes, many procedural justice criteria mimic many of the concerns raised by Robin West in her book CARING FOR JUSTICE:

> In her recent book Caring for Justice, Robin West argues that justice or some attribute of justice such as institutional consistency, personal integrity, or impartiality, and care are both required for moral decision-making. In using the word "care," West begins with the nurture of individuals: "When we nurture, we nurture particular persons, not groups, nations, or species, and when we nurture a particular person, we seek to make that person as fulfilled as possible." The "circle of care" can also extend to groups and be the basis egalitarian social order based on "a sense of brotherhood and sisterhood" rather than on "an abstract and bloodless zeal for consistency."

Becker, *supra* note 42, at 43 (citing ROBIN WEST, CARING FOR JUSTICE 69, 72, 88 (1997)).

96. Abrams notes,

> This last insight reflects a point made more recently by feminist theorists: Strict detachment from the perspectives of litigants, which many legal thinkers view as a feature of objectivity or independence, is not simply elusive but is also undesirable. Feminists and other critical scholars argue that what is sometimes lauded as salutary distance actually functions as a means of evading responsibility. A judge who does not fully contemplate the impact of a particular decision on the lives of litigants and those similarly situated . . . may fail to acknowledge the violence or pain imposed by his decision. Such a judge acts without full comprehension of the tangible meaning of his work. According to this view, an ability to foster a kind of imaginative interdependence—to put oneself in the course of judging in the position of each of the litigants whose case one resolves—may be a crucial aid rather than a barrier to sound adjudication.

Abrams, *supra* note 74, at 511.

97. When Lenore Weitzman first presented the results of her study on the California divorce system to judges, they denied that they awarded low amounts of alimony and child support and that they awarded more of the marital assets to husbands

than to wives. WEITZMAN, *supra* note 93, at 395–96. Weitzman then changed her approach and began her presentations by asking judges to resolve several hypotheticals that involved spousal maintenance, child support, and property division. She then collected and tabulated the results and traced the financial implications of the awards that the judges had made. She compared results of the awards to the actual costs of raising children, to state and welfare poverty levels, and to the husbands' disposable income after divorce. She examined women's employment prospects and compared the postdivorce incomes of husbands and wives. When judges realized that the awards they had made in the abstract created severe economic disadvantage for women and children, they proved far more receptive to entertaining the actual consequences of their decisions. *Id.* at 396.

98. *See* Elrod, *supra* note 53, at 524; Wallace J. Mlyniec, *A Judge's Ethical Dilemma: Assessing A Child's Capacity to Choose*, 64 FORDHAM L. REV. 1873 (1996) (arguing in favor of judicial education on child development and on children's capacity for rational choice). Although predictions about what custody and visitation arrangement optimally serves the needs of any particular child probably likely remain impossible, *see, e.g.*, JOSEPH GOLDSTEIN ET AL., BEFORE THE BEST INTERESTS OF THE CHILD (1979), certain basic observations might prove helpful. For instance, teenagers have social needs that differ from those of three-year olds. Visitation patterns that are insensitive to that difference probably do not fulfill the teenager's developmental needs. Placement of a child in the custody of the father who abused the child's mother in the child's presence probably does not serve that child's best interests. Judicial refusal to admit physical evidence of sexual abuse in a child visitation dispute probably disserves that child's interests. Although these suggestions might seem self-evident, currently their wisdom eludes many judges.

99. The education suggested here would sensitize judges to the lives of the people before them and to the real consequences of their decisions—in other words, it would foster judicial empathy. For discussion of the importance of emotion, particularly empathy, in judging, see MARTHA C. NUSSBAUM, LOVE'S KNOWLEDGE: ESSAYS ON PHILOSOPHY AND LITERATURE 78–82 (1990); Lynn N. Henderson, *Legality and Empathy*, 85 MICH. L. REV. 1574, 1651–52 (1987); Martha L. Minow & Elizabeth V. Spelman, *Passion for Justice*, 10 CARDOZO L. REV. 37, 44–48 (1988). *But see* Susan Bandes, *Empathy, Narrative, and Victim Impact Statements*, 63 U. CHI. L. REV. 361, 365 (1996) (arguing that the use of emotion and narrative in legal decision making must be tempered by an assessment of the context and the values to be advanced).

100. *See* Mlyniec, *supra* note 98, at 1874.

101. *See* Resnik, *supra* note 43, at 1925.

102. *See* Dreyfuss, *supra* note 57, at 378.

103. Judges in Hawaii's unified family court system note the value of reinforcing dialogue between judges who all are committed to similar values.

104. *See* Dreyfuss, *supra* note 57, at 378.

105. Gender bias task force reports reflect the pervasive belief that more education regarding domestic violence will help judges, lawyers, court personnel and

police make better decisions. *See, e.g., Missouri Gender Bias Report, supra* note 49, at 500. They also note that education already has influenced state officials, but that more training certainly is needed. *Id.* at 500–514.

106. *See* Revesz, *supra* note 52, at 1164.

107. *See* Dreyfuss, *supra* note 57, at 378.

108. Two specialized courts in the federal system reflect this wisdom. In 1942, Congress established the Emergency Court of Appeals. The court had exclusive jurisdiction over appeals from wartime price control decisions made by the administrator pursuant to the Emergency Price Control Act of 1942. For its success the price control program required a high level of voluntary compliance. The speed of disposition and the uniform application of price controls by the Emergency Court of Appeals inspired the respect of government and private attorneys as well as the voluntary compliance of parties. *See* Jordan, *supra* note 38, at 757–59. Likewise, the specialized U.S. Tax Court oversees the federal income tax system, which depends heavily on voluntary compliance for success.

109. *See, e.g.*, PHYLLIS CHESLER, WOMEN AND MADNESS (1972); Joan S. Meier, *Notes from the Underground: Integrating Psychological and Legal Perspectives on Domestic Violence in Theory and Practice*, 21 HOFSTRA L. REV. 1295, 1300–1312 (1993).

110. Teitelbaum explains,

> Classical research through experimental testing of hypotheses about custodial arrangements, marital dissolution, alimony and most other questions of public importance is simply impossible. Random assignment of children to one or another parent, or the random granting and denial of divorce petitions, is neither constitutionally nor socially acceptable. Second-choice methodologies, such as quasi-experimental research, are only relatively less difficult.

> Lee E. Teitelbaum, *Moral Discourse and Family Law*, 84 MICH. L. REV. 430, 437 (1985). Although I share Teitelbaum's concern about the difficulties and the potential invalidity of social science research, an assertion that social science can teach us nothing relevant to divorce claims too much. Social science research, for instance, has exposed the devastating effect that various forms of family violence has on children. Social science research has sensitized us to the psychology and needs of abused spouses. We understand that children's developmental needs change with age. Much of what today may seem conventional knowledge, then, is a product of previous scientific investigation.

111. *See* Carol S. Bruch, *Parental Alienation Syndrome and Parental Alienation: Getting It Wrong in Child Custody Cases*, 35 FAM. L.Q. 527 (2001); Richard Ducote, *Guardians Ad Litem in Private Custody Litigation: The Case for Abolition*, 3 LOY. J. PUB. INT. L. 106, 132–42 (2002); Cheri L. Wood, Note and Comment, *The Parental Alienation Syndrome: A Dangerous Aura of Reliability*, 27 LOY. L. REV. 1367 (1994). An article graphically illustrates this point. The author proposes a new statute to govern the admissibility of child hearsay testimony

in child sexual abuse prosecutions. In setting the stage for the presentation of this new statute, the author describes the tension between protecting a criminal defendant's constitutional rights and encouraging sexually abused children to testify. On this stage sits Dr. Richard Gardner, whom the author introduces as "a medical doctor and Columbia University professor who has written over 30 books on child psychotherapeutic technique . . . ." Robert G. Marks, Note, *Should We Believe the People Who Believe the Children?: The Need for a New Sexual Abuse Tender Years Hearsay Exception Statute*, 32 HARV. J. LEGIS. 207, 209 n.8 (1995). The author then quotes Gardner's belief that hundreds (and possibly thousands) of falsely accused child sexual abusers currently reside in our jails. *Id.* The author's respect for and reliance on Gardner is unwarranted. Gardner's own profession has discredited his views. *See* Bruch, *supra,* at 530–34. Gardner himself published many of his books and articles on child psychotherapeutic technique, *id.* at 535, presumably because no respected academic press would publish them. Gardner offered videotape and audiotape versions of his books and many of his lectures. Marks' deference to Gardner's opinion, then, makes obvious the danger inherent in naive acceptance of bad science. *See id.* at 536–40 (describing the damage Gardner has done in cases across the United States).

112. *See, e.g.,* Mary Ann Dutton, *Understanding Women's Responses to Domestic Violence: A Redefinition of Battered Woman Syndrome,* 21 HOFSTRA L. REV. 1191 (1993); Fischer et al., *supra* note 34 (describing a culture of battering that offers a more nuanced understanding of battered women); Meier, *supra* note 109, at 1303–22 (critiquing and offering several alternatives to the battered woman syndrome).

113. A related problem concerns the ability of those who organize judicial education to determine the validity of social science research and to package it in a form conducive to use by judges and other court staff. I would suggest that states turn to their educational institutions for assistance. Conceivably, a law school clinical program could offer judicial education, particularly if the state provided funding. Legal academics in clinical programs could include other relevant disciplines, such as sociology, psychology, and social work in their educational offerings. Moreover, state court systems should share information with one another. An annual national conference of those in charge of judicial education could conserve substantial state resources and foster enlightening debate and exchange. The more open and informed the development of the judicial education program is, the more difficult it becomes for shoddy research to gain a foothold.

114. Competence requires judges to apply legal rules to the facts of the case. *See, e.g.,* Cavanagh & Sarat, *supra* note 1, at 378, 383. The legal rule relevant to child custody and visitation issues is "the best interests of the child." This standard, however, provides no real principle for decision—it merely begs the question of what custodial or visitation arrangement best serves the child's interest. The judge must seek to give meaning to the general standard by recognition and employment of secondary principles of decision. The judge's

own knowledge gained from personal experience frequently will not apprehend a child's reality. Even if it did, personal knowledge usually lacks the generality and authority necessary for acceptance as a legitimate principle of decision. As a result, the judge must turn to some acceptable knowledge base and create a lower-level norm for purposes of decision. Social science knowledge provides secondary principles of decision. This process simply recognizes what Kelsen argues: "A legal system is a hierarchy of norms, where higher-level norms regulate the creation of lower-level norms. In other words, every legal norm (except those at the lowest level) must perform the function of conferring the power to create norms at the next lower level." Hans Kelsen, General Theory of Norms xxv (Michael Hartney trans. 1991).

115. See Zemans, *supra* note 69, at 642–44 (noting that a written judicial opinion of sufficient quality can help to legitimate particularly controversial opinions and foster judicial accountability).

116. Although rare in this country, other countries authorize close judicial scrutiny of divorce agreements. French divorce judges have considerable control over proposed settlements as well as the authority to investigate whether a spouse freely gave consent and whether the agreement adequately protects the children's interests. The judge can interview the parties and their lawyers and order third parties to produce relevant documents. The judge can refuse to accept the agreement, in effect refusing permission to divorce. The judge, in essence, has the power through successive rejections of an agreement to force the parties to adopt an agreement the judge "indirectly" authors. *See* Marie-Therese Meulders-Klein, *Financial Agreements on Divorce and the Freedom of Contract in Continental Europe, in* The Resolution of Family Conflict: Comparative Legal Perspectives 297, 301–02 (John M. Eekelaar & Sanford N. Katz eds. 1984). Even some settlement proponents recognize that settlement outcomes deserve scrutiny, particularly those that require court approval and involve the public interest. *See* Menkel-Meadow, *supra* note 25, at 2686.

117. *See also* Gail Frommer Brod, *Premarital Agreements and Gender Justice*, 6 Yale J. L. & Feminism 229 (1994); Bryan, *supra* note 17; Bryan, *supra* note 27; Bryan, *supra* note 20; Laurie C. Kadoch, *Five Degrees of Separation: A Response to Judge Sheldon's The Sleepwalker's Tour of Divorce Law*, 49 Me. L. Rev. 321 (1997); Sally Burnett Sharp, *Fairness Standards and Separation Agreements: A Word of Caution on Contractual Freedom*, 132 U. Pa. L. Rev. 1399 (1984); Katharine B. Silbaugh, *Marriage and Contracts and the Family Economy*, 93 Nw. U. L. Rev. 65 (1998); Judith T. Younger, *Marriage, Divorce, and the Family: A Cautionary Tale*, 21 Hofstra L. Rev. 1367, 1374–75 (1993).

118. *See* Sharp, *supra* note 117, at 1451–53.

119. *See* Kadoch, *supra* note 117, at 332–33.

120. Kadoch makes similar recommendations:

First, prior to the scheduling of all uncontested hearings, all parties desiring to proceed to divorce on an uncontested basis would be required to submit to the court, in addition to a request for hearing, the following documents: individual verified property lists and verified statements of income along with supporting documentation, a proposed settlement agreement, and a proposed judgment. There would be an accompanying form provided by the court that would provide a checklist and a list of questions to be completed separately by both parties. The questions, which would be aimed at ascertaining fair dealing, competence, understanding, and complete treatment of all the issues, could ask the following: Who drafted the agreement? Were the parties represented by counsel, and if so, what are the attorneys' names? Do the parties desire the agreement to be incorporated into the judgment and merged? This would be written in plain English. The checklist would include a list of all possible issues that should be covered by a settlement agreement, and the parties would indicate whether the item is relevant or not relevant, and whether it has been addressed in the agreement. The form would be signed and notarized.

Second, prior to the scheduling of the uncontested hearing by the clerk of the court, a judge (or possibly an appointed master) would review all the documentation to make certain that all items were covered and in order. That process would include filling out a checklist that would itemize all required documents. This list would be identical to the one filled out by the parties, but would include a space to note missing documents or questionable items as well as to ask questions. The reviewer would note internal inconsistencies and ambiguities in the agreement, as well as inconsistencies and ambiguities between the proposed agreement and the proposed judgment. A copy of the form would be returned to the parties, and they would be required to act in accordance with the directives of the judge or master.

Third, once the parties had complied with all directives, an uncontested hearing would be scheduled at which both parties would be required to appear. Any ambiguities that needed to be addressed by the court would be dealt with at the hearing. The parties would sign an exit form. The judge would make a brief statement and all documentation would become part of the record in the case.

Fourth, there would be mandated sanctions for parties and attorneys who were later found to have acted in bad faith or inconsistently with the public policies being promoted. Such actions would allow innocent parties to sue both the opposing party and either of the attorneys. Additionally, the agreement and/or the judgment could be altered by the court without disturbing the parties' divorce status.

Kadoch, *supra* note 117, at 341–42.

121. Mnookin and Kornhauser argue that a requirement that judges intensively review only those agreements that fall outside a broad range of acceptable outcomes would curb the judicial tendency to rubber-stamp settlement agreements. Robert H Mnookin & Lewis Kornhauser, *Bargaining in the Shadow of the Law: The Case of Divorce*, 88 Yale L.J. 950, 993 (1979).

122. *See* Sharp, *supra* note 117, at 1451.

123. *See* Bryan, *supra* note 17, at 1271 (noting that judges who refuse to vacate settlement agreements frequently acknowledge their unfairness). *See also, e.g., In re* Marriage of Bielawski, 764 N.E.2d 1254 (Ill. App. Ct. 2002) (acknowledging that the settlement agreement favored the husband, but upholding its enforceability); Seiffert v. Seiffert, 702 So. 2d 273 (Fla. Ct. App. 1997) (acknowledging that the settlement agreement might be unreasonable, but upholding its enforceability); Tubbs v. Tubbs, 648 So. 2d 817 (Fla. Ct. App. 1995) (acknowledging that the agreement may have favored the husband, but upholding its enforceability).

124. *See* Bryan, *supra* note 17, at 1153–55; Sharp, *supra* note 117, at 1451, 1457–60. Hadfield poses the feminist dilemma on contract enforcement:

> Contract law proceeds from the premise that obligation is established by the existence of voluntary and informed choice to enter into a contract. Hence, the defenses to the enforcement of a contractual obligation must demonstrate a defect in the circumstances of choice: a failure of voluntariness or an absence of adequate information. . . . It is the unlikelihood of success with these contract defenses that, in fact, crystallizes the feminist dilemma. For if women were the beneficiaries of special doctrines of mistake or coercion, they would thereby be identified, in the logic of contract, as less competent, and more deserving of "tender treatment," than the autonomous agent with whom the law ordinarily deals. . . . The law does not presume that people always choose wisely or in their own interests. Indeed, it establishes that contract enforcement is neutral and that responsibility for the consequences of a foolish choice ordinarily lie with the chooser. When a woman seeks release from a harmful contract, she argues that she is exceptionally diminished in her capacity to assume responsibility for her choice. There's the rub.

> Gillian K. Hadfield, *An Expressive Theory of Contract: From Feminist Dilemmas to a Reconceptualization of Rational Choice in Contract Law*, 146 U. Pa. L. Rev. 1235, 1247–48 (1998). Hadfield goes on, however, to argue for a conception of rational choice that does not see the failure to implement a person's earlier choice as a failure to respect her autonomy. *Id.* at 1257–63. She also argues against blind enforcement of divorce settlement contracts. *Id.* at 1270–76. I also note that the feminist dilemma has less salience in the specialized court. The court reviews all agreements for financial fairness and quality child placements, regardless of the parties' gender. State interests trump party autonomy in a gender-neutral fashion that does not implicate overtly women's generally disadvantaged position.

125. *See* Bryan, *supra* note 17. Certainly contract doctrine offers numerous examples of restraints on individual autonomy in contexts other than divorce. *See* Anthony T. Kronman, *Paternalism and the Law of Contracts*, 92 Yale L.J. 763 (1983).

126. As Hadfield notes regarding separation agreements: "[T]he price of respecting women's autonomy and 'encourag[ing them] to take full responsibility for their own lives and their own decisions' is that women are left to bear the full brunt, including potential poverty, of their now wasted marital investment." Hadfield, *supra* note 124, at 1244.

127. In her discussion of Stake and Rasmusen's proposal for marital agreements, Abrams notes,

> The fact that women bargain in the shadow of inequality, and in the shadow of ongoing social contention over women's changing roles, should counsel caution in treating marital choice as an authentic, univocal preference. Enforcing these choices uncritically may exacerbate this inequality by formalizing or institutionalizing it, a prospect that should at least deter us from treating the legal facilitation of "choice" as an unequivocal social or political good.

> Kathryn Abrams, *Choice Dependence, and the Reinvigoration of the Traditional Family*, 73 IND. L.J. 517, 522–23 (1998).

128. I am grateful to Judge Robert Hyatt, a District Court judge in Denver, Colorado, for this suggestion.

129. *See* Engler, *supra* note 26, at 2017–18.

130. Other commentators suggest a proactive rather than reactive role for family court judges. *See* Johnston, *supra* note 93, at 458–59.

131. *See* Cavanagh & Sarat, *supra* note 1, at 380–81 (1980). *See also* Richard Delgado et al., *Fairness and Formality: Minimizing the Risk of Prejudice in Alternative Dispute Resolution*, 1985 WIS. L. REV. 1359, 1368–69; Owen M. Fiss, *Against Settlement*, 93 YALE L.J. 1073, 1077 (1984).

132. Mauro Cappelletti & Bryant Garth, *Access to Justice*, 27 BUFF. L. REV. 181, 228–29 (1979).

133. *See* RONALD DWORKIN, LAW'S EMPIRE 225–44 (1989).

134. *Id.* at 227.

135. *See* S. Jay Plager, *The United States Court of Appeals, The Federal Circuit, and the Non-Regional Subject Matter Concept: Reflections on the Search for a Model*, 39 AM. U. L. REV. 853, 858–59 (1990).

136. *See, e.g.*, RICHARD A. POSNER, THE FEDERAL COURTS: CRISIS AND REFORM 156–57 (1985); Revesz, *supra* note 52, at 1162–63.

137. Revesz, *supra* note 52, at 1162.

138. Judge Plager also notes that narrowness of judicial vision results from the attributes of the individual judge rather than specialization. Plager, *supra* note 135, at 859.

139. *See, e.g.*, Mahoney v. Mahoney, 453 A.2d 527 (N.J. 1982); *In re* Marriage of Graham, 574 P.2d 75 (Colo. 1978); *In re* Marriage of Olar, 747 P.2d 676 (Colo. 1987). *But see* O'Brien v. O'Brien, 489 N.E.2d 712 (N.Y. App. Ct. 1985).

140. *See* Bryan, *supra* note 17, at 1191–92, 1206–12.

141. *See* Revesz, *supra* note 52, at 1154, 1166 (specialized courts subject to review by generalist courts of appeal do not pose as great a threat to quality output as specialized courts without such review).

142. For example, the availability of divorce might turn on the constitutionality of a state's residency requirement. *See* Sosna v. Iowa, 419 U.S. 393 (1975). A judge may face the full faith and credit provision of the U.S. Constitution in deciding whether to recognize another state's divorce decree. *See* Sherrer v. Sherrer, 334 U.S. 343 (1948). A state's exercise of personal jurisdiction over a nonresident spouse may require a court to determine whether a violation of the Fourteenth Amendment's due process requirements has occurred. *See* Kulko v. Superior Court of Cal., 436 U.S. 84 (1978). A state statute that authorizes third-party visitation might impermissibly invade the liberty interest of the parents in the care, custody, and control of their child. *See* Troxel v. Granville, 530 U.S. 57 (2000).

143. *See, e.g.,* Klein v. Klein, 745 N.Y.S.2d 569 (N.Y. App. Div. 2002) (finding that stock in a closely held corporation is marital property); Litvak v. Litvak, 479 P.2d 402 (Colo. Ct. App. 1970) (finding no abuse of discretion when a trial court awarded the wife a percentage of the husband's interest in a closely held corporation); Zelinski v. Zelinski, 735 N.Y.S. 2d 302 (N.Y. App. Div. 2001) (finding that half of the appreciation during the marriage in the husband's interest in a closely held corporation was marital property subject to division.).

144. *See* Harbaugh v. Sweet, 257 B.R. 485 (Bankr. E.D. Mich. 2001) (finding that federal law should control the interpretation of the term "alimony" when determining a debtor's ability to exempt income of a former spouse from his or her bankruptcy estate). *See also* Meridith Johnson, *At the Intersection of Bankruptcy and Divorce: Property Division Debts Under the Bankruptcy Reform Act of 1994,* 7 Colum. L. Rev. 91 (1997); Veryl Victoria Myles, *The Nondischargeability of Divorce-Based Debts in Bankruptcy: A Legislative Response to the Hardened Heart,* 60 Ala. L. Rev. 1171 (1997).

145. *See* Wadlington & O'Brien, *supra* note 10, at 573–79. For instance, spousal maintenance is taxable income to the recipient. Consequently, a spousal maintenance award of $1,000 per month may be worth only $700 after taxes. Spousal maintenance paid also is deductible from the income of the payor spouse. Consequently, the $1,000-per-month award may not reduce the payor spouse's after-tax income by that amount per month. To fashion equitable maintenance awards, courts must consider these tax consequences.

146. *See* Mansell v. Mansell, 490 U.S. 581 (1989) (addressing the federal Uniformed Services Former Spouses' Protection Act in a divorce case that involved distribution of military retirement pay); Steiner v. Steiner, 788 So. 2d 711 (Miss. 2001) (addressing whether the court could consider a husband's military disability benefits as income for purposes of spousal maintenance); Boulter v. Boulter, 930 P.2d 112 (Nev. 1997) (discussing the impact of the federal Social Security Act on the parties' divorce settlement agreement that divided the husband's Social Security benefits); *In re* Marriage of Rahn, 914 P.2d 463 (Colo. Ct. App. 1995) (finding that the federal Employee Retirement Income

Security Act did not preempt the state's ability to enforce the pension provisions of the parties' antenuptial agreement).

147. *See In re* Amberley D., 775 A.2d 1158 (Me. 2001) (discussing the jurisdictional criteria under the Uniform Child Custody Jurisdiction and Enforcement Act); *In re* Clausen, 502 N.W.2d 649 (Mich. 1993) (assessing the jurisdictional criteria under the Uniform Child Custody Jurisdiction Act); Friedrich v. Friedrich, 78 F.3d 1060 (6th Cir. 1996) (reviewing the Hague Convention and the International Child Abduction and Remedies Act, which provide the jurisdictional criteria in cases that involve children wrongfully removed from their country of habitual residence).

148. *See* Gangel-Jacob, *supra* note 28, at 827 (noting the complexity of divorce cases).

149. As Revesz notes, "It is reasonably clear that there are limits to how much generalist courts can continue to grow without some, perhaps substantial, deterioration in the quality of their output." Revesz, *supra* note 52, at 1120. The removal of divorce cases from the generalist docket actually might enhance the quality of judicial decision making in the remainder of cases. *Id.*

150. As Judge Plager notes,

> Judges confronted with large and highly diverse caseloads may tend to stereotype the cases, seeing little of the variation within rather than across subject matter. Consequently such judges may actually be more narrow in their approach to these cases. Judges who serve on a court of specialized jurisdiction, by contrast, may have presented to them a full range of cases covering a panoply of issues within that subject area. They may treat the merits of each case with greater care and understanding. Given the potential diversity of issues even within a single subject matter area and the vagaries of human character (judges being no exception), generalizations on this point are risky.

> Plager, *supra* note 135, at 859.

151. The appellate jurisdiction of the Court of Appeals for the Federal Circuit is more narrow than other federal courts of appeal, but actually covers a broad spectrum of cases. Its exclusive appellate jurisdiction extends to claims involving Native Americans, tax refunds, military discharges, property takings, government contracts, import law, trademarks, civilian personnel demotions and discharges, several federal employee issues, veterans benefits, and vaccine compensation. Plager, *supra* note 135, at 853 & n.1.

152. *See* Rochelle Cooper Dreyfuss, *The Federal Circuit: A Case Study in Specialized Courts*, 64 N.Y.U. L. Rev. 1, 7 (1989); Plager, *supra* note 135, at 854–55.

153. *See* Dreyfuss, *supra* note 152, at 14–20.

154. *Id.* at 21–23.

155. *Id.* at 54–55.

156. *Id.* at 52–59.

157. Conceivably the entire court bureaucracy could develop a bias in favor of substantiating child sexual abuse. However, the outside review by the commission

of each judge once every five years should intercept institutional bias. Data collection by the court administrator also remains a critical means of bias detection and interception. Certainly, those parents who lose custody of, and perhaps contact with, their children because of a finding of child sexual abuse will complain on their evaluations. And if the data collected indicates that custody evaluation teams have substantiated 100% of child sexual abuse allegations over two years, the court should consider the possibility, but not necessarily the truth, of institutional bias.

158. POSNER, *supra* note 136, at 150–51.

159. Plager, *supra* note 135, at 858. Moreover, some experienced family law judges acknowledge that family law cases are no more boring than other types of cases. *See* James Delaney, *How to Bring Legal Sanity to Domestic Relations: Civilizing Family Courts*, 2 FAM. ADVOC. 20, 21–22 (1980).

160. POSNER, *supra* note 136, at 153.

161. Dreyfuss makes this point in her study on specialized federal courts:

The repetitive nature of such a court's docket will always make appointment somewhat undesirable to the nation's best legal minds. Experience with past specialized courts demonstrates, however, that when the tribunal is organized to further an important public objective, extraordinary people do agree to serve. Indeed, anecdotal evidence suggests that appointment to a specialized bench composed of handpicked jurists can be a satisfying experience. The challenge in devising a common law to implement national policy is attractive, especially when there is general agreement on the policy.

Dreyfuss, *supra* note 57, at 417–18.

162. *See* Delaney, *supra* note 159, at 21–22.

163. *See* Dreyfuss, *supra* note 57, at 417.

164. As Professor Dreyfuss argues,

A new generalist court does not need public agreement to gain public trust. The heterogeneity of its docket makes it likely that there will be some issues that it can handle in a manner that validates the bench; indeed, the court need only receive and follow precedent to gain a measure of public acceptance. When the court then addresses controversial questions, its resolution may not be accepted, but its reputation will not be impugned. In contrast, when a specialized court is established in an area where there is no consensus, there is nothing for the public, practitioners, or other courts to measure its rulings against, and it becomes an easy target for those who disagree with its decisions.

Dreyfuss, *supra* note 57, at 415.

165. *See* POSNER, *supra* note 136, at 148 (refusing to argue that the creation of a specialized judiciary is fundamentally flawed and acknowledging its functionality in the Continental system).

6

MANDATORY DISCLOSURE, DISPUTE RESOLUTION EXPERTS, AND THE DISPUTE

Several procedures in the specialized court promote procedural and substantive justice. Mandatory disclosure, automatic sanctions, and the dispute resolution expert (DRE) who presides over the dispute assessment conference (DAC) play key roles, as does the DAC itself.

MANDATORY DISCLOSURES

The specialized court requires parties to file financial and custody affidavits early in the divorce process and just before final hearing. Presumably lawyers who represent clients in the specialized court will know of these disclosure requirements. Court personnel and printed forms inform all pro se petitioners of mandatory disclosure, and petitions for any form of relief in the specialized court must inform the opposing party of these requirements.

The court sets forth the form and content of the mandatory affidavits in an appendix to court rules. The affidavits anticipate two of the goals of the DAC: (a) temporary awards of custody and visitation, child support, spousal maintenance, and attorney fees pursuant to state statutory and case law; and (b) the DRE's preliminary assessment of the final disposition of the entire case.

The information required on financial affidavits must anticipate each state's unique statutory and case law on child support, temporary and permanent spousal maintenance, temporary and final attorney fees, and property distribution. Spousal maintenance statutes, for instance, typically require the court to consider the respective incomes of the parties, the length of the marriage, the age of the parties, the reasonable needs of the recipient spouse in light of the standard of living established during the marriage, and the ability of the payor spouse to fulfill those needs. Some states provide more elaborate criteria. Likewise, states statutes and case law recognize certain assets as property, distinguish between separate and marital property, and provide guidance for evaluation and distribution on divorce. Law that pertains to attorney fees typically considers the parties' respective needs and income, the property distribution, and the reasonability of the requested fees. Child support guidelines define each parent's gross and adjusted gross incomes. States authorize various adjustments to basic child support obligations based on child care, medical, educational, and special needs expenses for the child. A parent's unemployment or underemployment often influences child support. Although some commonality among state statutory and case law exists, substantial variation also occurs, which makes a comprehensive example of affidavits impossible here. States, however, have grown adept at the development of such forms. Consequently, I defer to the courts of each state to develop financial disclosure requirements that capture their unique laws.

Very importantly, the financial affidavits also must require each party to specify, explain, and justify the temporary and permanent child support, maintenance and attorney fee awards, and the property distribution that the party believes appropriate. Each party must identify each issue the party believes that the other party will or might dispute, as well as issues on which the parties agree.

Although financial affidavits require a comprehensive list and evaluation of all separate and marital property, this early disclosure cannot realistically expect parties to provide firm evaluations of complex property interests obtainable only after expert consultation or discovery. For instance, the affidavit can demand accurate evaluations of property interests such as stocks, bonds, and bank accounts, but it cannot expect the same for closely held corporations or professional practices 50 days after filing. It can, however, require disclosure of such assets, their classification as marital or separate, and the party's best good-faith estimate of their separate and marital values.

The information requested on the child custody affidavit reflects the particular state's unique approach to custody and visitation issues. At a minimum, these forms solicit the name, birth date, school, and grade of each child. Parents must identify the medical, psychological, and developmental needs[1] of, as well as the present custody, visitation, and child care arrangements for, each child. Specific questions[2] seek information about spouse or child abuse and the past and present physical and mental health of all parties and each child. Parents must identify any substance abuse and criminal activity of all parties and each child. Parties must describe the allocation of parental responsibilities that existed before the petition for custody and visitation and explain and justify thoroughly the temporary and permanent custody and visitation arrangements they think appropriate for each child. Each parent must identify areas he or she believes the other parent will or might dispute, as well as issues on which the parents agree.

Clients must sign the affidavits and attest to the truth and the comprehensiveness of the disclosed information. The lawyer, if one exists, must certify (a) that he or she has reviewed the financial information in the affidavits and all supporting documentation with the client, and (b) that the affidavit represents, to the best of the lawyer's knowledge, full and accurate disclosure of the required information. Custody affidavits must require similar certifications.[3]

The court specifies the time in which each party must file and serve the required affidavits. When a spouse files and serves a divorce petition, the other spouse generally files a responsive pleading within a time specified by procedural rules. Within 30 days of the filing of that responsive pleading, or within 60 days of the filing of the divorce petition if no responsive pleading is filed or required, each party must file with the court a custody and financial affidavit as well as pay stubs for the past three months and copies of federal and state personal, corporate, and partnership income tax returns for the past three years.[4] At the same time, each party must serve the other party with each of these documents, except that parties need not serve jointly filed tax returns if each party has possession or control of a copy of that return. A party can, 10 days before the date for disclosure, request that the court grant a time extension based on extreme hardship, although courts only rarely should grant extension requests.

Parties also must file and serve updated financial and custody affidavits three weeks before final hearing, even if they have settled all issues. These affidavits enable the court and custody evaluation teams to review settlements and to make preliminary assessments of disputed issues. Resubmission of custody affidavits also helps the court administrator to evaluate the parental education program. Presumably, the recommendations of some parents should better anticipate their children's needs and interests after parental exposure to an effective education program. If parties settle particular issues, they can, but need not, submit joint affidavits relevant to them.

Failure to submit initial mandatory disclosure, or incomplete disclosure, results in the automatic imposition of sanctions on the noncompliant party and possibly his or her lawyer.[5] The DRE sets the amount of sanctions pursuant to a predetermined formula based on a percentage of the noncompliant party's gross income. If the noncompliant party does not establish his or her gross income on the financial affidavit or at the DAC, the DRE uses the gross income for the noncompliant party indicated on the other party's financial affidavit. If neither party complies, the DRE exercises discretion and imputes gross incomes to both parties. Noncompliant parties and attorneys have one week after the DAC to provide mandatory disclosure. Continued noncompliance results in increasing fines against the party and the attorney. Ultimately, the DRE has discretion to dismiss the action or impose a default judgment against the noncompliant party.

A lawyer can avoid sanctions only if he or she withdraws as counsel before the DAC or satisfies the DRE that, despite his or her best efforts, the client refused to provide the requisite information or provided inaccurate information that the lawyer could not independently verify. A party can escape sanctions only if the party's lawyer failed to inform the party of the disclosure requirement.[6] The court uses the funds generated from sanctions to defray operating costs.

If both parties fail to file supplemental affidavits before the final hearing, the court imposes sanctions at the final hearing and refuses to grant the requested relief. If only one party complies, the court imposes sanctions on the errant party and has the discretion to grant relief based on the other party's affidavits.

Many procedural and substantive justice goals justify mandatory disclosure, certification, and sanctions. Disclosure and certification require lawyers to work with their clients early in and throughout the case.[7] In particular, the lawyer and client must work together to present data and to propose temporary and permanent orders in the affidavits. These interactions ensure client participation and voice in the process. Client inclusion honors family privacy and bolsters respect for decision maker authority. Disclosure also encourages the active participation of both pro se parties.

Mandatory disclosure and certification provide some assurance that decisions will rest on accurate information. This information in turn increases the likelihood that parties will enter more equitable divorce settlements. It levels somewhat the negotiation playing field, because it provides the dependent spouse with information that he or she might lack the resources or sophistication to formally discover. Moreover, the recommendations that lawyers help their clients to make and explain in their affidavits must survive review by a sophisticated DRE at the DAC with the client present. This exposure provides an incentive for lawyers to craft their recommendations with sensitivity to the client's interests and legal rights.

Mandatory disclosure also enhances efficiency, because it reduces the need for formal discovery and the associated court skirmishes that drain client and court resources. Early disclosure also encourages earlier settlements, because it requires lawyers and parties to begin, rather than neglect, the data collection and assessment process necessary for settlement. Moreover, the proposals that clients must make in their affidavits require lawyers to begin to adjust the unrealistic client expectations that discourage settlement. And, to avoid embarrassment at the DAC, a lawyer must encourage the client to make "fair" proposals in the affidavits that the DRE or judge will respect, rather than unrealistically high demands that alienate the other side and make settlement difficult.

Current practices and tactics suggest that lawyers and parties initially will resist mandatory disclosure. Because of the importance of disclosure, automatic sanctions provide the necessary incentive to comply.[8]

DISPUTE RESOLUTION EXPERTS

Within 30 days of the date on which the parties must file and exchange mandatory disclosure, represented clients and their attorneys as well as unrepresented parties must attend a DAC presided over by a DRE.[9] When cases contain allegations or disclosures of domestic violence, the DRE must meet separately with the respective parties and their attorneys.

The specialized court offers a particular selection and retention system for DREs. Court administrators initially screen applicants for DRE positions. Only lawyers can serve as DREs,[10] because only lawyers can give legal advice and command sufficient authority to legitimately impose sanctions and enter temporary orders. Administrators search for, but do not require, lawyers experienced in family law. Family law attorneys with mediation experience might provide a ready source of qualified applicants. Administrators, however, must ensure that traditional mediators, who focus primarily on securing settlements, can adapt to a different set of tasks. Administrators also seek DREs fluent in languages spoken by the court's constituents. Because judges and their DREs work closely with one another, each judge participates, to the extent the judge desires, in the actual selection of the DREs assigned to his or her courtroom.

The court administrator collects the same performance data on DREs as on judges. This data provides a basis for yearly review by the court administrator and the judge with whom the DRE works. The review culminates in a conference with the DRE and a written report that the administrator places in the DRE's employment file. If a DRE receives an unsatisfactory evaluation, the judge has the discretion to retain the DRE for an additional year. Two successive years of unsatisfactory evaluations result in dismissal. Yearly reviews provide quality control and ensure that DREs effectively implement system goals.

If the nominating commission refuses to retain the judge with whom a DRE works, the court assigns the DRE to the replacement judge for the first year. This assignment provides the new judge with qualified and experienced assistance and secures the DRE's employment. If, after the first year, the new judge prefers to work with a different DRE, the administrator assigns the DRE to another judge.

DREs receive the same training and education as judges and custody evaluators on relevant legal and social issues, as well as on procedural and substantive justice criteria. Because the court offers educational services to judges and custody evaluators, this training would not increase court costs. DREs receive additional training in counseling, negotiation, and mediation skills. Although education alone exposes a DRE to the importance of voice and participation and respectful treatment, the DRE needs additional skills training to implement those goals.

Such training proves critical in many instances. For example, if a DRE does not know the ground rules to set for client participation, the DAC might degenerate into a shouting match. A DRE must possess the skill to detect a party's interests that may lie hidden beneath wounded feelings or heated emotions. A DRE skilled in negotiation will discourage parties from taking hard-line positions on issues that require additional factual development and from making outrageous demands that alienate the other party. Education and training enhances the DRE's expertise and fosters respect for his or her authority, curbs bias, and promotes better results.

DISPUTE ASSESSMENT CONFERENCE

The DRE presides over the DAC at which he or she imposes sanctions, makes temporary awards, helps the parties and their lawyers to assess the case, and explains to parents how the court addresses custody and visitation issues. To decrease the time needed for the DAC, before their attendance the parties and their attorneys view a videotape that explains the conference's purposes. Before the DAC, the DRE reviews mandatory disclosure and computes sanctions,[11] identifies areas of dispute, and, to the extent possible, makes a preliminary determination of temporary awards and final disposition. The dispute assessment program assists the DRE. Before case referral to a DRE, personnel scan each case file for mandatory disclosure and flag deficient files. To the extent possible, employees also extract designated information from case files that the DRE needs for purposes of temporary awards and sanctions.

At the DAC, the DRE informs the parties and attorneys of any imposed sanctions, the time for payment of the sanctions, the new time period for compliance with mandatory disclosure, and the additional sanctions available for continued noncompliance. If a party or an attorney challenges sanctions, the DRE entertains argument and rules on the challenge. The imposition of sanctions could impair the DRE's relationship with the sanctioned individuals, who might thereafter suspect the DRE of bias against them. The matter-of-fact imposition of sanctions, however, makes the DRE's task more administrative than judgmental. Moreover the DRE's subsequent respectful treatment of the party should mitigate this perception. If, however, this practice proves problematic, a clerk can compute and impose sanctions.

The DRE then identifies, explains, and justifies to the participants the preliminary determinations he or she has made on temporary orders. The DRE listens to arguments and information from each side on each issue and adjusts preliminary awards, if appropriate, in response to these presentations. If a DRE imposes a temporary award that a party considers grossly unfair, the aggrieved party can appeal the award to the court. Before the court hearing on the appeal, however, the obligor spouse must make the temporary payments. Failure to pay results in the obligor's forfeit of the appeal. If the court confirms the DRE's award, the court may order the party who appealed to pay the other party's related attorney fees and costs.

The DRE need not address sanctions, temporary support, or attorney fees if the parties file a form verified by both attorneys and both parties that indicates that mandatory disclosure has occurred, that the parties have stipulated to temporary support and fees, that the stipulation meets the child support guidelines and the financial needs of the dependent spouse, and that the obligor has to date complied with the stipulation. The parties also must file the actual stipulation so that the DRE can assess its adequacy. The DRE modifies stipulations that he or she finds inadequate.

The DRE next employs his or her expertise to help the participants assess their case. The DRE uses his or her knowledge of the law and the judge's approach to specific issues to advise the participants whether a judge likely will accept their proposed resolution of undisputed issues. The DRE helps to define and narrow the issues in dispute, and he or she provides his or her evaluation of the participants' respective positions on disputed issues.[12] The DRE identifies additional information that the court undoubtedly will require at final hearing and suggests alternative final dispositions that the court might find acceptable. The DRE does not attempt to coerce settlement. Rational settlement at this early stage might prove impossible. The parties might need expert evaluations of complex financial interests, or dysfunctional emotional states might need time to abate. The DAC simply provides an early opportunity to assess the case through the eyes of a neutral expert.

The DAC and early support awards implicate several procedural justice goals. The DAC offers the parties an important opportunity for voice and participation.[13] Their contributions honor their authority within the private family and enhance their respect for decision makers.[14] The DREs treat parties respectfully and pay very careful attention to their legal rights. The DRE's appraisal of allegedly settled issues provides an opportunity for error correction. Mandatory disclosure provides the most accurate information available for the DRE's decisions. The mandatory attendance of all parties at the DAC offers procedural consistency. Early support awards reduce the hostility of dependent spouses,[15] because the awards protect them and the children from the adversarial tactics and financial disasters that sharpen anger.

The DAC and temporary awards enhance efficiency, because they facilitate settlement in several ways. To identify but a few—early awards decrease the wealthier spouse's incentive to delay settlement for tactical purposes. The DAC provides an opportunity for the DRE to adjust unrealistic client, and sometimes attorney, expectations that hinder settlement.[16] The DRE's case assessment educates clients whose lawyers delay case preparation, misrepresent legal positions, and seek protracted litigation to generate higher fees. The assessment also can make a protracted dispute seem futile. The presence of the parties at the DAC intercepts a lawyer's failure to accurately assess his or her client's interests, a failure that can cause a client to balk at settlement. The DAC provides attorneys with the opportunity to realistically assess their cases and their clients' representations of the other spouse. And, finally, the DAC provides substantial help to pro se parties who may lack the sophistication necessary to effectively negotiate.[17]

The DAC and early support awards also influence substantive justice. The DRE's assessment of the case might encourage one spouse to pursue his or her legal rights rather than accept a poor settlement offered by the other or encouraged by his or her own self-interested or incompetent attorney. The assessment also might deflate one spouse who hopes to coerce the other into a bad settlement.

Early awards enhance the likelihood of better outcomes. They can provide the dependent spouse with the resources needed for legal representation[18] and adequate preparation of the case. Dependent spouses can better withstand adversarial tactics that currently coerce them to accept poor financial settlements.[19] Early awards protect the well-being of children, because they mitigate their financial decline. Early awards also reduce children's hostility toward parents who might otherwise refuse to provide for them, which enhances the quality of the parent–child relationship. Awards that reduce parental hostilities also benefit children.[20] To come full circle, better settlements make final judicial review easier, which enhances system efficiency.

As the final DAC task, the DRE refers parents to the mandatory parental education program. If the parents dispute custody or visitation issues, the DRE explains that the court will automatically assign their case to a custody evaluation team if the disputed issues remain unresolved two weeks from the date they complete the parental education program. The DRE explains the qualifications of the team, the procedures the team will follow, and that parents must pay for the team's services in proportion to their respective gross incomes. Receipt of this information discourages frivolous and maliciously motivated custody disputes, which in turn offers the promise of efficiency, hostility reduction, and better outcomes.

These procedures might confound pro se parties. Consequently, a pro se program provides assistance to those without representation. It offers a videotape that all pro se parties must view at the time of filing for dissolution or within two weeks of service on them. The videotape explains court procedures, such as mandatory financial and child disclosure, the dispute assessment conference, the parental education program, custody evaluations, and early submission of settlement agreements for court review. Personnel also provide direct assistance with mandatory disclosure and, to the extent possible, child support guidelines. Although employees need not be lawyers, they can provide rudimentary legal advice, such as the marital or separate nature of specific property, the amount of child support dictated by the state guidelines and permissible deviations, the availability of spousal mainte- nance, and the criteria that teams use in custody evaluations.

Legal advice from nonlawyers is a controversial suggestion,[21] but many considerations support it.[22] Training and accountability to the court ensure the quality of advice. If a mistake occurs or a party misunderstands the law, the DRE can make necessary corrections at the DAC. Assistance and advice from court employees also provides an early indication of the court's respect for the parties' legal rights and enhances the voice and participation of less powerful spouses. The DAC can proceed more quickly if the parties appear with some legal knowledge. If parties understand their legal situation, settle- ment might occur earlier. Finally, settlement review becomes easier if agree- ments reached by pro se parties reflect their rights.

NOTES

1. *See* Risa J. Garon et al., *From Infants to Adolescents: A Developmental Approach to Parenting Plans*, 38 Fam. & Conciliation Cts. Rev. 168 (2000) (stressing the need for parenting plans that address the developmental needs of children).
2. For many reasons, general questions about the existence of child or spouse abuse ineffectively solicit domestic violence information. The abused spouse, for instance, may not identify extreme financial control, social isolation, jealousy, or even minor physical violence as abuse. The affidavits, thus, must ask specific questions that capture the multiple facets of abuse.
3. Others have proposed similar lawyer certifications. *See* Report, Committee to Examine Lawyer Conduct in Matrimonial Actions, State of New York 39 (1993) (hereinafter N.Y. Lawyer Conduct Report).
4. If the parties filed jointly for the past three years, they could agree between themselves which party bears the responsibility of filing the joint return. If the

parties cannot agree, to ensure that the court receives the information, both parties would be required to file the joint return.

5. Others have proposed similar sanctions against lawyers. *See* N.Y. LAWYER CONDUCT REPORT, *supra* note 3, at 39.

6. Other defenses available in any civil proceeding would remain available, such as the invalidity of a judgment based on the court's lack of subject matter jurisdiction or personal jurisdiction over the respondent party.

7. Sometimes lawyers assign this responsibility to paralegals. This practice, however, still fosters client participation. Moreover, lawyer certification requires that the lawyer personally review disclosures and their supporting documentation with clients to ensure disclosure accuracy and comprehensiveness.

8. Deterrence literature strongly suggests that the likelihood of punishment affects compliance with the law. *See* TOM R. TYLER, WHY PEOPLE OBEY THE LAW 21 (1990). The likelihood of punishment, however, falls short of a perfect prediction. Sometimes people comply with the law even when little chance exists that they will be punished for failing to comply. And sometimes people refuse to comply with the law even when the likelihood of sanctions is high. *Id.* at 22.

9. In some jurisdictions, resources and case load might require a longer period of time between the exchange of mandatory disclosure and the DAC. The court should, however, make every effort to schedule the DAC as soon as possible because of its importance to procedural and substantive justice.

10. Some might argue that lawyers will not apply for DRE positions. But many lawyers now serve in a similar capacity as magistrates assigned to divorce cases. Moreover, the position might prove attractive to numerous attorneys who express dissatisfaction with the overwhelming demands and narrow rewards of private practice. Also, DREs earn reasonable secure incomes and have attractive work schedules. Perhaps more importantly, the position offers the opportunity for constructive and rewarding service.

11. Alternatively, court staff can compute sanctions.

12. The dispute assessment conference offers many of the benefits of early neutral evaluation, see Deborah R. Hensler, *Suppose It's Not True: Challenging Mediation Ideology*, 2002 J. DISP. RESOL. 81, 98 (2002); Debra Cassens Moss, *Reformers Tout ADR Programs*, 80 A.B.A. J. 28, 28–29 (1994), but has additional functions. A much less desirable alternative would require a conference between the lawyers and the clients, much as Federal Rule of Civil Procedure 26 now mandates. For some highly competent attorneys, such a meeting might fulfill many of the purposes of the DAC. Attorneys could acquire information, define and narrow disputed issues, adjust unrealistic client expectations, and enhance client participation and voice. This meeting, however, would not result in necessary temporary awards or sanctions for noncompliance with mandatory disclosure. For less qualified attorneys, this meeting also might prove more dysfunctional than helpful. Uncontrolled adversarial posturing might occur, and uncontrolled client voice might degenerate into a destructive shouting match.

13. Client participation in the DAC has broader, although more subtle, implications for procedural justice. When the DRE models how to successfully include clients in cases, he or she encourages lawyers to attempt the same. A well-

managed, four-cornered negotiation session offers many of the advantages of the DAC and can provide an effective process to resolve divorce disputes. *See* Judith Ryan, *Mediator Strategies for Lawyers: The Four-Party Settlement Conference*, 30 FAM. & CONCILIATION CTS. REV. 364 (1992). My clinical students and I have used four-cornered negotiation to resolve divorce disputes and have found that the process is effective. Party participation facilitates brainstorming with the very people who know best what they want, even if the lawyer must temper that with what they need and realistically can get. Face-to-face communication frequently clears misunderstandings that inevitably arise when parties channel all communication through third-party lawyers. The participants can reach settlement without a recess to secure client approval. And although clients sometimes express an initial reluctance to meet with their spouses, they ultimately seem gratified by the experience and opportunity to participate. Several times, previously hostile spouses have left the negotiation talking to one another or have gone to lunch or dinner to celebrate their agreement.

14. As Menkel-Meadow notes,

> To the extent that certain kinds of settlement processes include more participation by the parties, they may also facilitate greater democratic participation in the legal system than the stylized ritual dominated by lawyers that is the formal adjudication system. . . . "control" of the dispute by the parties involved may make some forms of dispute resolution more responsive to the parties', rather than the professionals', interests.

Carrie Menkel-Meadow, *Whose Dispute Is It Anyway?: A Philosophical and Democratic Defense of Settlement (In Some Cases)*, 83 GEO. L.J. 2663, 2689 (1995).

15. Judge Delaney recognizes that the temporary support hearing can be critical to the future relationship of parents. James Delaney, *How to Bring Legal Sanity to Domestic Relations: Civilizing Family Courts*, 2 FAM. ADVOC. 20, 23 (1980).

16. Kressel notes that divorce lawyers complain that unrealistic client expectations substantially interfere with settlement and account for 50% of cases that go to trial. KENNETH KRESSEL, THE PROCESS OF DIVORCE: HOW PROFESSIONALS AND COUPLES NEGOTIATE SETTLEMENTS 160 (1985).

17. The Danish experience with an administrative divorce procedure indicates that unrepresented parties can manage their problems quite well after a single talk with a qualified administrative lawyer who serves many of the same functions of the proposed DRE. *See* Henrik H.H. Andrup, *Divorce Proceedings: Ends and Means*, in THE RESOLUTION OF FAMILY CONFLICT: COMPARATIVE LEGAL PERSPECTIVES 163, 175 (John M. Eekelaar & Sanford N. Katz eds. 1984). Andrup also suggests that a well-organized administrative procedure would reduce the need for parties to obtain legal representation. *Id.*

18. Early awards also will provide an incentive for lawyers to agree to represent dependent spouses.

19. The importance of an early and automatic forum for temporary support awards is particularly important in jurisdictions where a temporary support hearing

typically occurs months, or perhaps years, after filing. See Penelope Eileen Bryan, *Reclaiming Professionalism: The Lawyer's Role in Divorce Mediation*, 28 FAM. L.Q. 177, 177–88 (1994), for a case history that exemplifies the difficulties dependent spouses and children encounter when forced to negotiate from a position of financial desperation.

20. *See* LENARD MARLOW, DIVORCE AND THE MYTH OF LAWYERS 62–63 (1992) (describing the husband's common tactic of withholding support from the wife and the wife's reciprocal withholding of the children from the husband).

21. *See* R. Cavanagh & D. Rhode, *The Unauthorized Practice of Law and Pro Se Divorce: An Empirical Analysis*, 86 YALE L.J. 104, 110–15 (1976).

22. Cavenaugh and Rhode found that empirical evidence did not support the traditional justifications for lawyer opposition to legal advice by lay persons in divorce cases. *Id.*

7

CHILD CUSTODY PROGRAMS
AND PROCEDURES

The specialized court offers a parental education program and an expert team that evaluates each case in which the parties share children.

PARENTAL EDUCATION PROGRAM

The number of states that offer parental education in custody and visitation cases has burgeoned in the past two decades.[1] A 1998 survey indicates that 44 states have laws that authorize such programs.[2] Although they vary as to their mandatory nature and the authority responsible for implementation,[3] they all seek to educate parents on the negative effects that divorce can have on children and to provide parents with the knowledge and skills necessary to mitigate these problems.[4]

The programs set several goals: to (a) protect children from destructive parental conflict;[5] (b) reinforce quality parenting;[6] and (c) reduce divorce-related stress on children.[7] To fulfill these objectives, programs generally inform parents about constructive parenting practices,[8] typical and atypical adult and child reactions to divorce,[9] and children's developmental needs.[10] They acquaint parents with the detrimental effect on children of continued parental conflict,[11] particularly domestic violence and conflict over the children.[12] They caution parents to avoid the use of their children as pawns.[13]

They explain the legal process[14] and encourage parents to consider alternatives to litigation.[15] Some offer training on constructive communication and conflict resolution skills.[16] Several stress the importance of child support payment.[17] Programs typically combine live facilitators and videotaped presentations.[18] Proponents realize that successful programs require collaboration between mental health and legal professionals.[19] A small number of states also offer programs for children who experience the divorce of their parents.[20]

Some commentators object to parent education, because they believe that the programs will encourage parental cooperation when that cooperation might endanger a child or parent.[21] They also fear for the safety of domestic violence victims.[22] Programs have developed various methods to address these concerns. Program materials caution that domestic violence might make cooperative parenting inappropriate, that the physical safety of parent and child take priority over other concerns, that divorce from a violent marriage might promote a child's well-being, and that a parent should discuss parental or child abuse with counsel and bring it to the court's attention.[23] Sensitive programs do not assign one parent to the same small discussion group as the other and do not require joint parental attendance.[24] Where resources permit, some programs give parents the option to attend sessions on different days and provide security by uniformed court officers.[25]

Additional concerns about the content of parental education exist. When a program encourages mediation and settlement, it shows no sensitivity to the dangers these alternatives pose for less powerful parties, particularly women. Although the programs stress the negative impact that parental conflict has on children, their emphasis on the importance of the child's contacts with both parents may precipitate custody and visitation arrangements that address postdivorce parental conflict unrealistically. Nor do these programs seem sensitive to the interdependence between custody and visitation arrangements and financial issues.[26] The potential also exists for gender bias to invade educational content.[27] Unfortunately, research does little to quell these concerns.

Objective evaluations of program effectiveness prove rare or have limited scope.[28] Programs offered earlier rather than later in the divorce process[29] and those that offer skills training, however, seem to influence parents more than those limited to general education.[30] One study found that relitigation rates were lower for parents who attended education programs, whereas other studies found no difference.[31] Studies have yet to address whether education actually changes parental behavior or whether the behavior of educated parents differs from that of parents who lack such exposure.[32] And, attendance at voluntary programs remains poor.[33]

To the extent that these programs actually reduce parental conflict, induce the payment of child support, produce custody and visitation arrangements consistent with children's interests, and do not compromise the financial circumstances of dependent spouses, they serve both procedural and substantive justice goals. In these times of limited state resources, however, at the very least, objective assessment should accompany program continuation.[34]

In states that do offer parental education, the educational program in the proposed specialized court, in addition to the characteristics discussed earlier, explains custody evaluation procedures to parents. Courts without educational programs must inform both parents of custody evaluation procedures at the time a parent files a divorce or custody petition. In either specialized forum, the parents learn that a court-employed, highly trained evaluation team of a mental health professional and an attorney investigate all contested child issues. They also learn about the training the team has received, the investigative steps the team will take, the basic legal and social norms that govern evaluations, and the content and use of the team's final written report. Parents learn that they can challenge team findings and introduce other expert testimony, but they also learn that judges rely heavily on the team's report and testimony. Parents understand that they must pay for the team pursuant to a sliding scale and in proportion to their respective gross incomes. Parents who do not dispute child issues learn that they must submit their private agreements to the court before the final hearing and that the evaluation team and the judge will review, and have the authority to accept or reject, the settlement terms.

The education that parents receive about custody procedures promotes procedural goals. First, this knowledge lessens parental hostility. Frequently coached by their lawyers, parents who anticipate a courtroom custody battle tend to lock themselves into adversarial stances early in the divorce. Communication becomes strained or nonexistent. Experts on both sides distort parent–child relationships and exacerbate anger. In contrast, the even-handed procedures employed by neutral experts minimize the potential for either parent or their experts to distort the fact-finding process. Certainly parental posturing to gain advantage still will occur. The primary parent, however, should have less reason to fear, and thus to resent, such attempts. To the extent that this knowledge reduces parental hostilities, children benefit substantively.

Knowledge of custody procedures also enhances substantive justice. Parents who settle child issues in anticipation of team and judicial review should produce agreements that better reflect their children's interests. Knowledge also deters maliciously motivated or unmeritorious custody disputes. The parent with greater resources, for instance, learns that he or she can no longer distort the process through biased experts, which discourages groundless custody litigation and encourages sensible resolutions that better serve children's interests. Violent spouses understand that evaluators will discover their behavior and disfavor them as custodial parents, a deterrent to custody litigation that frequently favors the batterer to the child's disadvantage. Custody threats designed to force the probable custodial parent into a poor financial agreement will fall on deaf ears, which increases the likelihood of a fair financial resolution. The deterrent effect of this knowledge ultimately fosters system efficiency—another procedural goal.

Conceivably, however, parental knowledge of custody procedures might encourage rather than deter custody contests. The information might embolden a parent to seek custody even when his or her lawyer has suggested that he or she has little chance for success. Hostile, distrustful, or ignorant parents might trust neutral experts more than each other to fashion an appropriate custody arrangement. A battered spouse, for instance, might choose to have an expert team create a safety-sensitive visitation and custody plan rather than accept a plan driven by her fear or weakness in negotiations with her violent husband. If we take substantive justice seriously, however, the court should welcome these uses. A lawyer's bad advice should not defeat an involved parent's access to his children. Parental hostility, distrust, or ignorance should not govern custody arrangements. The court must protect the safety of spouses and children in violent families. Efficiency simply cannot trump substantive concerns. Moreover, parental payment for team services mitigates court costs considerably.

CUSTODY EVALUATION TEAMS

In addition to parent education, the specialized court employs custody evaluation teams. The custody evaluation teams consist of a lawyer and a mental health professional. To the extent possible, the team also consists of a male and a female, and the ethnicity of at least one team member corresponds with that of one or both parents. If either parent does not understand or speak English, one evaluator has facility with the relevant language, or the team works with a translator present. Whenever possible, after a specified period, team composition changes and members rotate to work with new individuals.

This composition serves several purposes. First, as noted earlier, the legal and mental health professions sometimes discriminate against the less powerful in society. The professions sometimes misunderstand minority and poor parents whose cultural experiences or poverty induce behaviors at variance with majoritarian values. Women, particularly those who live untraditional or violent lives, can fall victim to negative attributions. The likelihood of these biases may increase when expert teams act as agents of the conservative state. And custody cases expose the potential for bias when one third party wields too much authority. Decisions rooted in bias compromise procedural justice and work to the detriment of children. Team composition and rotation discourage these biases.

Team members must reach consensus on their recommendations or submit individual recommendations that explain why they disagree. During this process, each member must clarify and justify his or her individual conclusions to another from an entirely different discipline and gender.[35] Each member can challenge the normative, and perhaps inaccurate, assumptions that underlie the other's discipline. This process protects against bias and enhances the quality of the team's recommendations.[36] Team rotation also dispels bias, because it ensures that rigidity and routine do not govern the process of clarification and justification. Matching team composition with the ethnicity of the parent or parents fosters sensitivity and further parental acceptance of team recommendations.[37]

Some commentators express concern that mental health professionals too frequently fall victim to the fads and fantasies of their particular disciplines[38] and that they lack scientific expertise on what custody arrangements best suit children's interests.[39] Nonetheless, others conclude that mental health professionals, properly constrained, can offer courts helpful information peculiar to their unique training and expertise.[40] Team composition provides some of that constraint. Lawyers understand the concept of relevance and the legal criteria for the admissibility of expert testimony and will encourage their mental health colleagues to confine team recommendations and findings to the actual limits of team expertise. Lawyers also understand the due process concerns that underlie the statutory procedures and will promote team compliance with them.

The court administrator appoints team members to five-year renewable employment contracts subject to yearly review. The administrator searches for candidates with experience and knowledge relevant to child issues, including but not limited to family violence, the developmental needs of children, psychological testing, all relevant laws, and the psychology of divorce for adults and children. A candidate's openness to additional training, cultural sensitivity,[41] and commitment to the court provide additional criteria. Judges, to the extent they desire, participate in the evaluation and selection of candidates.

After appointment, team members undergo specialized training. They receive the same training as judges as well as education relevant to their unique tasks.[42] At a minimum, teams learn about

1. the common reactions of children, adults, and family systems to divorce;
2. the developmental needs of children and custody and visitation arrangements that anticipate them;[43]

3. the interdependence, or lack thereof, between children and parental needs;
4. the types, manifestations, ramifications of, and treatments for all forms of domestic violence;
5. the variations in family patterns between ethnic and social groups that reside within the court's community;
6. the potential contribution of extended family systems to a child's well-being;[44]
7. the unique conditions of poverty;
8. the current relevant research and its limitations;[45]
9. the strengths, weaknesses, and proper use of psychological tests in custody evaluations;[46]
10. the patterns of interaction between spouses that make face-to-face negotiations between them inappropriate;[47]
11. the interviewing, counseling, and dispute resolution techniques appropriate in custody evaluations;
12. the law relevant to custody and visitation issues; and
13. the legal criteria for the admissibility of expert testimony.

Experts sensitize team members to the potential for individual and professional bias to taint the evaluation process.[48] A poor mother who relies on the loving maternal grandmother for child care might provide a better home than a more detached father who can afford a day care center. Members learn the importance of self-monitoring to bias prevention. To further curb bias, educators encourage team members to balance their desire for consensus against the value of their independent judgments. For example, the lawyer who ordinarily might defer to the mental health professional's expertise learns that deference should occur only when the lawyer independently reaches the same conclusion or when his or her colleague has convinced him or her to alter his or her opinion based on the facts interpreted through the appropriate knowledge.

To the extent resources permit, the court can train teams in specific areas of expertise. A team, for instance, might become expert on child sexual abuse or spousal violence. The court assigns or transfers relevant cases to these teams, or the teams serve as consultants for other teams that confront such problems.[49]

Court officials explain the procedural and substantive goals of the court as well as their importance. Team members learn the procedures they must follow during evaluations and how those procedures implement the court's goals.

Specialized education and training address several procedural justice goals. Expertise enhances the legitimate authority of these decision makers and encourages parental respect for the outcomes they recommend. Education enhances the likelihood that accurate information, rather than, for example, irrelevant and unreliable tests, will underlie decisions. Training also sensitizes teams to the importance of impartiality, respectful treatment of parents and their rights, voice, hostility reduction, and procedural consistency. Recognition of these important concerns increases the probability that teams will conform their behaviors to them.

Education also enhances the likelihood of quality recommendations and decisions, a substantive justice goal.[50] Specialized knowledge, however, remains subject to the same caveats and qualifications noted previously with respect to judicial education.

A court administrator assigned to the custody evaluation division collects data on team members throughout the year, including feedback from parents and their attorneys as to team behaviors related to procedural justice concerns. The administrator also seeks information regarding parental perceptions of the quality of custody and visitation outcomes. This data, as well as the observations of the judge or judges a team member assists, provides the basis for yearly review. The administrator and involved judges perform the review and collaborate on a final report that contains specific findings. Team members receive a copy to help them adjust their conduct accordingly. Two consecutive poor reviews result in termination.

As noted previously, the unaccountability of those who currently assess custody issues[51] contributes to poor outcomes. Evaluation helps correct this deficiency. Evaluation also encourages team members to conform their behaviors to the court's procedural goals.

The "best interests of the child" standard should guide the team's custody investigation. As we have seen, each state has statutory and case law that sets forth the criteria the state considers relevant to children's best interests and that grant custody decision makers wide discretion. Team members, however, apply legal standards in light of their specialized knowledge. For instance, a team with expertise on the effects of domestic violence on children might recommend that the court award an "unfriendly" battered spouse primary residential custody, even though the state law favors friendly parents. The teams, then, temper the law with their expertise. In essence, in particular cases, the team's expertise and discretion somewhat insulates custody decision making from statutory standards that reflect interest group pressures rather than children's best interests.

The procedures the teams follow depend on whether the parents dispute or settle custody and visitation issues. Parents who settle their child issues submit a parenting plan to the court for approval. These plans must detail the custody and visitation arrangements for each child and provide thorough explanations for them. Evaluation teams review parenting plans in conjunction with the mandated child disclosures filed earlier by the parents. If the team accepts the plan, it so indicates with explanation and submits the plan for final court approval. If the court also accepts the plan, at final hearing the judge adopts the plan in its final judgment.

If the team or the court rejects the plan, the court refers the plan back to the parents with a thorough explanation of the reasons for rejection. Parents have the option to consult the evaluating team in preparation of a revised plan. Parents then can submit a revised plan that the court subjects to the same review and acceptance process. If the evaluation team or the court rejects the plan a second time, the team identifies the case as disputed, and the court subjects the case to the mandatory procedures described below.

In disputed cases the court specifies the mandatory procedures the custody evaluation team follows. The team first reviews the mandatory child disclosures and identifies areas of dispute or concern. If a case presents an isolated disputed issue, perhaps religious training or a special educational program for a child, the team confines its investigation to that issue and avoids unnecessary intrusion into the family.[52] Only when the team finds other provisions on which the parents have agreed problematic does the team expand its inquiry.

In more complex disputed cases, teams must conduct the following interviews: (a) each parent alone; (b) each parent with the child; (c) each child outside the presence of either parent; and (d) other significant people in the child's life that parents identify, and the team agrees, possess helpful information about the child's well-being, such as third-party caretakers, teachers, physicians, and extended family and friends of each parent and child. In all cases, evaluators spend equal amounts of time with both parents individually and with each parent in the presence of the child. Each parent can designate two people the team must interview, regardless of whether the team agrees. The team spends an equivalent amount of time with the people each parent designates. Each child also can designate a particular person the team must interview.[53] Teams thoroughly investigate all allegations or suspicions of any form of domestic violence as well as any indication of mental illness. If a team lacks the knowledge or skill necessary to investigate a particular issue, it consults with outside professionals or an expert team.

The personnel in the parental education and custody evaluation program provide assistance to custody evaluators. They help teams locate witnesses and relevant experts, coordinate calendars, schedule appointments, prepare written findings and recommendations, and initially review custody and visitation settlement agreements.

When, after investigation, the team believes a particular couple likely can reach agreement,[54] the team has the discretion to require the parents to meet with the team in an attempt to fashion a quality custody and visitation arrangement. The team cannot require such a meeting in any situation that involves any type of domestic violence.

Lawyers can request that teams keep them apprised of investigations actually performed, but not of the content of the investigations until submission of the team's final report. Lawyers also can submit recommendations, objections, or comments to the team in writing, but they also must provide the opposing counsel or party with a copy of any written communication.

The team prepares a report that details the procedures followed, the duration of each interview, and the factual findings, and expert impressions gained from each interview.[55] The report makes recommendations to the court. The team thoroughly justifies its recommendations based on the application of the facts to the law in light of expert knowledge. The report need not make an ultimate custody recommendation, but the team provides whatever guidance it comfortably can to the court. For instance, if investigation reveals that the father has abused the mother for several years, he presumptively becomes a poor custodial parent. On the other hand, if the two teenage sons have participated in the abuse, perhaps a custodial award to the mother makes little sense. In such a situation, the team can provide the court with relevant factual information and make expert predictions on the likelihood of successful treatment for the father and sons, but need not, and perhaps should not, make an ultimate custody recommendation.[56] In another instance, perhaps both parents exhibit some form of mental illness that equally inhibits their capacity to parent, the team can provide the court with the test results and explain how each parent's problems affect parenting, but can, and perhaps should, refrain from making an ultimate recommendation. Regardless of whether the team chooses to make a final recommendation, the factual thoroughness of and justifications in the report allows the court to knowledgeably review the team's recommendations and to alter them if the court deems alteration appropriate.

The team submits its report to both parents and the presiding judge well in advance of the final hearing. The judge reviews the report. If the judge finds any deficiencies, he or she informs the team and the parents and asks the team to correct them. If the court finds no deficiencies and the team has made recommendations, the court informs the team and the parents whether he or she preliminarily agrees with the recommendations. Once the judge accepts a report and indicates agreement with team recommendations, the parents have one week to accept or reject the report's findings and recommendations. If both parents accept the report in its entirety, the court seals the contents, and at the final hearing the court enters a custody and visitation order consistent with team recommendations.

If the team makes no final recommendation, or if the court rejects or if the parents challenge the team's recommendations, the court does not seal the report. The report becomes part of the official record and remains available to assist the court at the final hearing. In the above situations, parents can present argument and testimony, including additional expert testimony, at final hearing that support their respective positions. Parents also can cross-examine team members.[57] In the case of parental challenge of a court-approved report or recommendation, however, the court informs parents well before the final hearing that the team's report and recommendation carry a presumption of correctness that makes successful challenge quite difficult.[58]

Several goals justify these procedures. The assessment process inhibits bias and promotes error correction, because it (a) exposes evaluators equally to both parents, (b) involves the child's perspective, (c) demands thorough investigation of all domestic violence or mental illness allegations or suspicions, and (d) requires interviews with those designated by both parents and the child as well as those who have information relevant to the child's well-being. This broad exposure to various factual contexts provides an opportunity to intercept the formation of biases and to correct any erroneous impressions formed in one context by those gained in another. If either parent has concern that a team might harbor ethnic biases, for instance, that parent can require the team to interview a particular expert or an influential member of the relevant ethnic community. An Asian-American father assigned to a team of two Caucasian females, for instance, might request that the team consult an elder in his community or an expert who can explain his reluctance to participate in the evaluation process or how his parenting techniques might differ from those of middle-class White fathers.[59] Judicial review for deficiencies, judicial discretion to reject recommendations, and parental challenge provide additional mechanisms to expose bias and correct error. Although no person remains free of bias, at least these experts, who answer to no one but the court, offer more neutrality between parents than do the experts that parents employ.[60]

These procedures also reduce parental hostilities,[61] because teams treat parents evenhandedly and assuage any fear that one parent can employ superior resources to overwhelm the other. Parents no longer anticipate a heated courtroom battle with opposing experts and attorneys that distort their relationships with their children. In many instances, the court will seal reports and protect parents from the potential public ridicule that spawns defensiveness and anger.

The uniform procedures promote procedural consistency from case to case and ensure that teams and judges make decisions based on accurate rather than distorted information. Very importantly, the procedures ensure adequate parental as well as child voice and participation in the decision-making process. Inclusion, in turn, increases the decision maker's authority and encourage parental respect. Sealing the team's report in the event of judicial approval and parental acceptance honors the norm of family privacy.

The mandatory procedures promote efficiency, because they deter maliciously motivated custody claims and largely eliminate the need for contested custody hearings. A parent who knows, for example, that the team will discover the sexual abuse of a daughter and make custody recommendations accordingly, cannot hope to influence the custody decision with layers of biased expert testimony or threats of lawsuits against those scheduled to testify against that parent. The parent likely will not pursue custody in the first instance. Parents also know the difficulty, and perhaps the futility, of challenging court-accepted team recommendations, which in turn encourages them to forego litigation, particularly when they must pay additional attorney and expert fees.

Teams also substantially reduce the need for adversarial discovery and custody litigation, which, in turn, mitigate parental costs. Although parents must bear the costs of the evaluation, these costs should prove less burdensome than those incurred when parents pursue formal discovery and employ two sets of opposing lawyers and experts.[62] Only when parents challenge or the judge rejects team recommendations do parents incur discovery and litigation costs. Fewer contested discovery issues and less litigation also relieves the court and promotes system efficiency. Conceivably, as parents and lawyers adjust to the specialized court and begin to anticipate team recommendations, parents themselves more frequently will offer quality custody agreements for judicial approval that require minimal team involvement.

The tenuous nature of this efficiency claim must be noted, however. Greater court proficiency could lead to a heavier demand for services,[63] overwhelm evaluation teams, and compromise the speed of disposition. However, we do not yet know how parents will respond to teams, and program condemnation based on hypothetical fears seems overreactive. Moreover, because parents cover the cost of services, more frequent use simply requires more personnel. If indigent parents contest custody more frequently, the court can spread increased costs across users with the ability to pay.

Moreover, other efficiency gains noted earlier offset potential increased costs. And, finally, teams that inspire parental confidence and respect also might encourage voluntary compliance and minimize postdivorce litigation,[64] ultimately reducing long-term costs for courts and parents.

The procedures proposed here also contribute to substantive justice, because they increase the likelihood of quality custody and visitation decisions. To the extent that they deter custody litigation, teams also diminish the emotional stress children experience when their parents litigate custody and subject them to numerous psychiatric evaluations.[65] Team procedures also enhance the likelihood of fair financial terms in settlement agreements.

Threats of a contested custody battle designed to induce the more involved parent to accept an unfair financial settlement[66] should fall on deaf ears. These procedures, in essence, remove the custody chip from the bargaining table. Ultimately, because custody procedures fulfill both procedural and substantive justice goals, custody outcomes should command parental respect and encourage their compliance.

Objections, however, do exist. Attempts to encourage the use of court-appointed experts in other common law contexts largely have failed, primarily because of opposition from the bar. Trial lawyers claim that court-appointed experts have too much power and present insurmountable barriers to effective cross-examination. Critics claim that these experts undermine the adversary system by limiting participant control over the presentation of evidence and impart an aura of infallibility when, in fact, they have no greater expertise than other experts. Some fear that these experts will do a shoddy job as opposed to an adversarial expert.[67] None of these objections, however, proves persuasive in the context of the proposed specialized court.

The custody evaluation teams in the specialized court certainly would have a great deal of power. Safeguards provide appropriate limitations, however. Judges review reports and have the discretion to order additional work or reject the reports outright. Parties can challenge, cross-examine, and introduce their own experts. Perhaps parties will find it difficult to challenge a team's competence and integrity, but other types of cross-examination might prove easier.[68] Partisan experts have strong incentives to undermine opposing counsels, and their cross-examination can prove treacherous. Neutral experts have no reason to undermine either counsel and may more easily admit uncertainties and more openly explore new possibilities.[69]

Court-appointed experts do place constraints on the parties' ability to control the presentation of evidence. However, in the current system, courts already constrain party control when they assign custody evaluators, guardians ad litem, and special advocates to investigate cases. Attorneys might welcome the contrast of highly trained, neutral, and accountable teams. Moreover, the procedures that teams must follow provide ample party as well as attorney participation.

These procedures do limit somewhat the parties' ability to introduce "dueling experts." In this context, however, some constraint on party power seems a programmatic strength rather than a weakness. As noted earlier, judges make poor custody decisions partially because competing experts provide them with distorted and inaccurate information.[70] Surely the state's parens patriae power over the well-being of children warrants some reduction in party control over evidence presentation.

The claims that court-employed experts have no greater infallibility than other experts and that they likely will do a poor job have no credence in the family court context. We have every reason to expect teams to have greater competence than the alleged experts on whom the courts currently rely. Specialized training and continued accountability promote that expectation. Likewise no reason exists to believe they will perform in a shoddy manner. Mandatory procedures, specialized training, and accountability suggest that they will perform in a manner far superior to that of many, if not most, current custody evaluators, guardians ad litem, and special advocates.

Finally, worker's compensation administrative courts successfully have used appointed medical experts for decades.[71] Several reasons make the use of such experts easier in administrative proceedings than in trial courts. Administrative law judges with considerable expertise decide cases rather than juries. Procedures are less formal, and neutral experts usually write reports rather than testify.[72] Many of these features exist in the specialized court, suggesting the potential viability of appointed neutral experts in that court. Civil law courts also long have employed official experts who serve as consultants to the court rather than as witnesses.[73] Although this notion now seems foreign to our common law courts, in our earliest cases experts served as jurors or judges in these courts.[74] I do not suggest here that we should conform our common law courts to the civil tradition, or that we should return to the earliest of practices. I do note, however, that the suggestions made here do have support in other contexts and in history.

NOTES

1. *See* Jack Arbuthnot, *Court's Perceived Obstacles to Establishing Divorce Education Programs,* 40 FAM. CT. REV. 371, 371 (2002); Debra A. Clement, *1998 Nationwide Survey of the Legal Status of Parent Education,* 37 FAM. & CONCILIATION CTS. REV. 219 (1999); Linda D. Elrod, *Reforming the System to Protect Children in High Conflict Custody Cases,* 28 WM. MITCHELL L. REV. 495, 531–32 (2001); Joan B. Kelly, *Psychological and Legal Interventions for Parents and Children in Custody and Access Disputes: Current Research and Practice,* 10 VA. J. SOC. POL'Y & L. 129, 133–34 (2002). Andrew Schepard pioneered this development. *See* Andrew Schepard & Stephen Schlissel, *Planning for P.E.A.C.E.: The Development of Court-Connected Education Programs for Divorcing and Separating Families,* 23 HOFSTRA L. REV. 845 (1995); Andrew Schepard, *War and P.E.A.C.E.: Preliminary Report and a Model Statute of an Interdisciplinary Educational Program for Divorcing and Separating Parents,* 27 U. MICH. J. L. REF. 131 (1993).
2. *See* Clement, *supra* note 1, at 221–22. See *id.* at 228–36 for a summary of each state's provisions.
3. *See id.* at 220–22.
4. *See* Arbuthnot, *supra* note 1, at 371, 372–73; JoAnne Pedro-Carroll et al., *Assisting Children Through Transition,* 39 FAM. CT. REV. 377, 377, 380–81 (2001).

5. *See* Kelly, *supra* note 1, at 132; Pedro-Carroll et al., *supra* note 4, at 377–79.

6. *See* Kelly, *supra* note 1, at 132; Pedro-Carroll et al., *supra* note 4, at 377–81.

7. *See* Pedro-Carroll et al., *supra* note 4, at 377.

8. *See* Kelly, *supra* note 1, at 134; Pedro-Carroll et al., *supra* note 4, at 380–81.

9. *See* Pedro-Carroll et al., *supra* note 4, at 380–81; Andrew Schepard, *The Evolving Judicial Role in Child Custody Disputes: From Fault Finder to Conflict Manager to Differential Case Management*, 22 U. Ark. Little Rock L. Rev. 395, 412 (2000). *See also* Kelly, *supra* note 1, at 134.

10. *See* Risa J. Garon et al., *From Infants to Adolescents: A Developmental Approach to Parenting Plans*, 38 Fam. & Conciliation Cts. Rev. 168, 175–76 (2000) (stressing the importance of parental education on children's developmental needs); Pedro-Carroll et al., *supra* note 4, at 380.

11. *See* Pedro-Carroll et al., *supra* note 4, at 380, 382–83; Andrew Schepard, *Parental Conflict Prevention Programs and the United Family Court: A Public Health Perspective*, 32 Fam. L.Q. 95, 115 (1998).

12. *See* Pedro-Carroll et al., *supra* note 4, at 379.

13. *See id.* at 383.

14. *See* Pedro-Carroll et al., *supra* note 4, at 380, 383; Schepard, *supra* note 9, at 411–12.

15. *See* Kelly, *supra* note 1, at 135–36; Pedro-Carroll et al., *supra* note 4, at 383, 385–86.

16. *See* Pedro-Carroll et al., *supra* note 4, at 381–83. However, less than half of the programs in a 1998 survey offered skills training for parents. *Id.* at 380.

17. *See* Schepard & Schlissel, *supra* note 1, at 863–64.

18. *See* Kelly, *supra* note 1, at 136; Pedro-Carroll et al., *supra* note 4, at 381–82.

19. *See* Pedro-Carroll et al., *supra* note 4, at 381, 388–89; Schepard, *supra* note 11, at 116.

20. *See* Robin J. Geelhoed et al., *Status of Court-Connected Programs for Children Whose Parents Are Separating or Divorcing*, 39 Fam. Ct. Rev. 393, 393 (2001); Kelly, *supra* note 1, at 136; Pamela A. Yankeelov et al., *Transition or Not? A Theory-Based Quantitative Evaluation of Families in Transition*, 41 Fam. Ct. Rev. 242 (2003).

21. *See* Schepard, *supra* note 9, at 419.

22. *See id.*; Schepard & Schlissel, *supra* note 1, at 862.

23. *See* Schepard & Schlissel, *supra* note 1, at 862.

24. *See id.* at 863.

25. *See id.*

26. Many states, for instance, reduce the child support obligation of the nonresidential parent if that parent has a sufficient number of "overnights" with a child. *See, e.g.,* Fla. Stat. 61.30(11)(b) (2002); Colo. Rev. Stat. §14-10-115(10)(c) & 14(b) (2003).

27. In New York, however, the broad-based Statewide Advisory Committee constantly reviews the parental education curriculum for gender bias. *See* Schepard & Schlissel, *supra* note 1, at 862.

28. *See* Arbuthnot, *supra* note 1, at 371 n.7; Yankeelov et al., *supra* note 20 (presenting the results of an attitude and intention questionnaire based on pre- and post-program participation, but providing no information on changes in actual parental behavior post-program).

29. *See* Kelly, *supra* note 1, at 135.

30. *See* Elrod, *supra* note 1, at 532 & n.141; Kelly, *supra* note 1, at 136 & n.27; Pedro-Carroll et al., *supra* note 4, at 380.

31. *See* Kelly, *supra* note 1, at 135.

32. *See id.*

33. *See id.* at 134. Many claim that states must compel parent attendance in order to fulfill program goals. *See, e.g.,* Schepard, *supra* note 11, at 119–20.

34. *See* Pedro-Carroll et al., *supra* note 4, at 388 (noting that any new program deserves monitoring to refine practices and to facilitate goals).

35. For a discussion of how the perspectives of social workers and lawyers may differ and of the need for collaboration between these professionals in child-related legal proceedings, see Frank P. Cervone & Linda M. Mauro, *Ethics, Cultures, and Professions in the Representation of Children*, 64 FORDHAM L. REV. 1975 (1996). *See also* Janet R. Johnston, *Building Multidisciplinary Professional Partnerships with the Court on Behalf of High-Conflict Divorcing Families and Their Children: Who Needs What Kind of Help?*, 22 U. ARK. LITTLE ROCK L. REV. 453, 465 (2000) (recognizing the desirability of court-appointed, impartial, expert, multidisciplinary teams to evaluate custody issues).

36. Shuman suggests that an administrative tribunal comprised of experts might counteract the problems created by uncritical judicial reliance on individual mental health professionals. Daniel W. Shuman, *The Role of Mental Health Experts in Custody Decisions: Science, Psychological Tests, and Clinical Judgment*, 36 FAM. L.Q. 135, 161 (2002). The proposal offered here moves in that direction.

37. *See* Tom R. Tyler, *Multiculturalism and the Willingness of Citizens to Defer to the Legal and Legal Authorities*, 25 L. & Soc. INQUIRY 983, 983, 1002, 1004 (2000) (noting that people rely more strongly on procedural justice criteria rather than favorable results in deciding whether to accept and comply with a decision made by authorities from their own ethnic group).

38. *See, e.g.,* MARTHA ALBERTSON FINEMAN, THE ILLUSION OF EQUALITY: THE RHETORIC AND REALITY OF DIVORCE REFORM 87 (1991).

39. *See, e.g.,* Martha Fineman, *Dominant Discourse, Professional Language, and Legal Change in Child Custody Decisionmaking*, 101 HARV. L. REV. 727 (1988); Michael D.A. Freeman, *Questioning the Delegalization Movement in Family Law: Do We Really Want a Family Court?*, in THE RESOLUTION OF FAMILY CONFLICT: COMPARATIVE LEGAL PERSPECTIVES 7, 13–14 (John M. Eekelaar & Sanford N. Katz eds. 1984); Daniel A. Krauss & Bruce D. Sales, *Legal Standards, Expertise, and Experts in the Resolution of Contested Custody Cases*, 6 PSYCHOL. PUB. POL'Y & L. 843 (2000).

40. *See* Krauss & Sales, *supra* note 39, at 871–75. Krauss and Sales argue, for instance, that mental health professionals do possess the expertise to (a) screen

parents and their children for psychopathology, (b) assess whether a particular child has sufficient maturity to express his or her wishes and the weight a judge should give to that child's wishes, and (c) summarize current psychological research relevant to a particular custody situation. *Id.* at 871–73. Moreover, when two well-adjusted and loving parents share the responsibilities of child care, experts likely cannot predict what custody arrangement would best serve the children's interests. *See* Henrik H.H. Andrup, *Divorce Proceedings: Ends and Means, in* THE RESOLUTION OF FAMILY CONFLICT: COMPARATIVE LEGAL PERSPECTIVES 163, 172–73 (John M. Eekelaar & Sanford N. Katz eds. 1984). When a father abuses the mother or children, however, experts can use their knowledge of the effects of domestic violence on children to assist the court or make custodial recommendations.

41. The New York State Judicial Commission on Minorities suggests that all court personnel should show

> (a) the capacity to understand and appreciate different values, languages, dialects, cultures and life styles; (b) a capacity for empathy that transcends cultural differences; (c) avoidance of conduct that may be perceived as demeaning, disrespectful, discourteous or insensitive to persons from other cultural groups; and (d) a critical understanding of stereotyped thinking and a capacity for individualized judgment.

Gary B. Melton, *Children, Families, and the Courts in the Twenty-First Century,* 66 S. CAL. L. REV. 1993, 2022 (1993) (citing 2 REPORT OF THE NEW YORK STATE JUDICIAL COMMISSION ON MINORITIES 100–101 (Apr. 1991)).

42. Numerous commentators recognize the need for specialized training for those who make decisions about the welfare of children. *E.g.,* Annette R. Appell, *Decontextualizing the Child Client: The Efficacy of the Attorney–Client Model for Very Young Children,* 64 FORDHAM L. REV. 1955 (1996); Peter Margulies, *The Lawyer as Caregiver: Child Client's Competence in Context,* 64 FORDHAM L. REV. 1473 (1966); Jean Koh Peters, *The Roles and Content of Best Interests in Client-Directed Lawyering for Children in Child Protective Proceedings,* 64 FORDHAM L. REV. 1505 (1996).

43. *See* Joan B. Kelly & Michael E. Lamb, *Using Child Development Research to Make Appropriate Custody and Access Decisions for Young Children,* 38 FAM. & CONCILIATION CTS. REV. 297 (2000).

44. Professor Melton urges courts to enhance "natural networks" as a way to enhance support for troubled families, Melton, *supra* note 41, at 2023, but also cautions that the most troubled families might be isolated and attempts to strengthen their social networks might prove futile. *Id.* at 2024.

45. Krauss and Sales note that mental health practitioners frequently fail to acknowledge the serious limitations of research on which they rely in their custody evaluations. Krauss & Sales, *supra* note 39, at 864–65. Education eliminates, for instance, reliance on syndrome testimony that lacks scientific verification. *See* Daniel W. Shuman, *What Should We Permit Mental Health Professionals to Say About "The Best Interests of the Child"?: An Essay on Common Sense,*

Daubert, and the Rules of Evidence, 31 Fam. L.Q. 551, 564–65 (1997) (identifying scientifically unverified syndrome testimony as a problem in child custody cases).

46. Education ensures that psychologists would not use testing instruments improperly. *See* Marc J. Ackerman & Melissa C. Ackerman, *Child Custody Evaluation Practices: A 1996 Survey of Psychologists*, 30 Fam. L.Q. 565, 573 (1996) (expressing their concern that one third of the psychological experts they surveyed who performed custody evaluations used two tests, the MCMI–II and the MCMI–III, on divorcing parents even though the tests were designed for a clinical rather than a normal population).

47. For instance, Beck and Sales note the harmful nature of face-to-face negotiations between violent spouses and couples with enmeshed, highly conflicted, autistic, or "demand–withdraw" interactive patterns. Connie J.A. Beck & Bruce D. Sales, *A Critical Reappraisal of Divorce Mediation Research and Policy*, 6 Psychol. Pub. Pol'y & L. 989, 996–1000 (2000).

48. *See* Margulies, *supra* note 42, at 1496–97.

49. For instance, many argue for differentiated case management for high conflict families. *See* Schepard, *supra* note 9, at 413, 422–26; Elrod, *supra* note 1, at 521.

50. Studies indicate that attorneys who represent children perform more competently after specialized training. *See* Appell, *supra* note 42, at 1967–68.

51. Shuman notes that judges fail to demand accountability from expert witnesses in the areas of child custody and visitation. Shuman, *supra* note 45.

52. Johnston, *supra* note 35, at 464 (recommending that custody evaluators confine their investigations to disputed issues and avoid unnecessary and disruptive intrusion into family privacy).

53. The idea that children have participatory rights in a custody proceeding might seem strange to legal professionals in the United States. *See generally* Barbara Bennett Woodhouse, *Talking about Children's Rights in Judicial Custody and Visitation Decision-Making*, 36 Fam. L.Q. 105, 107–09 (2002). Yet, as Woodhouse convincingly relates, the United States lags significantly behind international developments in children's rights. *Id.* at 107–10. Participation empowers children by providing them voice in a process that directly affects their well-being, see *id.* at 118–20, without raising the alarm generally attached to recognition of more direct rights for children. Unsurprisingly, many advocates maintain that even very young children have a right to voice in custody proceedings even if indirectly expressed through testimony by guardians ad litem or attorneys. *Id.* at 123–24. *See also* Kelly, *supra* note 1, at 150–51 (noting the helpfulness of relevant input from children provided children have no actual decisional control).

54. *See* Beck & Sales, *supra* note 47, at 996–1000 (recognizing the harmful nature of face-to-face negotiations between certain types of couples).

55. Elrod, for instance, recommends the following:

> In reporting or testifying about their custody or visitation recommendations, mental health professionals should distinguish among their clinical judgments, research-based opinions, and philosophical positions. As

one scholar noted, mental health professionals lack the proficiency to specify what constitutes the best interests of other people's children. In addition, mental health professionals should summarize their data-gathering procedures, information sources and time spent and present all relevant information on limitations of the evaluation that result from unobtainable information, such as failure of a party to cooperate or the circumstances of particular interviews. Evaluation reports should be written in plain English without technical jargon or legal terms. The reports should accentuate positive parental attributes as well as negative ones and avoid adding to the family's shame by stigmatizing or blaming parents or children. Psychiatric diagnoses should not be used unless they are relevant to parenting. If making a recommendation to the court regarding a parenting plan, the reports should provide clear, detailed recommendations that are consistent with the health, safety, welfare and best interest of the child.

Elrod, *supra* note 1, at 542.

56. Many commentators urge custody evaluators to refrain from making ultimate custody recommendations and to confine their reports to information relevant to that decision. *See, e.g.,* Krauss & Sales, *supra* note 39, at 875.

57. Australia provides for cross-examination of welfare officers that prepare custody reports for specialized family court judges. *See* Frank Bates, *The Role of the Expert in Judicial Divorce Procedures, in* THE RESOLUTION OF FAMILY CONFLICT: COMPARATIVE LEGAL PERSPECTIVES 123, 127–29 (John M. Eekelaar & Sanford N. Katz eds. 1984). Cross-examination allows parties to test the reliability of the evidence, provides a safeguard against irregularities in the team's investigation or errors in the basis for the team's opinion, and facilitates a proper understanding of the evidence. *Id.* at 128. Moreover, welfare officers in Australia seem to welcome an opportunity to support and justify their conclusions before the court. *Id.*

58. The U.S. Supreme Court long has recognized that the Due Process Clause of the Fourteenth Amendment recognizes and protects parents' fundamental liberty interest in the care, custody, and management of their children. Santosky, II v. Kramer, 455 U.S. 743, 102 S. Ct. 1388, 71 L.Ed.2d 599 (1982); Lassiter v. Department of Soc. Servs., 452 U.S. 18, 101 S. Ct. 2153, 68 L.Ed.2d 640 (1981). When a state procedure threatens to substantially alter a parent's access to his or her child, the state must provide the parent with sufficient process. The procedures offered here provide sufficient parental participation, as well as numerous safeguards against state excess, to withstand any due process challenge.

59. *See* Melton, *supra* note 41, at 2016–18 (explaining a few of the unique qualities of the Asian-American culture).

60. Many commentators recognize that in contested custody cases the children's interests frequently become subordinated to the individual interests of the disputing parents. *See, e.g.,* Catherine J. Ross, *From Vulnerability to Voice: Appointing Counsel for Children in Civil Litigation,* 64 FORDHAM L. REV. 1571,

1583–86 (1996); Woodhouse, *supra* note 53. *See generally* John H. Langbein, *The German Advantage in Civil Procedure,* 52 U. Chi. L. Rev. 823, 835–40 (1985).

61. Commentators recommend that parents use a forum to resolve their child-related disagreements that does not alienate them from each other to the extent associated with adversarial combat in the courtroom. *See, e.g.,* Schepard, *supra* note 9, at 408.

62. In a replication and expansion of an earlier study, Marc and Melissa Ackerman found that a psychologist's fee for a custody evaluation ranged from $600 to $15,000, with an average of $2,645.96. The average fee has tripled in the past decade. Ackerman & Ackerman, *supra* note 46, at 575. Interestingly, although the family law attorneys in one survey doubted the helpfulness of mental health experts in making child custody decisions, they nevertheless hired these experts largely to discredit their opponent's expert. *See* Robert D. Felner et al., *Child Custody Resolution: A Study of Social Science Involvement and Impact,* 18 Prof. Psychol.: Res. & Prac. 468 (1987).

63. *See generally* Rochelle Cooper Dreyfuss, *Specialized Adjudication,* 1990 BYU L. Rev. 377, 382.

64. Kelly describes custody procedures in California that have some similar attributes as those proposed here. She explains,

> The most effective process for developing and implementing parent arbitrator programs is through the collaborative work of an interdisciplinary committee appointed by the family law judge and consisting of experienced family law lawyers, custody evaluators, and mediators. . . . The final order described the Special Masters' authority, provided quasi-judicial immunity, delineated procedures to be used, defined the term of service and procedures for termination, listed the type of disputes at each level, authorized ex-parte communications and meetings, and provided grievance processes for parents and fee collection provisions for Special Masters. Materials were developed for parents to describe the program, and to emphasize the extent of the authority that they would be transferring to the Special Master in situations where parents could not settle specific disputes on their own.

Kelly, *supra* note 1, at 146. Kelly acknowledges the extremely limited nature of empirical research on special master programs but notes that preliminary indications suggest a dramatic decrease in relitigation. *Id.*

65. *See* Bates, *supra* note 57, at 133–35 (noting an Australian contested custody case in which the children have been subjected to numerous psychiatric evaluations and interviews—even when tests showed the children to be entirely normal and when the children themselves protested continued testing).

66. *See* Elizabeth S. Scott, *Pluralism, Parental Preference, and Child Custody,* 80 Cal. L. Rev. 615, 265 (1992); Richard Neely, *The Primary Caretaker Parent Rule: Child Custody and the Dynamics of Greed,* 3 Yale L. & Pol'y Rev. 168, 171, 177–81 (1984).

67. *See* Samuel R. Gross, *Expert Evidence,* 1991 Wis. L. Rev. 1113, 1193–94.

68. *See id.* at 1196.

69. *See id.*
70. Judges frequently complain about the stress they experience in custody cases because they lack information relevant to a child's needs. *See* Garon et al., *supra* note 10, at 183. Langbein describes his own experience as an expert witness:

> Perverse incentives: At the American trial bar, those of us who serve as expert witnesses are known as "saxophones." This is a revealing term, as slang often is. The idea is that the lawyer plays the tune, manipulating the expert as though the expert were a musical instrument on which the lawyer sounds the desired notes. I sometimes serve as an expert in trust and pension cases, and I have experienced the subtle pressures to join the team—to shade one's views, to conceal doubt, to overstate nuance, to downplay weak aspects of the case that one has been hired to bolster. Nobody likes to disappoint a patron; and beyond this psychological pressure is the financial inducement. Money changes hands upon the rendering of expertise, but the expert can run his meter only so long as his patron litigator likes the tune. Opposing counsel undertakes a similar exercise, hiring and schooling another expert to parrot the contrary position. The result is our familiar battle of opposing experts. The more measured and impartial an expert, the less likely he is to be used by either side.

Langbein, *supra* note 60, at 835.
71. *See* Gross, *supra* note 67, at 1205–06.
72. *See id.* at 1206–07.
73. *See id.* at 1209; Langbein, *supra* note 60, at 835–40.
74. *See* Gross, *supra* note 67, at 1209.

CONCLUSION

The procedures presented here are based on their potential to enhance procedural and substantive justice. Moreover, they address many deficiencies that scar the psyches of the men, women, and children who pass through the system, and fulfill many of the goals of therapeutic jurisprudence. Finally, the formalized interdisciplinary approach to child issues offers much to many mental health professionals as participants and educators.

The proposed specialized court undoubtedly would prove costly for already strained state budgets.[1] As noted earlier, however, the economic and social costs that current practices impose on states, on our society in general, and on affected individuals far outweigh the expense of the proposed court system. We simply cannot ignore those costs and continue to operate as usual.

When I began this book more years ago than I like to remember, I also intended to alleviate system deficiencies through severe restrictions on judicial discretion. Statutory formulas for spousal maintenance, like those used for child support and recently proposed by the American Law Institute, could limit judicial discretion and ensure maintenance for dependent spouses. Presumptions in favor of an equal distribution of marital property and an expanded definition of marital property could stabilize property distribution and improve the postdivorce economic situation of dependent spouses. For several reasons, however, I no longer believe that rigid formulas should substitute for judicial discretion.

Families do present diverse social and financial circumstances. Rigid formulas frequently would fail to render "just" results.[2] For instance, a strong presumption in favor of an equal division of marital property might, on its face, seem fair. Yet one need not stretch the imagination too far to anticipate numerous situations in which an equal division would threaten the financial well-being of a dependent spouse. I prefer to rely on an educated and accountable judiciary, settlement review, early intervention by dispute resolution experts, and custody evaluation teams rather than rigid rules to promote substantive justice.[3] If the future proves my reliance on procedure an error, I then would recommend restrictions on the discretion of all important decision makers.

The current political climate also argues for retention of some indeterminacy in the law and some discretion in its application. The composition of our state legislatures is predominantly male.[4] These legislatures, understandably, show great reluctance to knowingly pass dissolution laws more favorable to women.[5] Moreover, many women who have ascended to powerful positions, such as to state representative, have done so partially through their adherence to masculine values.[6] They too might prove unsympathetic to less fortunate women.[7] If we depend on legislatures to pass laws that obviously compromise men's and favor women's interests, I suspect that little change will occur.[8] On the other hand, the procedural reforms proposed here appear more neutral, and state legislatures might offer less resistance to them.

Finally, we have seen throughout this book that many factors other than substantive law contribute to poor outcomes.[9] Better law, for instance, in the hands of incompetent and biased decision makers offers little relief.[10] Nevertheless, reliance on procedure does not eliminate the desirability of substantive reform. The law should better anticipate the financial vulnerability of postdivorce families. I certainly favor an expanded definition of marital property that captures assets such as professional degrees and enhanced earning capacity. I see no reason why "separate" property must remain separate when many couples, particularly in long-term marriages, plan their financial lives based on that property. Custody law should more accurately reflect social science research rather than political influence. Child support guidelines should better anticipate the actual costs of raising children, including postsecondary education. Spousal maintenance laws should anticipate the financial vulnerability of dependent spouses and encourage, rather than discourage, awards. We certainly should continue to push for these changes to substantive law that would complement the procedural reforms offered here.

NOTES

1. *See Developments: Unified Family Courts and the Child Protection Dilemma,* 116 HARV. L. REV. 2099, 2100 (2003) (noting that family court reform proposals undoubtedly will face financial scrutiny).

2. Penelope Eileen Bryan, *Vacant Promises? The ALI Principles of the Law of Family Dissolution and the Post-Divorce Financial Circumstances of Women,* 8 DUKE J. GENDER L. & POL'Y 101 (2001).

3. I am not alone in my preference for discretion over rigid rules. *See* Judith T. Younger, *Marriage, Divorce, and the Family: A Cautionary Tale,* 21 HOFSTRA L. REV. 1367, 1376–77 (1993).

4. The Center for American Women and Politics, Eagleton Institute of Politics, at Rutgers, The State University of New Jersey, published data indicating that, in 2001, women constituted 22.4% of the state legislators in the United States, with women holding 20% of state senate seats and 23.3% of state house or assembly seats. The 10 states with the highest percentage of women in state legislatures are Washington (38.8%), Arizona (35.6%), Nevada (34.9%), Colorado (34%), Oregon (33.3%), Kansas (32.7%), New Mexico (31.3%), Maine (30.1%), Connecticut (29.4%) and New Hampshire (29.3%). The 10 states with the low percentages of women state legislatures are Alabama (7.9%), Oklahoma (10.1%), South Carolina (10.6%), Kentucky (10.9%), Mississippi (12.6%), Arkansas (13.3%), Pennsylvania (13.4%), New Jersey (15%), South Dakota (15.2%) and Wyoming (15.6%). These number represent more than a fivefold increase since 1969. CENTER FOR AMERICAN WOMEN AND POLITICS, EAGLETON INSTITUTE OF POLITICS, RUTGERS, THE STATE UNIVERSITY OF NEW JERSEY, WOMEN IN STATE LEGISLATURES 2001, *available at* http://www.rci. rutgers.edu /~cawp/ pdf/stleg.pdf. The increase in women legislators, however, does not yet approach a sufficient percentage to successfully implement a women's agenda. Nor can we expect all women legislators to support such an agenda.

5. *See* Bryan, *supra* note 2, at 105 & nn.54–55.

6. *See* Mary Becker, *Patriarchy and Inequality: Towards a Substantive Feminism,* 1999 U. CHI. LEGAL F. 21, 25 & n.20, 34.

7. *See id.* at 25.

8. *See* Marsha Garrison, *The Economic Consequences of Divorce: Would Adoption of the ALI Principles Improve Current Outcomes?,* 8 DUKE J. GENDER L. & POL'Y 119, 123 (2001) (recognizing that political pressures may compromise the integrity of real-world legislation).

9. As Garrison notes,

> These various examples make it clear that the achievement of equitable outcomes when families break up cannot be achieved either through broad grants of discretion, or even through the substitution of rules for discretionary standards. Changes in the law of family dissolution will not produce equity improvements unless two preliminary criteria are met: legal change must reflect public values and familial expectations,

and it must also reflect a detailed understanding of current outcomes and the process by which they are produced.

Garrison, *supra* note 8, at 123.

10. Kadoch recognizes that inept judicial application of Maine alimony law, rather than the law itself, results in inadequate awards. Laurie C. Kadoch, *Five Degrees of Separation: A Response to Judge Sheldon's The Sleepwalker's Tour of Divorce Law*, 49 ME. L. REV. 321, 345–51 (1997). *See also* Gary Skoloff & Robert J. Levy, *Custody Doctrines and Custody Practice: A Divorce Practitioner's View*, 36 FAM. L.Q. 79, 79–85 (2002) (acknowledging numerous factors that influence custody outcomes and openly doubting whether custody doctrine can alter those factors).

AUTHOR INDEX

Abraham, J. H., 30, 86, 92
Abrams, K., 33, 163, 199, 233, 234, 236, 243
Ackerman, B. A., 29
Ackerman, M. C., 81, 275, 277
Ackerman, M. J., 81, 275, 277
Acock, A. C., 35
Alagna, S. W., 167
Alfieri, A. V., 153
Alfini, J. J., 231, 233, 234
Amato, P. R., 35, 37, 40, 46
Anderson, E. G., 165
Andrup, H. H. H., 43, 224, 257, 274
Appell, A. R., 274, 275
Arbuthnot, J., 229, 235, 271, 273
Arendell, T., 34, 35, 37, 38, 41, 44, 45, 46, 47, 48, 88, 89, 95, 156, 162
Atwood, B. A., 197, 198, 199
Aucamp, F. P., 230

Babb, B. A., 7
Bahr, S., 34
Baker, L. A., 91, 101, 179
Baker, M., 17, 18, 19, 30, 31, 32, 33, 34, 35, 40, 44, 45, 46, 48, 79, 89, 225, 228
Bandes, S., 237
Barnes, P. G., 230
Barrett-Howard, E., 52, 179
Barry, W. A., 164
Bartlett, K. T., 6
Bates, F., 231, 276, 277
Bayles, M. D., 85
Beck, C. J. A., 17, 76, 77, 105, 171, 174, 175, 177, 178, 225, 226, 227, 275
Becker, M. E., 7, 30, 97, 98, 99, 102, 103, 104, 156, 161, 166, 168, 169, 171, 228, 236, 281
Behrens, M. A., 231, 232, 233, 234, 235
Behrman, R. E., 16, 35
Belcher, D. I., 198
Beller, A. H., 19, 38
Beninger, E. S., 87

Benton, C. J., 166
Berger, J., 164, 177
Bersoff, D., 85, 151
Bianchi, S., 25, 35
Binder, D. A., 151
Bix, B., 198
Blakeslee, S., 26, 37, 39
Blakesley, C. L., 20
Blankenhorn, D., 21, 30, 47, 49, 86, 95
Blankenship, D., 28, 163
Block, J. H., 35
Blumstein, P., 156, 162
Bograd, M., 100
Boland, B., 233
Booth, A., 17, 46, 49
Boulding, K. E., 165
Bowker, L. H., 100
Bramlett, M. D., 16
Brandon, K., 78
Brandwein, R. A., 34, 44
Bray, J. H., 49
Brinig, M. F., 34, 44, 46, 48
Brod, G. F., 184, 197, 198, 199, 240
Brooks-Gunn, J., 34
Bross, D. C., 102
Browne, A., 42, 163, 168
Bruch, C. S., 83, 228, 238, 239
Bryan, P. E., 6, 30, 31, 76, 77, 84, 86, 95, 109, 156, 157, 158, 161, 162, 163, 164, 165, 166, 167, 169, 171, 176, 182, 183, 184, 193, 195, 198, 224, 225, 226, 227, 228, 240, 242, 243, 258, 281
Buchanan, C. M., 41
Buckner, E. T., 40
Bumpass, L. L., 16
Burt, R. A., 154
Buss, E., 83
Buzawa, E., 104

Cahill, M., 19, 32, 75, 77, 105
Cahn, R., 98, 99, 100
Caplan, P., 31, 101

Fineman, M. L. A., 14, 21, 31, 33, 77, 80, 87, 88, 91, 96, 101, 103, 104, 161, 162, 170, 236, 273
Finkelhor, D., 20, 41, 42
Finlay, B., 38
Finley, L. M., 161
Fischer, K., 76, 163, 168, 169, 170, 171, 226, 239
Fiss, O. M., 223, 243
Folberg, J., 226
Folger, R., 150
Fox, G. L., 35, 39, 41
Fredericks, L., 101
Freeman, M. D. A., 273
Friedan, B., 88
Friedman, L. M., 52, 53, 179
Frieze, I., 168
Fuchs, V. R., 87
Fuller, L. L., 16, 53, 151, 223
Furr, L. A., 39
Furstenberg, F. F., Jr., 34

Gable, J., 231, 233, 234
Gagnon, A. G., 171, 226
Galanter, M., 19, 32, 75, 77, 95, 105, 180
Galston, W., 29
Gangel-Jacob, P., 105, 160, 171, 178, 225, 226, 227, 245
Gardner, R., 214, 239
Garfinkel, I., 21
Garon, R. J., 80, 178, 255, 272, 278
Garrison, M., 6–7, 19, 34, 35, 65, 67, 76, 89, 90, 91, 92, 93, 94, 95, 109, 156, 281–282
Garth, B., 218, 243
Gatland, L., 16
Geelhoed, R. J., 272
Gelles, R. J., 167
Geraghty, A. H., 230
Gerber, R. J., 17, 105, 174, 178, 224
Gerencser, A. E., 171–172
Gergen, K. J., 52, 53, 178
Gerson, K., 91
Gibeaut, J., 232
Gifford, D. G., 165
Gilkerson, C. P., 97, 151, 152, 153, 154
Gilligan, C., 121, 162–163, 166
Girdner, L. K., 20, 80, 168
Glendon, M. A., 16

Glick, P. C., 48, 88
Goldstein, J., 237
Gondolf, E. W., 170
Goodman, E., 30
Graham, J. W., 19
Graham-Bermann, S. A., 100
Gray-Little, B., 101, 102, 169
Green, B., 80
Greenbaum, L., 151
Greenberg, J., 179
Greenberg, M. S., 52, 53, 178
Greenburg, J. C., 80
Grief, G. L., 20
Griffiths, J., 152, 153, 154, 177
Grillo, T., 76, 163, 226
Grissett, B., 39
Grodin, J. R., 233, 234
Gross, S. R., 173, 175, 277, 278
Guggenheim, M., 83
Guidubaldi, J., 35, 37
Guthrie, C., 106

Hadfield, G. K., 242, 243
Hahn, B. A., 38
Hall-McCorquodale, I., 31, 101
Hamby, S. L., 101, 102, 169
Hammer, H., 19, 20
Haralambie, A. M., 82, 83, 104
Harlow, C. W., 168
Harnett, D. L., 165
Harrison, F. L., 176
Hart, B. J., 76, 171, 226
Hart, H. L. A., 52
Hartney, M., 240
Hauser, B., 167
Hegar, R., 20
Helgeson, V. S., 166
Henderson, A. J. Z., 101
Henderson, L., 237
Henry, R. K., 18, 19, 30, 86
Hensler, D. R., 16, 52, 225, 227, 256
Hernandez, D. J., 19
Hershkoff, H., 227
Hershorn, M., 100
Hetherington, E. M., 17, 21, 32, 35, 37, 39, 40, 41, 43, 44, 45, 46, 48, 49, 88, 103
Heuer, L., 227
Hewlett, S. A., 103
Hochschild, A., 161

Hodges, W. F., 35, 37
Hoelter, J. W., 164
Hoff, P. M., 20
Hofstadter, S. H., 93
Holden, G. W., 100
Holmes, J. G., 165
Honeyman, C., 76, 226
Horner, M. S., 121, 166
Houlden, P., 150
Howard, J. A., 166
Howe, W., 6
Hyatt, R., 243

Jackson, T. D., 5, 85
Jacob, H., 79, 107, 108, 229
Jacobs, S. B., 97, 98, 105
Jacobsen, J., 87
Jaffe, P. G., 80, 82, 98, 99, 100, 101,
    102, 103, 104, 168, 169, 171
Jasinski, J. L., 168
Jayakody, R., 31
Jenkins, J. M., 35
Johnson, L. D., 98
Johnson, M., 244
Johnston, J. R., 41, 80, 177, 178, 236,
    243, 273, 275
Jordan, E. R., 227, 238
Jost, J. T., 165
Joy, P. A., 174

Kadoch, L. C., 41, 89, 174, 182, 240–
    241, 282
Kahn, A. J., 34
Kalter, N., 49
Kamerman, S. B., 34
Kantor, G. K., 168
Kass, A., 177
Katz, S., 5, 43, 75, 159, 163, 177, 184,
    224, 231, 240, 257, 273, 274, 276
Kay, H. H., 21, 30, 41, 89, 93, 160, 163,
    229, 236
Keenan, L. R., 97, 102, 169, 170, 171
Keith, B., 37
Keith, V. M., 38
Kelly, A. B., 91
Kelly, J. B., 17, 21, 30, 31, 32, 37, 38,
    39, 40, 41, 43, 44, 46, 48, 49, 50,
    88, 103, 177, 178, 226, 271, 272,
    273, 274, 275, 277

Kelly, R. F., 83
Kelsen, H., 240
Kiecolt, K. J., 35
Kilborn, P. T., 45
Kirp, D. L., 88, 162
Kitson, G. C., 45
Klein, C. F., 98, 168, 170
Kline, M., 41
Koffman, S., 164
Kornhauser, L., 107, 183, 241
Korobkin, R., 106
Kramer, L. D., 231, 232, 234–235
Krause, H. D., 21
Krauskopf, J. M., 173
Krauss, D. A., 29, 34, 37, 75, 78, 80, 81,
    82, 177, 178, 225, 226, 273, 274,
    276
Krein, S. F., 38
Kressel, K., 79, 155, 164, 167, 173, 175,
    177, 178, 226, 257
Kritzer, H. M., 77
Kronman, A. T., 242
Kurdek, L. A., 36, 39, 40
Kurtz, L. R., 98

Lamb, M. E., 274
Lamke, L. K., 101, 169
Langbein, J. H., 277, 278
Larkin, E. A., 231, 233
LaTour, S., 150
Lawrence, J. K. L., 6
Lehmann, P., 100
Leitch, M. L., 76, 101, 226
Lerman, L. G., 76, 171, 226
Leung, K., 52
Levendosky, A. A., 100
Leventhal, G. S., 52, 178, 179
Levin, L., 87
Levine, A., 166
Levittan, S. R., 93
Levy, R. J., 7, 77, 151, 152, 171, 174,
    180, 226, 282
Lin, S. -L., 48, 88
Lind, E. A., 52, 75, 105, 150, 151, 173,
    227, 228
Lips, H. M., 164
Livingston, C., 20
Locke, J., 78
Logan, R., 120
Lonsdorf, B. J., 165

Lowenstein, S. R., 83
Luban, D., 153, 227

Mabry, C. R., 31
Maccoby, E. E., 17, 21, 90
MacDougall, D. J., 5, 159
MacIntyre, A., 29
Macke, A. S., 164
Mackie, M., 164
MacKinnon, C. A., 103
Mahoney, M. R., 98, 101, 167, 168, 169,
    170, 171
Maisel, P., 151
Marcus, I., 93, 95
Margulies, P., 83, 274, 275
Mark, J., 174
Marks, R. G., 239
Marlow, L., 80, 83, 106, 179, 258
Marston, A. A., 197, 199
Martin, T. C., 16
Mason, A., 18, 103
Mason, M. A., 30, 96, 97
Mather, L., 17, 75, 77, 84, 85, 86, 95,
    105, 106, 107, 108, 109, 114,
    151, 152, 153, 154, 155, 163,
    175, 177, 178, 179
Mauro, L. M., 273
McArthur, E., 25, 35
McCant, J. W., 32
McCarrick, A. K., 167
McDonald, G. W., 164
McDonough, M., 233
McGraw, K., 151
McLanahan, S. S., 34, 37
McLindon, J. B., 35, 92
McNight, M., 6
McPhail, L., 183, 185
Meier, J. S., 98, 99, 100, 101, 102, 104,
    168, 171, 238, 239
Melli, M. S., 75, 76, 77, 80, 84, 107,
    108, 109, 155, 158, 159, 173,
    174, 180, 183
Melton, G. B., 6, 16, 17, 18, 33, 35, 39,
    49, 82, 224, 230, 274, 276
Menkel-Meadow, C., 107, 225, 227, 240,
    257
Menzie, D., 103
Mercing, S. C., 198
Merry, S. E., 78
Meulders-Klein, M. -T., 184, 240

Miller, B., 152, 153
Mills, J., 167
Milne, A., 226
Mincer, J., 87
Minow, M. L., 21, 89, 91, 94, 99, 103,
    170, 237
Mlyniec, W. J., 79, 85, 230, 237
Mnookin, R. H., 17, 21, 41, 75, 77, 89,
    90, 95, 96, 107, 160, 163, 180,
    183, 241
Moir, D. S., 43
Moore, J. C., Jr., 164
Morgan, L. A., 19, 35, 44, 45, 46, 48, 49,
    88
Moss, D. C., 256
Myers, L., 87
Myles, V. V., 244

Naiman, J., 177
Neely, R., 104, 160, 277
Nemeth, C. J., 164
Newman, J. O., 173
Nolan-Haley, J. M., 76, 226–227
Nozick, R., 29, 78
Nussbaum, M. C., 237

O'Brien, R. C., 224, 244
O'Connell, M. E., 192
O'Gorman, H. J., 154, 155
Oberdorfer, D., 20
Ohlin, L., 168
Okin, S. M., 17, 29, 30, 34, 35, 78, 156,
    159
Oldham, J. T., 198
Opie, A., 96
Orloff, L. E., 98, 168, 170
Ormrod, R., 20

Paasch, K. M., 35
Pagelow, M. D., 98, 100, 168–169, 170,
    171
Paltrow, B. L., 157
Pang, S., 13
Parry, R., 82
Partridge, S., 40
Pasto, J., 182, 184
Pateman, C., 29, 30, 162, 164, 165,
    193

Wood, C. L., 238
Woodhouse, B. B., 39, 43, 275, 277
Woods, L., 168, 227

Yankeelov, P. A., 272, 273
Yegge, R. B., 174, 176
Yllo, K., 100

Yngvesson, B., 165
Younger, J. T., 199, 240, 281

Zammit, J. P., 77, 78
Zelditch, M., Jr., 164
Zemans, F. K., 232, 233, 240
Zorza, J., 168, 170

SUBJECT INDEX

Abduction. *See* Kidnapping by parents
Abuse. *See* Child abuse; Child sexual
    abuse; Domestic violence
Affidavits. *See* Disclosure
Alimony. *See* Spousal maintenance
Alternative dispute resolution (ADR).
    See Mediation; Settlements
American Bar Association
    Commission on Separation of
      Powers and Judicial
      Independence, 232n
    proposal on Standards on State
      Judicial Selection (2000), 231n
American Law Institute, 279
Anger. *See also* Conflict of divorcing
    clients
    due to unfair results, 128–130, 177–
      178n
Antenuptial agreements. *See* Premarital
    agreements
Appeals, 132–133, 180–182n
Assertive bargaining tactics and gendered
    constraints, 121–122, 149, 165–
    167n
Associative obligation, 21n
Attorney fees, 158n, 173–174n
Attorneys. *See* Lawyers
Australia's specialized family court, 230–
    231n, 276n

Battered women. *See* Domestic violence
Best interests of the child standard, 72,
    82n, 178n, 204, 265
Bias of decision makers, 63–64, 85–86n
    custody issues, 67–71, 95–105n
    financial issues, 64–67, 86–95n

CAFC. *See* Court of Appeals for the
    Federal Circuit
California Equal Justice Report, 96n, 97n
Center for American Women and
    Politics, 281n

Certification of disclosures. *See* Disclosure
Child abuse. *See also* Child sexual abuse
    custody or visitation awarded to
      abuser, 27, 42n, 69, 101n
    judicial treatment of allegations of,
      69, 99n, 100n
    legal representation of children, 83n
    psychological effects of, 100n
Child custody
    bias of decision makers, 67–71, 95–
      105n
    divorced mothers without, 160n
    effect on custodial parent, 46n
    evaluators. *See* Custody evaluators
    frequency of dispute over, 89n
    judge's authority to decide, 58–59,
      75n
    lawyer's competence to handle, 61–
      63, 83–85n
    noncompliance with decrees and
      agreements, 13, 17n
    parental education program and,
      261–262, 273n
    participatory rights of child in
      custody proceeding, 275n
    women's fear of losing custody, effect
      of, 71, 104n, 117, 144, 160n
Child development
    blaming problems on mothers, 103n
    of children who witness abuse of
      mother, 99–100n
    of divorced children, 27
Children of divorced parents
    adjustment to step families, 49n
    criminal activity of, 27, 39n
    custody of. *See* Child custody
    financial situation of. *See* Child
      support; Hardship of divorced
      children and women
    legal treatment of, 3–4
    lives of, 3, 25–27, 34–43n, 49–50n
    participatory rights in custody
      proceedings, 275n
    support of. *See* Child support

Child sexual abuse. *See also* Domestic
   violence
   abduction to protect child from, 19n
   custody or visitation of parent who
      engages in, 27, 42n, 69, 104n
   guardian ad litem's lack of
      knowledge, 59–61, 83n
   hearsay admissibility in prosecutions,
      238–239n
   judge's lack of knowledge, 58,
      79–80n
   judicial treatment of allegations, 69,
      102n, 112
   NOW educational program for
      judges on, 30n
Child support
   contact with child and, 21n
   enforcement, 19n
   lawyer's competence to handle, 61–
      63, 83–85n
   noncompliance with court orders,
      12–13, 17–18n
      societal change due to, 21n
   paying, reasons for, 18n
   recommendations for national
      guidelines, 21–22n
   reduction due to remarriage, 21n
   resistance to paying, reasons for, 14–
      15, 21n, 58
Client–lawyer relationship. *See* Lawyers
Code of Judicial Conduct, 231n
Competitive bargaining in divorce
      proceedings, 121–122, 165–167n
Compliance issues, 12–15, 17–22n
Conflict of divorcing clients
   hostility reduction and, 128–130,
      177–178n
   judge's effect on, 228–229n
   lawyer's neutrality, 154n
   parental education program and, 261
   postdivorce high conflict behaviors,
      41n
   postdivorce relationship and effect
      on children, 204, 260
Constitutional issues
   divorce decrees and, 220, 244n
   right to parent–child relationship,
      78, 244n, 276n
Corporate Training Unlimited, 13
Correction of decisional errors, 132–150,
      179–199n

default judgments, 132, 133, 180n,
   182n
premarital agreements, 132, 147–
   150, 197–199n
reform proposal and, 217
settlement errors, 132, 133–147,
   182–197n
trial court errors, 132–133, 180–
   182n
Costs
   of experts, 116–117
   of judicial review of settlements,
      216
   of specialized divorce court, 279,
      281n
Court of Appeals for the Federal Circuit
      (CAFC), 220–221, 245n
Courts. *See* Judges and courts
Criminal activity of divorced children,
      27, 39n
Custody. *See* Child custody
Custody evaluation teams, as part of
      reform proposal, 262–271, 273–
      278n
Custody evaluators, 59–61, 83n, 124

DAC. *See* Dispute assessment
      conference
Decision-maker characteristics, 55–109
   advice from mental health
      professionals, 59, 80–82n, 103–
      104n
   custody evaluators, 59–61, 83n, 124
   custody issues, bias in, 67–71, 95–
      105n
   financial issues, bias in, 64–67,
      86–95n
   guardians ad litem
      authority of, 59–61, 81n
      bias in custody issues, 70–71,
         104n
   impartiality, 63–64, 85–86n
   inconsistency of, 129, 130–132,
      224n
   judges
      authority of, 56–61, 78–83n
      bias in custody issues, 67–70, 95–
         104n
      bias in financial issues, 64–66,
         91–94n

lawyers
    authority of, 61–63, 83–85n,
        84–85n
    bias in custody issues, 71, 104–
        105n
    bias in financial issues, 66–67,
        94–95n
    respect for disputants, 71–75, 105–
        109n, 129–130
Default judgments, 132, 133, 180n, 182n
Delay in divorce proceedings and
    settlements, 125
Depression. *See also* Psychological
    problems
    as gendered constraint on voice of
        women, 120–121, 165n
Disclosure. *See also* Discovery
    mandatory as part of reform
        proposal, 247–251, 255–256n
    standardized forms for financial and
        child issues, 216
Discovery
    delay and, 125
    failure to conduct, 145–147, 173n
    reform proposal and, 269
    requests for, 72–73, 74, 108–109n,
        116, 158n
Displaced Homemakers Network, 90n
Dispute assessment conference (DAC),
    216, 252–255, 256–258n
Dispute resolution experts (DREs), 251–
    252, 256n
Disrespect of disputants' legal rights, 71–
    75, 105–109n, 129–130
Divorce dispute resolution system
    accurate information and decision
        making, 124, 173n
    assessment of current status of,
        111–199
    correction of decisional errors, 132–
        150, 179–199n
        default judgments, 132, 133,
            180n, 182n
        premarital agreements, 132, 147–
            150, 197–199n
        reform proposal and, 217
        settlement errors, 132, 133–147,
            182–197n
        trial court errors, 132–133, 180–
            182n
    efficiency, 125–126, 173–175n

gendered constraints on voice of
    parties, 116–122, 156–167n. *See*
    also Gendered constraints on
    voice of parties
hostility reduction and, 128–130,
    177–178n
    parental education program, 261
judges as constraints on voice of
    parties, 112–113, 151n
lawyers as constraints on voice of
    parties, 113–115, 151–155n
procedural consistency, 129, 130–
    132, 178–179n
pro se actions. *See* Pro se
    representation
reform of. *See* Reform proposals
voice of parties, 111–124, 150–173n
Divorced men
    custody requests by and awards to,
        67–71, 95–96n, 160n
    lives of, 43–45n, 49n
    living standards of, 44n, 45n, 92n
Divorced women
    custody awards to, 67–71, 95–105n
    employment issues for, 27–28, 45n
    fear of losing custody, effect of, 71,
        104n, 117, 144, 160n
    financial situation of. *See* Hardship
        of divorced children and women;
        Spousal maintenance
    legal treatment of, 3–4
    lives of, 3, 27–29, 43–45n, 48–49n
    maintenance payments to. *See*
        Spousal maintenance
    voice of. *See* Gendered constraints
        on voice of parties
Divorce rates, 16–17n, 25, 34n
    of remarriages, 28, 49n
Domestic violence. *See also* Child abuse;
    Child sexual abuse
    child custody awarded to spousal
        abuser, 67, 69
    judge's knowledge and attitude, 58,
        68, 72, 98–99n, 123
    lawyer's treatment of, 123
    legal system's treatment of, 31n,
        42n, 122–124, 167–173n
    mental health professional's lack of
        knowledge about, 82n
    parental education program and,
        260, 272n

Domestic violence, *continued*
    posttraumatic stress disorder of
        abused women, 69, 101n
    psychological assessment of abuser
        and abused spouse, 70, 104n
    state custody statutes and, 98n
    voice of abused spouse in divorce
        proceedings, 122–124, 167–
        173n
DREs. *See* Dispute resolution experts
Duress, defined, 185n

Economic hardship. *See* Hardship of
    divorced children and women
Economic value of children, 14
Education
    of custody evaluation teams, 263–
        265, 274–276n
    of dispute resolution experts, 252
    of divorced children, 26, 37n, 39n
    of judges, 64, 212–215, 222, 235–
        239n
    of parents, 254, 259–262, 271–273n
    of pro se parties, 255
    of public about specialized divorce
        court, 223
Efficiency of legal system, 125–126, 173–
    175n
Election of judges. *See* Selection and
    retention of judges
Emergency Court of Appeals, 238n
Emergency Price Control Act of 1942,
    238n
Emotionalism of clients, 115, 125, 129,
    152n, 153n
Employee Retirement Income Security
    Act, 244–245n
Employment issues
    for battered women, 170n
    for divorced women, 27–28, 45n
Equal pay issues, 87n
Ethics of care, as gendered constraints on
    voice of parties, 119–120, 162–
    163n
Ethics of lawyers, 62, 105n
Evaluators
    custody evaluation teams, 262–271,
        273–278n
    custody evaluators, 59–61, 83n,
        124

Expectations
    as gendered constraints on voice of
        parties, 121, 165n
    inconsistency of decision makers
        and, 130–132
    unrealistic, 125
Experts, 81–82n. *See also* Custody
    evaluation teams; Mental health
    professionals
    cost of, 116–117
    wife's need for, 119

Fairness and procedural justice, 11, 15n,
    16n
Father–child relationship. *See* Child
    custody; Parent–child
    relationship
Father–mother relationship
    divorce's effect on, 14, 28
    postdivorce high conflict behaviors
        of, 41n
    postdivorce relationship and effect
        on children, 204
Fathers' rights groups, 23–24, 30n
Feminists
    on contract enforcement, 242n
    on divorce, 23
    on gender roles, 30n
    on marital property definitions, 94n
    on single-parent families, 24
    on spousal maintenance, 88n
Financial resources. *See also* Child
    support; Divorced men; Hardship
    of divorced children and women;
    Spousal maintenance
    disclosure and discovery of. *See*
        Disclosure; Discovery
    men's control of, as constraint on
        voice of women, 118–119, 161–
        162n
    women's lack of, 157n
        ability to hire counsel and, 156n,
            158n
        as constraint on voice, 116–117,
            156–160n
Florida child support enforcement
    statutes, 13
Florida Gender Bias Report, 42n, 86n,
    97n, 99n, 104n, 156n, 157n,
    158n, 159n, 181n

Fraud, defined, 185n
French court scrutiny of divorce
  agreements, 240n

Garnishment, 13
Gay and lesbian parents, 63
Gender bias of legal system, 63–71,
  86–87n
Gendered constraints on voice of parties,
  116–122, 156–167n
    abused wife's voice, 122–124, 167–
    173n
    assertive bargaining tactics, 121–
    122, 149, 165–167n
    depression, 120–121, 165n
    ethics of care, 119–120, 162–163n
    expectations, 121, 165n
    financial disparities, 116–117, 156–
    160n
    intangible resource disparities, 118,
    161n
    naive trust, 118–119, 161–162n
    self-esteem, 120, 164n
    status disparities, 120, 163–164n
    traditional homemaker role, 117,
    160–161n
Gender relations, 23–24, 30n
    state legislatures and, 228n, 280,
    281n
Georgia Commission on Gender Bias, 69,
  102n
Grandparents' abduction of child, 19n
Guardians ad litem
    authority of, 59–61, 81n
    bias in custody issues, 70–71, 104n

Hague Convention, 245n
Hardship of divorced children and
  women. See also Child support;
  Poverty; Spousal maintenance
    decline in living standards, 34–35n,
    44–45n, 47n, 92n
    effect of, 26, 28
    judge's failure to take into account,
    57–58, 64–66, 236–237n
    lawyer's failure to take into account,
    66–67
    remarriage of mothers, effect of, 39–
    40n, 48n, 88n

Health of divorced children, 38n
Hostility. See Conflict of divorcing
  clients
Housing
    effect on children, 38n
    family home as marital property,
    94n
Human capital theory, 94n

Illinois examples of petitions to vacate
  settlements, 136–147, 184–197n
Impartiality of decision makers, 63–64,
  85–86n. See also Bias of decision
  makers
Income tax deductions for child support
  payments, 13
Inconsistency of judges. See Procedural
  consistency
Individualism and marriage, 34n
Interest groups. See Special interest
  groups
International Child Abduction and
  Remedies Act, 245n
International child kidnapping, 13, 245n

Joint custody, 27, 30n, 102n, 103n
Judges and courts
    authority of, 56–61, 78–83n
    bias in custody issues, 67–70, 95–
    104n
    bias in financial issues, 64–66,
    91–94n
    coercing litigants, 58, 73, 75n, 206
    as constraints on voice of parties,
    112–113, 151n
    costs of judicial review of
    settlements, 216
    dislike of family law cases, 57, 72,
    78–79n, 105n, 229n
    education of judges, 64, 212–215,
    222, 235–239n
    inconsistency of decisions of, 129,
    130–132, 224n
    involvement in settlements, 58, 73,
    75n, 77n, 216, 240–242n
    naive trust of women in, 119
    opposition to continuing role in
    divorce case resolution, 203–205,
    217

Oregon Gender Fairness Report, 96n, 100n, 104n

ABOUT THE AUTHOR

Penelope Eileen Bryan, JD, has taught family law and civil procedure at the University of Denver College of Law for the past 16 years. She received her law degree and her master's degree in family sociology from the University of Florida. Her scholarship offers a unique blend of knowledge about family law and civil procedure, dispute resolution, the psychology and social condition of women and children, and domestic violence. In addition, she brings a wealth of practical experience to her scholarship. She has served as an expert consultant on numerous divorce cases, supervised students in a family law clinic, survived three divorces of her own, and raised four children, mostly as a single parent.